THE STRUGGLE FOR EGYPT

The Council on Foreign Relations (CFR) is an independent, nonpartisan membership organization, think tank, and publisher dedicated to being a resource for its members, government officials, business executives, journalists, educators and students, civic and religious leaders, and other interested citizens in order to help them better understand the world and the foreign policy choices facing the United States and other countries. Founded in 1921, CFR carries out its mission by maintaining a diverse membership, with special programs to promote interest and develop expertise in the next generation of foreign policy leaders; convening meetings at its headquarters in New York and in Washington, DC, and other cities where senior government officials, members of Congress, global leaders, and prominent thinkers come together with CFR members to discuss and debate major international issues; supporting a Studies Program that fosters independent research, enabling CFR scholars to produce articles, reports, and books and hold roundtables that analyze foreign policy issues and make concrete policy recommendations; publishing *Foreign Affairs*, the preeminent journal on international affairs and U.S. foreign policy; sponsoring Independent Task Forces that produce reports with both findings and policy prescriptions on the most important foreign policy topics; and providing up-to-date information and analysis about world events and American foreign policy on its website, www.cfr.org.

The Council on Foreign Relations takes no institutional positions on policy issues and has no affiliation with the U.S. government. All views expressed in its publications and on its Web site are the sole responsibility of the author or authors.

STEVEN A. COOK

THE STRUGGLE FOR EGYPT

EGYPT

*From Nasser
to Tahrir Square*

A Council on Foreign Relations Book

OXFORD

UNIVERSITY PRESS

OXFORD
UNIVERSITY PRESS

Oxford University Press, Inc., publishes works that further
Oxford University's objective of excellence
in research, scholarship, and education.

Oxford   New York
Auckland   Cape Town   Dar es Salaam   Hong Kong   Karachi
Kuala Lumpur   Madrid   Melbourne   Mexico City   Nairobi
New Delhi   Shanghai   Taipei   Toronto

With offices in
Argentina   Austria   Brazil   Chile   Czech Republic   France   Greece
Guatemala   Hungary   Italy   Japan   Poland   Portugal   Singapore
South Korea   Switzerland   Thailand   Turkey   Ukraine   Vietnam

Published by Oxford University Press, Inc.
198 Madison Avenue, New York, New York 10016
www.oup.com

Oxford is a registered trademark of Oxford University Press

Library of Congress Cataloging-in-Publication Data
Cook, Steven A.
The struggle for Egypt : from Nasser to Tahrir Square / Steven A. Cook.
p. cm.
Includes bibliographical references and index.
ISBN 978-0-19-979526-0 (alk. paper)
1. Egypt—Politics and government—1952–1970. 2. Egypt—Politics and
government—1970–1981. 3. Egypt—Politics and government—1981– I. Title.
DT107.827.C64 2011
962.05—dc22

2011016635

1 3 5 7 9 8 6 4 2

Printed in the United States of America
on acid-free paper

If the ruling class has lost its consensus, i.e. is no longer leading but only "dominant," exercising coercive force alone, this means precisely that the great masses have become detached from their traditional ideologies, and no longer believe what they used to believe previously, etc. The crisis consists precisely in the fact that the old is dying and the new cannot be born; in this interregnum a great variety of morbid symptoms appear.

Antonio Gramsci, Selections from the Prison Notebooks

Contents

Acknowledgments

Although my name appears alone on the cover and title page of this book and I alone am responsible for its content, *The Struggle for Egypt* is in many ways the product of a collective effort. I cannot thank Richard Haass, the president of the Council on Foreign Relations, enough for devoting so much time and effort helping me to figure out the kind of book I wanted to write and what I wanted it to say. James Lindsay, the Council's director of studies, picked up where Richard left off with encouragement and invaluable advice on the manuscript as it began to take shape.

I was fortunate enough to work with two extraordinarily bright and talented research associates—Lauren Linakis and Riad Houry—while drafting this book. They devoted remarkable amounts of time and energy to the manuscript. Not only were they adept at ferreting out facts and figures, and writing research memos, but they also offered expert advice on the book's overall argument. Lauren, in particular, deserves high praise and credit. She worked as if the project was her own and the book is better for it.

A group of outstanding interns, Michael Koplow, Jacob Friedman, Ayse Lokmanog˘ lu, Maysam Ali, Morgan Kaplan, Kate Powell, and Alexander Brock, worked extremely hard for no pay to help make this book possible. Ashraf el Sherif was an invaluable resource for me when I was unable to be in Cairo. Jessica Glover spent hours in the Library of Congress, retrieving articles and sources from the Middle East and Africa reading room. Laura Puls and the library staff at the Council on Foreign

Relations handled my many requests with aplomb. Lia Norton proofread my initial draft with tremendous concentration and good cheer.

Brian Dubie, the former lieutenant governor of Vermont and an American Airlines captain and U.S. Air Force Reserve Colonel (ret.) Charles H. Huettner graciously took time out of their busy schedules to review the technical details of the EgyptAir 990 crash for chapter 6.

To my Egyptian friends and colleagues, of which there are too many to name here, this book is the product of my admiration, respect, and love for you and your country. Thank you for the endless hours you have spent teaching me. Please know that while you may quibble or disagree with my arguments and conclusions, my intention is to give a broader audience what you have patiently given me: a nuanced, sophisticated, and compelling understanding of an extraordinary country.

I must thank a great group of friends and colleagues for their encouragement and advice. In particular, Joe Glicksberg, Michele Commercio, Julie Taylor, Amy Hawthorne, Marc Lynch, James Green, Hilary Price, John Crosson, Sue Adams, Alison Fargis, David Efron, Issandr el Amrani, Ashraf Swelam, Hassan el Sawaf, and Richard Vuernick. Bart Friedman and Imran Riffat offered their encouragement throughout from this project's conception to its conclusion. David Pervin has proven time and again to be a source of wise counsel. I am indebted to Erik Shawn and Brad Rothschild for reading a draft of the manuscript—in Brad's case twice. At CFR, I have benefitted from the advice of a terrific group of colleagues including Ray Takeyh, James Goldgeier, Charles Kupchan, Robert Danin, Adam Segal, Elizabeth Economy, Sebastian Mallaby, and Benn Steil. My friends and colleagues from the Clinton, Bush, and Obama administrations offered valuable advice and perspective on my work.

I am grateful to David McBride at Oxford University Press. He believed in this project from the very beginning and without his hard work, The Struggle for Egypt may have never seen the light of day.

The book would not have been possible without the generous support of three dear friends and patrons, Mahmoud Abdallah, and Peter and Susan McCall. I am forever grateful to them.

Thank you to my family. I am heartbroken that my beloved father, who died suddenly and unexpectedly while I was in Cairo in early 2008, is not here to read The Struggle for Egypt. I take solace knowing that his strong beliefs in justice and democracy were an inspiration for the project.

I am indebted to my extraordinary wife, Lauren, for her seemingly infinite patience and to our daughters, Madelyn and Mia, for reminding me every day how beautiful the world can be.

Map of the Greater Middle East. Courtesy of Christopher Robinson.

Map of the Arab Republic of Egypt. Courtesy of Christopher Robinson.

THE STRUGGLE FOR EGYPT

Introduction

Hassan

A FORD EXPEDITION? Isn't that the really huge one? I asked myself as I stood staring down Mohammed Mazhar Street on a mind-numbingly hot Cairo afternoon in late August 1999. Less than fifteen minutes before, I had fielded a phone call from a gentleman named Hassan telling me to wait for him in front of my apartment building, and that he would pick me up in his green Ford Expedition. I didn't think too much about it until I made my way down to the street. A Ford Expedition? I hadn't seen many of those. Cairo's thoroughfares were clogged with a variety of high-end Mercedes, BMWs, Range Rovers, and loads of more modest Mitsubishis, Skodas, Fiats, and Daihatsu minivans, as well as the odd ancient Russian Lada or two, but not a tank like the Expedition. I quickly did a rough calculation. To buy one of the biggest SUVs on the market in Egypt probably cost Hassan double what he would have paid in the United States. Couldn't be, I thought. I must have misheard him over the scratchy phone line.

My image of Hassan, whom I had met two days before via e-mail, was of one of those underemployed university graduates that one often comes across in Egypt. They are frequently found working some combination of odd jobs—in the post office, fixing watches, driving taxis—to help keep mothers, fathers, sisters, wives, and children fed. What led me to him was a short article he had penned in an English-language publication called *Civil Society* that, best I could tell at the time (and subsequently confirmed), enjoyed a miniscule readership. Even though I suspected that the magazine's limited circulation meant that Egypt's vaunted internal security services would largely ignore it, providing *Civil Society*'s publisher, editors, and writers some leeway, Hassan's poison pen was still shocking. On the eve of Hosni Mubarak's "election" (it was really a referendum) to a fourth term in office, Hassan minced no words in a forthright attack on the Egyptian regime and its defenders. His well-reasoned eloquence dripped with sarcasm and outrage over the follies of Egypt's corrupt power structure, and he voiced a deep despair over his beloved country's suffering and the long degradation and impoverishment of its people.[1]

The Expedition finally appeared, moving slowly, it drove by a *baqqel* (the Egyptian version of a bodega), some workers organizing a shipment of goods on the street, the neighborhood doormen congregating on the corner, the launderers making deliveries, and the knife sharpener whose workshop was a pushcart, before it stopped in front of me. I climbed aboard, extended my hand, and added "As-salaam Aleikum" out of respect. Hassan grunted something incomprehensible in return. I replied, "Thank you for picking me up. This is quite a car. You don't see too many of them in Cairo."

"Yes, I bought it to scare people away," he responded, laughing sardonically.

Over the course of that afternoon and many afternoons and evenings to follow, I learned that Hassan was the scion of a well-to-do family that had made money in imports and exports. He was a child of the elite; he had attended one of Egypt's best schools (the English School Cairo, renamed the Victory School Cairo in the early 1960s) and spent his summers playing at the pool in Agami (a resort area near Alexandria). Hassan could easily have settled into a life, like so many other Westernized Egyptian elites, in which he pursued his business interests and enjoyed all the benefits of his social status. Yet his conscience would not permit it. Although an elitist—he enjoyed creature comforts, lived in one of Cairo's new American-style gated suburban communities (more Palm Springs than Giza), and scoffed at my love for Egyptian street food—Hassan nevertheless dedicated himself, in his own ways, to exposing Hosni Mubarak's Egypt for its corruption and cruelty. This distinguished Hassan from his neighbors and the vast majority of people in his social class who, regardless of their views, were unwilling to criticize the regime publicly.

What seemed so tragic about Hassan was not only his near obsession with the perfidy of the Mubarak regime, but also his overpowering disappointment. While talking to him you got the sense that he took his country's troubles very personally. To Hassan, Egypt's situation at the time was dark, because of his conviction that its contemporary social and political development had been unnatural—the result of a historical accident that desperately needed correcting.

A little more than three years after our first meeting, Hassan and I sat in the back of his Mercedes (he had given up the Expedition as too impractical for Cairo's streets and employed a driver to preserve his sanity), stuck in an endless jam of cars, buses, and trucks, along the dusty, tree-lined Corniche on the east bank of the Nile. I gazed out the window, observing the parade of Egyptians who had descended on the Corniche seeking the odd cool breeze off the great river in the late September heat, as Hassan engaged in a soliloquy about the immorality of American military aid to Cairo. He must have noticed that I was only half listening—we'd had this argument many times before—because he stopped in midsentence. "You know, Cairo was once a very beautiful city. They used to wash the streets with soap and water every night. We didn't have all of these people. It was a wonderful place to live." This was the elitist in him. I had been traveling to Cairo regularly since 1993, and it was always a chaotic, ferocious, urban disaster. The preternatural charm and good humor of most Egyptians made the city fun. It was even somewhat of a rush for those not faint of heart, as Cairo tends to overload all five senses at once.

As we crawled along past the Foreign Ministry and the Ministry of Information in the direction of Tahrir Square (Liberation Square), Hassan elaborated on a theory that had been rolling around in his head. If not for the July 1952 coup d'état that brought Gamal Abdel Nasser and the Free Officers to power, Egypt would have become a flourishing democracy. Hassan was engaging in a bit of faith-based analysis and a fair amount of historical revisionism. There is no way of knowing whether the Albanian-Ottoman dynasty that ruled Egypt, beginning with Mohammed Ali in 1801, would have ultimately given way to a democratic political system.

This was not the only outside-the-mainstream theory, hypothesis, or proposition about Egypt that I heard from Hassan over the years. I remember one chilly evening in early 2000, I sat across from Hassan in an overstuffed chair of nouveau Arabesque design, sipping on Egypt's domestic brew (Stella), while he expounded on the idea that Egypt needed an Islamic revolution. Hassan was hardly an Islamist. I was, after all, drinking a beer and my host was enjoying a glass of wine. Indeed, few members of the Muslim Brotherhood reside in the gated community of Katamiyya Heights, with its infinity pools, golf course, and clubhouse. The residents of this exclusive enclave and the many copycats that ring Cairo's outer environs may have resided in Egypt, but they seemed increasingly removed from it. Hassan was not unaware of the irony of what he suggested. Rather, he reveled in it. To him, Iran demonstrated convincingly the folly of clerical rule, and the Iranian people would surely one day overwhelm the Islamic regime with demands for democracy. From Hassan's perspective, people needed to experience Islamist rule and its severe shortcomings. Confronted with all the difficulties he was sure would come with the "Islamic Republic of Egypt," Egyptians would in time demand democracy. Indeed, from Hassan's perspective, theocracy would be a small price to pay if it ultimately sped up Egypt's transition to a more open political system.

Hassan never actually advocated for an Islamic revolution. He was merely trying to drive home his belief that Egypt was trapped in a pathological-like state of authoritarianism, and that something dramatic needed to happen in order break the nondemocratic order. That's why in late 2003, before the insurgency in Iraq kicked into high gear, Hassan jokingly asked me why there were no plans for "Operation *Egyptian Freedom*." He had very little patience for evolutionary change, believing that it only played into the hands of the leaders of the regime, who invariably co-opted, deflected, and undermined otherwise well-intentioned American and European efforts to promote political change in partnership with Egypt. To Hassan, this kind of approach was little more than pure fantasy because it never required the Egyptian leadership to actually undertake any reforms. This was why he was an ardent opponent of Washington's annual economic and military assistance package to Egypt, which Hassan called "insidious" because there were no conditions on the aid, rendering the United States "an accomplice to the Egyptian regime's inexorable demolition" of his country.

I have always chalked up Hassan's advocacy for Islamic revolution and regime change at the end of a gun as a (successful) effort to be provocative. He is too serious a thinker to have ever believed that the imposition of political change by force would inevitably lead to democracy. There was no need to repeat the disastrous consequences of the invasion of Iraq. Suffice it to say that well before President George W. Bush left office, his administration dropped the notion of a democratic Iraq in favor of a country that could control its borders and was stable enough so the United States military could withdraw. Hassan continued to believe, however, that the peaceful emergence of an Islamic state would lead to democracy. Here he may have been reaching a bit. Despite the political ferment in Iran, especially after its disputed June 2009 presidential election, the advent of an Islamic state poses several possible outcomes, including democracy, but also a narrower, nastier dictatorship.

At the same time, the underlying insight of Hassan's counterfactual argument that Egypt would have developed a flourishing democratic system had a group of young disaffected military commanders never undertaken a coup in July 1952 seemed entirely plausible: the roots of Egypt's sixty years of military-dominated authoritarianism lies in the political and ideological struggles that emerged after the Free Officers disposed of the ancien régime. Gamal Abdel Nasser and his two successors, Anwar Sadat and Hosni Mubarak, never developed an appealing narrative of Egyptian society that was shared among the vast majority of Egyptians. Nasser and Sadat tried, but foundered because their rhetoric about social justice, economic change, and democracy never matched the everyday reality of the vast majority of Egyptians. Mubarak's Egypt was almost totally void of ideological content, instead the regime tried to elicit loyalty to the state through economic development, but fell back on coercion to maintain order. As a result, Egypt became a corrupt police state par excellence. This lack of a compelling vision generated a seemingly neverending political struggle about the nature of Egypt that has never been settled: Is Egypt a republic? A democracy? What roles should Islam, nationalism, and liberalism play in Egyptian politics and society? The inability of Egypt's leaders to answer these questions in a convincing way forced them to fill the void with violence, which ultimately led to the Egyptian revolution of 2011.

Hassan found both good news and bad news in the debate over the answers to these questions. On the positive side, liberal ideas about the sources of power, the role of the state, and the character of politics were central to this debate. Yet liberals themselves had become marginalized as President Mubarak's National Democratic Party (NDP)—which dominated the political arena until the 2011 uprising—the Muslim Brotherhood, and many of the political movements in between appropriated the discourse of reform and political change that echoed liberal principles. At the same time, these groups—the NDP, the Brotherhood, and Nasserists, for example—were not credibly liberal. Moreover, for all of their ideological differences, Egypt's political players alternatively sought to use each other's symbols and cooperate in the spheres of culture and society when their political interests dictated. To be sure, not all of Egypt's diverse political groups did this equally. The NDP and the government borrowed symbols from the Islamists and liberals far more than other political forces, which only underscored the point that Egyptian leaders failed to embed their own ideas about Egypt and its future trajectory in the minds of the people. This dynamic produced a set of ironies that, over time, became notable features of Egypt's political and social landscape: a constitution that identified Islamic law as *the* basis for legislation while the government brutally suppressed its Islamist opponents; the NDP's rhetorical commitment to liberal ideals and simultaneous institutionalization of its power under the guise of reform; and Muslim Brothers and Nasserists positioning themselves as the avatars of democratic change.

This state of affairs revealed a more nuanced view than what was often portrayed in the press, some scholarly work, and the accounts that formed the backdrop of U.S. policy, which tended to emphasize the conflict between the Egyptian state and the Muslim Brotherhood. The Islamists have indeed played an enduring and deeply influential role in politics. Yet even with all the attention on the seemingly singular struggle between the regime and the Brothers, the fight about what Egypt was, what the country stood for, and where it was going was actually broader than the two-dimensional snapshot of Islamists versus the state. Egyptians have long managed to carry on an ideological debate that was considerably richer than what either the Brothers or the defenders of the regime had to offer. Indeed, the liberal and leftist roots of Egypt's January 25, 2011, uprising provide some of the best evidence of the multidimensional nature of Egyptian politics in the late Mubarak era.

Although the unhappy state of affairs that led to the explosion of early 2011 was the product of Egypt's own internal problems and contradictions, there was also a foreign component. The British, the Soviets, and for the last three decades, the Americans, have all had an impact on the Egyptian political arena. In the 1970s, Washington, pursuing its Cold War interests, entered a strategic relationship with Cairo and became stuck. Over time, the United States became a critical yet largely negative factor in Egyptian politics. Washington provided financial, diplomatic, and political support to the leaders of a nondemocratic political system, who were either brutal or indifferent toward their own people. As a result, different political factions consistently sought to use the U.S.-Egypt relationship as a weapon in their domestic political conflicts.

What was at stake in Egypt from the time the Free Officers took over in 1952 boiled down not only to who controlled "The Chair"—that was obvious even to the casual observer—but also, more broadly and importantly, who got to define Egypt. This struggle had consequences beyond Egyptian domestic politics, however. Whoever defined Egypt also defined Cairo's relationships with its neighbors in the Middle East and with the United States. In the meantime, the revolution of 2011 has provided much hope that this struggle for Egypt—which had laid waste to the dreams of the Islamists, the descendants of the Free Officers, the Left, the Liberals, and the Nasserists—might be over. For Hassan, the popular uprising that brought an end to Hosni Mubarak's long reign was personally a moment of uncharacteristic jubilation. The push for Mubarak's departure, which had long been a seemingly lonely and Sisyphean cause, had suddenly become a national struggle. Yet, Hassan harbored doubts; Egypt's history and fractured opposition haunted him. The battle against Mubarak was over, but the struggle to define Egypt was entering a new phase, and he was not at all confident how it would turn out.

Understanding the uprising of January 25, 2011, when tens of thousands, and subsequently millions, of Egyptians took to the streets demanding political change, requires not only a detailed grasp of events in the weeks and months before this extraordinary moment, but also of the decades that preceded the uprising. It is impossible to draw a straight line from events in the distant past to the present, because history unfurls in many directions and human behavior is nothing if not complex. At the same time, however, throughout a country's history a set of ideas, questions, and themes tends to emerge that becomes central to the national conversation. In Egypt's case, there has been intense debate to define what Egypt is, what it stands for, and what its relation to the world is.

These issues are the central concern of this book, which begins with the stirrings of Egyptian nationalism that can be traced back to the 1880s, through the Free Officers' coup of July 1952, and ends with the extraordinary events in Tahrir Square in early 2011. In between, this volume critically examines how the underlying and unanswered questions of Egyptian politics and society shaped the political battles of the Nasser, Sadat, and Mubarak years. The latter part of the book sheds light on how Washington contributed to the struggle to define Egypt, what it stands for, how the country should be governed, and its place in the world. Indeed the role of foreigners runs like a live wire through Egyptian politics. Against the broad sweep of contemporary Egyptian political history, the demands for change from Tahrir Square are yet another manifestation of the struggle for Egypt that has been going on since at least the late nineteenth century. As the final chapter demonstrates, Egyptians now have an opportunity to finally answer these questions. To do so in a way that appeals to the vast majority of Egyptians will likely be a complicated, long, quite possibly painful, but ultimately necessary, process for Egypt to become an economically dynamic and politically vibrant society.

Egypt for the Egyptians

aluja Pocket. Al-Naqab Desert. December 1948. Trenches. There is no escaping them. They have become the dominant feature of a bleak landscape. They are home and prison for the soldiers and officers of the Fourth Division. The enemy pounds away with incessant attacks from both the air and the ground. This is what it has come to. The initial dash across the Sinai into the Naqab had been relatively successful. Half the force branched to the east, attacking through the Bedouin town of Beersheba, and as far north as Bethlehem, threatening to link with Jordan's Arab Legion in an assault on al Quds, or Jerusalem. The other half moved up along Palestine's western coast within striking distance of Tel Aviv—a city of two hundred thousand people. Success on either front would spell the ignoble end of the Zionist project.

Yet King Farouk and his advisors were not interested in destroying Israel. By December 1948, whatever gains had been made since May were mostly lost. Four of Egypt's five brigades were barely in Palestine at all, with two brigades (between 6,000 and 10,000 men) clustered around the town of Rafah in the southern Gaza Strip and another two brigades parked at al Auja just north of the border. The last Egyptian element—three regiments of the Fourth Division—was holed up thirty-five miles north at the strategic crossroads of Faluja—the gateway to the coastal towns of Ashkelon, Ashdod, Tel Aviv, and Jerusalem to the north and east. In a series of meetings at the nearby Kibbutz Gat, the Israeli commander, a thirty-year-old named Yigal Allon, had given his Egyptian counterpart, Colonel Mahmoud Sayed Taha (or Taha Bey) the opportunity to withdraw his forces safely to Sinai. The Egyptian was unyielding, however. With his young aide, Major Gamal Abdel Nasser, at his side, Taha Bey told Allon, "One thing I shall be able to save [is] the honor of the Egyptian army. And therefore I shall fight to my last bullet and my last man."[1]

The ensuing Israeli assaults on the Faluja fortifications were withering. The ceasefire of July 1948 provided an opportunity for the ragtag Israeli forces to arm themselves adequately. World War I era guns and rifles gave way to second-hand artillery, tanks, and even American-made bombers. The Israelis, sensing a victory that would give the new state some 600 square miles more than it had been allotted in the 1947 UN partition plan, threw everything at the Egyptian holdouts, who never withdrew, returning to Egypt only after the armistice negotiations of March 1949.

In the mud and despair that had become Faluja, however, the young officers serving Taha Bey continued developing a movement that had begun to crystallize some years earlier. The Zionists may have represented the mortal enemy of the moment—as artillery shells, mortars, and bombs rained down on them—but the threat of Zionism was a symptom, not a cause, of the unhappy situation in which they found themselves. Impending defeat in the Naqab was oddly liberating, as it provided an opportunity to meditate on Egypt's political, social, and economic malaise, penetrated as it was with corruption, political intrigue, and foreign influence. For Major Nasser and fellow junior-grade officers like Salah Salim, Zakariyya Mohieddin, and Kemal al Din Hussein, their experience in Palestine would fuel a determination to redeem Egypt's greatness.[2]

Cairo. July 23, 1952. As the light begins stretching from the east across the Sinai Peninsula to the Giza plateau, where the great Pyramids stand as testimonials to the singularity of Egypt, Cairo is bathed in an odd, washed-out tone of white. The mist off the Nile—a product of the midsummer humidity—creates an odd sense of foreboding and anticipation. The armored vehicles make their way through the still-quiet streets (in 1952, Cairo was not the megalopolis of fifteen million souls that it is today) and pass Ataba Square, where four tanks have been standing sentry since the predawn hours when the order was given to deploy at sensitive locations throughout the capital.

From Ataba Square, the caravan of armored cars makes its way to Elwi Street and the studio of Egyptian Broadcasting. Among the officers who descend upon the main studio is a slight, young, dark-complexioned colonel named Anwar el Sadat. More professional agitator than distinguished officer, Sadat's career had been marked by stints in jail for his political activities, including flirtations with Nazi Germany and the Muslim Brotherhood. Now he was responsible for letting the nation know of the army's plan that would finally bring sovereignty and dignity to Egypt.

This was to be one of Egypt's finest moments. Yet shortly after the broadcast began at 6:30 a.m., the transmission was interrupted. The Free Officers, as the coup plotters referred to themselves, had not established complete control of the country in the six hours since their coup began. The governor of Cairo and forces loyal to the king had cut the power to the Abu Zaabal relay station. In short order, troops acting on behalf of the Free Officers seized the communication facility. At 7:30 a.m., Sadat began his announcement:

Egypt has passed through a critical period in her recent history characterized by bribery, mischief, and the absence of governmental stability. All of these were factors that had a large influence on the army. Those who accepted bribes and were thus influenced caused our defeat in the Palestine War. As for the period following the war, the mischief-making elements have been assisting one another, and traitors have been commanding the army. They appointed a commander who is either ignorant or corrupt. Egypt has reached the point, therefore, of having no army to defend it. Accordingly, we have undertaken to clean ourselves up and have appointed to command us men from within the army whom we trust in their ability, their character, and their patriotism. It is certain that all Egypt will meet this news with enthusiasm and will welcome it.

As for those whose arrest we saw fit from among men formerly associated with the army, we will not deal harshly with them, but will release them at the appropriate time. I assure the Egyptian people that the entire army today has become capable of operating in the national interest and under the rule of the constitution apart from any interests of its own. I take this opportunity to request that the people never permit any traitors to take refuge in deeds of destruction or violence because these are not in the interest of Egypt. Should anyone behave in such ways, he will be dealt with forcefully in a manner such as has not been seen before and his deeds will meet immediately the reward for treason. The army will take charge with the assistance of the police.

I assure our foreign brothers that their interests, their personal safety, and their property are safe, and that the army considers itself responsible for them. May God grant us success.[3]

This announcement, remarkably guarded in tone and modest in goals, represented the decisive moment in contemporary Egyptian history. With Sadat's 187-word-long soliloquy, the political trajectory of Egypt changed. The "Blessed Revolution"—the appellation the officers gave to the coup—set in motion the political processes, patterns, and dynamics that would make an indelible impact on regional and global politics.

The Officers' intervention in July 1952 was the culmination of seventy years of nationalist agitation that gripped Egypt since 1882, when another group of soldiers under the leadership of Colonel Ahmed al Urabi rebelled against the Egyptian monarchy. Urabi and his followers had become increasingly dismayed as Egypt, burdened with a crushing external debt to British and French banks, fell under European control during the previous decade. In response to Urabi's challenge, London and Paris dispatched naval forces to the Egyptian coast off the port of Alexandria. The French, who were reluctant to occupy Egypt, backed out of an outright confrontation with Urabi, who had just wrested control of the government; however, London remained determined to protect British interests. As a result, on July 11, 1882, British warships shelled Alexandria and landed thousands of soldiers in Egypt.[4] Urabi's forces put up an unexpectedly stiff resistance to the British invasion. In August, the Egyptian army fought the British to a draw in a bloody battle at Kafr el Dawwar, a town in the Nile Delta just northwest of Cairo. A month later, the British finally subdued Urabi's forces in a town called Tel el Kebir, part way between Cairo and the city of Ismailiyya.

Until that time, the British crown had been an influential, though primarily external, player in Egyptian politics. Yet, with the tens of thousands of soldiers deployed to put down Urabi's revolt, the British were in every sense "in" Egypt—though London never colonized the country in the same way that it took possession of, for example, India, Rhodesia, Kenya, and Singapore. It was only in 1914, after the start of World War I, that Egypt became a protectorate of the United Kingdom. Nevertheless, the British regarded Egypt as a strategic asset in its ongoing competition with France and Russia and in the related issue of securing London's colonial crown jewel in South Asia: India.[5] Indeed, the completion of the Suez Canal in 1869—a triumph of French engineering and financing—invested Egypt with strategic importance in international trade and security well beyond its natural resources and assets. In 1875, the British sought to gain a controlling interest in the operation of the Canal when London purchased all of Egypt's shares in the Suez Canal Company from the Egyptian ruler.[6] Upon announcing the purchase, British Prime Minister Benjamin Disraeli made it clear to the House of Commons that his government's policy toward Egypt was to strengthen its hold on India, among other colonial possessions. Urabi's revolt five years later was a warning sign of the instability of the country the Khedive Ismail—the grandson of Mohammed Ali, the founder of the Ottoman-Albanian dynasty that ruled Egypt beginning in 1805—ruled. Yet it was also an opportunity for the British crown.[7] Establishing a British presence in Egypt would ensure Egyptian stability and secure Britain's unfettered access to the Suez Canal. London's concern with stability and access to the Canal foreshadowed a policy that would guide the pax-Americana in the Middle East a century later.

In 1882, the British found themselves in an extremely awkward position as they began their administration of Egypt. London's goal was to ensure "native sovereignty," which technically rested with the Ottoman Sultan, Abdulhamid II, in Constantinople.[8] Yet by the late nineteenth century, Egypt's connection to the Ottoman Empire was tenuous at best. Mohammed Ali, who was an officer in the Ottoman military, had ruled Egypt on behalf of the sultans with the assistance of bureaucrats who hailed from various parts of the realm including Turks-Circassians, Balkans, and Arabs.[9] Yet the descendants of Mohammed Ali were not always loyal servants of the sultans. Ismail, for example, harbored thinly veiled pretensions of Egyptian independence. After the American Civil War, he employed officers from the Union and former Confederate armies to train the Egyptian military so it would be prepared to fight should the Ottomans seek to assert direct control over Egypt.[10] Still, the Khedive Tewfiq—Ismail's eldest son—enabled Britain's 1882 invasion as a means to do away with Urabi and his nationalist revolt, which was as much a threat to Khedival rule as it was to Britain's need to secure a vital waterway to India. Despite London's standing policy of restoring Ottoman sovereignty, Britain's presence in Egypt only served to further weaken ties between Cairo and Constantinople.

As with all projects of foreign intervention, London sought an indigenous political class that was willing to participate in the British penetration of the country. In Egypt's case, Tewfiq, his courtiers, and

Egyptian politicians had little choice but to submit to the British, given the ragged state of official finances that the Khedive inherited from his father. Still, there was a constituency for Britain's new, more direct role in Egypt, particularly among the Turco-Egyptian, Circassian, and Balkan political elite, who regarded Urabi's nationalist agitation as a threat to their material and political interests.[11] For his part, Tewfiq was caught in the unenviable position of needing foreign intervention to save his throne, compromising him politically among a population that had begun to embrace nationalist values.

THE POWER OF THE PRESS

In the decade before Urabi's revolt, the Egyptian press had been actively agitating against Europe's ever-increasing penetration of Egypt. Of all the countries in the Arab world, Egypt has the longest history of an active and independent press. The emergence of newspapers and journals in Egypt dates back to Napoleon's invasion of Egypt in 1798 and France's subsequent brief occupation of the country in 1801. French colonial officials arrived in Egypt with the tools "to civilize" Egyptian society. Yet the French version of the "white man's burden" was not the primary motivation for the intervention. Paris sought—at the expense of its British competitors—to secure for itself the fastest route from Europe to the Indian subcontinent. Nevertheless, among the instruments of occupation that arrived with French bureaucrats, anthropologists, engineers, surveyors, and scientists was the printing press. French authorities used this technology to disseminate official decrees and to produce the newspaper, *Le Courier de l'Egypte* (*Egyptian Post*), and an Arabic publication, *Al-Tanbih* (*The Notice*). Although an Egyptian edited the latter, the two papers reflected the sensibilities and outlook of the French political project in Egypt.

In 1828, Egypt's ruler Mohammed Ali established *al-Waqai al-Misriya* (the *Egyptian Official Gazette*, often referred to as the *Official Gazette*) as a means to communicate government policy. Five years later, the *Military Gazette* began publication alongside periodicals from other government ministries. The press remained in the hands of Egyptian officialdom until 1863, when Ismail took the reins of power. Under Ismail, an indigenous press began to flourish with significant assistance from the royal court. No doubt Egypt's new ruler, who was the tender age of thirty-three when he assumed the throne, intended to advance his own political agenda through his patronage of the press,

but he also saw himself as a great reformer and understood the importance of newspapers, journals, and periodicals to a modern society. In
addition to Ismail's official mouthpiece, *Wadi al Nil* (*The Nile Valley*), a
variety of publications emerged expressing support for diverse causes
and ideological inclinations ranging from Islamic reform and Egyptian
nationalism to support for Europe's project in Egypt. By 1870, Egypt
boasted sixteen journals, of which ten were published in Arabic.

Ismail's initial sponsorship of the press did not, however, shield
him from its withering criticism. His prodigious spending on royal
extravagances, such as his attempt to redevelop Cairo in the image
of Paris and his insistence that important infrastructure projects like
the national railway and the Suez Canal be completed quickly, undermined Egypt's balance sheet, and the country fell further under the
sway of Paris and London.[12] In 1876, Ismail was forced to accept the
joint British and French Commission on Public Debt, which supervised repayment of the Khedive's obligations to European financial
institutions. Egyptian journalists and editors responded to this perceived disaster with little regard for royal deference or diplomatic
niceties. The newspaper, *al Ahram* (*The Pyramids*), which two Lebanese
Christians founded in 1876, criticized the monarchy for its increasing subordination to the West. Similarly, *Jaridat Misr* (*Egypt Journal*)
editorialized against European control.[13] The press was hardly exag-
gerating French and British influence. In 1879, the British and French
governments forced Ismail from the throne after Cairo defaulted on its
loans, making way for the pliable Tewfiq to do their bidding.

During Urabi's revolt, the Khedive and his British overlords sought
to rein in the press, sending editorialists and journalists into exile. Yet
even the Press Law of 1881, which forced the closure of certain papers,
did little to undermine nationalist feelings. In the two decades that
followed Urabi's uprising, Egyptian newspapers nurtured a national
conversation, pitting pro-monarchists and pro-British elements against
nationalists who sought an "Egypt for the Egyptians."[14] In this effort
the Egyptian papers were greatly aided by two events. The death of
Tewfiq in 1892 led the way for Abbas Hilmi II (sometimes referred
to as Abbas II) to assume the Egyptian leadership. Tewfiq's son was
considerably less inclined toward the British than his father, and
he used the press to advance his own nationalist goals. In addition,
the repression of the Egyptian press was an unsustainable policy for
Britain's Foreign Office, given European sensibilities about personal
and political freedom, including freedom of expression. As a result,
by the beginning of 1890 the British consul general in Cairo, Lord

Cromer, permitted exiled journalists to return to Egypt, where they picked up where they had left off, agitating against Britain's presence in their country.

ISLAMIC REFORMISM

Although the Egyptian press played an important role both in contributing to and reflecting the stirring of Egyptian nationalism, there were other critical actors in this seven-decade-long drama. Among them were Egypt's Islamic intellectuals and activists. The issue of Islam and politics is deeply controversial, particularly in the post-9/11 era, in which concepts like *jihad*, *salafism*, and *Wahhabism* have become familiar, if not entirely well-understood, terms for many. Yet it is important to underscore that Islam is a critically important cultural and political touchstone that has helped shape Egypt and the modern Middle East.

In the late nineteenth and early twentieth centuries, leading Islamic intellectuals like Jamal al Din al Afghani (who was Shi'i and ethnically Persian), his disciple Sheikh Mohammed Abduh, and, in turn, Abduh's student Rashid Rida raised a series of fundamental questions about Egypt, the Muslim world, and Europe: Why, they asked, is Muslim civilization so backward? Why, given Islam's history of "social and individual development" and belief in reason, had the Muslim world fallen so far behind the West?[15] What is the Muslim world's response to the West? And, perhaps most important, what is the relationship between Islam and modernity?[16] Although these questions had little to do with nationalism per se, the answers that al Afghani, Abduh, Rida, and others provided were critical to the development of Egyptian nationalist sentiment prior to the Free Officers' coup of 1952.

To Islamic reformers, the condition of Muslims was a function of their collective ignorance, deficit of public morals, and lack of unity. They did not hate Europe per se; both al Afghani and Abduh spent time in Europe and admired its achievements. Abduh, in particular, recognized the importance of European-inspired educational, political, and civil reforms that Khedive Ismail undertook, but these reforms produced a range of problems that Islamic law (*shari'a*) was ill-equipped to handle. His prescription was not to graft European law onto Egyptian society, but rather to develop a system of thought or a set of principles that would reconcile Islam with modernity.[17] For Abduh and other reformers, Egyptian and Muslim societies in general could not just give themselves up to Western conceptions of what society should look like. Thus, Islam must act as a brake or "controlling factor" on society.[18] Ultimately, Abduh believed that in order to arrest the decay of Egypt, it needed a just ruler who governed in accordance with the law and in consultation with the people.

Abduh spawned a robust following of disciples who sought to extend and interpret his ideas further. The most prominent among these were Ahmad Lutfi al Sayyid, Rashid Rida, and in particular Saad Zaghlul, who was to play the central role in Egypt's nationalist struggle until his death in 1927. There was, however, a significant difference in the way these three figures interpreted Abduh's thought and how they sought to apply it to Egypt's problems. For example, Lutfi al Sayyid was not necessarily as committed to the centrality of Islam as Abduh, al Afghani, or his contemporary Rida. He acknowledged that a religious society is morally superior to a nonreligious one, but he did not believe that "an Islamic society is superior to a non Islamic" society.[19] Lutfi al Sayyid was more interested in wrestling with the relationship between Islam and nationalism, which he ultimately decided were incompatible. Nevertheless, he shared with Abduh an abiding interest in the development of a moral relationship between citizens and rulers. He thus objected to the British presence and the Khedive on the grounds that they ruled absolutely.

At the opposite end of the spectrum from al Sayyid was Rashid Rida, who, in 1898, began publishing a journal called *al Manar* (*The Beacon*), which was to become the tribune of Islamic reformism. For Rida, the answer to the central question, "Why are Muslim countries backward?" was society's deviation from Islam. Rida appreciated the technological prowess of the West, but he believed there was a direct link between the moral principles of Islam and the healthy development of society.[20] If Islam was properly understood and practiced, then prosperity, development, and strength would surely follow. Rida was clearly responding to the work of two important Islamic thinkers, Ahmad ibn Hanbal (780–855) and Taqi al Din ibn Taymiyya (1263–1328) who laid the groundwork for *salafism*, which posits that true Islam is the combination of principles contained in the Quran and in the practices by which the Prophet Mohammed and his companions lived.[21] The vast majority of *salafis* are peaceful, but echoes of Rida's (and earlier *salafist* theorists) ideas and those, in particular, of ibn Taymiyya, can be found in the justifications and prescriptions that Islamic extremists have often invoked to defend their violence.[22]

Yet Islamic reformism should not be damned for the way in which Rida chose to interpret (or misinterpret) Abduh and al Afghani. He had, as the great historian of the Arab world, Albert Hourani, has sneeringly written, "the spirit of a disciple."[23] Rather, the central insight of the reformists—giving Islam pride of place—turned predominant thinking about nationalism on its head. Whereas the European experience indicated the need to break from religion as a guiding principle of society, the Islamic reformers emphasized religion as central to realizing the Muslim world's twin goals of independence and recovery of lost greatness.

SAAD ZAGHLUL AND THE WAFD

By far the most well-known and influential of al Afghani's disciples was Saad Zaghlul. Born to a moderately prosperous family in the Nile Delta in either 1857 or 1860, Zaghlul came of age when Islamic reformism was at its apogee and European penetration of Egypt began in earnest. In 1871, Zaghlul graduated from al Azhar, the ancient mosque and university that had been the center of Sunni learning and scholarship since the tenth century. An acquaintance of Abduh's during his time at al Azhar, Zaghlul subsequently worked for him as the deputy editor of the *Official Gazette*—the journal in which the government published decrees, laws, and regulations—before earning a law degree and serving on Egypt's Court of Appeals. In 1906, the politically ambitious Zaghlul married the daughter of Prime Minister Mustafa Fahmi Pasha, which provided him with a much needed entrée into the rarefied world of the Egyptian ruling class and their British overlords. The same year, Zaghlul managed—with the assistance of British Consul General Lord Cromer—to have himself appointed minister of education.

Notwithstanding the association with Abduh and al Azhar, Zaghlul's worldview was largely secular. Yet, he did share with many of Abduh's other followers the insight that educational and legal reforms were necessary components of Egypt's drive for independence. During his time at the Education Ministry, he sought to increase literacy, replace English with Arabic as the language of instruction, and increase the number of schools. Zaghlul's tenure as minister of education lasted until 1910, when he was appointed minister of justice, where his major achievements were the establishment of a school to train justices in the application of Islamic law and the founding of the Egyptian

Bar Association—an organization that has, in a variety of ways, remained deeply influential in Egyptian politics. Yet Zaghlul's time at the Justice Ministry was relatively brief. Although he had developed a good relationship with Lord Cromer, who assumed by dint of his family ties to the pro-British Mustafa Fahmi Pasha that Zaghlul held similar views, he did not get on well with either of Cromer's immediate successors.

Zaghlul opposed the efforts of Sir Eldon Gorst, who replaced Cromer in 1907, to grant the Khedive the ability to exercise more power—albeit not independently from British interests—at the expense of the government. Prior to World War I, Zaghlul and other leading intellectuals and politicians who had emerged from Abduh's circle were pragmatic about the British in Egypt. Zaghlul, and especially Ahmad Lutfi al Sayyid, recognized the need to accommodate themselves to the political reality of Britain's presence. At the same time, they sought to extract whatever gains they could while the British remained in Egypt, hoping these changes would ultimately serve the cause of an independent Egypt. Reconciled as they were to Britain's presence, their primary objection was to London's absolute rule through the Khedive. Even after Lord Kitchener replaced Gorst as consul general, Zaghlul became increasingly embittered toward the British. Over the course of the following two years, the minister repeatedly clashed with the consul general on both a personal level and on matters of policy, leading to Zaghlul's resignation in 1913, so that he could run in the elections for the newly created Legislative Assembly—one of those reforms that nationalists hoped would prepare Egypt for a democratic future once it achieved its independence.[24]

Zaghlul won his election handily, and his peers voted him vice president of the assembly. Although the proto-parliament had very limited powers, Zaghlul became the leader of the opposition to the government and, by association, the British. The assembly was abolished when World War I broke out in 1914 and London declared Egypt a protectorate. This change fundamentally altered the nature of Britain's presence in Egypt. What had started out in the 1880s as an effort to ensure the financial stability of Egypt in the service of European banks had become a grander project requiring thousands of British troops and hundreds of government advisors embedded within the Egyptian bureaucracy. While the foreign presence in Egypt was always a source of controversy, friction, and ideological contestation, British conduct during the war only intensified these problems and generated entirely new challenges.

Prior to the establishment of the protectorate, British interaction with Egyptian society was largely confined to the elite. The impact on the rest of the population was not excessively brutal. There were, of course, exceptions, such as the notorious "Dinshawi incident" of 1906 in which a squabble between British soldiers and Egyptian villagers led to the sentencing of fifty-two Egyptians to either hard labor, public flogging, or, in the case of four of the accused, death. Despite this episode, which galvanized the population against the British, in some ways London's policy proved beneficial to Egypt's rural population in particular. Over the course of thirty years, British consul generals, especially Lord Cromer, undertook a range of administrative initiatives intended to improve the well-being of the population that had a profound socioeconomic effect on Egyptians. Agricultural reforms led to greater prosperity among Egypt's rural farmers and peasants. This afforded their children greater access to educational opportunities in secondary, professional, and technical schools, which were also expanded at the behest of the British. Yet the exigencies of ensuring British interests against the Central Powers (Germany, the Ottoman Empire, Austria-Hungary, and Bulgaria) after 1914 placed a heavy burden on Egypt's rural masses. The *fellahin*, most of whom were tenant farmers, and as such obligated to pay a significant tax to their absentee landlords, were forced to surrender animals and crops to the British to support the war effort. Many men from Upper Egypt were conscripted to be laborers for British forces in Egypt and Palestine. Indeed, the war altered the entire complexion of the British presence in Egypt as tens of thousands of additional "Tommies" were deployed to Egypt.

The combination of the war and the unintended consequences of British policy added impetus to the nationalist agitation that had begun thirty years prior. Lord Cromer's introduction of administrative and agricultural reforms in the 1880s had not only an economic impact on Egypt's rural population but also a political effect. Notably, a new technocratic class with deep ties to Egypt's masses emerged. It was this group of newly minted professionals, relatively wealthier farmers and administrators, that formed the crucible of Egypt's independence movement.[25]

Immediately after the armistice in November 1918, Egyptians began to press their nationalist demands in both London and Paris, where the final disposition of the outcome of the war was to be determined. Zaghlul and other members of the defunct Legislative Assembly proposed sending a delegation, or *wafd*, under their leadership to present British officials with Egypt's demands.[26] Zaghlul and his colleagues—whose group became known as *"al Wafd"*—opposed the participation of the actual Egyptian government of Prime Minister Hussein Rushdi Pasha. From the Wafd's perspective, the prime minister and the members of his government had served Britain's wartime interests, compromising their ability to make nationalist demands on the British and victorious powers. Yet London did not look favorably on negotiating with a group that had, from the perspective of the Foreign Office, no official standing. Strictly speaking, this was indeed the case. Zaghlul and his colleagues, Abd al Aziz Fahmi and Ali Shaarawi, had been legislators in a body that had not met in almost five years and even then wielded little or no influence on the government. This was a convenient cover for British officials who were, no doubt, reluctant to deal with Zaghlul's group, which was demanding an end to martial law, the abolition of Britain's protectorate, and representation at the Peace Conference in Paris as a prelude to independence. Despite or perhaps because of London's objections, the Wafd garnered strong public support. Nevertheless, the British continued to refuse the group's participation in the Paris peace talks.

At the same time that Zaghlul was lobbying British officials in Egypt for permission to travel to Paris, Cairo was rife with rumors that the Foreign Office had approved another delegation under the leadership of the Egyptian prime minister. Recognizing both Zaghlul's popularity and how damaging the rumors were to him and his government, the prime minister declared that unless the Wafd was invited to negotiate in London, he would quit. Still the British refused to include the Wafd. The prime minister kept his word and on March 1, 1919, Hussein Rushdi Pasha resigned, leaving Egypt without a government. In response to the increasing political agitation of the Wafd and its supporters, the British authorities declared the organization a threat to public order. They also exiled Zaghlul, Ismail Sidqi—an ambitious politician who had served as agriculture minister during World War I and who would later break with Zaghlul and the Wafd—and another leader of the organization, Hamad Basil, to Malta. British efforts to suppress the Wafd only served to enrage the Egyptian population, setting off demonstrations and riots that would last from the early spring through the summer, leaving twenty-nine British soldiers and more than eight hundred Egyptians dead.

If the Foreign Office needed any evidence that the Wafd commanded popular support, the convulsion of protests and violence that swept the country during the "nationalist revolution of 1919" should have been a clear indication. London's only response was to replace the ineffective Sir Reginald Wingate with its victorious commander in Palestine, Field Marshal Edmund Allenby, as its point man in Cairo. As high commissioner, Allenby's position regarding the Wafd was more forthcoming than his predecessor.[27] Indeed, on taking up residence in Cairo in October 1919, the new high commissioner appealed to religious leaders for help in restoring calm to Egypt's streets. He also met with Wafdist politicians in an effort to reach an accommodation with the group. Yet, London's continued refusal to deal with the Wafd, combined with its insistence that the protectorate remain in place, undercut Allenby's efforts to restore order.

Even as the Foreign Office was taking a hard line on the protectorate, British Foreign Minister Lord Curzon was shifting his position on the Wafd, if ever so slightly. Once Curzon was assured that Britain's wartime Allies would recognize the legitimacy of extending the protectorate, the foreign minister reasoned that there would be no harm in allowing the Wafd to go to the peace talks and releasing Zaghlul from exile. With support for the protectorate assured, Curzon concluded that Egyptian demands at the Peace Conference would come to naught, regardless of who spoke for Cairo.[28] On this issue, the Foreign Office was quite correct. American President Woodrow Wilson may have articulated the right for national self-determination in his famous Fourteen Points speech to a joint session of Congress in January 1918, but Washington recognized the British protectorate over Egypt, as did all the other victorious powers.[29] The only issue that London was willing to negotiate was some form of Egyptian autonomy under the protectorate—far less than the independence that the vast majority of Egyptians desired.

The ongoing popular protests in favor of the Wafd and independence forced the government of Hussein Rushdi Pasha—he had been brought back to government on April 9—to resign once again. Allenby and the Foreign Office then turned to the former prime minister and rival to Zaghlul, Mohammed Said Pasha, to form a government in late May. The Wafdists and their followers interpreted this move as a British effort to once again defy public will and sow additional fissures among Egyptian elites in the hope that the national movement would succumb to infighting. At about the same time, the British declared their intention to investigate the disturbances that had rocked Egypt for the better part of the spring. The Commission of Inquiry charged with investigating the violence in Egypt—the Milner Mission, named after Lord Alfred Milner, who led the effort—arrived in Cairo in December 1919 and stayed until the following April. Despite the five-month stay, most political leaders and groups boycotted the Mission at the behest of the Wafd. Yet Zaghlul's public position was quite different from his private intentions. In what was no doubt an effort to embarrass the Mohammed Said Pasha government and Allenby, Zaghlul made his way to London in June and undertook negotiations with Milner. They were able to achieve a draft memorandum on the basic points of a treaty between Egypt and Great Britain that would abolish the protectorate and recognize Egypt's independence so long as certain British critical interests in Egypt were secured.

The memorandum represented a marked step forward in Egypt's drive for independence, but the two governments failed to enter negotiations to draft a formal treaty. Zaghlul was opposed to any other individual or group taking credit for what would ultimately be a great national achievement and thus he refused to take part in any negotiations that included the government. The Egyptian prime minister, now Adli Yakan—a descendant of Mohammed Ali—did not want to enter negotiations without Zaghlul, recognizing the enormous popular prestige the Wafd leader commanded. Nevertheless, by May 1921, Yakan determined that he would send a delegation to Britain to negotiate without the participation of Zaghlul and his organization. In order to head off Zaghlul's almost certain efforts to incite his followers against the government, High Commissioner Allenby sent the Wafd leader into exile again. The resulting explosion of violence forced London's hand, however. On February 22, 1922, Allenby announced the "Declaration of the British Government to Egypt" in which Egypt was offered independence so long as four issues were "reserved" for London's control: the security of imperial communications, defense of Egypt against foreign aggression, the protection of minorities and foreign interests, and Sudan.

QUASI-INDEPENDENCE

The declaration was an achievement in many respects. The protectorate was terminated on March 15, 1922, freeing Egyptian leaders to set their own goals and national priorities. The institutions of the state were quickly handed over to Egyptians, including the military. The struggles of the previous forty years finally seemed to be coming to a close. For the first time in more than a century, Egyptians were in control of their own national destiny. For all the promise of the early days after independence, however, the role of Great Britain and its four "reserved points" would remain a critical factor in Egyptian politics for the next thirty years. Given the nationalist battles of the preceding years, particularly the bloody months of 1919, ensuring one's nationalist credentials became paramount for Egyptian politicians. As a result, almost immediately after Egypt's independence, its leaders sought to undo the reserved points, believing quite correctly that these provisions undermined Egypt's claims to sovereignty. A draft version of the April 1923 constitution went so far as to proclaim King Fuad—who had become monarch in 1917—the ruler of Egypt *and* Sudan, in violation of the agreement with Britain that reserved Sudan for future consideration. The provision was removed from the final draft when London reacted strongly to the Egyptians. It was this type of capitulation—or the perception of it—to British demands that would do much to complicate Egyptian politics in the ensuing decades.

Egypt's problems during this period were not solely a function of Great Britain's continued presence, however. Egyptian politicians, in particular the Wafdist leadership, pursued an agenda that was based primarily on self-aggrandizement and the pursuit of power. When the Wafd came to power after the general elections, securing 90 percent of the seats in parliament, its distinguished history of struggle against oppression did not carry over to governing. Although often described as liberal, the Wafd distinguished itself for wielding anti-democratic measures in the same manner that British and royal officials had done between 1881 and the declaration of February 1922.[30] For example, in response to criticism from the opposition press, Zaghlul—who was now prime minister—brandished the notorious Press Law of 1881, which had been amended in 1909. The law allowed the government to refer journalists and editors to the criminal courts instead of charging them with misdemeanors. The prime minister also revealed his authoritarian impulses when he sought to close down newspapers that were offensive to him and the Wafd. Zaghlul also retained the Law of Associations, which forced political parties and other groups to seek permission from the government before they could meet.[31]

The situation did not improve after Zaghlul's untimely death in August 1927. Although prominent and popular among the party faithful, Zaghlul's successor, Mustafa al Nahhas, was largely ineffective, hamstrung by the continued British presence in Egypt. Despite the blatant attempt to unilaterally maneuver Egypt out from under the reserved points in the draft constitution four years earlier, the Egyptian government sought primarily to alter the situation through negotiations. The status of those negotiations became a constant source of friction in Egyptian politics as competitors for power consistently used the British presence and the inability of al Nahhas to do anything about it to undermine his rule. Indeed, al Nahhas's government fell in June 1930 over the breakdown of Anglo-Egyptian talks.

Al Nahhas's failure led to the emergence of Ismail Sidqi as the strongman of Egyptian politics. Sidqi had been a supporter of Zaghlul and went into exile with the Wafdist leader in Malta in March 1919. He ultimately broke with Zaghlul over the leadership of the Wafd and became head of the Liberal Party, serving as the interior minister in a short-lived coalition government that the Liberals joined in the mid-1920s. When King Fuad tapped him to form a government in 1930, Sidqi was widely regarded to be "pro-Palace." Confronted as he was with a range of unprecedented economic and social problems stemming from the Great Depression, Sidqi was determined to prevent the constitution from getting in the way of what he regarded as effective governance. In collaboration with the Palace, Sidqi ruled Egypt for the next five years by decree.

Sidqi's authoritarian rule produced a strong reaction from the Wafd and others in the opposition who began to pressure King Fuad for a return to constitutional rule. The Palace assented to these demands in April 1935, but it would be another eight months before the 1923 constitution was reestablished due to British opposition. The Foreign Office was concerned that if the constitution were reestablished it would also mean the return of the Wafd, which London regarded as inimical to its interests. But Britain's heavy hand backfired, resulting in rioting and demonstrations to protest London's interference in Egypt's domestic affairs. The momentary instability gave the king requisite political cover to issue a decree reinstating the constitution and forcing a new round of negotiations between Cairo and London over the four reserved points.

Those negotiations, conducted on the Egyptian side by al Nahhas—who became prime minister again—resulted in the Anglo-Egyptian Treaty of August 1936. Although the treaty ostensibly dealt with all four points, in reality the agreement only addressed Britain's protection of minority and foreign interests effectively. The new Anglo-Egyptian military alliance that the pact established was little more than a semantic upgrade from the reserved point concerning Britain's protection of Egypt against foreign aggression, leaving a garrison of ten thousand British troops in the Canal Zone—an issue that would play a critical role in the Free Officers' so-called revolution sixteen years later. Finally, the treaty left Sudan's sovereignty to the Sudanese people, which ran counter to Egyptian demands for unity of the Nile Valley. Still, al Nahhas could boast a number of achievements. The treaty bolstered Egypt's independence, as the British high commissioner became an ambassador, thereby paving the way for the further Egyptianization of the government.

Despite these successes, Egypt's domestic politics remained unstable and deeply polarized. The internecine power struggles of Egypt's leading politicians further damaged an already deteriorating political environment. In a striking display of cynicism, al Nahhas, determined to remain in power for the duration of parliament's four-year tenure, organized a paramilitary group called the Blue Shirts to intimidate opponents and mobilize support for the Wafd. Throughout 1937, the relationship between the newly crowned King Farouk and the Wafd grew increasingly difficult, with the government intent on ensuring that the Palace neither exercise power at its expense nor garner popular support. For his part, the king, who ascended the throne in 1936 after Fuad's death, grew increasingly concerned about what he perceived to be the Wafd's own power grab and looked upon the emergence of the Blue Shirts with alarm. In response, Farouk fought the Wafdist government on a range of issues including appointments to parliament, the budget, military commissions, and who controlled the religious institutions of the country.[32] The latter was especially important as Farouk sought the assistance of religious authorities, in particular the leaders of al Azhar, in his struggle with al Nahhas and the Wafd. At the same time, an organization called Misr al Fatat (Young Egypt) emerged with its own paramilitary shock troops, the Green Shirts. This fascist organization was often deployed in the streets and at Wafdist demonstrations to rally support for the Palace through slogans like "Country, Islam, and King." The fusing of nationalist and religious sentiments with the monarchy inherent in these slogans was no accident. It was clearly intended to emphasize that the Palace, in contrast to the Wafd, was the proper steward of both the nation and Islam. The struggle became so intense and the political environment so fraught that a member of the Green Shirts, Ezzedin Abdel Qader, who was the grandson of Ahmad Urabi, attempted to assassinate Prime Minister al Nahhas while he was traveling to a political rally in the Shubra section of Cairo. A month later, the king achieved what Abdel Qader's bullets could not when the government, fatally wounded from its incessant battles with the Palace, proved weak enough for Farouk to dissolve it.

THE MUSLIM BROTHERHOOD

The most important group to emerge in Egypt during the interwar years was a religious society that was to have a profound and lasting impact on Egyptian, Middle Eastern, and global politics: the Society of Muslim Brothers, also known as the Muslim Brotherhood. The society was founded in March 1928 when six laborers who toiled for the British in Ismailiyya—a city in the Suez Canal Zone—implored a twenty-two year-old primary school Arabic teacher named Hassan al Banna to lead them in an effort to reestablish the dignity and honor of Arabs and Muslims. It was no accident that these workmen sought out al Banna, who devoted most of his life, despite his young age, to Islamist activism.

Born in 1906 in the town of Mahmudiyya, about a two-hour drive northwest of Cairo, Hassan al Banna was steeped in the principles, values, and teachings of Islam from a very young age. His father repaired watches as a vocation, but was also the *muezzin* and imam of the local mosque. Al Banna joined the first of an extensive list of religious societies when he was twelve years old. The "Society for Moral Behavior," which al Banna eventually led, was intended to educate young boys about Islam's moral proscriptions. At the same time, he became interested in Sufism—the central tenet of which is the belief that Muslims can achieve a union with and perfect understanding of God through a ritual called *dhikr*, or remembrance of God. In this ritual, participants induce themselves into a trancelike state through the repetition of religious phrases, drumming, and taking stimulants.[33] Sufis are organized around "orders," fraternity-like organizations called *tara'iq* that follow a charismatic leader. When he was thirteen years old, al Banna became the secretary of a local Sufi order that advocated for Islamic morality and enlisted local residents to resist the work of Christian missionaries in the area. He eventually became a full member of the Hassifiya Order of Sufism three years later.

After a short time at the Primary Teachers Training School in the Nile Delta town of Damanhur, al Banna moved to Cairo, where he enrolled in Dar al Ulum. Founded in 1873, the school was intended to provide an education in the sciences to aspiring Egyptian teachers.[34] When al Banna arrived in Cairo in 1922, the political ferment that had led to the nationalist "revolution" of 1919 had hardly abated. The political machinations of the Wafd, the Palace, the British, and other smaller political parties accounted for the significant tension and polarization that had become a regular feature of Egypt's post–World War I political arena.

To al Banna, the state of Egyptian politics reflected the pernicious effect of secularism buffeting Egyptian society, whether it was the orientation of the university, the cultural milieu that celebrated secularism, or direct attacks on religious orthodoxy that emerged in Egypt.[35] The perceived appeal of secularism deeply concerned al Banna, and as a result he sought out the religious authorities at al Azhar for their counsel about what could be done about Egyptian society's apparent pulling away from Islam. His interviews with al Azhar leaders and others proved disappointing, however. Al Banna came away from those meetings convinced that Egypt's men of religion were resigned to the social changes going on around them and were thus not inclined to stem the tide of secular values and ideas. He came to the conclusion that Egypt needed a cadre of like-minded Muslims who could bring the faith back to the people.[36] Toward that end, after his assignment to a primary school in Ismailiyya, al Banna sought to build this group through teaching, lecturing, and no small amount of politicking. New to Ismailiyya, al Banna sought to ingratiate himself with local religious leaders, politicians, and leading families.

Ismailiyya was paradigmatic of the problems that plagued the whole of Egypt. Due to the city's strategic location along the Suez Canal, Ismailiyya hosted large numbers of British forces and offices of the Suez Canal Company—tangible evidence that Egypt remained under foreign domination despite the country's formal independence.[37] Compounding the perception of humiliation was the extraordinary gap in the living standards and quality of life between Egyptians and the foreign economic elite who called Ismailiyya home. Al Banna's call for Muslims to return to their religious values and roots was necessary to reverse their degradation and that of Egyptian society at the hands of foreigners. Clearly, al Banna's message, which emphasized the centrality of Islam in resisting the depredations of foreigners, tapped into the widely held resentments and frustration of Egyptians. After all, there were many religious societies in Egypt at the time, but most were quite small, local affairs with little in the way of what could be considered a national following. Yet, within four short years, the Muslim Brotherhood established branches in the main cities of the Canal Zone besides Ismailiyya—Port Said and Suez—as well as an office in the small town of Abu Suwayyr along the route from Ismailiyya to Cairo.

At this time, al Banna and his lieutenants made the decision to shift the Brotherhood's base of operation to Egypt's capital. There was little point to the Brotherhood's advocating and agitating for the return of religious values in regional cities. The organization had been successful in establishing a core following, but to have any chance of altering the trajectory of Egyptian society, it was imperative for the Brothers to bring their message to Cairo. The city was not only Egypt's political, economic, and cultural capital, but also that of the entire Middle East. Movements, ideologies, knowledge, and culture tended to reverberate from Cairo in concentric circles to the rest of Egypt then to the Levant and to the Persian Gulf beyond.[38]

When al Banna set up shop in Cairo in 1932, he had honed the ideas that were to become central to the Brotherhood's message of social and political reform that would in the ensuing decades transform Egyptian politics and affect nearly every country in the region. At the heart of the Brotherhood's emerging set of principles were three related ideas. First, Islam is a "total system," meaning that classic Western-liberal notions of a separation of church and state did not apply in the Muslim world. In the type of Islamic society that the Brotherhood advocated, politics was always sacred. Second, for the Brothers, Islam is based on two primary sources: the holy Quran, which is God's revelation to his messenger on Earth, the Prophet Mohammed, and the compilation of the sayings and actions of Mohammed known as the Sunna. This was the key to understanding Islam and building a Muslim society. Finally, "Islam was applicable to all times and places"—a notion that reinforced the centrality of religion in all aspects of a Muslim's life.[39]

Armed with a growing and increasingly influential organization, al Banna moved forcefully into Egypt's political fray, as his entire project of reform required the mobilization of the Brotherhood. Initially, al Banna and his colleagues hoped to achieve an Islamic society working through the Palace and King Farouk. The monarch was quite popular at the time of his coronation and, in particular, the leadership of the Brotherhood regarded him as a potential ally. The sixteen-year-old Farouk was under the tutelage of the well-respected rector of al Azhar, Sheikh Mustafa al Maraghi, and Ali Mahir, who served as the head of the royal court and prime minister. The pro-religious, anti-Wafdist outlook of both al Maraghi and Mahir provided an opportunity for the Brotherhood. This was not universally popular among the rank and file, however.[40] Yet al Banna's relationship with the court was hardly the most controversial issue confronting the organization. There were among the growing membership of the Brotherhood those who advocated using force to promote an Islamic society. Al Banna rejected this course, causing defections from the organization that resulted in the emergence of radical offshoots. It is important to underscore that while al Banna eschewed violence in the late 1930s, he was not at all opposed to arming the Brotherhood. Still, the controversial question of the Brotherhood's use of political violence was not to become a serious issue until after World War II.

WORLD WAR . . . AGAIN

The outbreak of war in Europe in 1939, Egypt's strategic position in the Middle East, and the exigencies of the British war effort combined to have a significant impact on Egyptian politics. The Palace and successive governments continually sought to balance their treaty obligations to the British government with the demands of Egypt's nationalist camp, which either sought neutrality or alignment with the Axis powers. The situation in Egypt was decidedly tense as German forces advanced through North Africa toward Egypt. The British Foreign Office pressed for change in Cairo as the government of Ali Mahir refused to declare war on Germany and did only what was minimally required under its treaty commitments to London and nothing more to assist the British war effort.[41] Under heavy pressure from the British, Mahir was dismissed in favor of Hassan Sabri who was, in turn, succeeded by Hussein Sirri. British military successes in Egypt's western desert helped relieve the pressure on the Egyptian government for the better part of 1941. Prime Minister Sirri's decision on January 6, 1942, to break relations with Vichy France precipitated another political crisis. Already predisposed toward the Axis powers due to sixty years of Britain's uninterrupted presence in their country, the Egyptian population reacted negatively to Sirri's move. Widespread demonstrations shook the Sirri government, ultimately bringing it down.

In an astonishing irony, the British then demanded that the king appoint a Wafdist government. Initially, Farouk objected, calling instead for a coalition government. On February 4, the monarch found British soldiers and a squadron of Stuart M3 tanks surrounding the Abdin Palace in an open display of British hostility to Egypt's national sovereignty. King Farouk succumbed to London's ultimate threat and appointed al Nahhas prime minister. Although al Nahhas penned a note to the British ambassador claiming that the circumstances of his appointment in no way indicated his or his party's support for Great Britain's interference in Egypt's internal affairs, the damage was done.

Egypt's nationalists never forgave al Nahhas or Farouk for their unwillingness to resist British pressure.

Against the backdrop of these events, which led to a souring of relations between the Palace and the Muslim Brotherhood—the organization advocated a strict policy of non-belligerency in World War II—al Banna was continuing to expand the scope of the Brotherhood's activities and contacts. In 1940, the Brotherhood leader met with a young army officer named Anwar Sadat.[42] Second Lieutenant Sadat, along with another officer, Abd al Munim Abd al Rauf, became the primary liaisons between a discontented group of officers and the Brotherhood. During their periodic meetings, Sadat and al Banna shared details of their respective organizations. For example, Sadat learned that al Banna had been collecting weapons for the Brotherhood. In return for disclosing this closely guarded secret, Sadat offered details on the rapidly coalescing group of officers who were distressed over the political polarization and corruption of Egyptian politics. Although al Banna had previously rejected "forceful reform," his admission to Sadat about the Brotherhood's weapons only told part of the story. By 1941, al Banna began establishing paramilitary groups within the Brotherhood known as *al jihaz al sirri* (secret apparatus) also referred to as al *nizam al khass* (special section). Army officers who were attracted to the Brotherhood's message made up the ranks and were responsible for training the armed cadres. Despite the cordiality of relations between the Brotherhood and the officers, which included a discussion of merging the two groups, al Banna reportedly demurred when asked if the Brotherhood could be relied on to assist the officers should they make a move against the government.[43] Al Banna saw the situation as quite the opposite from his military interlocutors. He believed the Brotherhood's status as a mass movement consecrated upon the organization sole leadership of the drive for national reform and independence from the British.

For its part, the al Nahhas government, cognizant of al Banna and the Brothers' prestige, sought to placate the group. For example, in exchange for al Banna's agreement not to stand in the 1942 elections, al Nahhas's government cracked down on alcohol consumption and prostitution and permitted the Brotherhood to resume its newspaper and periodical publications, a privilege that al Nahhas had revoked earlier that year.[44] Within the Wafd itself there were competing ideas about how to deal with the challenge the Brothers presented. One faction believed the Brotherhood was beyond the pale and should be repressed. Others advocated leveraging the prestige of the Brothers in the Wafd's struggle with their common foe, the communists who gained political ground in Egypt during the war years. Generally, the Wafd approached the Brotherhood's challenge with a keen sense of the party's own short-term interests, which dictated periodic accommodation and confrontation with al Banna's organization.

From 1944 through most of the immediate post–World War II period, a series of "minority governments" ruled Egypt, which only heightened the political maneuvering among the Wafd, Muslim Brotherhood, Palace, government, and British.[45] The Palace clearly wanted to avoid tapping yet another Wafdist government, even though the minority parties were typically offshoots of the Wafd whose leadership split from the party for reasons having less to do with policy than personality differences. Among these smaller parties, King Farouk most often turned to a faction that dissident Wafdists founded called the Sa'adist Party.

In October 1944, Ahmad Mahir (not to be confused with his brother Ali) led the Sa'adists into government. Mahir opposed the Brotherhood and openly supported the Allied war effort. His position on the war was no doubt motivated by the tide of the fighting in Europe following the Allied invasion of France the previous June. Indeed, by the time Mahir assumed the prime ministry, World War II in Europe would last only another eight months. Mahir wanted to secure Egypt's place at whatever postwar settlements conference was to come and was thus determined to declare war on the Axis powers, despite the profound opposition of Egyptian nationalists of all stripes. On February 24, 1945, Mahir was assassinated in parliament as he read out Egypt's declaration of war. Al Banna and other leaders of the Brotherhood were suspected in the plot, but were subsequently cleared of the crime, which a member of the Nationalist Party perpetrated.

In Mahir's place, King Farouk appointed Sa'adist party leader Mahmoud Fahmi Nuqrashi. The assassination of Mahir, and the intense nationalist agitation of the Wafd and the Brotherhood in the months after the war, compelled Nuqrashi to request negotiations with London over Britain's evacuation from Egypt and the disposition of Sudan. The British response in January 1946 represented the paradigmatic diplomatic nonresponse, which committed London to nothing in the way of either negotiations or withdrawal. The popular anger with British high-handedness temporarily unified the Brotherhood, communists, and Wafd in the streets. On February 9, students representing these groups sent a memo to King Farouk demanding negotiations with Britain and followed it with what was supposed to be a peaceful march to the Abdin Palace on the same day to emphasize their position. The demonstration turned into a massacre as a confrontation between the police and unarmed students ended in bloodshed on the Abbas Bridge as the protestors made their way from the Egyptian University to the palace. Shaken by the events, King Farouk held a conference at the palace the next day during which he repudiated the violence and expressed support for the students' efforts. The Nuqrashi government was summarily dismissed, and former Prime Minister Ismail Sidqi—who had ruled by decree in the 1930s—was asked to form a new government.

Relations between the government and the Brotherhood improved during Sidqi's tenure, which spanned from February 1946 until the following December.[46] Given the instability of Egyptian politics, the prime minister was forced to focus on his short-term political fortunes. Surveying the political landscape, the prime minister, the king, and no doubt the British regarded the Wafd as the primary impediment to their interests. Consequently, Sidqi established an implicit understanding with the Brotherhood, the only other organization in Egypt besides the Wafd that could claim a mass, national following. Restrictions on the Brotherhood, which was placed under surveillance after the Mahir assassination, were loosened. The organization's publications began to appear, and the organization was permitted to purchase newsprint at a favorable rate. Brotherhood cadres that were trained to ensure cohesion within the movement and intimidate supporters of other groups were also permitted to operate openly. Yet events outside of Egypt would conspire against continuation of the tacit agreement between Sidqi's government and the Brotherhood.

PALESTINE

As the Jewish community in Palestine moved toward statehood in the 1940s, political conditions simultaneously deteriorated in Egypt. By mid-decade, al Banna and the Brotherhood had been involved in the affairs of Palestine for ten years. There was a clear pan-Islamic strand to the early Brotherhood's worldview; thus, it was only natural for al Banna and his organization to become actively involved in what they perceived as the usurpation of Muslim lands. During the 1936–1939 strikes and violence that gripped the Arab and Jewish populations in Palestine, the Brotherhood was deeply involved in raising awareness of the perceived dangers of Zionism to Palestine. Al Banna funneled funds from Brotherhood coffers to the Palestinians. In addition, the Brothers published pamphlets and distributed leaflets, and al Banna included Palestine in his speeches and advocacy work at the time.

Yet, the Brotherhood's advocacy on behalf of Palestine and its Arab inhabitants was also intimately linked to Egyptian nationalism. The Brothers shared the concern with the Islamic reformers that the weakness and disunity of Muslims invited foreign intervention and societal problems. Zionism, which emerged in the late nineteenth century and provided both the ideological and operational bases for a Jewish redemption in Palestine, was regarded—inaccurately—as an instrument of European colonialism. In this way, the plight of Palestinian Arabs was linked to that of Egyptians who were contending with powerful foreign forces bent on exploitation. For Egyptian nationalists, confronting Zionism was hardly distinguishable from their struggle with Britain's presence in Egypt.

The situation in Palestine, the British presence in Egypt, and Egyptian nationalism came to a head in 1947. At the end of 1946, Ismail Sidqi's premiership gave way in December to yet another Nuqrashi-led government. The cause of Sidqi's fall was his inability to quell a series of riots, demonstrations, and boycotts that Egyptian nationalists had undertaken against Britain and British interests in Egypt. Nuqrashi, confronting a track record of failure on the part of successive Egyptian governments to come to an agreement with Great Britain bilaterally, decided to pursue an altogether different track by taking Egypt's grievances to the newly created UN.

Looking back, from more than six decades later, this decision was a gross miscalculation. After all, Great Britain was a leading member of the recently victorious world powers. In a competition between British interests and those of Egypt in the UN Security Council, the odds were surely stacked heavily against Cairo. Yet, in the postwar environment infused with the heady promise of the United Nations, the exhaustion of the European powers after engaging in six years of total war, the rise of the United States, and the beginnings of decolonization, Nuqrashi and his advisors could hardly be faulted for seeking redress of their grievances at the UN. As it turned out, the Security Council adjourned in September 1947 without resolving the conflict between Egypt and Britain. The decision of the Security Council not to adjudicate the conflict was reminiscent of Woodrow Wilson's decision to recognize the British protectorate over twenty-eight years prior at the postwar settlement conference in Paris. To add to Egyptian frustration, two months later the United Nations General Assembly voted to partition

Palestine, paving the way for the fulfillment of Zionist dreams—the establishment of the state of Israel.

Even before the Security Council's decision, al Banna had told the Brothers to prepare for jihad in Palestine.[47] Now the secret apparatus and other volunteers began training with the help of the disaffected army officers who had made contact with al Banna earlier in the decade. On April 25, 1948, the Brothers sent a "battalion" to el Arish in the northern Sinai in preparation for the conflict that would ultimately begin the following week.[48] Ahmad Abd al Aziz, an army officer on leave, led the group. Two other officers, Kemal al Din Hussein and Salah Salim, who would go on to be members of the original nine Free Officers, also joined the Brotherhood battalion. When the battle was joined on the first of May, the Brotherhood's units engaged Israeli forces near Beersheba, but they were largely ineffective. Later in the war, they took part in Arab operations in Jerusalem and Bethlehem, though again they were nonfactors. The Brothers did, however, distinguish themselves during the last stage of the war when they undertook the task of resupplying the Egyptian forces that were trapped in the Faluja pocket. Despite this heroism, the Brotherhood could not entirely escape Cairo's fraught political environment. In November 1948, the Nuqrashi government outlawed the group for allegedly planning an "imminent revolution."[49] On the battlefield, the Egyptian commanders gave the Brotherhood volunteers a choice: they could be returned to Cairo, where they would almost certainly face imprisonment, or remain in the conflict zone under the strict control of the Egyptian armed forces. Most elected to stay.

PRELUDE TO A COUP

The government's decision to outlaw the Brotherhood was actually long in coming. The Brothers, along with the Wafd, had played a central role in destabilizing Egypt. Between 1945 and Nuqrashi's order, Ahmad Mahir was assassinated, there had been an attempt on Mustafa al Nahhas's life, the wartime minister of finance was murdered, there was random violence against British personnel and interests, and two Cairo cinemas were bombed, not to mention the deaths of demonstrators at the hands of police during the periodic convulsions of mass protest in Cairo and other cities. Notwithstanding the bloody nature of Egyptian politics and the Brotherhood's role in these disturbances, it was not until 1948 and the discovery of the secret apparatus that led to the outright ban of the Brothers. During that year, two members of the Brotherhood's armed wing assassinated a well-respected judge for sending one of their colleagues to prison for attacking British troops. Then there was what became known as the "Jeep incident" in which members of the Brotherhood were caught transporting weapons and explosives in Cairo. The Brotherhood argued that the cache was intended for its volunteers in Palestine, but the discovery raised suspicion in the government that the Brothers were planning a domestic insurrection. Finally, two additional plots to assassinate the Wafd's leader, Mustafa al Nahhas, were revealed.

Although Nuqrashi's decision to dissolve the Brotherhood was taken to stabilize the political arena by staving off further violence, it did anything but. With the organization's closure, al Banna simply no longer maintained control of the Brothers. Communication was disrupted, making it difficult for him to exert his influence on his hardcore followers.[50] Untethered from al Banna and his well-developed political instincts, the armed cadres of the secret apparatus and other members reeling from the dissolution of their organization were free to seek revenge on the government as they saw fit. And, indeed, on December 28, 1948, a Brother named Abd al Majid Ahmad Hassan murdered Prime Minister Nuqrashi. Egypt's next prime minister, Ibrahim Abd al Hadi, avenged Nuqrashi's murder. All opposition groups and leaders were subject to official repression. The hardest hit was the Brothers, four thousand of whom were sent to prison. What was described as "official terror" reached its height when al Banna himself was assassinated outside the building housing the Young Men Muslim's Association on February 12, 1949, as he got into a taxi. The government was widely believed to have sanctioned the killing.

In January 1950, the Wafd returned to power after five years. Given the damage to the party—much of it self-inflicted—in the political struggles of the previous twenty-five years, the Wafd immediately sought to shore up its nationalist credentials. Toward that end, the Wafd reopened negotiations with London over Britain's status in Egypt and pursued policies to address the yawning socioeconomic problems of the country. The talks with the Foreign Office lasted until October 1951 when, frustrated with the British, Prime Minister al Nahhas unilaterally abrogated the 1936 Anglo-Egyptian Treaty. Along with celebrations, al Nahhas's actions set off a round of strikes, work stoppages, and slowdowns designed to make life as difficult as possible for the British and their interests in the country.[51] There was also an uptick in violence against British personnel, particularly in the Canal Zone between November 1951 and January 1952. The Wafdists were caught off guard by the public demonstrations and the fierce response of British forces to the provocations in the Canal Zone. Despite public demands to do so, there was no way the government was going to deploy the Egyptian armed forces against the mighty British. This unwillingness in turn fueled anti-Wafd sentiment, leading to riots and demonstration against both al Nahhas and King Farouk.

In the midst of this ferment, British forces in Ismailiyya began to clear the city of all armed groups, including the Egyptian police. On January 25, the British commander, General George Erskine, informed the deputy governor of Ismailiyya to surrender his and his officers' arms and leave the city. Under orders from the Interior Ministry, the Egyptians refused to abandon their post. In response, the British shelled the police compound, killing fifty officers and gendarmes. This latest offense to Egypt's sovereignty led to mass rioting. On January 26, Cairo burned in an orgy of anti-British outrage. Al Nahhas was dismissed for the last time in favor of Ali Mahir—the wartime prime minister and brother of the late prime minister, Ahmad Mahir—who was charged with restoring order. Mahir's government lasted less than two months. In March, a lawyer and former minister of education under al Nahhas, named Nagib al Hilali replaced Mahir.

Throughout the political upheaval of the post-Palestine-war period, the clandestine organization of officers that Sadat divulged to Hassan al Banna began to reveal itself. Gamal Abdel Nasser and his associates, deeply embarrassed by the defeat in Palestine, were able to leverage that experience into a nationalist narrative that placed blame not only for that defeat, but also for Egypt's general political instability on King Farouk, the Wafd, political parties, the royalist senior command, and the British. This message represented a unique challenge to all the forces in the country that had vied for political supremacy.

The first open confrontation between the officers and the king occurred when Nasser and his comrades sought control of the influential Officers Club in December 1951. Sensing a challenge in which his loyalists were unlikely to prevail, the king ordered that the club's elections be postponed. In a prelude to the outright sedition that was to come months later, the Free Officers pressed 300 to 400 of their colleagues to hold the elections in early January despite the king's wishes. Armed with an eloquent denunciation of the status quo under Farouk, Nasser and his colleagues swept the poll. The Free Officers, virtually unknown to most Egyptians, thus burst onto the chaotic political scene as a formidable force. Not only were they armed, but the Free Officers were suddenly politically dangerous.

Licking his wounds from the success of the group of upstarts, the king sought to purchase the political quiescence of the armed forces. Farouk ordered Prime Minister al Hilali to raise the pay of the entire officer corps. Yet al Hilali's government resigned in late June when it became clear that the king wanted a government that would be reliably pro-Palace.[52] As a former Wafdist turned political independent, al Hilali clearly did not fit the bill. Instead King Farouk turned to Hussein Sirri—a political independent who had served variously as foreign, interior, and prime minister since the 1930s in addition to a brief tenure as the king's director of cabinet affairs—to become prime minister. The new cabinet was Egypt's thirty-fourth since the country's formal independence three decades earlier, but Sirri's premiership would not last long. The prime minister had his own ideas about how to defuse the growing crisis between the Palace and young commanders. Sirri wanted to appoint General Mohammed Naguib to be minister of war in an effort to mollify the Free Officers.[53] Naguib led the Officers Club at the behest of Nasser and his colleagues until July when Farouk suddenly dismissed the board and replaced it with a group of loyalists. Naguib refused Sirri's offer and in any case Farouk appointed Colonel Ismail Shirin—his brother-in-law—to the post.[54] In response to this rank nepotism that was sure to compound the friction with the Free Officers, Sirri resigned on July 20. The elevation of Colonel Shirin indicated that Farouk was intent on reimposing control over the officer corps. Should the king and his new minister of war prevail, it would surely mean the arrest of the Free Officers for their open insubordination of royal authority. Time was most certainly up, forcing Nasser and his colleagues to act.

The Rise of the Officers

W HEN ANWAR SADAT finished informing Egypt and the
world of the Free Officers' coup, he and his colleagues
began the search for what to do next. Their communiqué
was remarkable for its lack of bombast typical of successful coup plotters and, importantly, for the absence of anything that resembled a plan
for the future of Egyptian politics. It reflected the parochial interests
of young officers who believed that poor leadership, profiteering, and
politics had burned them in the Palestine conflict. It was not ideology
or some grand project that drove the Free Officers' intervention, but
rather anger, shame, and fear of arrest that led them to put tanks and
troops on the streets in the wee hours of July 23. Sadat's reference to
"mischief-making elements" was an implicit reference to the political
parties and movements that had done much to destabilize the political
arena between the time of Egypt's nominal independence in 1923 and
the morning of July 23, 1952, but this was a rhetorical device intended
to elicit support for the Officers, not the hint of an agenda for post-
coup Egypt.

REFORM, NOT REVOLUTION

Three days after seizing power, the Free Officers ordered the royal
yacht to convey King Farouk to exile in Italy, yet the Officers did not
immediately abolish the monarchy. Initially, Nasser and his associates did not seek a direct role in ruling the country primarily because,

despite not having a well-developed plan, their inclination was to undertake reform rather than regime change. Although the Officers disbanded the parliament, they left governing to a civilian prime minister and cabinet, whom the soldiers nevertheless sought to influence. Still, they had no program, no means, and no framework of thought to turn abstract notions about reform into a reality.

Essentially, they made it up as they went along.[1] The Officers' distinct lack of a guiding ideology combined with the unintended consequences of their intervention and the hard realities of Egyptian politics produced something quite different from the reform the Free Officers claimed they wanted. Indeed, instead of a renewed parliamentary system, the Officers oversaw the development of an authoritarian political order that endured, albeit in modified form, until early 2011.

This is not to suggest that the Officers did not stand for anything. In general, they shared the same basic views as all the other political players of the era, including the Wafd, the Muslim Brotherhood, factions of the Left, and a bevy of small parties and political independents—the parliamentary system needed reform, the British had to go, and changes were necessary to improve the socioeconomic standing of the vast majority of Egyptians. Of these, there was clearly a consensus on the status of the British, but there were different interpretations of what a "clean" parliamentary order entailed and of the best way to improve the lot of Egypt's rural poor, workers, and urban laborers. For the Officers, the goal was to forge a reformed political system along roughly the same lines of the parliamentary system they had just turned over, but with significant safeguards against the corruption and excesses that plagued Egyptian politics prior to the coup. As part of this process, they believed the old-guard political elites should stand aside, voluntarily or otherwise, and make way for a new, younger, more responsible party leadership. In essence, the Officers were looking for people just like them—men who, with their sense of mission, would work to ensure that Egypt fulfilled its potential.

The core group of nine Free Officers—Lieutenant Colonel Gamal Abdel Nasser, Major Abdel Hakim Amer, Lieutenant Anwar Sadat, Major Salah Salim, Major Kemal al Din Hussein, Wing Commander Gamal Salem, Squadron Leader Hassan Ibrahim, Major Khalid Mohieddin, and Wing Commander Abdel Latif al Boghdadi—came of age almost two decades after the 1919 Revolution and were among the first cadets admitted to the military academy after a Wafdist government opened it to all social classes in 1936. The two best-known officers (in the West), Nasser and Sadat, came from decidedly modest

origins while their colleagues were sons of minor officials, professionals, and small landowners.[2] This gave the Free Officers a certain
middle-class cast, though they actively cultivated the romantic notion
that most of them were from the hardscrabble towns and cities south
of Cairo or the Nile Delta region.

The Officers also nurtured the notion that theirs was a common
enterprise. Though in many important respects this was accurate, it is
clear that it was Nasser who stood out as the leader among the young
commanders who made up the Free Officers. Hagiographical accounts
of Nasser's life make much of his ostensible courage, organizational
capacity, political cunning, and great compassion for the Egyptian
people. There are, of course, grains of truth in these accounts, but
Nasser was far more complicated than the veritable superhero that he
was to become. He was, and remains for some, a towering figure in
Egyptian and Middle Eastern politics, having played a central role in
crafting a regime that was, to varying degrees, emulated in Tunisia,
Libya, Syria, Iraq, and Algeria. This was an unlikely trajectory for a
postal clerk's son, who lost his mother at eight years old. Despite what
his biographers claim was a strong intellectual curiosity from early on,
Nasser barely graduated from high school and failed out of law school
before entering the Military Academy (on his second try) in 1937. By
all accounts, Nasser's great talent was not his military acumen—though
his reflections on the Palestine war of 1948 suggest that he was competent at soldiering—but rather a complicated mix of political agitation,
conspiracy, opportunism, and leadership.[3]

Nasser was caught up in the political fervor gripping Egypt throughout his early years, having been attracted to the nationalism of Mustafa
Kamil (not to be confused with founder of modern Turkey who had a
similar sounding name) and his National Party, and to the thought of
the Islamic reformer, Mohammed Abduh. The consistent theme that
ran through the ideas of each of these thinkers was how the Muslim
world could rid itself of foreign domination. The 1936 Anglo-Egyptian
Treaty was, in particular, a marker for Nasser, who saw it as Cairo's
further submission to London's interests. As a result, his subsequent
political career was inextricably linked to Egypt's complicated relations
with the great powers. Although a nationalist and by most measures
deeply committed to justice, Nasser, as circumstances required, was
quite capable of compromising both principles. His political beliefs
and ability to lead drew like-minded young men into his orbit, among
them Sadat and Abdel Hakim Amer, who he met on deployments
to the garrison town of Mankabad in Upper Egypt and the Sudan,

respectively. The other six members of the original Free Officers were classmates of Nasser at the Military Academy.

With the exception of Khalid Mohieddin, who was a committed leftist, the Free Officers demonstrated an ideological opportunism both before and after the coup. This allowed them to consort with the Muslim Brotherhood, who regarded the Officers as a subgroup within their larger movement; the Left, which influenced the Officers' collective thinking concerning social justice; and even the exemplar of the parliamentary system that had failed so miserably, the Wafd.[4] In these contacts and consultations, the Officers sought to not only appropriate ideas from their interlocutors but also cultivate individuals within these groups who would be loyal to the Free Officers.

GREAT BRITAIN ON THE WAY OUT

Beyond social justice and reform, virtually all Egyptians wanted a resolution of the so-called national question, meaning the vexing issue of Great Britain's presence in Egypt and the status of Sudan, which Egyptians regarded as an integral part of their country. The historical affinity that Egyptians held for Sudan was based on a variety of factors, from cheap manpower and livestock to national aggrandizement, but there was also a strategic imperative that has long been a central feature of Egypt's domestic and foreign policies: security of the Nile. This continued to be a priority in Cairo's foreign policy agenda, which is why, prior to his fall, President Hosni Mubarak shielded Sudanese leader General Omar Bashir from the International Criminal Court for his alleged role in the Darfur genocide, resisted a new water-sharing agreement among the nine countries of the Nile basin, and opposed the early 2011 referendum on Sudan—though he accommodated himself to the inevitable result that would divide that country. Although it has become cliché, the river, which winds its way south to north from its headwaters in Ethiopia 4,132 miles to the Mediterranean on Egypt's north coast, is literally Egypt's lifeline. The vast majority of the country's arable land falls along a narrow strip on the banks of the river. Sudan's importance to Egypt stems from the fact that it is one of the few locations where the river could be dammed in a way that effectively reduces the Nile's flow, threatening Egypt's livelihood. The Egyptians have thus sought either to control the country themselves or ensure a friendly government in Khartoum, Sudan's capital.

Indeed, the status of Sudan was among the many problems between Cairo and London that undermined any goodwill—if any ever existed—between the Egyptians and the British. Over the course of seven decades, London demonstrated an unwillingness to acknowledge Egypt's popular will. The inability of Egypt's rulers to reconcile the desire among the vast majority of Egyptians for national sovereignty with British strategic interests fatefully destabilized the political arena. In order to remain in power, Egyptian politicians were forced to square the circle of British demands for certain rights and privileges against Egyptian popular sentiment that the country be permitted to determine its own political, social, and economic trajectory. The most painful episode, of many over the course of Britain's presence in Egypt, came in February 1942 when the British forced a Wafdist government on King Farouk.

A decade after this searing incident, however, Britain was compromised. The British presence in Egypt had morphed from one essentially concerned with commercial matters—the repayment of Cairo's debt and secure access to South Asia—to, over the course of two world wars and the dawn of the Cold War, one of national and Western security interests. Although victorious in World War II, Britain paid a heavy price in that global conflict. Weakened materially, and confronting the nationalist movements throughout the empire, London was forced to let South Asia go in 1947. The emergence of independent India and Pakistan in August of that year was followed quickly by the end of the British Mandate in Palestine, and the emergence of independent states in formerly British-controlled Sri Lanka and Burma. Despite these critical changes, Britain remained deeply invested in the remnants of the empire, especially in the Persian Gulf, with its vast reservoirs of oil and gas.[5] As a result, Egypt remained critical to the defense of Western interests in the Gulf, primarily because the Suez Canal provided the fastest and most reliable way for oil and gas to reach Europe and the primary means to flow forces to the region in the event of a crisis there. In the early 1950s, however, despite London's abiding interest in the region, it no longer had the wherewithal to shape developments in the Middle East. That role increasingly fell to the United States and the Soviet Union.

The rise of Moscow after World War II and the apparent depth of communist support in both the developed and less developed world, including in Egypt, were of deep concern to Washington. Yet American policymakers maintained a different approach to securing Western interests in the Middle East than their British counterparts. London sought to hang on to its protectorates as that ultimate guarantor of regional security, whereas Washington believed that not only was the British presence no longer necessary, it was also counterproductive to an overall strategy to meet the Soviet challenge. To be sure, the policy divergence between Washington and London was relatively small— after all, both Americans and British saw the value in establishing client states in the region—yet the differences between the two allies were politically important.

The conventional and romanticized view of Washington in the immediate postwar era suggests that America's own war for national self-determination fought between 1775 and 1783, combined with the alleged distaste among American political elites for colonialism shaped U.S. policy in Asia, Africa, and the Middle East. Although this narrative conveniently scrubs Washington's sometimes ugly history in places like the Dominican Republic, Haiti, Nicaragua, and the Philippines, it is largely accurate in the Middle East. Still, the fact that the United States was not a colonial power in the region had little to do with Washington's view of the British presence in Egypt. American officials regarded Britain and its position in Egypt as a complicating factor in their efforts to cultivate the new regime of military officers, which Washington looked on with enthusiasm. The United States wanted reliable, pro-Western client states in the region to help confront Soviet efforts to extend its influence in the Middle East.[6] The fact that the British had demonstrated a capacity to destabilize the Egyptian political arena, which, in turn, had the potential to sour the Officers' predisposition toward the West, made it clear to Washington that the British had to go.[7] As a result, despite the special relationship between Washington and London, the Eisenhower administration nudged, if ever so gently, its British allies to come to terms with a withdrawal from Egypt. Yet, agreement with the British would have to wait until the Free Officers consolidated their power.

BREAKING THE POWER OF THE LANDED CLASS

In addition to the ever-present and vexing problem of Egypt's relationship with Great Britain, the Officers, like so many other Egyptian political elites at the time, also strongly advocated social justice. Precisely what that meant, of course, was subject to the interpretation of different groups. The forces of the Left had a significantly different set of prescriptions to Egypt's economic problems than did the Sa'adist Party, for example, which represented business and large agricultural interests.[8] For their part, as the Free Officers coalesced in the late 1940s, they "implicitly accepted much of the social critique of the Left."[9] Yet in the immediate aftermath of the coup, the Officers were too preoccupied with politics to address Egypt's wide-ranging economic problems, including a large and growing gap between rich and poor, little investment in the manufacturing sector, foreign domination of what industry existed, and Egypt's vulnerability to world prices stemming from its single-crop—cotton—economy.[10] As a result, in July and August, the Free Officers did little to alter the prevailing liberal economic policies of the ancien régime. Thus, Egyptian economic policy continued to encourage private investment, including from foreign sources, offered tax relief for industrial companies, allowed profits to be transferred out of the country after five years, and actually reversed laws requiring 51 percent Egyptian ownership of firms.[11] They also focused their immediate efforts on shoring up the budget and holding the line on inflation.

Yet even as the Free Officers continued the liberal economic policies that had guided the Egyptian economy for the previous seven decades, they were developing plans to address Egypt's socioeconomic problems in an altogether different way. The primary instrument to achieve this goal was agrarian reform. With the help of leftist intellectuals, the Free Officers developed a plan for land reform that they sought to put in place within six weeks of seizing power. The Officers decided on an arrangement that limited landowners to a maximum of two hundred feddans—about 210 acres—though the authorities would permit an additional allotment of one hundred feddans if the owner had any children. Although more radical changes to the Egyptian economy were to come later on in the decade, the plan was severe enough to produce a political crisis. The Officers' handpicked prime minister, Ali Mahir, opposed land reform. Powerless to stop the change, however, Mahir sought to influence the extent of the redistribution of private property, arguing that the Officers should set the ceiling for landholdings at five hundred feddans—this was a position that the Wafd and other landowning interests supported. At the time, less than one-half percent of total landowners held approximately 35 percent of all the cultivable land, while the vast majority of the remaining landowners controlled five feddans or less each.[12] The issue came to a head in early September, and when Mahir continued to resist the Officers' two hundred-feddan proposal, he was sacked in favor of General Mohammed Naguib.

The general was a natural choice for the Officers. Although they did not know him well, they liked his profile. Born in the Sudanese capital, Khartoum, Naguib hailed from a long line of military officers. He was commissioned as an artillery officer in 1918 and posted to Sudan. Like his younger colleagues among the Free Officers, Naguib was quickly disillusioned with both British domination of Egypt and Sudan and the dismal state of the armed forces. Although he was rotated through a number of positions due to his politics and outspoken opposition to the British, Naguib was consistently promoted, rising to brigade commander during the war in Palestine. He earned a reputation as a competent officer and garnered significant support within the military, especially among the artillery officers. The fact that Naguib was one of the few senior commanders who performed well in Palestine was also an asset to the Free Officers. In addition, the general seemed to share their politics, leading Nasser and his colleagues to believe that it would not be difficult to control Naguib. That belief proved to be erroneous sooner rather than later, but in the period before the coup when he served as the Free Officers' front man in the battle with King Farouk over control of the Officers Club and in the early months after the intervention, General Naguib seemed loyal to the Free Officers' movement.

Naguib assumed the prime ministry on September 8, 1952. His cabinet was composed of civilian technocrats, including two associates of the Muslim Brotherhood. The new minister of justice, Ahmad Housni, had been a Brotherhood fellow-traveler but never an actual member of the organization. Sheikh Ahmad Hassan Baquri's appointment as minister of *awqaf*, or religious endowments, was a far more controversial selection that would have repercussions for Brotherhood-Free Officer relations down the road. In the fraught aftermath of Hassan al Banna's assassination in early 1949, Sheikh Baquri challenged Hassan al Hudaybi's bid to be the Muslim Brotherhood's next supreme guide. Baquri ultimately lost, but the battle within the Brotherhood's main decision-making body, the Shura Council, was bruising, sowing profound mistrust between Baquri and al Hudaybi.

Ali Mahir's departure indicated that, at least initially, governments under the new regime were not supposed to be an independent policymaking body, but rather the implementer of the Free Officers' desired initiatives. As intended, Naguib's new cabinet passed land reform the day after the general took the reins of the prime ministry. In a testament to the Officers' intention to break the power of the landed class and in the process improve the lot of Egyptian agricultural laborers, the law not only limited land ownership, but it also fixed wages, allowed for the establishment of cooperatives and unions, limited land rents, and improved tenancy regulations.[13] A month after the agrarian reforms, the Officers began to dabble in state-directed development with the establishment of the Permanent Council for the Development of National Production. The council was supposed to spur a shift away from agriculture to industry and manufacturing. If this was in fact the primary goal of the council, it failed. Yet, like the land reform that immediately preceded it, the effort to shift the basis of the Egyptian economy was part of a broad effort to undermine the prevailing economic elite—a primary constituency of the monarchy and parliamentary order that the Free Officers had just overturned.

Still, with the exception of well-developed ideas concerning the national question, the Officers' approach to economic and political reform was ill-defined at best. To be sure, the Left's critiques of the old order were the inspiration for the vaguely socialist impulses of the early months of the new regime, but the Free Officers were neither committed communists nor leftists. Similarly, the Officers disliked the old parliamentary order, but not necessarily because they were authoritarians inherently opposed to representative government. The elusive nature of the Free Officers' beliefs actually served them well in the immediate aftermath of their intervention. All of Egypt's competing political factions and movements could claim the Officers as their own, which insulated Nasser and his associates from having to confront a broad-based opposition to their coup, at least temporarily. In a relatively short time, however, the distinct lack of ideological agenda contributed to the political struggles that the Officers would encounter in the first 18 to 24 months of their rule.[14]

BRINGING THE PARTIES TO HEEL

On the same day that the Agrarian Reform Law was passed—September 9—the government approved the Party Reorganization Law. In a foreshadowing of future laws regulating the establishment, leadership, and acceptable ideological dispositions of political parties, this initiative was central to the Officers' effort to control the parliamentary system, which had been in a state of suspension since the coup. The new law required the dissolution of the parties and ordered them to apply for recertification to the Interior Ministry by October 7. This process required the parties to submit a platform, a roster of party leaders, and their financial records to the government. The law also disqualified those party figures who were accused of corruption from serving, essentially allowing the Interior Ministry to pick and choose party leaders.

Although the Officers claimed that those parties permitted to reopen would compete in an election the Officers promised to hold in early 1953, the law strained an already complex relationship between the Free Officers and party leaders. As noted earlier, there was a general consensus that the parliamentary system was broken and that the coup was necessary for reform. Yet, beyond these areas of broad agreement, the Officers diverged from the leadership of the political parties on the exact nature of reform. These differences were not terribly surprising since Nasser and his colleagues wanted the parties to undertake "voluntary purges" that would retire old-guard leaders in favor of a new generation of politicians.[15] Some of the parties complied with this demand, while others, notably the Wafd, demurred. Mustafa al Nahhas, the four-time prime minister and doyenne of the Wafd who was seventy-three years old at the time of the coup, simply refused to comply. Al Nahhas's opposition was both principled—he believed the Officers should restore parliament and end their tutelage of the political system—and parochial, given long-standing allegations of financial chicanery among the party leadership.[16] Opening the party's books to the leaders of the new regime was sure to be dangerous and damaging. Al Nahhas's deputy, Fuad Sirag el Din, who was widely regarded to be the real power in the party due to the leader's advancing age, had come to represent all that was corrupt and craven about the parliamentary period.[17] Consequently, Sirag el Din, like al Nahhas, initially sought the path of resistance against the Officers. At the same time, younger party activists—the very people that Nasser had hoped to cultivate—frightened by a potential showdown with the Free Officers, prevailed upon al Nahhas to accept the Party Reorganization Law. They believed that if the party demonstrated some flexibility in the face of the Officers' demands for internal reform, the longevity of the Wafd would be ensured.[18]

For their part, the Officers chose to avoid a direct confrontation with al Nahhas and Sirag al Din.[19] After all, the two men represented the party of Saad Zaghlul and the 1919 Revolution. Although its nationalist credentials were compromised in February 1942 and subsequent revelations of corruption and other improprieties further eroded the party's standing, the Wafd still commanded a significant following that could be deployed in the streets to create uncertainty and instability.[20]

In an environment where the Officers had yet to consolidate their power, they did not need a political conflict that would throw open to question their command of the political arena.[21]

During the month-long recertification period, the Ministry of Interior declared that there was evidence of corruption against al Nahhas, disqualifying him from serving as party leader. A deal was ultimately brokered between the party and the government, in which al Nahhas would be permitted to serve as "honorary" president.[22] However, when the Ministry of Interior recertified the Wafd and six other groups, the Officers reneged on the agreement, hoping to split the party between supporters of al Nahhas and Sirag al Din and the younger group of party stalwarts who had previously counseled caution and cooperation when it came to the new regime. As it turned out, the Wafd's second-tier leadership and its rank and file chose to support al Nahhas as the party took its grievances to the State Council—the highest administrative court in Egypt.[23] The case was never fully adjudicated, however. Perhaps fearing a ruling that would not be in their favor, the Free Officers outlawed all political parties on January 17 only a few days after the judges recessed to consider the case.

At the turn of 1953, the Officers confronted a legal challenge from the Wafd and were at odds with the Left over the government's handling of violent labor unrest in Kafr al Dawwar the previous August. Indeed, the Kafr al Dawwar incident, during which the army killed four and injured an undetermined number of striking textile workers, is among the uglier episodes of the early post-coup era. The army's use of lethal force—despite being fired on first—to put down the strike, the arrest of about five hundred workers, and the execution of two alleged leaders of the strike led the Democratic Movement for National Liberation (DMNL)—supporters of the coup—to declare the new regime "fascist."[24] For their part, throughout late 1952 and the earliest days of 1953, the Muslim Brotherhood remained noncommittal, neither offering its full support to the Officers nor assailing them. Supreme Guide Hassan al Hudaybi, who was perhaps a more astute political operator than Hassan al Banna, understood that his and his movement's best interests were served by staying above the fray.

By mid-January the Officers had had enough of the political forces buffeting them. In addition to dissolving the parties, they announced a three-year transition period, transformed the Free Officers' executive committee into a Revolutionary Command Council (RCC), and declared that Prime Minister Naguib would rule in the name of this newly formed body. They also announced that a committee of fifty prominent political figures would draft a new constitution.[25] The Officers intended to build support for their new course while simultaneously tamping down on opposition to their dissolution of the parties.[26] In an indication that the Officers had begun to think more ambitiously, they began referring to the July coup as a revolution. In February 1953, Nasser declared that reforming the parliamentary system had become "a minor objective compared to the wider aims of our revolution. The latter [objective] seeks to change the political system."[27]

In place of political parties, the RCC established the Liberation Rally.[28] The name of the organization, with its conscious tip to the nationalist sentiments that had been brewing in Egypt for the previous seven decades, was a dead giveaway for the Rally's ultimate goal, instilling the Free Officers' movement—now revolution—with a veneer of popularity. Egyptians were to unite within the Rally to continue the heroic work of the Officers and collectively strive to achieve both the goals of the revolution and Egypt's nationalist aspirations.[29] Toward that end, the Officers unveiled an eleven-point program that would guide government policy: withdrawal of foreign forces from the Nile Valley; self-determination for the Sudan; development of a new constitution; establishment of a system of social welfare; ensuring the redistribution of wealth; rule of law and the protection of personal as well as political freedoms; educational reform; good relations with Arab states; formation of an all-Arab military force; goodwill with friendly countries; and an upholding of the principles of the UN charter.[30]

Beyond the third-worldist rhetoric of liberation and nationalism that trumpeted the Rally, the Officers had another unstated, but nevertheless critically important, objective for creating the organization. Given the difficulties they had encountered with Egypt's traditional political parties in the six months since they sent King Farouk packing, the Liberation Rally was intended to be an instrument of political control. The Rally, it was hoped, would provide the Officers with an ability to both shape political debates and watch over the political arena to ensure conformity to the Revolutionary Command Council's wishes.

It is unclear how much the RCC actually invested in the Liberation Rally, but it failed to be the mechanism of political mobilization that its founders hoped it would be. Despite this grab bag of commitments and principles aimed at a broad spectrum of Egyptians, the political parties, the Left, and the Brotherhood continued to enjoy the loyalty of the vast majority of Egyptians at the expense of the Rally. To be fair, the Rally was not a total failure; it was able to deploy thugs from among its ranks to either stage street demonstrations supporting the Officers or face-off against Wafdists, leftists, or Muslim Brothers when necessary. Finally, in subsequent years, the organization served as the model for successor organizations called the National Union and the Arab Socialist Union (ASU).

A REPUBLIC IS BORN

The move from "coup" to "revolution," combined with the measures the Revolutionary Command Council took in 1953 to impose discipline on the political arena, did little to mitigate a range of problems that threatened to undo the Officers' July 1952 intervention. University students—an important constituency given their history of political activism—remained decidedly ambivalent toward the Officers. Cairo University was split between Wafdists and Muslim Brothers, with a relatively smaller faction of students loyal to the Liberation Rally. Egypt's working class, which was a potentially potent source of anti-regime activity, was still susceptible to leftist organizing. The Officers had taken some measures to improve the pay in this sector, but had made little headway eliciting widespread support.

By June of 1953, Nasser and his fellow conspirators had delivered little tangible in the way of addressing the public's political and material needs, putting a drag on the revolution that the Officers announced six months earlier. In order to arrest this decline and capture the imagination of the Egyptian people, the RCC took the bold step of abolishing the monarchy and declaring Egypt a republic. Prime Minister Naguib was elevated to president and five prominent Free Officers assumed ministerial portfolios. Nasser became deputy prime minister and minister of interior, Wing Commander Abdel Latif Boghdadi assumed the Ministry of War's portfolio, Major Salah Salim was appointed minister of guidance and minister of state for Sudan affairs, and Major Abdel Hakim Amer was named commander and chief of the armed forces, a ministerial-level post. Three months later, Nasser gave up the Interior Ministry to Lieutenant Colonel Zakariyya Mohieddin, the fifth officer to enter the government. The remaining ministers, ten in all, were civilians with technocratic backgrounds.[31]

The establishment of the republic did not impress the Left, particularly the communists. Not only were they skeptical of the Officers' willingness to return Egypt to representative government, but they were deeply opposed to the new regime's relationship with the United States. There was no denying the fact that a certain intimacy quickly developed between Washington and the Officers. The first official meeting between American Ambassador James Caffery and the Officers came just two days after the coup, and by all reports the ambassador was impressed with the young commanders. The following day, Caffery saw King Farouk off at Alexandria's harbor, ensuring the former monarch's safe passage to Italy while making certain that the Officers' intervention remained peaceful.[32] In the days and months after the coup, Caffery cultivated Naguib while Nasser maintained a line of communication with the embassy's political counselor, William Lakeland. In addition, the CIA's Kermit Roosevelt Jr.,—who played a central role in the August 1953 coup d'état that brought down Iranian leader Mohammed Mossadegh—was dispatched to Cairo to help the Officers develop their own clandestine intelligence service.[33] Washington also made its influence felt on Egyptian politics. In one instance, Ambassador Caffery pressured the new regime to block Rashad al Barawi—who was one of the leftist intellectuals who helped the Officers craft the Agrarian Reform Law—from joining the cabinet.[34] More than anything, Washington—in what would become a hallmark of its approach to Egypt beginning in the mid-1970s—sought stability in Egypt and was reassured by the message that Egypt's new rulers would suppress communism at home and would consider incorporating Egypt into Western regional security initiatives. At around the same time, the Egyptians appealed directly to Washington for both economic and military aid.

To the Left, it seemed that Nasser and his colleagues were all too willing to exchange the relationship with Great Britain for one with the United States, which from where the communists and other leftists factions sat was no difference at all. If, for example, Caffery could veto the Officers' appointments, how different was he from Lords Cromer, Gorst, and Kitchener, who ensured that London's interests came before those of Cairo? Presaging events that would take place two decades later, the burgeoning of U.S.-Egypt ties resulted in ever-intensifying criticism from the Left, which accused the Free Officers of being instruments of imperialism. This went well beyond what the Officers were willing to tolerate, however. Demanding the return of constitutional life and social justice was one thing, but openly questioning the Officers' nationalist credentials was quite another because it struck at the very heart of the junta's claims to legitimacy. Consequently, the Left, especially the communists, was subjected to waves of arrests and other forms of repression from which it never fully recovered.

When it came to the Muslim Brotherhood, the Officers remained on cordial terms with the Islamists through mid-1953, but beneath the surface there was significant mistrust on all sides, which the announcement of the republic did little to ameliorate. The Islamists felt that the new leadership had intentionally slighted them throughout the first year after the coup. The appointment of Sheikh Ahmad Hassan Baquri to Naguib's cabinet as minister of religious endowments was, whether intended or not, an affront to Supreme Guide al Hudaybi. More broadly, Nasser had reneged on what the supreme guide believed to be a pre-coup commitment that the Officers would coordinate with the Brotherhood before undertaking major policy initiatives.[35] Al Hudaybi and his associates thus came to the bitter conclusion that they would not be able to influence the trajectory of Egyptian politics directly, as they had hoped.[36] The Officers had every reason to keep the Brotherhood at arm's length, however. The movement commanded a far greater following among Egyptians than the new regime, making it difficult for the Officers to impose their control on the group. The uneasy relationship between the Brothers and the Officers seemed to transform into a total breach when, in January 1954, a commemoration of those killed in the Canal Zone in 1951 and 1952 turned into a riot.[37] The authorities used the violence as an excuse to arrest 450 Muslim Brothers and ban their organization.

At the same time that they founded the republic to win popular support, the Officers established a Revolutionary Tribunal charged with adjudicating cases of treason and corruption to frighten the opposition. The three judges appointed to hear the cases were Sadat, Boghdadi, and Squadron Leader Hassan Ibrahim, none of whom had any professional legal experience. The defendants, many of whom were accused of collaborating with foreign powers and efforts to undermine the revolution in order to restore the ancien régime, faced the possibility of capital punishment.[38] The first to be tried was former Prime Minister Ibrahim al Hadi, who had overseen a widespread and brutal crackdown on almost every political faction and group in Egypt after the assassination of Prime Minister Nuqrashi in December 1948. The excesses of al Hadi's campaign of repression made him a reviled figure across the political spectrum. Al Hadi was sentenced to hang, but his sentence was ultimately commuted later to life imprisonment.

The Wafd's Fuad Sirag al Din, the party's deputy leader and long-time power broker, came before the tribunal next. For the entirety of the previous year, the Officers circled Sirag al Din warily, arresting him in the fall of 1952 only to release him a short while later.[39]

He would have no such luck with the Revolutionary Tribunal. Despite his best efforts to embarrass the new regime during the trial, Boghdadi, Sadat, and Ibrahim found Sirag al Din guilty of manipulating the price of cotton, negligence during the January 1952 Cairo fire, "granting irregular favours to the king," and "inadequately planning the abrogation" of the 1936 Anglo-Egyptian Treaty.[40] The Tribunal sentenced Sirag al Din to fifteen years in prison, though he was quietly released shortly thereafter and placed under house arrest.[41] In the end, however, the establishment of the republic and the show trials of politicians who were inextricably linked to some of the worst excesses of the parliamentary order failed to achieve the intended goals. Both the opposition and average Egyptians remained dissatisfied with the Free Officers.

SHOWDOWN

At the end of 1953 and beginning of 1954, the opponents of the new regime from across the political spectrum, both civilians and soldiers, continued to agitate against Nasser and his colleagues. The combination of cross-cutting political pressures and cleavages among Egypt's main political actors, combined with the Free Officers' inability to garner popular support, ultimately forced the Revolutionary Command Council's hand. By early 1954, the Officers came to the conclusion that the time had come to clear the political field once and for all and consolidate their power.

Yet for all of the Free Officers' political struggles with the Wafd, Muslim Brotherhood, and the Left, the RCC's relationship with the general officer corps in 1954 was one of the most important tests of the Free Officers' staying power. The ties between the RCC and the military were complex and exceedingly delicate—after all, the military remained the only organization capable of employing enough force to topple the new regime. Although in the early days after the coup, the Officers cashiered some 450 soldiers and officers, the purge went no further.[42] The RCC was of the military, but the Free Officers only ruled Egypt on behalf of or in the name of the armed forces in official pronouncements and rhetorical flourishes. Only later when the consolidation of power was complete could Nasser and his associates credibly claim that the military was one with the Free Officers. Among the various factions, political groups, cells, and networks within the Egyptian armed forces at the time, the Free Officers were actually among the smallest, dwarfed by both the communists and the Muslim Brotherhood. Consequently, it was initially in the interest of the Free Officers to keep the military as far away from politics as possible.

Although early on there was significant tension between the Free Officers and their own network of followers within the different branches of the armed forces, the first big test of the new regime's relations with the military came in December 1952. At that time, artillery officers took on Nasser and his associates over the rough treatment of one of their own, a retired colonel named Rashad Mahanna. Egypt's new leaders had unceremoniously dumped Mahanna—a strong supporter of their coup—after he sought to empower the Regency Council the Officers established for Farouk's son, the infant King Ahmad Fuad.[43] In response to the high-handedness of Nasser and his colleagues, the artillerymen sought changes to the Free Officers executive, proposing that five members of the body should be elected and another five drawn directly from the original July 1952 conspirators. This was a nonstarter for the new leaders who rejected the proposal out of hand. The following month, after the artillery group mounted a challenge to Egypt's new leaders at the Officers Club, the Free Officers placed thirty-five conspirators under arrest and charged them with a plot to overthrow the regime.[44] Yet the effort to decapitate the artillery corps backfired, creating further unrest within the general officer corps. The situation was only defused after four hundred officers staged a sit-in at their barracks and Nasser promised an investigation into their grievances.

The Free Officers also encountered problems with General Naguib, their designated front man. They hoped that Naguib—recognizing that his source of power was directly related to his relationship with them—would play the Free Officers' game. He was to give the lieutenant colonels, majors, and wing commanders a veneer of adult supervision and gravitas while he did the young Officers' bidding. But they underestimated Naguib's genuine popularity. To the Egyptian public, Naguib was the new prime minister who ostensibly led a movement that toppled an unpopular king, vowed to end the instability of the previous thirty years, and, importantly, promised to terminate Great Britain's occupation of Egypt.

By the time the Free Officers declared the Republic in January 1953, they had tired of Naguib who, out of a lack of any viable alternatives, had been named to the new post of president. The friction was based on Naguib's penchant for using his personal prestige to go beyond the bounds of what the Free Officers expected of him. For example, the president opposed the Officers' appointments to the first republican cabinet, including Nasser's close friend and confidant Major Abdel Hakim Amer as commander and chief-of-staff of the armed forces. The tension over cabinet appointments was merely emblematic of the Free Officers' resentment over Naguib's determination to take his presidential duties seriously.

Nasser succeeded in forcing Naguib's resignation in February 1954, but not without a fight. Wafdists, Muslim Brothers, much of the Left, the general public, and non-Free Officer military officers preferred Naguib to the Revolutionary Command Council and opposed Naguib's ouster. This time the military's armored corps took center stage. In a show of force that threatened again to open a major fissure between the general officer corps and the RCC, the leaders of the armored corps demanded Naguib's return.[45] Confronted with a choice between bringing Naguib back or a full-scale mutiny among the armored corps, Nasser backed down. The RCC eventually squelched their opposition within the armed forces with the help—ironically—of the artillery corps, but the problem of Naguib remained.

When the general was restored to the presidency just a few days after his resignation, Egyptians took to the streets to rejoice. The apparent support of the president from students, the Muslim Brotherhood, Wafdists, and other political factions unhappy with the authoritarian drift of the Free Officers placed Nasser on the ropes. In what seemed like a last-ditch effort to rescue the Officers from their suddenly precarious position, Nasser released political prisoners and announced elections for a parliament that would finish drafting a new constitution. In addition, martial law would be lifted.

By now, Naguib was under the impression that he was the master of Egypt's political arena. Yet even as the president was conspiring to consolidate his power, the Free Officers were moving to undermine him. They organized a showdown between themselves and Naguib at the Officers Club. Nasser and his colleagues won the day and the allegiance of the general officers, yet the president still managed to cling to his position. With the support of the armed forces virtually assured and Naguib greatly weakened, the RCC sought to dispose of the opposition. The Officers were determined to offer Egyptians a choice: a return to the corruption of the old guard or the economic progress, social justice, and national sovereignty that the Free Officers promised.

Toward that end, Nasser and his associates sought to stir up Egypt's political environment. On March 20, there were six explosions in

Cairo, which was almost certainly the work of agents of the Free Officers to foment fear of instability. Then five days after the bombings, the RCC announced that all politicians and political parties that were previously banned would be permitted to resume their political activities unfettered. It did not take very long for these groups to fall back into old and very bad habits, raising the specter of the unprincipled and corrupt political practices of the pre-1952 era.

At the same time, the regime's mouthpieces in the press stirred up trouble, alleging a plot among old-guard figures like the much reviled former prime minister, Ibrahim Abdel Hadi, Mustafa al Nahhas, and supporters of President Naguib, that would revive the old-guard politicians of the ancien régime. In response, on March 26, pro-regime unions called a general strike to protest against the old-guard politicians and parties. Over the following two days, protests and counterprotests gripped Cairo. After two full days of demonstrations—the atmosphere thick with the anticipation of a crackdown—the Free Officers stepped in and declared their intention to ensure order.[46] The well-timed action to defuse the crisis of their own making gave Nasser and his colleagues the permanent upper hand in the battle to control Egyptian politics.

Naguib was unable to muster the political forces necessary to confront the Officers. Exhausted from the stress of the near-constant political struggle, the president was hospitalized and remained a nonfactor in politics until he was formally deposed the following November. After the Officers' demonstration of force, the political parties were in no position to make demands on the Revolutionary Command Council. It mattered little anyway. Two weeks later, the party leaders were stripped of all their political rights.

At the same time the Officers were undermining the old guard, they were—in a rare moment of political finesse—working to ensure that the Muslim Brotherhood did not join the fray. On March 25, the Officers ordered about two hundred members of the organization, including the supreme guide who had been arrested in January, released from prison. Nasser then arranged a meeting with Supreme Guide al Hudaybi, during which he allegedly promised the supreme guide that the Muslim Brotherhood could resume its activities and the government would—in a presumed act of contrition—publicly explain the reasons for the organization's dissolution the previous January.[47] These promises kept the Islamists safely on the sidelines of the events of March 26–28, but it came with a cost to the Officers. They completed their consolidation of power, with one important exception. The deal with al Hudaybi meant that the Muslim Brotherhood, an organization that in its relatively short history had become deeply intertwined and influential in Egyptian society, remained beyond the Revolutionary Command Council's control. Yet Nasser never honored his promise to al Hudaybi that the Brotherhood would be legalized, and within a few months of the March showdown, the Islamists began agitating against the regime.

DISPOSING OF THE BROTHERHOOD

Foreign policy had not ranked very high on the Free Officers' list of concerns except for the settlement of the national question. Given that both the status of Sudan and the British presence in Egypt were among the central issues that vexed Egyptian politics over the course of the previous seventy-two years, the final disposition of both these issues was critical to the Free Officers' legitimacy. The negotiations with London that had gone on in fits and starts since Egypt's formal independence in 1923 often foundered on the question of Sudan. Intent on not allowing this issue to complicate the negotiations over the British presence in Egypt proper, the Officers ultimately moved away from demanding "the unity of the Nile Valley" to accepting the notion of Sudanese self-determination.[48] The British, with Washington's help, were atypically amenable to this idea. The newfound flexibility of both sides led to the February 1953 Anglo-Egyptian agreement on the Sudan.[49]

With the thorny issue of Sudan no longer hampering negotiations, the Free Officers then turned their attention toward ending the British occupation of the Canal Zone. Although it would no doubt have helped them enormously with public opinion, the Officers never moved to abrogate the Anglo-Egyptian Treaty of 1936 unilaterally, though they were strong supporters of such a policy when Mustafa al Nahhas did the same in October 1951. The Officers were decidedly unwilling to take such a dramatic step for fear of British retaliation—a confrontation they could ill afford. Further, even though the Anglo-Egyptian Treaty limited the number of British troops in the Canal bases to ten thousand, the Officers made little of the fact that London maintained many times that amount.

With general agreement on how to proceed with the Sudanese question hammered out the previous February, the new regime entered into negotiations with the British on April 27, 1953. Almost immediately the negotiations ran into trouble, and they were suspended ten days later. In response the RCC ordered attacks on British forces and interests in the Canal area to pressure London to be more forthcoming without precipitating a major military response.[50] These guerilla-style attacks would subsequently wax and wane with the progress of negotiations.

Despite the apparent initial difficulties in the negotiations, there was much to which the parties agreed. For example, the Egyptians accepted, in principle, Britain's assertion of its right to protect Western interests in the Middle East and also assented to a timetable for the British departure, rather than demanding an immediate withdrawal as some Egyptians desired. Cairo committed itself to keeping the Suez Canal bases in good working condition and agreed to allow British technicians to assist in this process. The Free Officers were also willing to allow British forces to return to Egypt in the event of a crisis in the Middle East. The differences between the parties lay in two seemingly minor but symbolically important areas for the RCC. First, the Officers objected to any remaining British personnel donning military attire. The presence of the British armed forces was, after all, the most visible manifestation of Egypt's circumscribed sovereignty during the preceding decades. The Egyptians' second objection had to do with the inclusion of Turkey as a trigger for Britain's reentry to the Canal Zone. It was one thing to agree to draft language that permitted Britain access to the Canal bases in the event of an attack on a member of the Arab League, which of course included British protectorates in the Persian Gulf, but London's insistence on including Turkey in this contingency was quite another. The inclusion of the Turkish Republic—a member of NATO—would link Egypt, albeit a step removed, to the West and its security interests.[51]

Despite Egyptian objections to Turkey's inclusion—or more precisely an attack on Turkey as a justification for the return of British forces to the Canal Zone—and separately the attire of the remaining British technicians in Egypt after Britain's withdrawal, Cairo and London reached an outline agreement in July 1954. The "Heads of Agreement" was made possible by a simple deal between the Free Officers and their British interlocutors. The Egyptians were willing to drop their objections to Turkey so long as London agreed that its personnel would be restricted to civilian clothing at all times. The agreement set June 1955 as the timeline for a British withdrawal, though the British were granted access to the Canal Zone for an additional seven years.

While the Officers may have considered the deal a diplomatic triumph, others did not share their enthusiasm. Even though they were the last men standing after the March 1954 showdown, al Hudaybi and the Brothers had almost immediately after that incident begun calling for the reestablishment of the parliamentary system and freedom of the press.[52] When the details of the Heads of Agreement were released, it provided further opportunity for the supreme guide to disparage the Officers. He took Nasser and the Officers to task over the very issue on which they staked their claim to power and legitimacy in the first place—nationalism.[53] From al Hudaybi's perspective, rather than delivering Egypt from the British, the Heads of Agreement did little more than effectively extend the Anglo-Egyptian Treaty of 1936.

Nasser obviously could not allow the Brotherhood to question the Officers' nationalist credentials. Consequently, the RCC embarked upon a propaganda campaign against the Islamists over the six weeks between the draft agreement and the finalization of the accord in late October 1954. Nasser's offensive first and foremost sought to delegitimize the prestige and moral authority of the Brotherhood. Toward that end, al Hudaybi and his followers were accused of complicity with the communists and Zionists and the British.[54] Recent history clearly suggested otherwise. The Brotherhood was both steadfastly anti-communist and anti-British. Collaboration with Zionists was equally absurd given the Brothers' activism on behalf of Palestinian Muslims dating back to the 1930s. Nasser and the press also accused al Hudaybi of engaging in a bid for power, insinuating that the Islamists sought to sow instability in Egypt's political arena through violence and disorder.

The Islamists were largely correct on the principles—the agreement made a number of concessions to London that were vulnerable to criticism on nationalist grounds—but ultimately it mattered little, given the force at the disposal of the Officers. The crucial moment came on October 26, when the regime called a rally at Manshiya Square in Alexandria to celebrate the formal signing of the Anglo-Egyptian agreement. As Nasser regaled the gathered crowd with an account of Egypt's nationalist struggle, a tinner and member of the Brotherhood from the Imbaba district of Cairo named Mahmoud Abdel Latif fired eight shots at the Egyptian leader.[55] Either Abdel Latif was a poor marksman or, as some suspect, the assassination attempt was staged in order to discredit the Islamists. Despite his close range, Nasser was unscathed and went on to finish his speech to the thunderous approval of the gathered crowds.

The extraordinary boost in popularity that the failed assassination attempt gave Nasser and the Free Officers provided the regime with wide latitude to deal with the Muslim Brotherhood once and for all. Liberation Rally activists were dispatched to destroy the Brotherhood's Cairo headquarters. In the Canal Zone, regime supporters sacked businesses affiliated with the Islamists. Three days after Abdel Latif missed him, Nasser publicly denounced the supreme guide and stepped up a fierce propaganda campaign against the Islamists. The press went after the Brotherhood's paramilitary organization—the secret apparatus (al jihaz al sirri)—alleging that the Brotherhood sought to use this group to topple the regime.

In the ensuing security sweeps, the Brotherhood's leadership was taken into custody and brought before a newly created People's Tribunal over which Salah Salim, Anwar Sadat and Hussein Shaf'ei presided. An additional two thousand Brothers were sent to prison. The proceedings in the People's Tribunal were also used to undermine whatever was left of Mohammed Naguib's prestige. The Free Officers' former front man and first president of the republic was alleged to have plotted with the Muslim Brotherhood against the new regime. Naguib was, in turn, placed under house arrest, where he remained until his death in August 1984. In the end, the Brotherhood survived the onslaught, but barely. For the remainder of the Nasser period, the Brothers were either underground or imprisoned. In the short run, this rendered the Islamists a relative nonfactor in Egyptian politics, but the showdown between the Officers and the Muslim Brotherhood in 1954 and the subsequent consolidation of the regime would have a profound impact on Egyptian politics for decades to come.

INSTITUTIONALIZING THE NEW REGIME

Through 1954, the Officers' rule was marked by a certain amount of experimentation and ad hoc policymaking. As threats and opportunities developed, the Officers discovered—through trial and error—how to deal with these challenges most effectively. Although in January 1953 Nasser began invoking "revolution" to describe the Officers' movement, this was mostly for rhetorical purposes. It was only after the crisis of mid- and late-1954 that led to the consolidation of the Free Officers' power that the improvisation of the previous few years gave way to a broader effort to dramatically alter Egypt's political system. There were, of course, brief glimpses of this revolution, of sorts, during the first two years of the Free Officers' rule—land reform, the political parties law, and the various tribunals that prosecuted ancien régime figures—but at that time Nasser and his comrades had not intended to remake entirely the social, political, and economic landscape of the country.

The Free Officers' move from reform to revolution was a function of circumstance and context. Confronted with a range of internal and external enemies, even after the crisis of March 1954, the Officers sought both the means to retain their power and to minimize future challenges to their dominance, thereby helping them to consolidate their power further. They did this through the development of what social scientists often refer to as "institutions" and the rest of the world calls rules, laws, decrees, and regulations. Generally speaking, institutions shape the behavior, expectations, and experiences of people as they navigate society. The political, economic, and social institutions forged during the Free Officers' era established the red lines of society, laying out for Egyptians what was acceptable behavior in the new order.

Yet it is the nature of these institutions and thus the kind of political system that the Officers founded that is crucial to understanding Egypt's subsequent political development and ultimately the uprising of January 25, 2011. The question of institutions, where they came from, and how they change, is a hotly debated topic among scholars. One image suggests that institutions are the result of the conscious efforts of a group of elites or other political actors who have determined that existing rules, regulations, laws, and decrees do not suit their interests.[56] Another school of thought takes issue with the notion that somehow institutions "flow effortlessly from the design table of omniscient rulers."[57] The development of Egypt's institutions was not effortless and, importantly, these laws, rules, decrees, and regulations preserved the power, prestige, privileges, and resource advantages for the Free Officers and their allies at the expense of society.[58]

Moreover, the institutions that Nasser and the other Officers founded continued to shape Egyptian politics. Other than through revolutions, which are quite rare, institutional change tends to be evolutionary, taking place within the context of existing institutions and previous institutional development.[59] Thus, the series of political party laws that Egyptian leaders promulgated in recent decades corresponded in a variety of details to the original 1952 Party Reorganization Law. To be sure, Egypt changed between the mid-1950s and the January 2011 uprising, but the country's prevailing political order during that time clearly reflected the authoritarian system that the Free Officers founded in the political maelstrom during the early years of their rule.

That system was the source of the ensuing six-decade-long struggle in Egypt over the central ideological and organizing principles of the state and society. Although the Officers rigged Egypt's institutions to serve their interests, they were never able to embed in the minds of Egyptians a set of ideas around this political order. The Officers' distinct lack of ideological convictions or anything but the most rudimentary guiding principles made them vulnerable to other political forces selling more comprehensive, emotionally and materially satisfying notions of what Egyptian society and politics should look like. The consequence was a seemingly never-ending political conflict between the defenders of the political system the Free Officers founded and their opponents that produced no small amount of political alienation, economic dislocations and—at times—violence.

Setback and Revolt

W HATEVER PROBLEMS THE Free Officers encountered consolidating their power in the eighteen months after they deposed King Farouk, by the mid-1950s they commanded Egypt's political arena through a combination of bribery, coercion, and normative appeals to support the revolution based on its ostensible successes. The internal struggles that occurred between the summer of 1952 and the spring and early summer of 1954 pulverized the opposition and provided Nasser and his colleagues with the freedom to build their regime. There were three decisive events during this time that contributed mightily to both the process of constructing a political system and, importantly, a political environment conducive to the Officers' project. The first was Mahmoud Abdel Latif's failed assassination of Nasser, which seemed to transform the way Egyptians viewed their heretofore mercurial leader. Almost overnight, Nasser went from a somewhat shadowy, fearsome figure to a courageous, beloved son of Egypt. To be sure, there was still much to fear from Nasser and the government, but his sudden charisma was of significant political value to him and the political project that he led. Second, beyond Nasser's newfound popularity was the sense among Egyptians that the Officers were delivering on their promises to address social injustices, promote economic development, and build Egypt into a regional power. Much of this change was more apparent than real, but for a time it seemed as if the difference between the RCC's revolutionary rhetoric and reality was small indeed. This period was relatively short-lived, however, lasting only about a decade. Yet it was during this era, when the regime seemed most secure, that the seeds of Egypt's subsequent ideological struggles were sown.

The third decisive moment was Nasser's nationalization of the Suez Canal on July 26, 1956. The sequence of events that led Nasser to take this dramatic step is among the most important and infamous of the early Cold War. It was the nationalization of the Canal that led officials in Washington, London, and other Western capitals to conclude that Cairo was firmly in Moscow's camp. Ironically, the roots of Nasser's decision resided in an effort between the Egyptian and American governments to forge a strategic relationship that would place Egypt at the center of U.S. efforts to counter the Soviet Union. As noted in chapter 2, both the Free Officers and the American government looked for ways to develop relations between their countries. Shortly after the coup, Cairo sought military aid from Washington, but the Eisenhower administration found considerable resistance to this from the British. Washington was pulled between London and Cairo, especially after the Egyptians requested $100 million in military and economic assistance in August 1954. The U.S. president and his advisors seemed to share Ambassador James Caffery's assessment that the Free Officers would be good partners in pursuit of American security interests in the region. Had Cairo's potential strategic utility been Washington's only consideration, this would have facilitated the transfer of the requested assistance to the Egyptians. Yet Eisenhower had to tend to his relationship with the British (NATO allies) who objected to a large aid package for the Egyptians while London was negotiating with the Free Officers over the terms of Britain's future access to the Suez Canal. British Prime Minister Winston Churchill argued that a unified American-British stance on the aid request would pressure the Egyptians into an agreement that was more favorable to London.

Hamstrung between its desire to develop ties with Cairo and its obligation to support London (however reluctantly), the Eisenhower administration struggled to split the difference between the Free Officers and Churchill. Yet the relationship between the Americans and the British on the one hand and the Egyptians on the other subsequently lurched from efforts to develop cooperative relations to misunderstandings and provocations. These difficulties were most pronounced from mid-1955 to the latter part of 1956. In May 1955, after attending the Bandung Conference in Indonesia, Nasser declared that "positive neutralism" would be the defining feature in Egyptian foreign policy. Bandung, which was the first of a series of conferences bringing newly independent African and Asian countries together in what would later become the Non-Aligned Movement, declared collective opposition to colonialism and the perceived predatory policies of the new global powers, the United States and the Soviet Union. Cairo's new foreign policy posture was, in part, a response to events that occurred earlier in the year. In early 1955, the Baghdad Pact, which was an effort to establish a regional security system that included Iraq, Iran, Turkey, and Pakistan, began to take shape and was regarded in Cairo as a Western effort to isolate Egypt.

In addition, shortly after negotiations to establish the Baghdad Pact began, the Israelis launched an attack on the Egyptian military presence in the Gaza Strip. The raid killed thirty-eight Egyptian soldiers, wounded another twenty-four, and destroyed Egypt's Gaza military headquarters. The immediate cause for Israel's attack was the large number of increasingly brazen Egyptian-sponsored attacks that Palestinian militants carried out against Israeli infrastructure in the southern Negev. Yet it was also an effort to demonstrate Israeli resolve and military superiority after a period in which its leadership had chosen to absorb terrorist attacks from Gaza with minimal retaliation.[1] The unintended consequence of Israel's brigade-sized raid into Gaza was, however, a massive Egyptian military buildup. In August, the Egyptians inked an agreement to purchase 200 tanks, 150 artillery pieces, 120 fighters, 50 bombers, 2 destroyers, 2 submarines, and thousands of rifles and automatic weapons from the Soviet satellite, Czechoslovakia. Although the weapons bound for Egypt were a mix of Czech and Soviet manufacture, there was never any doubt—despite a Soviet and American agreement to reduce the flow of arms to Middle Eastern belligerents—that Moscow was behind the deal. Cairo may have harbored concerns that the British and Americans were trying to isolate Egypt through the establishment of the Baghdad Pact, but the real target of the developing security organization was the Soviet Union. As a result, the Soviets had to act and the Israeli raid on Gaza provided ample justification. The transfer of arms to the willing Egyptians was also an opportunity for the Soviets to demonstrate that, notwithstanding U.S. and British efforts to keep it out of the region, Moscow would pursue clients and influence in the Middle East.

The Czech arms deal aside, Nasser attempted to stay true to his rhetoric about positive neutralism while he sought Western financing for the centerpiece of the new regime's development strategy—the Aswan High Dam. In 1902, after three years of work, the British engineering firm Sir Alexander Gibbs & Partners completed the first Aswan Dam. Located three miles south of Aswan, the dam proved incapable of creating a large enough reservoir area either to control Nile flooding or to produce adequate hydroelectric power. Even with renovations that raised its height twice (in 1907–1912 and 1929–1934), the Aswan Dam was wholly inadequate for its intended purpose. In light of these problems, one of the first development tasks that the Free Officers sought to undertake was the construction of a new dam about four miles upriver from the original. This new "High Dam" would expand agriculture by a third—providing enough reclaimed land for five hundred thousand families—and produce 10 billion kilowatts of electricity for industrialization. In early 1956, the International Bank for Reconstruction and Development (IBRD, the precursor to the World Bank) agreed to provide $200 million toward financing the High Dam while Washington and London committed a combined $70 million for the project. Yet the Eisenhower administration reneged on its commitment on July 19, resulting in both the British and the IBRD doing the same. The immediate cause of this turnaround was Nasser's recognition of the People's Republic of China at the follow-up to Bandung, held in Brioni, Yugoslavia, in July 1956. Washington and the West were committed to the anti-communist nationalists who had fled mainland China in 1949 for the island of Taiwan. Nasser's recognition of Peking (known to many beginning in the 1980s as Beijing) only confirmed for Eisenhower that after the accumulation of events over the previous eighteen months, Egypt's foreign policy posture had become irrevocably opposed to U.S. interests.

The Egyptians struck back a week later. Returning to Manshiya Square in Alexandria—the same place where he survived Mahmoud Abdel Latif's assassination attempt in 1954—Nasser gave a three-hour address before an enormous crowd. The speech reviewed the regime's achievements four years after the coup, affirmed Egypt's determination to fulfill the goals of the revolution, justified the Czech arms deal, and presented a withering critique of the IRDB's terms under which the bank offered to finance the Aswan High Dam. In the closing section, Nasser revealed that the French and British had been relieved of their controlling interests in the Suez Canal, declaring:

> The Suez Canal was one of the facades of oppression, extortion, and humiliation. Today, citizens, the Suez Canal has been nationalized and this decree has in fact been published in the Official Gazette and has become law. Today, citizens, we declare that our property has

been returned to us. The rights about which we were silent have been restored to us.[2]

The Canal, Nasser declared, was to be an asset solely for the benefit of Egypt and its people and henceforth, revenue from Canal tolls would be dedicated to financing the Aswan High Dam. Since 1875, when Khedive Ismail was forced to sell Egypt's shares in the Canal to the British crown in order to settle a part of his crushing debts, foreign control of the waterway had been an affront to Egyptians. The importance of the Canal to London's geostrategic calculations produced a situation in which British decision makers became vested in Egyptian stability, resulting in ever-greater penetration of Egyptian political and economic life over the course of Britain's seven-decades-long presence in Egypt. Tossing out the British, in contravention of the Anglo-Egyptian agreement of 1954, was the ultimate expression of Egyptian nationalism.

The French connection to the Suez Canal also ran deep. It was, after all, Ferdinand de Lesseps, a French diplomat, who conceived of the Canal and was the driving force behind its construction.[3] French nationals held 50 percent of the outstanding shares in the Suez Canal Company, which was headquartered in Paris. Yet, by the mid-1950s, under the leadership of Prime Minister Guy Mollet—a member of the French resistance during World War II—Paris regarded Nasser as another Hitler bent on both dominating his region and slaughtering Jews. As a result, Mollet drew France closer to Israel, believing the French had a historic responsibility to help ensure Israeli security.[4] Yet there was a dynamic at play that went beyond the nationalization of private French interests or solidarity with Israel. By the time Nasser nationalized the Suez Canal, France was well into the second year of what would turn out to be a bloody eight-year battle with Algerian nationalists who were trying to throw off 130 years of French colonial rule. Paris erroneously believed that Nasser was a primary source of arms and money for the Algerian insurrection.[5]

Immediately after Nasser's nationalization of British and French interests in the Canal, the British press, in particular, began pounding the drums for war. Even so, it was Prime Minister Mollet who began preparations for hostilities against Egypt with Israeli Prime Minister David Ben Gurion. For his part, British Prime Minister Anthony Eden was uncomfortable with Israel's participation, fearing it would complicate London's relations with the Arab world, though he ultimately relented. While the Europeans had a limited aim—reversing the nation-alization of the Canal—the Israelis actually harbored larger goals. Ben Gurion and the Minister of Defense, General Moshe Dayan, clearly sought to exploit the tension over the Canal to inflict damage on the Egyptian army, which was deployed in the Sinai uncomfortably close to Israel; to demolish Palestinian terrorist bases in Gaza; and to break Egypt's control of the Strait of Tiran. Under Egypt's Law 32 of 1950, the Egyptians formally closed this strategic waterway that separated Tiran Island and the southern tip of the Sinai Peninsula to Israeli and Israel-bound shipping. The reality was quite different from the restric-tions laid down in the law, which the Egyptians only enforced hap-hazardly until 1955, when they progressively tightened restrictions on cargo to and from Israel's port of Eilat.[6] This posed a threat to Israel's economic development as the strait was the only way in and out of the Gulf of Aqaba.

The result was the October–November 1956 Suez War, known to Egyptians as the Tripartite Aggression. The week-long conflict was a military defeat, but a political triumph for Nasser and Egypt. It began on October 29 with an Israeli military thrust into the Sinai, including a daring daytime drop of five hundred paratroopers deep into central Sinai near the Mitla Pass. Israeli forces encountered some stiff resis-tance at the Mitla Pass itself and in northern Sinai at a place called Umm Qataf. On October 30, the British and French issued an ulti-matum to *both* Egypt and Israel to cease hostilities and withdraw their forces ten miles east and west of the Canal, respectively. The diplo-matic missive also demanded that Egypt ensure freedom of naviga-tion of the waterway for all nations. If these conditions were not met, Her Majesty's government and France would temporarily occupy the Canal. Of course, this was all a ruse to which Ben Gurion, Eden, and Mollet agreed before Israel's invasion. The ultimatum was written in a way to ensure that Nasser would reject it, providing justification for Allied military action, which began on the evening of October 31 with French and British attacks on Egyptian air bases.

It was not until November 5, however, when French and British paratroopers landed at Port Said at the northern entrance to the Canal, that the Anglo-French-Israeli plan was fully underway. In response, Egypt's ally, the Soviet Union, threatened retaliation against the conspirators. A diplomatic note to the Israelis warned them to cease military operations while "there was still time."[7] To prove they were serious, Soviet MiGs intercepted and disabled a British reconnaissance aircraft high over Damascus on November 5. At the same time, NATO intelligence officials were noticing an unusually high level of Eastern bloc military communications.

The Soviets were not the only ones who were angry at the French, British, and Israelis. Despite the fallout in U.S.-Egypt relations from the Czech arms deal, Egypt's recognition of the People's Republic of China, and suspicions of Nasser's friendly intentions toward Moscow, the Eisenhower administration reacted poorly to the Anglo-French-Israeli aggression. Just two days before their push into the Sinai, President Eisenhower warned the Israelis not to invade and reminded Prime Minister Ben Gurion that Israel's long-term interests lay with Washington, not Paris and London. This was in all likelihood a hard sell for Eisenhower. Although he was surely correct, France was Israel's staunchest ally at the time and the Israel Defense Forces were equipped with significant amounts of French-manufactured equipment.

As for the Europeans, throughout the previous summer of consultations, American officials made it abundantly clear to their British and French counterparts that Washington would not support military action against Egypt. A crisis in the Middle East involving two founding members of NATO so close to the November 6 presidential election might also complicate Eisenhower's reelection bid. More broadly, its close ties to Great Britain and France notwithstanding, the United States was resolutely opposed to Europe's efforts at holding onto the last vestiges of its empires. The Eisenhower administration calculated (correctly) that to the extent that its European allies were trying—often violently—to maintain their grip on colonial possessions in the Middle East, Africa, and Asia, nationalist groups within these places would gravitate toward the Soviets.

Of additional immediate concern, however, was the awkward position in which the Tripartite Aggression placed President Eisenhower, who was simultaneously contending with the Soviet military action against a nationalist uprising in Hungary. On November 4, one thousand Soviet tanks entered the Hungarian capital, Budapest, while Soviet aircraft and artillery bombarded the city. How could the White House denounce Moscow's aggression against Hungary while its own allies were doing seemingly the same in Egypt? Indeed, Secretary of State John Foster Dulles bluntly told the French ambassador in Washington, Hervé Alphand, that the Anglo-French-Israeli invasion of Egypt was no different from the Soviet aggression in Hungary.[8]

Eisenhower went to the UN Security Council to resolve the crisis in the Middle East only to be thwarted by British and French vetoes—which further enraged the American president. The American administration then turned to the UN General Assembly, where it secured a resolution (by a sixty-four to five vote) demanding a cessation of hostilities and an immediate withdrawal of all foreign forces from Egypt. At the same time, Washington informed the Israelis that they should not necessarily expect American help if the Soviets made good on their promise to retaliate. The State Department reiterated to the French in no uncertain terms that the only solution to the crisis was the withdrawal of all foreign forces from Egypt and the deployment of UN peacekeepers.[9] Finally, Eisenhower refused to support London's application for a $1 billion loan from the International Monetary Fund. Given Prime Minister Eden's desperation to secure these funds in light of the significant economic troubles on his hands, the British capitulated, bringing an end to the Anglo-French-Israeli alliance.

All forces were withdrawn from Egyptian territory by December, though Israel secured guarantees that the new ten-country United Nations Emergency Force (UNEF) being dispatched to the Sinai would keep the Strait of Tiran open.[10] Washington's stand against Great Britain, France, and Israel bolstered Cairo's position on the Canal, essentially legitimizing the waterway's nationalization; effectively ending any further British efforts to directly influence the course of Egypt's domestic politics; and instilling Nasser with even greater self-confidence at home and on the regional and global stages.

RHETORIC AND REALITY

During the mid-1950s and early 1960s, the Egyptian economy, which was being transformed from what was essentially a feudal system to a state-directed one, was improving. Overall gross domestic product increased dramatically in the early 1960s before declining sharply in 1966. Income per capita also improved modestly and steadily throughout the decade before declining in 1966, though it rebounded in 1968 and 1969.[11] The plight of the Egyptian worker was markedly improved—at least for those who were gainfully employed. Job creation remained a nagging problem, growing only 2.75 percent during the 1960s. Even so, in the fifteen years between the coup and the June 1967 war, the income of Egyptian workers in the professional, technical, commercial, and clerical sectors of the economy nearly doubled.[12] Also, by the mid-1960s, the wealthiest Egyptians' share of national income declined 10 percent, while the bottom 60 percent increased its share by 12 percent. These economic changes coincided with a dramatic expansion of educational opportunities. Whereas before the coup, less than half of school-aged children received a primary education, within a decade 90 percent of urban children and three-quarters of rural children were enrolled in school.[13] In the decade and a half between the Free Officers' consolidation of power and 1969, the life expectancy of Egyptians increased by three to four years. It was during this time that the leaders of the new regime came closest to achieving their goal of successfully embedding the ideas that animated their so-called revolution into the minds of Egyptians. It is important to underscore that the economic performance was relative. Taken as an aggregate, the economy's overall growth rate was no better than 4 percent, the increase in per capita income was a modest 2 percent, and Egypt remained deeply in debt.[14] Yet, in comparison to the period before the coup, it seemed that the Free Officers were able to generate significant economic development and address a variety of social and economic ills, giving the regime a powerful normative appeal on which to continue their efforts to build a new Egypt.

Central to this effort was a demonstration of Egypt's power and influence abroad, which, in addition to social justice and reform, was one of the commitments the Free Officers had made to the Egyptian people. Nasser's rhetoric about pan-Arab solidarity and the perfidy of the West to thwart—primarily through the establishment of Israel—Arab power found a willing audience among nationalists at home and across the region, lending additional luster to the new regime. Egypt's "Sawt al Arab" ("Voice of the Arabs") gorged on Arab nationalism in its daily broadcasts, thrilling audiences from Rabat and Ramallah to Ramadi and Riyadh. This came at a time when the old political order in the Arab world was increasingly under attack, with Nasser leading the charge. The decolonization of North Africa was well underway. Tunisian nationalists declared a republic in 1957 and the country's leader, Habib Bourguiba, pursued a range of policies that were similar to those of his Egyptian counterparts. In Algeria, a war of liberation that began in 1954 cost the lives of perhaps a million people by the time Algeria won independence from France in 1962. In the Levant, Lebanon was the stage for political intrigue among different ideological, ethnic, and sectarian factions; and, Syria was lurching from one government to the next in a debilitating series of coups and counter-coups. In 1958, Iraq shook off the vestiges of British tutelage when Colonel Abdel Karim Qassem overthrew King Feisal, scion of the Hashemite rulers of Jordan, whom London had placed on the Iraqi throne. In each of these places, new leaders sought to emulate Nasser and the Free Officers, albeit tailored to their own specific political contexts.

Syria's political class did not just seek to emulate Egypt, but to unify the two countries. By the late 1950s, a weak government under the leadership of Shukri al Quwatly concluded that there was no domestic solution to the country's tribulations, and he sought to inject stability into Syrian politics through a merger with Egypt. Yet ideology also motivated Syria's leaders. Most commonly associated with Saddam Hussein's Iraq, Ba'athism is primarily of Syrian origin—an ideological response to the negative impact of French colonial policy on that country. The central theme of Ba'athism's early theoreticians—Zaki al Arsuzi, Wahib al Ghanim, and especially Michel Aflaq and Salah al Din Bitar—was the kindling of an Arab awakening (literally, the Arabic word *ba'ath*). This revival was to be realized through a renewed sense of pride in the past achievements of Arab civilization; a recognition that certain features and aspects of contemporary Arab societies—sectarianism, tribalism, and the status of women—were responsible in part for the backwardness of the Middle East; an appreciation of the European enlightenment; an embrace of socialism; and the resistance to colonialism, which created unnatural divisions among the Arabs. Aflaq, a Maronite Christian, and his collaborator in the full elaboration of Ba'athist ideology, Bitar, reconciled the seemingly secular underpinnings of their doctrine of Arab renaissance with Islam, suggesting that the two were inextricably linked and thus posed no contradictions and problems.

The primary tenets of Ba'athism were similar in many ways to the principles that had ultimately come to guide Nasser and his associates as they constructed their new regime. Unlike the Ba'athists, however, Nasser regarded Arab unity as a rhetorical device for domestic and regional aggrandizement rather than a project that could be carried out practically. Nasser wanted Egypt to lead the Arab world against what was widely believed to be the West's ill-intended designs on the Middle East, but this approach did not require deconstructing the state system that had become a fact of life in the region. Still, in mid-January 1958, Nasser received fourteen Syrian military officers who had traveled to Cairo to urge the Egyptian leader to form a "United Arab Republic" consisting of the two countries (with the possible later addition of Iraq). Nasser was not initially enthusiastic about the prospects of conjoining the two countries. Not only would there be practical challenges made more difficult by geography—Cairo is almost four hundred miles from Damascus—but the Egyptian leader also under-stood the complexity of Syria's domestic political struggles and wanted no part of them.[15] Still, the Ba'athist appeal for Syrian-Egyptian unity was difficult for Nasser to dismiss out of hand. Rejecting the merger would reveal his pan-Arab rhetoric to be hollow, thereby jeopardizing Egypt's claim to Arab leadership. Ultimately, Nasser calculated that the costs of forgoing a union were too great and that he would take his chances with the vicissitudes of Damascus politics. The creation of the United Arab Republic on March 6, 1958, was greeted with such enthusiasm in Syria that whatever lingering doubts he had were swept away in the din of cheering throngs upon Nasser's arrival in Damascus after the union was consummated.[16]

By mid-1958, Nasser was the undisputed master of Egyptian poli-tics and he sought to do the same for Cairo in regional politics. The Syrians had gone to him precisely because he was "the greatest Arab" of the era.[17] In roughly the decade between the nationalization of the Suez Canal and the late 1960s, the Egyptian capital was the epicen-ter of Arab culture, higher learning, and politics, outpacing its tradi-tional rival, Baghdad. The trends that were set and the ideas that were developed in Egypt reverberated throughout the Arab countries across the North African rim to the Persian Gulf. Coinciding with Nasser's "Voice of the Arabs" was an intellectual ferment about the possibilities of Arab nationalism and republicanism that had swept new leaders into power. Indeed, those leaders often sought moral and material support in Cairo. It was no accident, for example, that Algerian nationalists turned up in Cairo seeking Egyptian assistance during their brutal war with the French. After Algeria won its independence in 1962, it was not Iraqi, Saudi, or Syrian teachers who were dispatched to Algiers to help the new government pursue its policy of Arabization, but Egyptians. Later, when a young Libyan colonel named Mu'ammer Qadhafi over-threw King Idriss in September 1969, he followed the model of the Free Officers who had come to power almost two decades earlier.

Egypt was also experiencing a period of unprecedented influence beyond the Arab world as Nasser joined a triumvirate of powerful non-aligned leaders including India's Jawarhalal Nehru, Yugoslavia's Tito, and Indonesian President Sukarno. Nehru was India's first postcolonial leader and emerged as an important moral force in the battle against colonialism and the right to self-determination. In Yugoslavia, Tito, a hero of the anti-fascist movement of the previous decades, staked out a position truly independent of both Washington and Moscow, despite his socialism. Sukarno was the leader of Indonesia's independence movement against the brutality of Dutch colonialists. Nasser's associations with these global figures was a clear indicator that both he and Egypt had arrived.

Still, despite Nasser's achievements at home and abroad, Cairo's effort to dominate the pan-Arab political arena was proving to be a challenge. Saudi Arabia, the Gulf emirates (all of whom remained under British tutelage), and Jordan were all conservative monarchies whose leaders regarded Egypt's republicanism, vague socialism, drift toward Moscow, and bid to lead the Arab masses as a threat to their stability and power. Egyptian radio broadcasts heaped venom not just on Israel and Zionism, but also on Egypt's Arab antagonists. Nasser, his supporters and associates in Egypt, and leaders of the new republican regimes considered the monarchies to be reactionary and thus by their very nature an impediment to Arab progress. In contrast, Cairo led a "revolutionary" camp that espoused nationalist and reformist ideas that, while borrowed from the West, were deployed against Europe, the United States, and their allies.

Even within the different Arab groups there was significant discord, presenting a further challenge to Egypt's bid for regional leadership. Among the monarchies, the Jordanians were deeply distrustful of the Saudis, who only a generation earlier had forced the Hashemites from the Hejaz region of the Arabian Peninsula and, in the process, assumed control of the holy cities of Mecca and Medina. Without this source of influence and power, the Hashemites were left adrift and dependent on British support. Weak and located between a hostile Israel and—as of 1958—an equally hostile Iraq, Amman was subject to the malevolent influences of Baghdad, Riyadh, and Cairo. For their part, the small Gulf states were hardly players in the inter-Arab arena given their continued dependence on London. Kuwait, in particular, was subject to Iraqi irredentism that claimed the country as its nineteenth province, forcing the British to deploy additional forces to the Persian Gulf in 1961 to protect the ruling family.

The situation was not much better and even a good deal worse among the republics. The Algerians were recovering from their bloody revolution and were already preoccupied with the emerging competition with Morocco for leadership in North Africa. Abdel Kareem Qassem's coup in Iraq revived the perennial rivalry between Cairo and Baghdad for regional leadership. By far, the most debilitating problem among the new republics was the failure of the Egyptian-Syrian experiment in unification just three short years after the two countries merged. Ironically, the Syrians, who had solicited Nasser to create the

United Arab Republic, were the ones to sue for its dissolution. The divorce was a function of wildly different expectations of the parties; the practical difficulties of merging two countries with different histories, political institutions, and economies; and the ham-fisted way in which the Egyptians sought to bring Syrian politics to heel.[18] To the Egyptians, the creation of the UAR was not the union of two equals, but rather absorption of Syria into Egypt's political system. Nasser was to preside over the union as its president with four vice presidents, an all-union cabinet that presided over national issues such as defense, foreign affairs, and education, and two regional cabinets for issues related to Egypt and Syria, respectively. Syria's ministries of defense and foreign affairs were appended to their counterparts in Cairo, as was the Syrian intelligence service, which became a subsidiary of Egypt's General Intelligence Directorate. Soon after the merger, the Syrians were chafing at Nasser's effort to render their country a province of Egypt.

Although the hard feelings between Egyptians and Syrians continued for the following two years, it was a series of incidents in 1961 that ultimately led to the UAR's dissolution. First, the Egyptians sought to extend their statist economic model to Syria, nationalizing banks, insurance companies, and other concerns. In addition, higher taxes were levied on individuals, maximum salaries were capped, and workers were granted representation on boards. Any Syrian official who protested these measures was sacked or transferred to Cairo. Second, an ongoing power struggle between Field Marshal Abdel Hakim Amer—UAR vice president, war minister, and ultimately Nasser's supremo in Syria—and Colonel Abdel Hamid Sarraj, the head of Syria's intelligence service, forced Sarraj's resignation in mid-September. A little more than a week after Sarraj's exit, the Syrian military staged a coup d'état demanding redress for unspecified grievances and a modernization of the armed forces. Nasser rejected these demands, but soon realized that his personal appeal among average Syrians would not carry him through the crisis if the military was opposed to him. On September 29, Amer and other Egyptian officials were put on a plane to Cairo and a new civilian government under a Syrian lawyer named Ma'mun al Kuzbari was established in Damascus. Despite the dissolution of the union and the bitterness the entire experience caused, in early 1963 the Syrians and the Iraqis approached the Egyptians about a merger of the three countries. His great reluctance notwithstanding, Nasser entered into an agreement in April promising eventual union. Yet the agreement foundered quickly over struggles between the Iraqi and Syrian branches of the Ba'ath parties and a failed coup in Syria that sought to replace the government with pro-union Nasserists. The attempted coup and the subsequent death sentences for the coup plotters further poisoned relations between Cairo and Damascus—a conflict that would dominate inter-Arab politics in the ensuing years.[19]

If Egypt and Syria were engaged in political intrigues and a form of rhetorical warfare, this paled in comparison to the actual conflict to which Nasser committed Egyptian forces in Yemen in October 1962. The previous month, army officers under Brigadier General Abdallah Sallal undertook a coup d'état and, in the process, believed that they had killed Yemen's leader Imam Mohammed al Badr when the military bombed his palace. The imam survived, however, and organized an insurgency against the new republic with the help of tribal groups in the northern part of Yemen. The Saudis and Jordanians committed to help Imam al Badr with both finances and arms. In response, Sallal and his fellow officers appealed to the Egyptians for assistance. Given his commitment to export the Egyptian revolution and his ongoing confrontation with the "reactionary" monarchies of the region, Nasser agreed to support Yemen's republicans. That commitment would last the better part of five years, at its height involve 60,000–70,000 Egyptian soldiers and officers—of whom as many as 26,000 are estimated to have been killed—and leave a lasting stain on the Egyptian armed forces for its use of chemical weapons against Imam al Badr's forces during the campaign.[20] Ultimately, it was only the emergency of the June 1967 war that prompted Egypt to bring its forces home.

While foreign policy buffeted Cairo's bid for regional leadership, Egyptian domestic politics had become complicated, if decidedly less volatile. As noted earlier, the improvement in a variety of socioeconomic indicators combined with nationalist triumphs, like the dispossession of British and French interests in the Suez Canal, generated significant political support for the new regime. This gave Nasser the confidence and political will to pursue more thoroughgoing changes in Egyptian society and politics. It was during this era that Egypt's economy took on a decidedly socialist cast, despite Nasser's and the Free Officers' rejection of leftist dogma in the immediate period after the coup. Widespread nationalization of the economy began with the July 1961 decrees that brought significant parts of the economy under direct state control. The government assumed 100 percent ownership of all banks and insurance companies as well as fifty heavy industrial and shipping concerns. In addition, the decrees enjoined public utilities, textile manufacturers, food processors, department stores, hotels, and a variety of other businesses to cede anywhere from 10 percent to 50 percent ownership to the government.[21] The scale of the nationalization was significant, but a sizeable portion of the economy remained in private hands. This was to change in 1964, when Nasser ordered another round of nationalization. Those firms that had only been partly nationalized three years earlier now came under exclusive government control. Sectors that had been spared altogether in 1961 such as pharmaceuticals and construction were also nationalized.[22]

The statism of the economy coincided with a dramatic expansion of the state into areas that had heretofore been independent. For example, the Egyptian government stripped al Azhar—the university and mosque that served as a training ground for Sunni ulema from all over the Muslim world—of its religious endowment and did away with shari'a courts.[23] In the summer of 1961, Law 103 brought al Azhar's faculty formally under state control. Nasser appointed nonclerics to the university's board and added medicine, as well as engineering and agricultural sciences to al Azhar's core curriculum.[24] The takeover of al Azhar was consistent with an environment—which actually predated the Free Officers' coup—that, while not overtly hostile to religion, was secular in tone. For example, the 1962 National Charter, which came eleven months after al Azhar became a ward of the Egyptian state, was respectful toward Islam, as was the subsequent 1964 constitution. Still, Nasser's leftward shift was clearly emphasized in these two documents at the expense of religion.

Similarly, the government sought to bring the universities and workers under its control. Although both groups supported the coup and the goals of the new regime, they were also potential sources of trouble. In the early days after the Free Officers' coup, Egyptian workers— in the form of the Founding Committee for a General Federation of Egyptian Trade Unions (FCGFETU)—indicated their support for a return to parliamentary rule.[25] Moreover, it is important to recall that the Officers' first encounter with popular opposition to their rule was after the army put down striking textile workers at Kafr al Dawwar in August 1952. The position of the FCGFETU only fueled the Officers' suspicion of organized labor, which the majority of the RCC considered to be a bastion of communism.[26] In general, however, it was not solely an issue of the workers' ideological proclivities that mattered to the Officers, but the very fact that the labor movement was beyond the grasp of the Revolutionary Command Council. A basic feature of authoritarian political systems is the unwillingness of nondemocratic leaders to countenance the existence of alternative centers of power.

As a result, Nasser and his associates went about bringing Egyptian labor under their control. This entailed a crackdown on the communists, purges within the trade union leadership, demonstrations of force against striking workers, and, importantly, appealing to workers in a way that would establish support for the regime within the labor movement.[27]

In April 1953, the Officers gave workers job security when they made it harder for employers to fire their staff without cause. This was followed in December with the Law of Individual Contracts, which increased severance pay, extended annual vacations, offered free transportation for workers employed in distant factories, and provided health care to workers and their families. These material benefits came with conditions, however. Workers were no longer permitted to strike and were required to accept arbitration in all labor disputes.[28] The benefits the Officers offered in exchange for these restrictions were acceptable to many workers who chose not to oppose the government's new policies. In a further effort to impose discipline on labor, the Free Officers permitted unions greater latitude to organize. Counterintuitive as it seems, this had the ultimate effect of weakening the Egyptian labor movement because it sparked a proliferation of unions that diluted the power and influence of larger organizations like the General Federation.[29] Although these measures had an important effect on the relationship between the Officers and working class, the regime continued to confront opposition from labor until 1961 and the promulgation of additional legislation, which favored workers.[30]

As far as the students were concerned, the Free Officers were well aware of recent Egyptian history. University and secondary students had been politically active from the 1919 nationalist revolution through the parliamentary period and remained so as Nasser and the RCC struggled to consolidate the new regime. Indeed, at critical moments throughout Egypt's nationalist struggle, whether it was the 1919 uprising , the protests over King Farouk's February 1942 acquiescence to British demands for a Wafdist government, Black Saturday (January 1952)—the day angry crowds burned parts of Cairo after British forces shelled an Egyptian police compound in Ismailiyya—or any other important public protest, Egypt's students were present. They may not have been decisive in determining the outcome of these events, but they were a force with which the Palace, parties, the British, and ultimately the Officers had to contend.

Cairo and Alexandria universities, as well as newer additions such as Ain Shams University (founded in 1950 as Ibrahim Pasha University) located in the Abbasiya area of the Egyptian capital, were hotbeds of political activity and ideological contestation. Prior to the coup, student union elections—which typically pitted Muslim Brothers against Wafdists—were high-stakes affairs that at times turned violent. Once in control of the country, the Officers found themselves at a distinct disadvantage on the campuses. Although they had gone to great lengths to organize a network within the armed forces, they had no affiliated student organization. No doubt this was a function of the clandestine nature of their enterprise; but without students, the Free Officers were missing a critical constituency. In contrast, the Muslim Brotherhood, the Democratic Movement for National Liberation, communists, and the Wafd all maintained student cadres. Still, because students and many of their professors had been part of the nationalist struggle, these groups threw their support behind the Free Officers, believing that the young commanders represented an opportunity to achieve reform, social justice, and national independence.[31]

Immediately following the coup, university students pledged support for the Officers. Despite this, Egypt's new leadership was unable to translate the early support of Egyptian campuses into an asset that it could leverage to its advantage against the regime's opponents. Indeed, as the Officers sought to consolidate their power and repress competing political factions, student opposition grew. While students—like virtually all Egyptians—shared the Officers' goals, many were opposed to a military dictatorship. Student activists at the time of the coup had come of age during the parliamentary period and thus believed in the virtues of civilian rule and democracy. As a result, the students at Cairo University reversed their support for the regime and established a front to oppose military rule. This is not to suggest that the regime's support on campuses dissipated completely. The Youth Bureau of the Liberation Rally, which was established in 1953, maintained a following for the new regime, but like the Rally itself, there was a distinctly contrived nature to the group. In reality, the Youth Bureau consisted of government-sanctioned thugs who sought to intimidate student Wafdists, Muslim Brothers, and leftists. In order to keep the universities in line, the RCC employed a combination of what was called the "University Guard" (policemen stationed in each university department); the Ministry of Interior's state security agents; the military police; and informants within the student body, faculty, and administrators to complement the activities of the Youth Rally.[32] These repressive measures kept student opposition activists under constant surveillance and threat. Even so, the students proved to be tenacious. At Cairo

University, for example, student opponents of the regime continued to battle for months after their adult counterparts succumbed to the Free Officers' drive to consolidate their power in March 1954. Indeed, the RCC was unable to pacify the university until well into that summer.

Intent on not allowing Egypt's universities to become centers of anti-regime activity after 1954, the government undertook a broad range of indirect strategies to depoliticize the campuses. At the level of faculty and campus administration, the new regime created a Ministry of Higher Education and a Council of Higher Education in order to better control the flow of resources and personnel into the universities, end the practice of electing faculty deans, and created incentives—notably, plum government positions—for faculty and administrators to acquiesce to the new political order. The depoliticization of students was conducted through the creation of campus organizations dedicated to supporting the regime and a conscious effort to draw young people into activities that were geared more toward youth welfare and sports instead of politics.[33] Prominent among these was the Socialist Youth Organization, which fell under the umbrella of the Arab Socialist Union. The union was the successor to the Liberation Rally and the National Union that existed during unity with Syria, and, like these organizations, it was a mechanism of political control and the sole source of regime-sanctioned politics.

There were, however, two additional factors that contributed to the quiescence of Egyptian universities between the mid-1950s and the late 1960s. First, the regime could point to a decade of success. Strides in economic development, educational opportunities, progressive social change, and Cairo's global political influence gave credence to Nasser's claims about the achievements of the revolution. There were a great many students who responded to these claims with unbridled support for the regime. Second, students—like their professors and Egypt's workers—responded to the material benefits that the regime offered. In the students' case, the promise of a free education and the guarantee of employment upon graduation bound them to the regime. Thus, by the early to mid-1960s, Nasser had done much to assimilate critical constituencies through a combination of normative appeals about the nature of Egyptian society and strategic distribution of resources.[34]

As momentarily successful as Nasser seemed to be, however, the guarantor of the regime's stability was coercion. Throughout the British presence in Egypt, the country was under martial law—a situation that Nasser and his fellow Free Officers sought to leverage to their political advantage. In October 1954, the Officers rewrote the British-era military regulations as part of their effort to ensure the newly consolidated power of the RCC. The product of that effort was not—as some had hoped—an easing of the many restrictions of the existing law, but rather an expansion of the powers and purview of the military authorities.[35] Four years later, the regime promulgated a more comprehensive "Emergency Law." Officially known as Law 162 of 1958, the law gave the government extraordinary powers under a state of emergency. These included censorship and closure of newspapers and periodicals, restrictions on union activities, and strict limitations on political organizations, which could only meet at the discretion of the Ministry of Interior. The law also established a parallel judicial system, called State Security Courts, intended to adjudicate crimes related to public safety and national security. These courts, which do not exist in any of Egypt's founding documents, lack basic guarantees such as due process and limit a defendant's right to appeal.[36]

BROTHERS IN PRISON

The codification of the Emergency Law came at a time when the regime confronted no organized opposition and was clearly intent on keeping it that way. By 1958, Egypt's political landscape was bleak at best. The RCC dissolved the political parties in January 1953, mercilessly repressed the Left, and expanded its powers to ensure that no autonomous centers of power emerged. The Officers, however, reserved their greatest wrath for the Muslim Brotherhood. Within six weeks of the attempt on Nasser's life—what became known as "the Manshiya incident" (for the square where the incident took place)—the People's Tribunal handed down the death sentence to seven members of the Brotherhood, including the would-be assassin Mahmoud Abdel Latif and the organization's Supreme Guide Hassan al Hudaybi. The Brotherhood's leader was, however, ultimately spared the gallows and sentenced to life in prison. All told, an additional nine Brotherhood activists were condemned to death (all commuted to life in prison) and 1,100 others sent to jail, not to mention an additional 1,000 Brothers who were incarcerated without being formally charged.

Those who were sent to prison were dispersed in facilities across the country, the Brothers who escaped the police dragnets lived on the run and in hiding, and the organization's leadership was effectively silenced. These circumstances, combined with the order of December 5, 1954, disbanding the Muslim Brotherhood, brought an effective—though temporary—end to the group's activities. Suddenly, there was no organizing, no agitating, no strategizing, and no politicking. This was the way it was to remain for the Brotherhood until late 1957 and early 1958. Yet while Nasser and the Officers could repress the Brothers in an effort to eliminate its physical presence, they were unable to erase entirely the sentiments, principles, and ideas that animated the organization and its activists. The reemergence of the Brotherhood in the late 1950s suggests a certain resilience borne of the conviction in the establishment of an Islamic society above all.

As it happened, the ability of the Brotherhood to start organizing again was a function of Nasser's hubris. Riding high from the early economic and social successes of the revolution, as well as Egypt's exalted status among many in the Arab world and beyond, Nasser calculated that he had prevailed. In many ways, Nasser's view was largely consistent with what was happening in Egyptian society. The Egyptian leader was at his zenith: his emphasis on nationalism, pan-Arab solidarity, and a vague form of socialism clearly resonated with many Egyptians. As a result, Nasser relaxed his grip (ever so slightly) on the Brotherhood. He ordered second- and third-tier activists who had been charged with lesser crimes or no crimes at all to be released from prison.

Nasser's ostensible magnanimity had an important unintended consequence that would both rebound on the regime and ultimately contribute to a rift within the Brotherhood that would have significant consequences in the ensuing decades. The suppression of the Brotherhood in the preceding three years was so severe and thoroughgoing that Nasser and his advisors calculated that the coercive power would intimidate the newly released Brothers from any political activity. Once more, even had they wanted to organize, the regime ensured there was no longer a coherent movement around which these Brothers could resume their activities. On both accounts, Nasser was only half correct. The awesome power of the state had, indeed, broken the Brotherhood—but not for good. Between 1954 and 1957, the Islamists ceased to be a force in Egyptian politics. Against these odds, however, the released activists began rebuilding their shattered organization.

The reconstitution of the Brotherhood had actually been in the works for some time from behind bars. The effort was, at first, ill-defined and progress was made possible only by happenstance. The Muslim Sisterhood, an organization about which there is little known, played a central role in nurturing the Brotherhood's rebirth. The Sisters served as an informal prison-support network, but they were actually much more than that. They provided a link between the different prisons where Brothers were held, carrying messages and ideas that helped sustain the organization after the regime sought to decapitate it.[37] In addition, the structure and organization of the Egyptian prison system at the time facilitated communication between Brothers who had been intentionally dispersed throughout the country. In particular, prisoners requiring medical attention were all sent to a central infirmary in the Tora prison complex southeast of Cairo. One of the patients in the facility was a Muslim Brother named Sayyid Qutb who suffered from chronic respiratory problems.[38]

Sayyid Qutb Ibrahim Hussein Shadhili was born in 1906 in a village called Musha in Upper Egypt to a landowning family. Although Qutb's father enjoyed the status of a wealthy man, his affluence diminished over time as he cared for his large extended family. Qutb's mother enrolled him in Musha's state-run elementary school, which maintained a curriculum based on Western pedagogical methods. Qutb's primary education was interrupted briefly during a short and unhappy stint at a private Quran school. Even so, religion along with Egyptian nationalism—his father was a member of the Nationalist Party—and social justice were intertwined in Qutb's formative years, providing a basis for his subsequent intellectual development.

In 1921, Qutb left Musha for Cairo, where he enrolled in the Dar al Ulum Preparatory School and, after completing his studies there, went on to Dar al Ulum, where he earned a degree in Arabic language and literature. Upon his graduation in 1933, the Ministry of Education hired Qutb. He spent the next six years teaching in primary schools in Cairo and several provincial towns before moving back to the Cairo area and settling in the southern suburb of Helwan. After moving to Helwan, Qutb left the classroom in favor of an administrative position within the ministry. In addition to his new bureaucratic post, Qutb found time to devote himself to literary writing and criticism. During this time he wrote a novel titled *Thorns* (1947) and famously challenged the work of Taha Husayn—one of Egypt's towering intellectuals and a leading man of Arabic letters. In his 1937 critique of Husayn's *The Future of Culture in Egypt*, Qutb dismissed Husayn's contention that Egypt should reclaim its alleged Hellenic past as Europe had done. He argued forcefully that while Egypt would benefit from emulating some organizational aspects of Western civilization, the country had never been an integral part of the Hellenic world and thus should be careful not to sacrifice its own unique civilization and culture in favor of an alien one.[39] In this way, Qutb was expressing sentiments that were not terribly different from the adherents of Islamic reformism and the disciples of Mohammed Abduh.

It was not until after World War II that Qutb's writing took on a more specifically religious cast. In *Social Justice in Islam* (1949), Qutb argued that because the very bases of Islam were equality, social cohesion, and community, it alone could ensure justice.[40] He was clearly responding to events swirling around him as publication of the book coincided with the deterioration of Egypt's political climate over the nationalist issue, the establishment of the State of Israel, and the generalized political agitation against King Farouk and the monarchy. Yet Qutb ended up observing some of the most intense moments in Egypt's prolonged political tumult from afar. In early November 1948, he departed for a twenty-one-month visit to the United States on an Egyptian government grant to study modern teaching methods. Qutb first spent some time in New York City and Washington, where he studied at Wilson Teacher's College—a precursor to the University of the District of Columbia. He left Washington for Greeley, Colorado, and the Colorado State College of Education. After six months at the foot of the Rocky Mountains, Qutb moved on to his final stop, California and Stanford University. Although Qutb believed he benefited from his studies in the United States and was impressed with the scale of the country's advanced economic development and technology, his American experience disturbed him.

In a lament on his stay in the United States written after his return to Cairo called *The America I Have Seen: In the Scale of Human Values* (1951), Qutb evinces a tone of both bewilderment and sadness that Americans, who had reached the zenith of development and thus prosperity, were simultaneously "abysmally primitive in the world of senses, feelings, and behavior."[41] He attributed this backwardness to the particulars of America's founding. According to Qutb, the first Americans' belief in "science alone," "desire for wealth," and a criminal element among the first pioneers led inexorably to a "deformed American character." This abiding flaw was manifest in America's violent pastimes—football, in particular—its history of warfare, Americans' indifference to the suffering of fellow humans, and their recklessly cavalier attitudes toward sex.[42]

After Qutb's return to Egypt in August 1950, he went back to the Ministry of Education, where he served as an inspector of elementary schools. He soon left the ministry to devote himself to advocating for the islamization of society. Toward that end, Qutb joined the Muslim Brotherhood and immediately became ideologically influential. In this capacity, Qutb was prolific, penning some eighty articles, columns, and commentaries (including his reflections on the United States) as well as two books, and the first installment of his eight-volume magnum opus, *In the Shadow of the Quran*, between late 1950 and 1954. When it came to the Free Officers, Qutb was initially enthusiastic about the coup and, like so many other Egyptians, hopeful that the young commanders would rid the country of corruption, political intrigue, and foreign influence. Yet Qutb was no passive observer of events. As head of the Brotherhood's propaganda section, he briefly served the Revolutionary Command Council as a cultural advisor.[43]

When the Free Officers took down the Brotherhood after the attempted assassination of Nasser, Qutb was rounded up with the rest of the organization's leadership. He was sent to Tora prison, where he spent most of his time revising *In the Shadow of the Quran* and extending the ideas of the influential South Asian Islamist theorists, Mawlana Maududi and Abul Hassan Ali al Nadwi. With Supreme Guide Hassan al Hudaybi effectively muzzled, the Brotherhood was literally adrift, left with neither ideological guidance nor leadership. In time, Qutb and his ideas increasingly filled these vacuums. The Brothers that were released from prison in 1957 and 1958 began to organize themselves into cells and looked to him for guidance. When these groups merged into a subgroup of the Brotherhood, they appealed directly to Qutb to become their spiritual leader.[44] Given his background in education, Qutb developed a curriculum for this vanguard that would fuel its ideological ardor. Among the works of classical Islamic thinkers such as Ibn Hanbal and Ibn Taymiyya, Qutb included his own *Milestones Along the Way* (1964), which he wrote specifically for these Brothers. Much of the book is extracted directly from *In the Shadow of the Quran*, with some new material written specifically for the vanguard.

Over the course of twelve chapters, Qutb set forth an ambitious argument about the nature of Islam; the inherent shortcomings of modern society, including those considered "Muslim societies"; and the appropriate solution to the problems that humanity confronts. Qutb's point of departure was that Islam was not merely a religion to be consigned to the reality of individual conscience and belief, but was rather a total system that governed life and, if applied in the manner that God prescribed, through his messenger the Prophet Mohammed, humanity would experience peace and harmony. Indeed, Islam is a "system [that] extends into all aspects of life; it discusses all minor or major affairs of mankind; it orders man's life—not only of this world but also of the world to come; it gives information about the unseen as well as the visible world; it not only deals with material things but also purifies intentions and ideas."[45] Islam, according to Qutb, would endow people "with such high ideals and values as have so far remained undiscovered by mankind, and which will also acquaint humanity with a way of life which is harmonious with human nature, which is positive and constructive, and which is practicable."[46] In other words, according to Qutb, Islam—which literally means "submission"—would set men free.

This call—in fact, requirement, in Qutb's worldview—to submit oneself to God in order to be free poses what seems to be a central contradiction in *Milestones* and the work that it inspired. How, opponents of Qutb's vision ask, can there be freedom in a system that requires one either to surrender to the will of Allah or face grave consequences? Yet, the "submission to God is the path to freedom" paradox is far less problematic than it seems at first blush. Qutb's central claim was that a society that does not follow the dictates of God as revealed to Mohammed is in *jahaliyya* (state of ignorance or an impious society). This ignorance was manifest in societies that lacked social justice; placed material well-being above all else; valued science over spirituality; and, importantly, bound men to other men, rather than God.[47] In this context, the Muslim creed, "*La ilah illa Allah*" ("There is no God but God")—also known as the *shahada*, or testimony of faith—took on a decidedly political, even revolutionary, significance. When Qutb invoked the shahada in *Milestones*, and when his followers subsequently followed suit publicly, they were not just invoking the unity of Islam, but rather declaring the illegitimacy of societies that placed man-made law above that of God's—to Qutb "a rebellion against God's sovereignty on Earth." Racial problems, nationalist rivalry, ethnic competition, poverty, injustice, and indeed the panoply of pathologies that humanity confronted were a function of jahaliyya—man's sovereignty over other men, a hallmark of societies found in both the West and the East. In contrast, Islam transcends race, ethnicity, and nationality; its only criteria is belief.[48] As a result, a true Muslim society is inclusive, free, and thus better able to realize its human values.

Harkening to the earliest Islamic community—a "community of belief"—at the time of the Prophet, Qutb writes:

They all came together on an equal footing in the relationship of love, with their minds set upon a single goal; thus they used their best abilities, developed the qualities of their race to the fullest, and brought the essence of their personal, national and historical experiences for the development of this one community, to which they all belonged on an equal footing and in which their common bond was through their relationship to their Sustainer. In this community their "humanity" developed without any hindrance. These are characteristics which were never achieved by any other group of people in the entire history of mankind![49]

In this way, Qutb regarded his vision of Islam as neither retrograde nor radical, but rather progressive; it held the keys critical to unlocking man's liberation and all the ills that befell him in the state of jahaliyya.

Milestones was not merely an academic exercise illuminating a particular interpretation of Islam and the deficits of modern society but, rather, a call to action. It is important to remember that Qutb was writing for members of the Muslim Brotherhood who sought his guidance and leadership. Whether he was referring to this group when he recognized the need for "a vanguard which sets out with this determination [to forge an Islamic system] and then keeps walking on the path, marching through the vast ocean of jahaliyya which has encompassed the entire world" is unclear. Yet, at the end of his introduction, in an unmistakable nod and wink to his followers, Qutb admits, "I have written *Milestones* for this vanguard, which I consider to be a waiting reality about to be materialized."[50] In this light, *Milestones* was less a metaphor than a guide for Qutb's followers, offering them insights into the nature and importance of their project and the appropriate way to proceed.

Indeed, how was this call to action to be operationalized? Qutb's answer was straightforward: the Muslim community must marshal its resources to confront the jahili system with which there could be no compromise.[51] Islam was at fundamental odds with societies organized around man's sovereignty over man, which was the source of mankind's many travails. Thus, Qutb declared:

This movement [i.e., the Islamic movement] uses the methods of preaching and persuasion for reforming ideas and beliefs; and it uses physical power and jihad for abolishing the organisations and authorities of the jahili system which prevents people from reforming their ideas and belief, but forces them to obey their aberrant ways and makes them serve human lords instead of the Almighty Lord. This movement does not confine itself to mere preaching to confront physical power, as it also does not use compulsion for changing the ideas of people. These two principles are equally important in the method of this religion. Its purpose is to free those people who wish to be freed from enslavement to men so that they may serve God alone.[52]

Jihad, or holy war—along with preaching—was thus an indispensable tool in helping to create an environment in which Islamic society could flourish and Muslims could realize the lofty goal of living in harmony with true human values. For Qutb, jihad was inherently offensive in nature. Islam, he believed, endowed Muslims with the "initiative" to establish the conditions for freedom on Earth through holy war. This meant that Muslims not only had a responsibility but also a divine-given right to take up arms "to establish God's sovereignty on the Earth, to arrange human affairs according to the true guidance provided by God, to abolish all the Satanic forces and Satanic systems of life, to end the lordship of one man over others, since all men are creatures of God and no one has the authority to make them his servants or to make arbitrary laws for them."[53] Indeed, with the resources available to the forces of jahaliyya, the Muslim vanguard would have little hope to create the condition in which an Islamic system would flourish without employing jihad.

Qutb derided his contemporaries who argued that Islam stipulates war only in circumstances when the Muslim community was under threat as "the product of the sorry state of the present Muslim generation" whose grasp of the Quran and Islam was limited.[54] To think of jihad in only defensive terms would, according to Qutb, negate the cosmic mission of Islam, which is to liberate man. He also rebuked "the orientalists" (Western, predominantly European, scholars of Islam) whom he believed intentionally distorted the true nature of jihad because they claimed that Islam used violence to impose itself on nonbelievers, rather than liberate the people from their servitude to false gods—especially man. To Qutb, embracing the faith was a matter of personal choice, yet it was one that he was sure people would make once the institutions of jahaliyya were destroyed. This was all a matter of practicality for Qutb. He was setting the record straight about the essence of Islam which was, to be sure, a religion but also a practical and fully realizable way of life.

Within Qutb's conception of an Islamic society, shari'a—or Islamic law—would regulate life. Contemporary discussions of shari'a tend to focus on the specific obligations that are required under Islamic law, but this was not Qutb's interest. His discussion of shari'a in *Milestones* was broader and consistent with his emphasis on the absolute sovereignty of God. In this way, shari'a was "part of that universal law which governs the entire universe, including the physical and biological aspects of man."[55] Following shari'a will then place man in "harmony" with nature as opposed to the conflict that arises when man abides by laws of his own making. In an important theological innovation, Qutb offered the bold claim that the present and next worlds "are not two separate entities, but are stages complementary to each other." When man follows shari'a, the benefits of this obedience are experienced in the present world rather than delayed until the next, though Qutb admits that these advantages "reach their perfection in the Hereafter." Qutb is implying—he is not specific in this area—that following Islamic law will produce an environment akin to paradise on earth.

In July 1965, the authorities discovered the Brotherhood vanguardists and accused them of planning the assassination of President Nasser and the overthrow of the regime. Given the central themes of *Milestones*—possession of which became a criminal offense—it is abundantly clear why Nasser sought to repress the group. In the context of Qutb's discussion of jahaliyya and the absolute sovereignty of God, Egypt's authoritarian regime—which had become the archetype for the republics of the Middle East—was clearly ripe for jihad. The subsequent military tribunal handed down death penalties to Supreme Guide Hassan al Hudaybi, Sayyid Qutb and two of his associates, Abdel Fattah Ismail and Mohammed Yusuf Hawwash. Like his sentence in the mid-1950s, al Hudaybi's punishment was commuted to life imprisonment, but Qutb, Ismail, and Hawwash were hanged in August 1966.

The July crackdown was critical in the future trajectory of the Brotherhood. After the vanguard's founding in the late 1950s, the supreme guide, under house arrest, was kept apprised of the group, tacitly supporting its activities and acknowledging Sayyid Qutb's spiritual leadership of the group. Al Hudaybi saw the emergence of the group in strategic terms.[56] With the supreme guide under house arrest and his organization largely in disarray, the activism of Qutb's followers was important in keeping the Brotherhood alive during a period of great stress. After the new round of repression, al Hudaybi was far more circumspect and ultimately distanced himself from the vanguard. The split was intertwined in both politics and doctrine, specifically differences related to concepts such as jahaliyya, the absolute sovereignty of God and, especially, *takfir* (excommunication). Although there is no denying Qutb's influence on this group when it came to these ideas, there is no direct reference to takfir in *Milestones*. Qutb may have implied that non-Islamic societies, including Egypt's, were in a state of ignorance, but he never specifically called for excommunication or a declaration of nonbelief. This concept was clearly a doctrinal innovation of Qutb's followers and those who read and interpreted *Milestones* in the years after Qutb's death.

Al Hudaybi well understood that the innovations in Islamist thought that Qutb extended in *Milestones* and the way Qutb's followers embraced them could ultimately prove fatal to the longevity of the Brotherhood, which under al Hudaybi sought to avoid direct confrontations with the regime after the Brotherhood was repressed in 1954. For the supreme guide, the primary goal was the preservation of the Muslim Brotherhood, and thus there was no choice but to reject what the vanguardists had come to represent. Even as Qutb's followers rejected accusations that jahaliyya, the absolute sovereignty of God, and takfir were central to their thought, the supreme guide's decision to turn away from them had a profound and enduring effect on Islamist politics in Egypt. To Qutb's followers, al Hudaybi's rejection of their group compromised the supreme guide's integrity and his claim to spiritual leadership of the Islamist movement.

The ideas contained in *Milestones* that became central to radical Islamist groups may have crystallized in the early and mid-1960s, but there was little that its adherents could do to operationalize their theological innovations. Nasser and the regime remained firmly in control, as the nascent movement had been decapitated with the hangings of Qutb, Hawwash, and Ismail. Yet the remnants of the vanguard so concerned al Hudaybi and the Brotherhood's leadership that they felt it necessary to respond to *Milestones*. Al Hudaybi had begun that process when he directly questioned Qutb's followers about whether the concept of takfir was central to their worldview. Yet the full elucidation of the supreme guide's response to Qutb's followers would not come for several years, and only after the most momentous event to rock the Middle East since the founding of the state of Israel in 1948.

SETBACK

On the evening of June 9, 1967, President Gamal Abdel Nasser appeared on Egyptian state television to address the nation. Egypt's armed forces lay in ruins. The officer corps was humiliated. The country, it seemed, was at the mercy of Israel and the goodwill of the superpowers. In his statement, Nasser reminded Egyptians that it was their "tradition" to sit together during both good times and bad. In the culmination of his 1,600-word address, he stated:

> We have now come to an important point in this exposition by asking ourselves: How are we to carry responsibility for this setback [*al naqsah*]? I am saying to you my friends—despite efforts to stop the crisis—that I am prepared to accept responsibility for it and I have taken a decision that I want you all to support me in: I have decided to resign completely and fully from any official position and political role and that I return to the ranks of the citizenry, to do my duty as any other citizen.[57]

The announcement of Egypt's crushing defeat came as a great shock to Egyptians. In the earliest hours of the conflict on June 5, Egypt's radio dispatches gloried in battlefield victories of Egyptian warriors. Reality set in shortly thereafter, however, as the scale of Israel's victory became clear. The outcome of the conflict did not dishearten Egyptians when it came to Nasser, however. He had given them regional and global stature, a modicum of economic and social progress and, most important of all, an Egypt ruled by Egyptians. They rejected Nasser's resignation. According to the *New York Times*' Eric Pace, Nasser's announcement produced "pandemonium on the streets" as millions of Egyptians spontaneously poured out of their homes, cafes, and stores to express support for their wounded leader, calling him back to the presidency. Some fifteen hours after Nasser bid the Egyptian people farewell, Anwar Sadat—the deputy speaker of the National Assembly—appeared before parliament and read a statement on behalf of now-citizen Nasser, who was himself unable to reach the assembly due to throngs clogging Cairo's arteries. Nasser via Sadat declared, to the relief of millions, "I was convinced of the reasons for my decision, at the same time the commanding voices of the masses and our people could not be resisted therefore I decided to stay in my place and my position that the people wanted until a time that we can rid ourselves of the enemy aggression."[58]

Despite the emotional outpouring for Nasser, the events of early June were, as he had said, a setback. The "Six Day War," as the conflict is commonly known, is a misnomer. (See the Six Day War map in this chapter.) The Egyptians were actually routed in about seventy-two hours. In those three days, the Israelis destroyed more than 300 aircraft—many while the planes were still sitting on the aprons of Sinai airbases—more than half of Egypt's 900 tanks in the Sinai were smashed or abandoned, and 500 (of 1,000) artillery pieces were captured, along with 10,000 vehicles. The human toll of the war was staggering as well. The Egyptian military suffered 10,000–15,000 killed in action, among them senior officers, and another approximately 5,000 were captured. This meant that more than 10 percent of all the Egyptian soldiers and officers in the Sinai at the beginning of hostilities on June

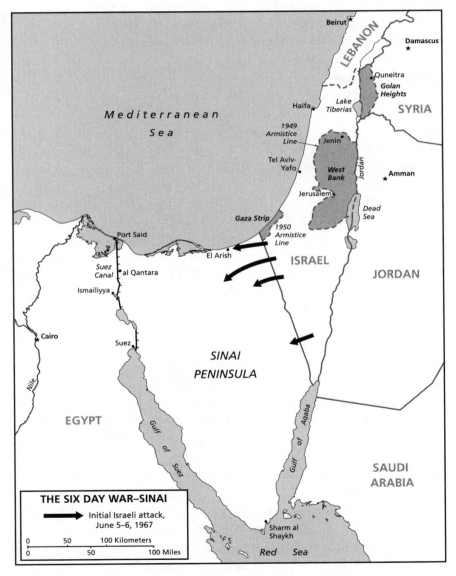

Israel's Attack in Sinai. Courtesy of Christopher Robinson.

5 were either killed or captured by the time a ceasefire was announced on June 9. In addition, by the time Israeli forces approached the Suez Canal on the night of June 8, the fighting had produced about 250,000 refugees from populated areas along the waterway and in the Sinai proper.[59]

The geostrategic consequences of the June War were enormous. When the guns finally fell silent on the Syrian front on June 11, Israel controlled the entire Sinai Peninsula and Syria's Golan Heights, placing the Israel Defense Forces (IDF) within easy striking distance of Cairo and Damascus. On the Egyptian front, the Israelis stopped their advance at al Qantara—about one hundred miles northeast of Cairo—before fanning out along the East Bank of the Suez Canal. On the Golan, Israeli tanks had seized control of the small city of Quneitra, placing them now only forty miles from the Syrian capital. From the rocky escarpments above Quneitra and the summit of Jabal al Shaikh (known commonly in English as Mount Hermon) just to the north, the Israelis could literally look down on and listen into Damascus. On the eastern front of the war zone, Israel now controlled all of Jerusalem. Prior to the outbreak of hostilities, the city was divided into an Israeli (Western) zone and a Jordanian (Eastern) zone. Jerusalem had been a consolation prize for the Hashemite family that had been run out of the Hejaz and the holy cities of Mecca and Medina in the Arabian Peninsula and placed on a British-fabricated throne in the backwater of Amman. The loss of the historic walled Old City, with the golden Dome of the Rock—the place where the Prophet Mohammed took his night flight to heaven—and al Aqsa Mosque, which sits upon the Temple Mount and the adjacent Western Wall, was a devastating blow to Jordan's King Hussein. Beyond Jerusalem, the Israelis took control of the territory on the West Bank of the Jordan River stretching from the town of Jenin in the north along the spine of the Judean and Samarian hills to the south, where the Afro-Syrian rift meets the Negev desert. With the conquest of the West Bank, combined with its takeover of the Gaza Strip at the corner of the Sinai and Mediterranean Sea, the Israelis suddenly controlled—and by international law—were responsible for 1.25 million Palestinians, including 750,000 refugees from the fighting in 1948.[60]

In addition to Israel's territorial gains, the battering of the Egyptians and Syrians was a victory for Western (mostly French) arms over Soviet equipment and clearly tipped the balance of power in favor of the Israelis. As for the United States, although the Johnson administration initially proceeded with discretion—counseling the Israelis against unilateral action, cautioning the Egyptians, and seeking a multilateral way to head off the march to war—once hostilities got underway and Israel's victory became clear, the United States sought to capitalize on the Arab defeat.[61] To be sure, the conflict posed serious complications for President Lyndon Johnson. This was particularly so after the Israelis attacked a U.S. Navy surveillance vessel, the USS *Liberty*, in international waters off the coast of el Arish on June 8, killing 34 American sailors and injuring another 171. The attack on the *Liberty* sparked an intense debate about Israel's motives that remain unsettled more than forty years later.[62] Yet while the historical record is not entirely clear about what happened on the morning of June 8 off el Arish, it does reveal that President Johnson was not going to allow the attack to complicate the new diplomatic opportunity that Israel's victory afforded Washington.

Like its predecessors and each of its successors, securing comprehensive peace between Israel and its Arab neighbors was a central component of the Johnson administration's Middle East policy. Yet Washington had little leverage in its efforts to make this laudable goal reality. Israel's victory and the territorial gains that went with it altered President Johnson's calculation. The Israelis now had something the Egyptians, Syrians, and Jordanians wanted—territory—that could be traded for a comprehensive settlement of the conflict. Thus, rather than forcing an Israeli withdrawal from the Sinai, Gaza, the Golan Heights, East Jerusalem, and the West Bank, the Americans threw their support behind Israel, reckoning that this maximal position would persuade the Arab parties (and in the Egyptian and Syrian cases, their Soviet supporters) to the negotiating table. Washington's assumption that the demonstration of Israeli military superiority and temporary—it was hoped—territorial aggrandizement would render the Arab side more flexible proved to be erroneous, however. At the August 1967 Arab League summit in Khartoum, leaders committed themselves to "unit[ing] their political efforts at the international and diplomatic level to eliminate the effects of the aggression," yet they rejected negotiating directly with the Israelis.[63] What became known as the "three no's"—no to negotiations, peace, and recognition—effectively stalemated the conflict, setting the stage for another eruption that would come in October 1973 and providing opportunity for Israelis to settle on the land they now occupied.

Even if the Arab countries refused to come to the table as the United States had hoped, Washington remained in a position of strength in relation to the diminished Soviets as a result of the war. For these circumstances, however, Moscow had only itself to blame. The origins of the June 1967 war and the motivations of its central participants are the subject of much scholarly debate. What did the Egyptian leader believe about Israeli intentions? What role did the Soviets play in sparking the conflict? Did Nasser actually seek war? Were the Israelis merely looking for another *casus belli* to take on the Egyptians? Whether Nasser wanted war remains unclear, but his actions nevertheless created a cascade of events that ultimately led to Israel's preemptive strike on June 5. Nasser's strategic errors were all his own, but his calculations and decisions during the critical weeks leading up to the conflict were shaped largely in response to a Soviet warning received in mid-May. Echoing Damascus' own reports of Israeli troop movements, which the Egyptians had discounted, Moscow indicated that the IDF was moving anywhere from eleven to thirteen brigades to the Syrian border. The Soviet intelligence dispatch had an immediate effect on Cairo, encouraging the Egyptians to take notice and ultimately respond to Israel's alleged escalation.[64] There were no Israeli troop movements, however. The Soviet report was bogus, but historians have yet to determine why Moscow issued the warning.[65]

The military and regional political contexts were also important in shaping Nasser's analysis. There had been considerable tension on the Syrian-Israeli border for years, but the Egyptians—despite wanting to demonstrate their regional leadership—had scrupulously avoided getting into a conflict with Israel over relatively minor cross-border skirmishes between Israeli and Syrian forces. The situation took a dramatic turn to the serious when, in April 1967, Israel's air force downed six Syrian MiG-21s. At the time, the Israel Defense Forces chief of staff, General Yitzhak Rabin, cryptically warned that the "lesson" (for the Syrians) of this limited incident could be "applied to other areas."[66] Divisions within the Arab world also played a role in Nasser's decision making. The Egyptians' regional rivals, notably the Saudis and Jordanians, had come to use the presence of the UN Emergency Force (UNEF) that had been deployed to the Sinai after the Tripartite Aggression as a cudgel against Nasser. They accused the Egyptian leader of hiding behind the UN in order to avoid—using the Egyptian leader's own rhetoric—his pan-Arab duty against Zionist imperialism.

Amidst the Soviet warning, tension between Israel and Syria, and regional politics it seems clear that Nasser sought to split the difference between two lamentable options: do nothing, which would make him look weak, or enter a war for which he was manifestly unprepared, given that a large number of Egyptian forces were bogged down in Yemen.

Needing to improve his regional standing, which had taken a hit from the long conflict in Yemen and the attacks on him from Amman and Riyadh, Nasser took a strong stand against Israel that was just short of war. On May 14, Egyptian forces were put on alert and large numbers of troops and equipment were deployed to the Sinai. Two days later, General Mohammed Fawzi—the Egyptian chief of staff—requested that the commander of the United Nations Emergency Force withdraw his forces from the Sinai. On May 18, Foreign Minister Mahmud Riad followed Fawzi's request with a letter to UN Secretary General U Thant, informing him that Egypt would no longer accept the UNEF presence in the Sinai and the Gaza Strip. By most contemporary accounts, Nasser had not made the determination to go to war when he ordered UNEF out of the Sinai. Rather, the Egyptian president, though not necessarily his military commanders who were making plans for airstrikes and commando raids, believed Israel would refrain from attacking Syria if there was a risk of war with Egypt—a far more potent adversary than the Syrians.[67] Yet events began to spiral toward war once U Thant acquiesced to Foreign Minister Riad's letter.[68]

During a visit with Egyptian pilots at an airbase in the Sinai on May 22, Nasser announced the closure of the Strait of Tiran. If Nasser did not want war, it remains a mystery why he took this fateful step. Since the 1956 crisis, the Israelis had made it clear that they would go to war if the Egyptians shut down the waterway to Israeli and Israeli-bound shipping. There are two plausible interrelated explanations for Nasser's miscalculation. First, Nasser, carried away with the war fever that was gripping the region and enjoying the rehabilitation of his status by taking a strong stance on Israel, gambled that he might actually get away with his provocation. Second, Israel had yet to respond strongly to Egypt's moves. Initially, the Israelis believed that Nasser's saber rattling was just that—a demonstration of force for the benefit of the Arab world.[69] There was precedent for this type of action. In late February 1960, the Egyptians sent two divisions into the Sinai over (false) reports that Israel was mobilizing against Syria, but less than two weeks later those forces were withdrawn. Although Egypt's brief remilitarization of the Sinai had caught the Israelis by surprise, in hindsight the IDF regarded the Egyptian deployment as an elaborate bluff. The 1960 incident was the prism through which Israel's leadership initially interpreted Nasser's latest dispatch of forces into the peninsula. General Rabin's veiled warnings and the IDF's mobilization aside, the Israeli response to Egypt's moves was at first muted—so much so that, even after Israel called up eighty thousand reservists, there was much public criticism of the government's seeming inability to confront the Egyptian challenge. Even after the Israelis undertook a general mobilization on May 20, Nasser, it seems, closed the strait in part because he had come to believe that he could do so without tremendous risk.[70] This was a significant miscalculation, but Israel's response would not come for another two weeks.

In that time, the Israeli prime minister publicly emphasized his desire not to use force to open the strait, while Foreign Minister Abba Eban traveled to Washington to take measure of the Johnson administration's approach to the crisis. On May 30, the situation took a dramatic turn. On that day, King Hussein, heretofore a bitter rival of Nasser, turned up in Cairo and signed a joint defense treaty with Egypt that placed Jordanian forces under Egyptian command. The king, who had enjoyed good clandestine relations with the Israelis until that point, clearly felt the regional pressure for conflict building and decided to throw his lot in with the Egyptians. He also repaired his relationship with Palestinian Liberation Organization leader Ahmad Shukairy and gave the green light for Iraqi troops to enter Jordan for the ostensible purpose of joining the fighting that was to come. The war was on six days later.

In the decades since the June War, it has become accepted wisdom that along with an estimated twenty thousand Egyptians, Syrians, Jordanians, Palestinians, and Israelis who died on the battlefield, so did Arab nationalism.[71] This conclusion seems only half correct, however. It is certainly true that Arab nationalism was much diminished as a result of the June War. Yet the animating beliefs of Arab nationalism survived the setback, notably a general awareness that "Arab" marked a unique identity forged in a common language and religion that produced broad feelings of kin. To be sure, the Arab world is notorious for its intramural rivalries pitting countries against each other in regional political struggles; but, at one end of the identity repertoire for Egyptians, Palestinians, Saudis, Jordanians, Syrians, Algerians, Moroccans, Tunisians, Qataris, Libyans, Bahrainis, Omanis, and others is the sense that these people separated by nationality are at a basic level all Arabs. These ideas were clearly at work in the Khartoum summit's final communiqué and the subsequent oil embargo of 1973, the Arab world's rhetorical solidarity with the Palestinian people, and even the Arab refusal to assist the United States in rebuilding Iraq after the 2003 invasion of that country.

Instead of killing Arab nationalism, the June War destroyed Nasserism. Here it is important to underscore several points developed in the previous two chapters. The origins of Egyptian nationalism are varied, but because of Egypt's own experience with European penetration, the nationalist project in Egypt was deeply intertwined with the situation in Palestine. Egyptians regarded Zionism as an extension of Europe's effort to colonize and dominate the heart of the Middle East and, thus, the struggle against Jewish claims to Palestine were connected to Egypt's own efforts to free itself from British domination. The Free Officers' coup was intended to rectify the ill effects of Great Britain's presence in Egypt, fusing the new regime's legitimacy with nationalism—an issue that would become a recurrent theme of more contemporary debates about Cairo's relationship with Washington. Egyptians were told that the political system the Officers built and the set of policies and principles that became known as Nasserism—nationalism, a vague socialism, and a strong central government—were necessary to achieve the goals of the revolution. Consequently, Egyptians were asked to sacrifice political and personal rights for the benefit of these important collective goods. Yet Egypt's shattering defeat seemed to strip bare the justifications for the regime and the nature of the political system. The accumulation and centralization of state power that Nasserism represented failed Egypt at that critical moment when it confronted "Zionist colonialism" directly. To be sure, the regime produced—as noted earlier—a modicum of progressive change that benefited society, but at what cost? The smoldering wreckage of the Egyptian armed forces made the political order founded after July 1952 seem hollow.

Despite the enthusiasm with which the Egyptian people called President Nasser back to office, they also wanted accountability for the defeat. How, they asked, could Egypt be defeated so soundly in just a few short days? During the fighting, Nasser had tried deflecting the shortcomings of the armed forces when he accused the Johnson administration of directly assisting the Israelis. The presence of the USS *Liberty* off el Arish momentarily gave this story an air of plausibility, but Washington made it clear to Cairo, Moscow, and all other interested parties that it had nothing whatsoever to do with Israel's battlefield successes. In the end, it was evident that while Egyptian armed forces had not performed poorly across the board, inadequate planning, substandard leadership on the battlefield, and an inability to leverage its superiority in hardware both in terms of raw numbers and technology plagued the Egyptians and led to their ignominious defeat.[72] This was a function of Egypt's army-dominated regime, which was geared less toward protecting the country's borders and projecting power and more toward running the day-to-day affairs of the country and ensuring domestic political control. To be sure, there were competent professionals in the Egyptian military who made good decisions during the conflict, but the shortcomings of the political environment in which they operated, combined with the very real limitations of their forces, conspired against these officers.

Because of a growing call from the Egyptian public for accountability for the defeat, Nasser laid responsibility on eight hundred military officers, including the commander of the armed forces, Field Marshal Abdel Hakim Amer, who he sacked on June 11, 1967. The field marshal had been one of Nasser's closest confidantes and was the exemplar of the shortcomings of the Egyptian armed forces. Amer had been less interested in the armed forces as a fighting force than as a political force, and as the military became more deeply involved in the day to day governance of the country after 1954, Amer used his exalted position to build a political and personal fiefdom.[73] Even as Nasser drifted further left in the mid-1960s and Amer led the Committee for the Liquidation of Feudalism, the field marshal and his associates within the military parlayed their predominant positions in the political arena to amass personal wealth. This combination of political power and financial resources made Amer and the officers loyal to him a "center of power" unto themselves.[74] It was as much for this reason as it was personal loyalty that Nasser was unwilling or unable to relieve Amer of his command prior to June 1967, though the field marshal's performance in 1956, his high-handed approach to Syria during the union with that country from 1958–1961, and the military's problematic expedition to Yemen clearly demonstrated Amer's limitations as an officer.

The scale of the defeat in June 1967 was so great and the military so compromised as a result that Nasser was able to bring an effective end to Amer's career. But, the story did not end with the field marshal's dismissal. In late August, Amer, along with 150 military officers and a handful of former government officials, was arrested for plotting to overthrow the government. Amer provided refuge to some of these individuals in his Giza home after they were dismissed for their role in the "setback." There, in Amer's villa, this group plotted both their revenge and their return to power. When Nasser got wind of these plans, he ordered the arrests. Rather than stand trial, Amer, after trying and failing the first time, eventually took his own life by swallowing pills. This version of events is, however, widely disputed. Amer's supporters long argued that officers loyal to Nasser gave the field marshal a choice: he could stand trial with the others and face certain humiliation or he could end his life honorably and swallow the pills Nasser's men provided. Amer's second wife, Berlanti Abdel-Hamid, argued that the field marshal was never actually given the choice but that Nasser had his former friend and colleague poisoned.[75] There is no definitive answer to what became of Amer, but there are few Egyptians who give credence to the regime's version of events.

REVOLT

The officers and officials who were arrested along with Amer—a group that included Minister of War Shams Badran and Chief of Intelligence Salah Nasser—were not the specific scapegoats for the 1967 defeat. To be sure, Nasser held them responsible, hence their collective dismissal along with hundreds of others. Still, Egyptians demanded scalps, and they got them in the four air force officers who were brought before a military tribunal in November 1967 to explain themselves and the defeat. On February 21, 1968, the court handed down its verdicts. Air Marshal Mohammed Sidky Mahmoud and his deputy, Air Vice Marshal Ismail Labib, received fifteen and ten years in prison respectively, but the chief of staff of the air force, Air Marshal Gamal Afifi, and Air Vice Marshal Hamed al Dogheidy were acquitted. The relatively light sentences for Mahmoud and Labib and the acquittals of Afifi and al Dogheidy, in particular, did not match their alleged transgressions, which had brought dishonor to Egypt on the battlefield and resulted in Israel's humiliating occupation of the Sinai Peninsula. Outraged at the trial, workers at a munitions factory in the Cairo suburb of Helwan walked off the job and took to the streets to express their anger. There, the workers confronted the police, resulting in a melee. The following day, students at Cairo and Alexandria universities also mounted demonstrations protesting the verdicts. Reflecting on those events four decades later, one participant remembered wistfully with a hint of anger, "We were sophomores at Cairo University and totally frustrated after the setback. We were expecting a fair trial and strong [verdict] for those responsible for the setback, however, we were shocked and in a state of disappointment. Was Gamal [Abdel Nasser], the one we demonstrated for [to come back to office], bluffing us? We started our demonstrations in the universities, then into the Cairo streets."[76] They stayed there for five days, during which two people were killed, 223 injured (including 146 policeman), and 635 arrested.

The intensity of the student protests led to a meeting between student representatives of Cairo University's Faculty of Engineering and the speaker of the parliament, Anwar Sadat. The regime had hoped that the audience with Sadat would defuse the tension and send the students back to class. Although Sadat allayed the concerns of the students, promising that they would not be arrested for their activism, they were taken into custody that evening. The students were not intimidated, however. The next day they took over the Faculty of Engineering, staged a sit-in there, and battled riot police who attempted to retake the building. Once again, the students were granted an audience with Sadat. Over the previous week—the students were scheduled to see Sadat on February 28—the government claimed that the students were responding to the verdicts in the "air force case," but it had become clear that what had been an expression of anger over the court's sentences quickly became a collective statement on the nature of Egyptian politics. Indeed, in the five days that the students stayed in the streets of the capital and Alexandria, they took the opportunity to develop a set of demands that went well beyond the verdicts.

In Cairo, the engineering students offered Sadat seven specific demands: the release of all arrested students; removal of domestic intelligence agents from university campuses; an investigation into the police's role in universities; a full government accounting of the air force officers' responsibility for the June 1967 defeat; freedom of expression and of the press; laws protecting political freedoms; and parliamentary reforms. In Alexandria, the student activists proffered a strikingly similar set of demands about political and personal freedoms with a few additions, including the dismissal of Nasser's brother from the local leadership of the Arab Socialist Union, punishment for those responsible for repressing the Helwan workers on February 20, abolition of "paid full-time work in political organizations," and the reinvigoration of youth organizations.[77]

At his meeting with the students representing Cairo University on February 28, Sadat rejected the students demands completely. He scolded them for their insubordination, suggesting obliquely that the proper role for the Egyptian student was to support the regime. In turn, the government sought to discredit the student activists, labeling them reactionaries who wanted nothing more than to roll back the gains of the revolution to benefit the old landed classes from which the regime claimed they hailed.[78] In an effort to turn public opinion away from the student demonstrators and their demands, representatives of the regime purposefully twisted the students' calls for parliamentary reforms, implying that these calls for change were nothing more than an attack on the composition of the National Assembly, specifically the mandated representation of workers and peasants in the legislature. The argument did not wash, for several interrelated reasons. First, as part of the Free Officers' vague commitment to social justice, they had swung the universities' gates open to young Egyptians from all social classes. Although there is no breakdown of the backgrounds of the student demonstrators or their leaders, it stands to reason that the eruption of anger at the regime in February 1968 was a broad-based affair. Second, although the Left was clearly influential in the demonstrations and the formulation of demands, the student protests were not an ideologically driven affair. Students of every political stripe participated in the demonstrations, and, while the Left played a prominent role, neither it nor the Muslim Brotherhood nor the Wafd nor any other faction drove the students into the streets.[79] The Brotherhood, after all, was unable to muster any kind of organizational leadership after the 1965 crackdown, and the Wafd remained outlawed. Rather, the bulk of the demonstrators were there because they advocated social and political change and were united in the perceived shortcomings of the revolution.

The eruption of student anger in February 1968 and a subsequent set of student protests the following November placed the regime on the defensive for the first time since the Free Officers consolidated their power in early 1954. To be sure, Nasser had faced challenges before from students. In 1966, for example, postgraduate students engaged in protests against the regime over the war in Yemen, the lack of political freedoms, and faltering economic and social development. Yet this demonstration of dissatisfaction was limited and defused relatively easily when Egyptian students living abroad—who had instigated the criticism of the regime—met with Nasser. The context of the 1968 demonstrations was quite different, however. Unlike 1966, the protests were broader based, including students as well as workers, two potentially potent political adversaries. And, of course, the disturbances came on the heels of the 1967 defeat, the scale of which greatly weakened Nasser and the regime's defenders.

At their core, the demonstrators' demands for political and personal freedoms, parliamentary reforms, and a reining in of police and intelligence services on university campuses challenged the sources of power and legitimacy of the regime. In a startling change of fortune for the Egyptian president, within eight months of demanding he rescind his resignation, Nasser and Nasserism were no longer above reproach. The regime's normative appeal—which was based on universal education, guaranteed employment, economic and social development, and geopolitical power—lost its luster. Indeed, Egypt's university students and their allies recognized the growing gap between the promise of these revolutionary goals and the objective reality of what the regime was actually able to deliver. By the mid-1960s, the momentum of state-directed development had begun to flag, undermining the goodwill the regime had accrued due to the economic and social progress earlier in the decade. Although the regime's coercive capacity had long been well-developed, the deterioration of its normative appeal in the wake of bad economic news; the pullback from socialism, which raised the specter of the return of the wealthy and landowning classes; and the drubbing in the Sinai all forced Nasser to rely more heavily on the security forces to maintain order. Yet the students at Cairo and Alexandria universities made it clear that they were no longer willing to pay the price in terms of personal and political freedoms for a regime that failed to achieve any of its stated objectives. In withstanding the police assault on Cairo University's engineering faculty, continuing to make demands—even as student "provocateurs" were arrested—and refusing to be intimidated during their second encounter with Sadat, the students signaled that their newfound enthusiasm for challenging the regime would not be dampened until their demands were met.

Confronted with the unenviable prospect of cracking down further on the students and potentially risking the stability of the regime, Nasser pursued a path typical of authoritarian leaders who suddenly find themselves in political trouble. He positioned himself as a reformer and sought to meet the demands emerging from Egyptian society without ever risking the core authoritarian institutions of the political order. This move was accomplished through the retrial of the air force officers and the "March 30 Program," which diagnosed the problems that contributed to the defeat, outlined Egypt's achievements over the critical months since the setback, and established a blueprint for the future. The statement identified "powerful actors"—Field Marshal Abdel Hakim Amer and the cadre of senior officers and officials tied to him—as the primary cause for both the military's poor battlefield performance and the apparent deficiencies of the Egyptian political system.

Yet, Nasser also asserted in the March 30 Program that the struggle to recover both Egyptian land and honor lay not just with military preparations, but also with the mobilization of Egyptian society to achieve democracy and social justice. Nasser thus outlined a ten-point program for a new constitution that underscored the importance of such basic individual rights as freedom of expression, thought, and opinion, as well as freedom of the press.[80] While affirming the supremacy of the law, the March 30 Program went a step further, proposing a High Constitutional Court vested with the power of judicial review. This was on the face of it an important step given the centrality of this concept in democratic polities. On the whole, the document stressed the necessity of deepening Egypt's democratic practices as a primary means of confronting the problems the country encountered and that the June 1967 war had laid bare.

On May 2, 1968, the government announced that 99.98 percent of voters approved the March 30 Program in a referendum. Despite what was clearly a government-manufactured result, the program seemed to usher in a genuinely more open period in Egyptian politics in which there was a modicum of free expression and a measure of self-criticism. Although it is often overlooked as one in a series of statements and revisions to revolutionary themes that were promulgated between 1954 and the early 1970s, the political impact of the March 30 Program should not be underestimated. Although the regime was never in danger as a result of the events between June 1967 and March 1968, the program allowed Nasser to regain his footing after the students openly questioned the regime's central principles. This new roadmap for national redemption acknowledged the government's mistakes while making a clarion call for unity and national sacrifice in preparation for a decisive battle with Israel. Implicit in this call for reform was the message that the student-worker demonstrations of February risked creating societal divisions, which would only make it harder to expel the Israel Defense Forces from Egyptian land. In essence, Nasser harnessed the deep nationalist affront of Israel's presence on the East Bank of the Suez Canal, which now numbered twenty thousand troops, to deflect and even delegitimize the criticism of the government and political system during a time of national crisis.[81]

While the March 30 Program may have provided a way out of the immediate challenge of the February demonstrations, Nasser remained personally and politically diminished. Indeed, the regime remained vulnerable to further challenges. Another eruption of student protests occurred in November 1968, though the cause of these disturbances— an effort to tighten educational standards at the secondary school level—was considerably less lofty than that of the previous February. Still, the outburst was instructive on one important level: it demonstrated once again the gap between the regime's ostensible principles and the objective reality of its coercive practices. At the time of the November protests, regime-affiliated intellectuals criticized the students for taking to the streets instead of addressing their grievances to the appropriate authorities.[82] Yet there was very little reason to believe that had student leaders done so, their demands would have been met.[83] After all, the previous February, Cairo University's student-leaders had gotten nowhere when they addressed the speaker of the parliament, who first had his interlocutors arrested and then, during a second meeting, summarily rejected the students' demands.

The problem of that gap between principle and practice would continue to plague the regime well after the challenges of the 1968 protests passed. The March 30 Program is a valuable case in point; although some student activists expressed satisfaction with the political environment, especially on university campuses, where the predatory policies of the police and intelligence services were curtailed in the months after Nasser unveiled the program, once the government was no longer on the defensive the document meant very little in practical terms. To be sure, liberal aspects of the March 30 Program were incorporated into the 1971 constitution, but Egypt's authoritarian political order remained intact.[84] For example, formal restrictions on personal and political freedoms continued, the Arab Socialist Union still dominated the political arena, and Egyptians were still subject to the caprice of their political leaders without any mechanism to hold these politicians accountable.

Importantly, Israel, or more specifically Israel's occupation of the Sinai, was useful politically for Nasser in this regard. Without question, Israel's presence on Egyptian land was the foremost and most immediate security threat to Egypt, which provided justification for the imposition of a state of emergency that placed Egyptians under formal military rule, if not martial law. As noted before, the Emergency Law that was central to these political circumstances suspended the formal rights and seemingly democratic principles that the 1964 constitution granted the Egyptian people. Thus, the police state that Nasser and his associates built in the years after they consolidated their power continued uninterrupted. Even the armed forces—despite the January and February trials of military officers, the earlier sacking of some eight hundred commanders, and the civilianization of the cabinet after the student demonstrations—retained its pride of place as the source of power and legitimacy for the regime. The complete demilitarization of the Egyptian political system was impossible as the entire country mobilized for a decisive battle with Israel.[85]

The student activists and leaders looking back with four decades of perspective recognize that the March 30 Program was little more than a tactical move to release the immediate pressure on the regime rather than a step toward meeting their demands for a more open and democratic political order. There is a strain of melancholy in their reminiscences given the durability of Egypt's nondemocratic system. Yet the June 1967 defeat and the student uprising that it sparked represented the first significant political blow to the regime. In the first decade after March 1954, the Free Officers seemed to have delivered on their promises of social justice, economic development, and national prestige. To be sure, there were confrontations with the Muslim Brotherhood vanguard in 1965, student dissent in 1966, and slowing economic development on the eve of the June War, but at least in the first two instances, the defenders of the regime were able to dispose of these challengers with relative ease and minimal damage to the leadership's prestige. The economy was a longer term challenge that Nasser had not effectively addressed. This problem, combined with the defeat and the students' expression of dissatisfaction, which Egypt's workers shared, marked the beginning of the end of the regime's ability to elicit the loyalty of large numbers of Egyptians without resorting to either patronage or force. Despite regaining his footing with the March 30 Program, the students had set a precedent: Nasser's regime and the principles by which he ruled Egypt were now subject to public scrutiny. Egypt's leadership would time and time again try to rectify this situation, but it was never able to regain the political advantages of its normative appeal, relying ever more on patronage and coercion to ensure the integrity of the political order.

Hero of the Crossing

T HE JUNE 1967 war never actually ended. From Lebanon and Jordan, Palestinian groups consistently launched hit-and-run raids into Israel and its newly occupied territories. In the Sinai, there was an almost continual exchange of fire between the Egyptians and Israelis across the canal. These clashes were largely contained through the end of 1967 and 1968, but they escalated in early 1969, leading President Nasser to formally announce a "War of Attrition" in March. Egypt's strategic objective in this conflict was for its newly reequipped armed forces—the Soviets had fully replaced the equipment Egypt lost in the June War within a year of the cease-fire—to demonstrate to Israel that the occupation of the Sinai would not be cost free. Toward that end, the cadre of senior officers who survived the post–June War purges devised an effective strategy for dealing with the Israeli challenge that matched Egypt's strengths against Israel's weaknesses. The Egyptians sought to keep the Israel Defense Forces (IDF) under constant pressure with a seemingly ceaseless barrage of artillery fire. Nasser's officers hoped that this would keep the Israelis at a high level of mobilization, placing a drag on the Israeli economy. Given Israel's small population and Israeli society's particular sensitivity to combat deaths, the Egyptians also sought to inflict as many casualties on the Israelis as possible in an effort to persuade Israel of the high price of staying in the Sinai.[1]

In some areas, the Egyptians were successful. The tenacity of the Egyptian personnel dispelled the notion among the Israeli public that the Egyptians could not fight—something Israel's military commanders already knew was a myth. The operations also instilled a sense of pride, purpose, and esprit de corps throughout the Egyptian ranks. Nasser was able, particularly after he managed to convince Moscow to commit its latest air-defense systems and personnel (including combat pilots) to Egypt's defense, to put the Israelis on the defensive. Still, Nasser's advantages were not enough to dislodge the Israelis from the Sinai or even the immediate area along the Canal. In fact, quite the opposite happened. The so-called Bar Lev line—a network of thirty forts built in 1968–1969 and named for Israel's then chief of staff, Haim Bar Lev—proved to be an effective defense against Egypt's incoming fire.[2]

Stalemated and without additional superpower military support beyond which they already enjoyed, in the summer of 1970 the two sides agreed to the "Rogers Initiative," which called for the Egyptians and Israelis to "cease-fire and standstill" for ninety days.[3] During this time, the United Nations' special representative to the Middle East, Swedish diplomat Gunnar Jarring, would resume his efforts to convince the Israelis, Egyptians, Jordanians, Syrians, and Lebanese to implement the November 1967 UN Security Council Resolution 242. The core of the resolution, which remains the basis for Arab-Israeli peace negotiations to this day, calls for Israel's "withdrawal . . . from territories occupied in the [1967] conflict" and the "termination of all claims or states of belligerency and respect for and acknowledgement of the sovereignty, territorial integrity and political independence of every State in the area."[4] Jarring's mission ultimately went nowhere as the parties traded accusations of cease-fire violations and the Arabs objected to direct negotiations with the Israelis.[5] Nasser took a tough and principled (from the Egyptian perspective) stand on Jarring's efforts, expressing Egypt's desire for peace but insisting that the IDF withdraw to its June 4, 1967 positions before negotiations on any of the other issues should commence. This was a move the Israelis, with Washington's backing, refused to take. The result was continued recriminations and deep mistrust as Cairo accused the Israelis of territorial aggrandizement while Jerusalem claimed the Egyptians were violating the cease-fire.

Within a month of the cease-fire standstill agreement, Nasser was confronted with another foreign policy issue that would have far-ranging consequences for Egypt and the region. Since 1965, the Palestinian Liberation Organization (PLO) had grown increasingly influential in Jordan; its cadres openly carried weapons and donned their own uniforms as the organization more generally took on the role of a state within a state, developing its own political and social institutions.[6] On September 6, 1970, a faction of the PLO called the

Popular Front for the Liberation of Palestine hijacked Pan Am, TWA, and Swissair flights over Europe. (Hijackers were thwarted on a fourth plane, an EL AL flight.) The Pan Am 707 landed in Cairo, and after releasing the passengers, the terrorists blew up the plane. The TWA and Swissair jets were forced to land at an airfield in Zarka north of the Jordanian capital, where they were joined on September 9 by a newly hijacked British Overseas Airways Corporation—the forerunner of British Airways—flight.

After the safe release of all the hostages, King Hussein took the opportunity to destroy the PLO's presence in the kingdom. The war threatened to destabilize the region, inviting Syrian, Iraqi, Israeli, and even potentially American and Soviet intervention. The crisis was, however, an opportunity for Nasser and Egypt. The Egyptian leader played a central role in mediating between PLO leader Yasser Arafat—who succeeded Ahmad Shukairy in February 1969—and King Hussein. After strenuous rounds of negotiations held in Cairo over the course of two days in late September, Tunisian Prime Minister Bahi Ladgham and his Sudanese counterpart General Gaafar Numeiry secured a cease-fire agreement with Nasser's assistance. Yet, even as the draft cease-fire was being finalized, the Jordanian military was intensifying its operations against the Palestinian forces. It was here that Nasser and his personal prestige played the greatest role in the conflict. He cajoled Arafat not to undermine the talks and encouraged King Hussein to consent to a fourteen-point agreement that would restore order in the Hashemite Kingdom.[7] This was a triumph for the Egyptian leader, who avoided a potentially irrevocable schism in the Arab world and burnished his flagging leadership credentials. Yet the stresses and strains of what became known as "Black September," combined with the extreme difficulties of the previous three years, took a heavy toll on Nasser. The day after the reconciliation was finalized, September 28, Nasser was dead from a heart attack—his second in twelve months.

Nasser's death was greeted with an outpouring of emotion from the Arab world and beyond. Announcement of the Egyptian leader's passing brought demonstrations in Beirut, forced the cancellation of U.S. naval exercises in the Mediterranean, and shook the U.S. bond market out of fear of prolonged instability in Egypt and the Middle East. In Cairo, "hundreds of thousands" turned out into the streets asking collectively, "Who will lead us, Gamal?" Millions of Egyptians attended Nasser's funeral.[8] In both life and death, Nasser achieved iconic status. It is not hard to understand why. He had given Egyptians the gift of an independent country that in the space of a few short years went from being British-occupied to being an influential voice in the developing world. The very fact that Egypt led the Arab states in their confrontation with Israel gave Nasser and Egypt even more cachet among the newly independent states of Asia and Africa. Egypt's military expansion underwrote its newfound regional and global prestige. Prior to the July 1952 coup, the armed forces were poorly trained and employed a hodgepodge of mostly outdated and ineffective equipment. By the late 1950s, however, Egypt boasted the largest and most technically advanced weapons systems in the region.

Domestically, the new regime that Nasser led was able, for a time, to generate the economic and social change that so many Egyptians craved during the deeply corrupting British-monarchical-parliamentary era. In a relatively short time, Nasser and the Revolutionary Command Council were able to forge an entirely new regime that broke the power of the traditional political and economic elites. The Officers had seen to it that the playing field was leveled, offering education and jobs to the sons and daughters of the heretofore powerless. The improvisation of the first eighteen months after the coup gave way to a regime that had a sense of coherence. To be sure, the principles of the revolution came only after the Officers consolidated their power, but land reform, "positive neutralism" in foreign policy, and the nationalization of the Suez Canal gave the new leadership and the political system they were constructing some momentum.[9] Egypt, after decades of European domination and royal chicanery, for the first time, it seemed, stood for something.

Yet, with all that had been achieved in Egypt in the eighteen years between the coup and Nasser's death, the Egyptian leader's legacy was decidedly mixed. The economic performance that produced impressive GDP growth in the early 1960s tailed off in the middle and latter part of the decade before picking up steam again during Nasser's last year of life. The emphasis on social justice and the emergence of a middle class notwithstanding, Egypt remained a place of vast asymmetries in wealth, health, and education. Even as the Officers undertook redistributive initiatives like the land reforms of September 1952, the nationalizations of 1961 and 1964, and the establishment of the Committee for the Liquidation of Feudalism, certain groups were well-positioned to leverage their proximity to power into new riches. Field Marshal Abdel Hakim Amer and the officers, as well as civilians around him, were notorious for what was widely suspected to be their ill-gotten gains. Moreover, those private enterprises that could be useful to the new regime remained influential. Prominent among these was the Arab Contractors Company and its principal, Osman Ahmed Osman. The company got its start in the 1940s building infrastructure projects for the British in the Canal Zone. After six years in Saudi Arabia and the Gulf, Osman returned to Egypt in 1956 and promptly went to work constructing the Aswan High Dam. In 1961, the Arab Contractors Company was nationalized, but Nasser understood the importance of the firm for Egypt's long-term development and permitted Osman to run the now state-owned company as a private firm. As of 1964, the company was exempt by law from a range of regulations stemming from nationalization that governed wages and terms of employment. Osman—like other wealthy businessmen deemed important to the regime—was permitted to establish private consulting and small-scale firms that partnered with Arab Contractors.[10]

When it came to the world around Egypt, the ignominious end to Egypt's expedition to Yemen after the crushing defeat in June 1967 and the fractious relations with Syria, Iraq, Saudi Arabia, and the Gulf states compromised Nasser's claims of Arab solidarity and Egyptian leadership of the region. Cairo derived considerable prestige from its rhetorically uncompromising stand against Israel, but at each and every confrontation between Egypt's armed forces and those of Israel, the Egyptians performed poorly. There were momentary triumphs such as the sinking of the destroyer *Eilat* in October 1967 or the November 1969 commando raid that sank three Israeli transport vessels, but Israel bested Egypt in every major battle during Nasser's leadership. This inability to deal effectively with Israeli military superiority forced Nasser to compromise his nationalist rhetoric as he drew ever closer to Moscow for military and diplomatic support.

Finally, from the struggle to consolidate power between July 1952 and March 1954, the Officers developed a set of nondemocratic laws, regulations, and decrees to ensure their power. Force, and the fear it produced, buttressed these political institutions, thereby keeping the Egyptian population in line. During that decade of economic growth and social progress between roughly 1955 and 1965, coercion was an important component of regime security, but the economic slowdown that began in 1966 combined with the setback of June 1967 resulted in the first major popular unrest since 1954. Consequently, despite promises of a modicum of liberalization, surveillance and intimidation of the population continued and even intensified. This state of affairs indicated, above all, that the ideological appeal of the regime, which was deeply intertwined with both Nasser's ability to deliver on the social contract that the Officers offered the Egyptian people and Egypt's geopolitical standing, was failing. There was no denying that Nasser forged a degree of social change; Egypt nevertheless remained largely poor, authoritarian, and dependent on a global power—circumstances similar to those that existed on the eve of the July 1952 coup.

THE EMERGENCE OF SADAT

Western newspaper accounts at the time of Nasser's death warned of a potentially troubled leadership succession. Citing the lack of a clear successor, American diplomats and intelligence analysts predicted a period of instability that would, among other negative consequences, set back peacemaking efforts. In the estimation of U.S. diplomats, Anwar Sadat, who had been named vice president in November 1969, was too weak to transform his provisional leadership into a bid for lasting power.[11] According to American press reports at the time, officials in Washington speculated that a collective leadership composed of senior military officers such as the minister of war, General Mohammed Fawzi, and the minister of interior, Sharawi Guma, along with the chief of military intelligence, would rule Egypt in the short run.[12] Other reports focused on Ali Sabri, the head of the Arab Socialist Union and the Soviets' man in Egypt, and Zakariyya Mohieddin, an original Free Officer, who had served as deputy premier until March 1968, as likely candidates to succeed Nasser.

The American analysis of Sadat's prospects was in some ways accurate, but it failed to consider the political calculations of the new president's adversaries. Although a first-tier Free Officer who enjoyed a long association—friendship even—with Nasser, he did not occupy a senior ministerial position throughout the 1950s and 1960s. He had been the editor of the regime's mouthpiece, a minister of state, and the speaker of the parliament. Among his peers and competitors, these positions were hardly of primary importance. Yet it was precisely the low opinion of Sadat among this cohort that made him an attractive candidate to succeed Nasser. Moreover, Washington overlooked the tendency among authoritarian elites to situate their actions within the established legal structures of the political system, even if it is not democratic. As a result, the sitting vice president was the most appropriate person to succeed Nasser in a strictly legal sense. Thus it was without much fuss or debate that the Supreme Executive Committee (SEC) of the Arab Socialist Union quickly settled on Sadat's candidacy.

There were no other serious contenders for the presidency anyway. Hussein Shaf'ei, who also had a Free Officer pedigree and had served Nasser in a variety of ministerial positions and as vice president (1961–1970), reportedly coveted the top job, but he had no power base beyond his relationship to the now dead president. Shaf'ei would ultimately serve as vice president to Sadat from 1970 until 1975. For the three most powerful men in Egypt—Sabri, Guma, and the minister of state for presidential affairs, Sami Sharaf—Sadat was intended to be little more than their front man. Between them and their allies, such as General Fawzi, these men controlled the state's coercive apparatus and as leaders of the ASU, they held seemingly unrivaled political sway. They also took steps to ensure that the new president would not be able to rule in his own right, enjoining Sadat to agree to five conditions before the Supreme Executive Committee would put his name forward. The most important of these was Sadat's commitment to rule collectively, which in practice would mean that the SEC and Central Committee of the ASU would have a say on all issues of importance, and a majority vote of both bodies was required in order to undertake policy initiatives. Under the agreement, the National Assembly—where Sabri, Guma, and Sharaf had support—would also have a vote on all significant matters of policy. The new president could not simultaneously hold the prime ministership, and ministers would not be permitted to act in areas beyond their ministerial competence.[13] Sadat agreed to these stipulations and was thus nominated to be Egypt's next president.

Egypt's third president was born on Christmas day in 1918 in Mit Abu al Kom, a village in the Nile Delta. Mohammed Anwar Sadat's father was a petty bureaucrat and later a translator for a British medical team in Sudan. Sadat was educated in Mit Abu al Kom's Quran school and then attended a Coptic school in the nearby town of Toukh. When he was seven years old, his family moved from the Delta region to Cairo. After graduating from secondary school, Sadat took advantage of the Wafd's policy of opening the military academy in 1936 to young men of the lower classes. He entered the academy in 1937 and, owing to an accelerated curriculum, graduated at the rank of second lieutenant in just one year. His first post was in Manqabad, a town along the western bank of the Nile just northwest of Asyut—a middle-sized city—in Upper Egypt. At the base, Sadat became acquainted with Nasser and another future Free Officer, Khalid Mohieddin. In 1940, Sadat was transferred to a post in the Cairo suburb of Ma'adi. While in Ma'adi, he married Eqbal Afifi with whom he had four daughters.

It was during his time in Ma'adi that Sadat made two important connections. The first was with Hassan Izzat. Like Sadat, Izzat resented the British and was part of a group of air force officers seeking to assist the Germans during World War II. In 1941, Sadat, Izzat, and Izzat's air force colleagues sought to smuggle General Aziz Ali al Masri—the armed forces chief of staff—out of Egypt so that the general could lend his support to a German-backed coup in British-controlled Iraq. The plot failed, and although he was suspected of taking part in it, Sadat was permitted to return to his unit without any punishment. The year after the al Masri incident, Sadat's anti-British conspiracies continued when he sought to raise an army to fight alongside the Germans who occupied Egypt's western desert up to El Alamein, 160 miles northwest of Cairo. He attempted to send word to the German commander, Field Marshal Erwin Rommel, that he and his fellow officers would lend their support to the Third Reich if Germany would guarantee Egypt's independence.[14] Sadat's message never made it to the German field marshal, however, since the Germans shot down the plane—mistaking it for a British military aircraft—carrying the note. Sadat was arrested in 1942 for his anti-British activities and expelled from the armed forces. He spent the next two years in prison. The flirtation with Nazi Germany was clearly a function of Sadat's deep hatred of the British, given their occupation of Egypt, but some of his later actions raise questions about his early views of Nazism, Jews, and Adolf Hitler's "Final Solution" for the Jewish community in Europe. Notably, in the early 1950s, Sadat penned an admiring letter to Hitler in the Egyptian magazine *al Musawwar*.[15]

Also during his time in Ma'adi, Sadat became acquainted with Hassan al Banna—the founder of the Muslim Brotherhood. The Palace had given al Banna access to the military barracks, hoping that the Brotherhood's message would counteract the appeal of King Farouk's archrival, the Wafd. After convincing al Banna that he was not a palace spy, Sadat and the supreme guide developed a relationship of sorts. According to Sadat, the two men drew close enough that he revealed to the Brotherhood leader that nationalist officers were biding their time before they would overthrow the monarchy, and al Banna in return revealed the existence of his organization's paramilitary force. In Sadat's account, al Banna pledged his and his organization's "cooperation" to the Officers' efforts.[16]

Sadat was arrested again in 1946 for allegedly taking part in the conspiracy to assassinate a Wafdist official named Amin Uthman, who had declared that separating from Britain was impossible. After two years in jail, the court found Sadat not guilty in 1948. During this time in prison, Sadat divorced Eqbal. Upon his release, he traveled with his old friend Hassan Izzat to Suez, where he met fifteen-year-old Jehan Ra'uf. Sadat married her the following year. In 1950, Sadat was permitted to return to the military—he was dismissed after his arrest in 1942 for nationalist activism—with the rank of captain after appealing to the commanders in chief of the armed forces and, according to one account, directly to King Farouk.[17] He became a member of the Free Officers sometime in 1951, though there is some controversy over when this actually happened. In his memoirs, Sadat implies that Nasser invited him to join the clandestine organization upon his reinstatement into the armed forces. Mohammed Hassanein Heikal, a confidant of both Nasser and Sadat, claims that the invitation did not come until much later because some of the Free Officers voiced concerns that Sadat had been part of the Iron Guard, an anti-Wafd group that was established at the behest of the Palace in 1942. The Guard was suspected of being directly involved in an attempt on Prime Minister Mustafa al Nahhas's life on September 6, 1945.

Although Nasser chose Sadat to announce the Free Officers take-over on the morning of July 23, he played a minor role in the actual coup. The night before, Sadat went to the movies with Jehan, and only after returning home did he heed messages from Nasser to make his way to fellow conspirator and future armed forces chief of staff Abdel Hakim Amer's apartment. Consequently, there was constant speculation among his rivals and co-conspirators that Sadat's evening out was intended to be his alibi if the attempted coup went badly. These allegations are certainly plausible. It is important to note that the Free Officers made a series of blunders during the night of July 22 and in the wee hours of the morning of July 23, owing to the fact that they were forced to accelerate their intervention, for fear that the plot had been discovered and their arrest was imminent. Nevertheless, the rumors of Sadat's possible subterfuge on the eve of the coup underline the distrust with which some of Sadat's own colleagues viewed him.

Sadat was a founding member of the Revolutionary Command Council, but he resigned in late 1953 over the intense politics and infighting within the Council. He then founded the newspaper *al Gumhuriya* (*The Republic*), which was to be the tribune of the new regime. Sadat returned to the RCC in 1954 and served as minister without portfolio. In that post, Sadat was one of three judges—the others were Abdel Latif al Boghdadi and Hassan Ibrahim—to preside in the Revolutionary Tribunal against the Muslim Brotherhood after the attempted assassination of Nasser in March 1954. He was also tapped to be the secretary general of the Islamic Congress, which the Officers founded in September 1954. Sadat's outward religiosity—his forehead bore a callous that some deeply religious Muslims develop from prostrating fervently during their daily prayers—and his known connection to the Muslim Brotherhood were useful in deflecting criticism that the leaders of the new order were irreligious or anti-Islam. Sadat returned to *al Gumhuriya* in 1955, but Nasser pushed him out shortly afterward when Sadat insulted U.S. Secretary of State John Foster Dulles in print at a time when the Egyptians were seeking aid from Washington.[18]

When the union with Syria was consummated on February 1, 1958, Nasser tapped Sadat to become the deputy speaker of the United Arab Republic's parliament. After the split with Syria in 1961, he became the speaker of the National Assembly until 1969, when Nasser named him vice president of the republic. His elevation to the vice presidency was almost certainly not an indication that Nasser intended Sadat to succeed him. Heikal, who fell out with Sadat in the 1970s, remarked in his book, *Autumn of Fury*, that Nasser claimed it was time to give Sadat a chance to serve in the post because everyone else had already done so. Heikal should be taken with some skepticism, however. After all, Sadat imprisoned him in September 1981 for endangering the "unity and security of the country," though he was only guilty of being harshly critical of the president.[19] Still, most observers agree that Nasser was not setting in motion a succession plan when he named Sadat his vice president.

Upon his nomination to the presidency on October 7, Sadat committed himself to upholding the principles and policies that guided his predecessors. He declared to the National Assembly:

> I consider your decision to nominate me for the Presidency of the Republic as a direction for me to pursue the path of Gamal Abdel Nasser. And if the vote of our masses in the general plebiscite will be "Yes," I shall consider this as an order to me to pursue the path of Gamal Abdel Nasser, which I declare before you, in all honesty, that I will continue to follow, whatever the case may be and from whatever position.[20]

In the same address, Sadat vowed to liberate Arab lands from Israeli occupation, to "safeguard, fully, the rights of the Palestinian people," and to work toward Arab unity. He also defined the enemies of the

Arab nation—not surprisingly Israel, international Zionism, and world imperialism. The new president reaffirmed Egypt's policy of non-alignment, which he emphasized, did not contradict Cairo's strategic relations with the Soviet Union. Finally, Sadat reminded the assembly that the Egyptian people were "part of the great national liberation movement with its progressive socialist trend" and that "preserv[ing] the socialist gains" of the previous eighteen years was of utmost priority.[21] On October 15, Egyptians went to the polls in a national referendum on Sadat's candidacy. The (assuredly predetermined) results—six million votes for the president designate and approximately 700,000 against—were intended to create the impression that Sadat had an overwhelming mandate to rule.

When Sadat entered office, Egypt's economic performance was uneven. Although annual GDP growth in the year before Nasser's death had been a healthy 6.8 percent, it slowed in 1970 to a still respectable 5.6 percent, before falling further in subsequent years. Annual per capita income also began to slide during Sadat's first year in office. Exports and imports as a percentage of GDP remained essentially flat as Egypt ran an overall trade deficit. Particularly worrisome was Egypt's external debt, which was almost 25 percent of gross national income. Moreover, Egypt had only enough reserves to cover a little more than 9 percent of that debt. Reliable employment statistics are hard to come by, but it is clear that the promises of Nasserism, with its guaranteed employment for university graduates, had its limits as Egypt wrestled with increasing underemployment. A bright spot was inflation, which was 3.75 percent in 1970, but fell to 2.1 percent by 1972. Overall, when Sadat succeeded Nasser, the economic picture was decidedly mixed with growth slowing, employment becoming a problem, and indebtedness increasing.[22]

The uncertain economic picture compounded the anxiety that Egyptians felt over Egypt's primary foreign policy challenge—the stalemate along the Canal. Despite the cease-fire standstill agreement that was well into its second month by the time Sadat took office, the Israelis seemed intent on settling in for a long stay in the Sinai. As early as October 1967, the Israelis began developing plans to establish settlements in the Sinai. They announced that they were repairing the oil installation at Abu Rudeis for Israel's use and elements of the Israel Defense Force's Nahal brigade encamped at Buhereit el Baradwil—which the Israelis called Nahal Yam—in northwestern Sinai.[23] By the time Sadat became president, four small Israeli settlements had begun to dot the Sinai landscape, especially in an area the

Israelis called the Rafiah (i.e., Rafah) Plain south of the Gaza Strip.[24] Within the first year of his presidency, another two were established along the Gulf of Aqaba that were intended to be holiday resorts.[25] Israel's effort to establish a seemingly permanent presence in the Sinai only reinforced Egypt's apparent impotence in the face of Israeli power. This unhappy situation for the Egyptians would prove to be a source of significant domestic friction and would ultimately lead Sadat down the path of war.

CORRECTING THE REVOLUTION

It was against the backdrop of these policy problems that Sadat sought to get out from under the collective leadership to which he had agreed. If he played his hand well, he could take a step toward resolving Egypt's outstanding economic and foreign policy challenges in the process of consolidating his power. Indeed, Sadat would prove to be far more agile than Sabri (who was one of two vice presidents), Guma, Sharaf, and the Americans expected. In retrospect, the conclusion that Sadat would be easily manipulated seems misguided. To be sure, his colleagues and associates considered him to be a lightweight who owed his vice presidency to Nasser's magnanimity, but Sadat had spent his entire adult life in politics and was, if nothing else, a shrewd operator.

Beginning in January 1971, Sadat simultaneously began to pursue policies independent of the Arab Socialist Union's Supreme Executive Committee and to cultivate critical constituencies. Chief among these was the armed forces. Since the 1967 defeat, the military had withdrawn from day-to-day governance and politics, but it remained an influential organization, if for no other reason than the armed forces had the power—if they so chose—to dispose of presidents, governments, and influential politicians they did not like. Sadat, even if he was not much of a military professional as a Free Officer, had significant cachet within the military, and as a result he began cultivating a rung of officers just below General Fawzi. Among these were the chief of staff, General Mohammed Sadiq, who would become minister of war, Lieutenant General Saad el Shazly, commander of the Red Sea district, who would fill Sadiq's seat; and Major General Mohammed Abdel Ghani el Gamasy—the officer responsible for overall training after the 1967 defeat—who was promoted to chief of operations. Sadiq, el Shazly, and el Gamasy were well respected among the general officer corps for their competence.

Yet it was not just Sadat's background or the post-1967 military's commitment to remain outside of politics that would seal the Officers' support for Sadat. Despite their reputations for professionalism, the president's personal commitments to advance the careers of Sadiq, el Shazly, and el Gamasy surely helped to secure their loyalty. Sadiq, in particular, was known to covet General Fawzi's job. At the same time, the officers were likely amenable to Sadat regardless of what incentives he offered—though it is clear he felt he needed them. General Fawzi was not well liked within the military, and the leaders of the ASU were positively despised for their role in scapegoating the military after the events of June 1967.[26]

The president's efforts did not stop with the armed forces, however. His strategy was to hem in Sabri, Guma, Sharaf, and their supporters by broadening his constituency. As a result, Sadat reached out to individuals and factions that opposed them on either policy or personal issues and nurtured relations with groups that should have been well disposed toward his rivals. Sadat turned his attention to the police, who were under the direct supervision of Guma in his capacity as minister of interior. Like General Fawzi, Guma was unpopular among police commanders, and Sadat subtly signaled that change was possible at the ministry if he had their support.[27] Next were members of the Left and communists who had suffered so much under Nasser's rule. They deeply resented the power brokers atop the ASU for both the repression they experienced and the widespread belief in leftist circles that the leadership of the union was far from committed to the socialist ideals it preached. Even though Sabri was close to the Soviets, he had been the primary conduit between the Free Officers and the American Embassy before and after the July 23 coup. To the Left, this history smacked of political opportunism more than anything else. Yet Sadat was no different when he appointed prominent leftist Ismail Sabri Abdullah as minister of planning in his first cabinet. Still, the appointment provided the president with a valuable amount of goodwill among a constituency that would help him cover his flank in any showdown with the Sabri-Guma-Sharaf faction.

Paradoxically, at around the same time that he was courting leftists and communists, Sadat began to step slowly away from the socialist drift that began under Nasser in 1961. After two waves of nationalization and the articulation of a five-year plan in 1960 (developed in 1958–1959), Sadat, it seems, would encounter significant problems in any effort to steer the economy toward free market reforms. Yet the regime's official rhetoric concerning socialism was considerably different than its actual economic policies. Nasser had, in fact, begun moving away from socialist-inspired economic policies as early as 1966 when it became clear that they were not producing the hoped for economic performance.[28] Growth had been strong during the early part of the decade, but it had slowed and other economic problems including a large debt burden persisted. Rather than deepening the regime's commitment to socialism, however, Nasser quietly loosened the reins on the private sector. The government encouraged state-owned banks to increase lending to private business and provided incentives for the private sector to increase exports.[29] This required a fundamental change in Egypt's overvalued exchange rate, which hurt exporters.[30] Sadat continued Nasser's modest pullback from statism including returning some private property, easing restrictions on foreign investment, and establishing the Egyptian International Bank for Trade and Development.[31] Not only did this make economic sense given the fact that Egypt's version of socialism seemed to have reached its limits, but it also provided a political benefit for Sadat as he sought to develop a constituency among the middle, upper, and wealthy professional and business-owning classes.

To an extent, Sadat's pivot was a gamble. The beginning of the shift away from socialism may have very well upset the Left. Yet there were three factors working in Sadat's favor. First, as noted, the Left's considerable distaste for ASU power brokers was palpable, which meant that there was little that Sadat could do at the time that would force them to throw their support in the direction of Sabri and others. Second, Sadat was hard to pin down ideologically. Although he was regarded as somewhat of a liberal, the Left did not believe he was in the thrall of private business interests and landowners.[32] Finally, in the grand scheme of things Sadat had not yet jettisoned the socialist economy; that was to come three years later. But in 1971, he remained committed rhetorically to statism in one form or another.

Within nine months of entering office, Sadat forced a showdown with the triumvirate of Sabri, Guma, Sharawi, and their supporters.[33] The central issue was Sadat's effort, beginning in January 1971, to pursue policies independent of the ASU Supreme Executive Committee. This first took the form of Sadat's decision—contrary to what had been agreed on among the leaders of the ASU that there would be collective decision making—not to go to war with Israel after the ninety-day extension of the cease-fire on the Suez Canal expired. In early February 1971, he unfurled a proposal before parliament that would extend the cease-fire through March 7. If Israeli forces redeployed from the Suez Canal Zone (to locations undetermined in the written text of Sadat's speech) during that time, Egypt would reopen the waterway to international shipping.[34] Nothing ever came of Sadat's offer, but it clearly put the president's partners in the collective leadership on notice that he had no intention of honoring the deal they struck the previous September.

Sadat then upped the ante with the ASU executive and declared that Egypt would seek union with Libya and Syria. The ASU's leadership was still rhetorically committed to pan-Arab unity despite the failed experiment of the United Arab Republic, the false start with Syria and Iraq in 1963, and the June 1967 defeat, which supposedly brought the era of pan-Arabism to an end. In mid-April, the three countries announced their intention to establish a Union of Arab Republics. Sabri, Guma, Sharaf, and the other ASU leaders opposed Sadat's unity initiative on the grounds that it would detract from the coming battle with Israel. The ASU Executive Committee also believed that Sadat was trying to outflank them on the Arab unity issue in order to push them from power and remake the political system in a way that was more conducive to his ability to rule alone. Sabri and his allies were entirely correct. Sadat was trying to expose the Sabri faction and draw them into an open confrontation.

The situation came to a head on May 1, when Sadat faced a hostile crowd of workers in Helwan that supported his rivals within the ASU Supreme Executive and shared the growing frustration with the status quo on the Canal. During his address, the president called out the Sabri faction, labeling it a "power center"—a term that had become synonymous with the excesses of Amer, the June 1967 defeat, and more generally, groups of people who held their own interests above those of Egypt. Sabri was subsequently pushed from the vice presidency and resigned his leading position in the ASU. Then, on May 11, Sadat learned from domestic intelligence sources of what he and his advisors believed to be a plot to overthrow him. Before responding to the apparent threat, Sadat reaffirmed the support of the armed forces and the Republican Guard—a special force that is charged with protecting the presidency and the regime. As a result, Sadat felt emboldened enough to turn his attention to ridding himself of Guma, Sharaf, and Fawzi. On May 13, he swore in a new minister of interior—a police official named Mamduh Salem—before demanding and receiving Guma's resignation. Sadat then gave Sharaf a choice. The longtime minister of presidential affairs could side with Sadat or his rivals. Sharaf chose the latter and was summarily sacked. With Guma and Sharaf pushed out, General Fawzi was easily dismissed from the armed forces.

In turn, the entire Sabri-Guma-Sharaf group within the ASU resigned en masse, hoping that it would apply pressure on Sadat, given the Sabri faction's known support within the National Assembly. The now ex-vice president and his supporters hoped that the parliament would reject both Sadat's unity scheme and the mass resignations among the ASU executive. Sadat's rivals badly miscalculated, however. They had a reservoir of support within the assembly, but Sadat—given his long tenure in parliamentary affairs going back to the late 1950s— had developed strong ties with members who were willing to do his bidding. With this group of supporters, the president was able to defeat the Sabri faction, freeing Sadat to exercise power independently. Sabri, Guma, Sharaf, and General Fawzi and their collaborators all went to prison for the alleged conspiracy against Sadat.

With his rivals successfully pushed aside in what amounted to a palace coup, Sadat then went about ensuring his power through what he called the "Corrective Revolution." He argued that this "rectification" was necessary to remedy the excesses of the previous two decades, which were harming Egypt's development. He also justified the reforms on the grounds that they were perfectly consistent with what Nasser had planned prior to his death. Politically, it remained important for Sadat to signal continuity with the Nasser era. Although Sadat now controlled the most important levers of power Nasser had reached iconic status, and an immediate and total break from him was impossible. Thus, when he dissolved the Arab Socialist Union on May 20 and took over its assets under the guise of preventing the reemergence of "power centers" and called for new elections to both the ASU and the National Assembly, Sadat claimed that Nasser too had intended these changes.[35] In July, the ASU voting took place, and not coincidentally, very few incumbents were returned to their positions in the organization. Throughout the rest of the late spring and summer, Sadat went about dismantling the sources of the Sabri group's former power.

The Socialist Youth Organization of the ASU was restructured. Its new leader, Kamal Abu Magd, was a lawyer with strong ties to the Muslim Brotherhood.[36] The new minister of interior, Mamduh Salem—a police officer by profession—announced that his ministry was pulling back from the universities. The country was renamed the "Arab Republic of Egypt," elections for a new "People's" Assembly (as opposed to National Assembly) were scheduled for November, and a new constitution was promulgated. Overall, the new document did not depart radically from previous iterations, but there were two important innovations. The 1971 constitution formally established due process—a hallmark of democratic polities—and Article 2 specified that "the principles of Islamic shari'a are a principal source of legislation."[37] The government also announced that five thousand landowners whose property had been taken in the 1969 land reform, which lowered the legal limit on land ownership to fifty feddans per person, would be compensated over the ensuing decade. Elections for the Supreme Executive Committee were never held, and in an effort to ensure that the union would not challenge his authority, Sadat placed one of his closest advisors, Sayyid Mar'ei, atop the organization in January 1972. Mar'ei was a former minister of agriculture under Nasser, future presidential in-law, and a landowner, which was important in Sadat's overall strategy to develop the landowning classes as a pillar of political support.

Even after the political and institutional reengineering of the summer of 1971, Sadat felt the need to broaden his constituency in an effort to further consolidate his power. Toward that end, he allowed the Muslim Brotherhood to resume some of its activities. This was a significant *volte face* for a regime that had reserved its harshest treatment for the Brotherhood. Upon coming to power, however, Sadat shrewdly perceived the potential benefits of reaching out to the organization. This surely had something to do with his own religiosity—which would grow ostentatiously later on—or his relationship with Hassan al Banna in the 1940s, but political considerations were paramount.

As much as his piety and ties to al Banna may have helped, there were parts of Sadat's post-coup history that might have complicated his appeal to the Brotherhood. After all, he was the chairman of the Islamic Congress, which was intended to either co-opt or freeze out the Brotherhood, and he was one of the three judges who passed sentence on the Brothers and the group's leadership after the attempted assassination of Nasser. Still, the Brotherhood welcomed Sadat's overtures. The group may have ceased to be an organized presence after its brutal subjugation by Nasser in 1954 and 1965, but Sadat seems to have understood the Muslim Brotherhood's pull. Even though it was a shadow of itself, the Brothers could claim the legacy of a truly mass movement and thus remained a potential political and social force. For Sadat, relieving the pressure on the Brotherhood would not only help enlarge the president's constituency (even if the Islamists remained wary of the government), but also—and more importantly—the Brothers could be an asset in the de-Nasserization of politics and society.

After the regime began releasing members of the Brotherhood from prison in 1971—a process completed four years later—Sadat and the Brothers began working in parallel. Consequently, without legalizing the organization, he permitted the Brotherhood to reestablish its press, including the Brother's flagship publication, *al Da'wa* (*The Call*); allowed it to proselytize openly; and gave the Islamists wide latitude to organize on university campuses. In his role as head of the Socialist Youth Organization, Abu Magd emphasized Islamic values. Outside of the universities, Sadat named prominent Islamist Ibrahim Shukri—though not a member of the Brotherhood—director of the Professional Associations Syndicate.[38] The Islamist influence that began with Shukri would have a profound effect on Egyptian politics, as the Muslim Brotherhood would, over the course of the 1980s and early 1990s, take control of the prestigious engineers, doctors, lawyers, scientists, and pharmacists professional associations.[39]

For all the cooperation between Sadat and the Muslim Brotherhood, however, there was significant mistrust between the two. Although reliably anticommunist, the organization was openly critical of the excesses of what would become one of Sadat's signature issues—economic opening, or *infitah* (discussed later). The Brotherhood also sought to work around the state's efforts to control the religious sphere, establishing private mosques and seeking to alter the official discourse that dominated public ones.[40] The biggest problem was, however, the Brotherhood's concern that the government, while seeking to work collaboratively with the organization, was simultaneously trying to undermine it. The proliferation of smaller Islamist groups raised suspicions within the Brotherhood that Sadat was trying to split or discredit the Brothers.[41] It is true that under Sadat's leadership, the government encouraged these organizations but it is unclear whether this was part of a ploy to discredit the Muslim Brotherhood specifically or a continuation of the broader policy of undoing Nasserism. Regardless, by the late 1970s, the government and the Brothers developed a mutual interest in countering extremist groups like al Gama'a al Islamiyya (the Islamic Group) and Takfir wa-l Hijra (Excommunication and Exodus), which murdered the minister of religious endowments in 1977. It is no coincidence that the same year, the book *Du'at la Qudat* (*Preachers not Judges*) was published. Written in 1969 under the byline of the Brotherhood's then-Supreme Guide Hassan al Hudaybi—though widely believed to be a collaborative effort by other leading Brothers and al Azhar scholars—the work was a refutation of both the theoretical framework that Sayyid Qutb developed in *Milestones* and the extremist tendencies that developed subsequently.[42]

In addition to reaching out to the Brotherhood, courting the police, and co-opting the traditional upper classes, Sadat began to make direct appeals to the Egyptian public that were sure to garner him support outside regime power brokers, leftists, and indispensable state organizations like the armed forces and the police. Sadat appealed to the latent desire for changes to the police state that had been in the making since the coup and the Free Officers' struggle to consolidate their power. The sentiments for change ran deep, despite the regime's ability to buy off workers, co-opt students, and repress all other potential rivals. Notwithstanding almost universal support for the July 1952 coup, each of Egypt's political factions also supported a return to a properly functioning parliamentary system. Egyptian politicians may have come to this as a consequence of tactical political maneuvering in their struggle against the Free Officers and each other, but that they perceived this position to be politically profitable suggests that there was broad support for the idea of a more open and representative government. Moreover, there had been indicators of this desire well after the coup. The immediate cause of the student riots in November 1968 may have been the lenient sentences handed down to air force commanders deemed responsible for the June defeat, but the core of the protestors' anger was related to the authoritarian nature of the Egyptian state.

Sadat played on these sentiments as he began calling for the establishment of a "state of institutions." He first employed this concept in a September 16, 1971, speech broadcast on Cairo Radio: "Our departure is the new Permanent Constitution . . . which stipulates that our supreme authority belongs to the Alliances of the Toiling Popular Forces . . . the Law is sovereign . . . and that the state is founded on institutions, not individuals."[43] The following spring, Sadat again invoked the same idea before a committee of the ASU when he declared: "With a view of pursuing the course of the May 15 Movement [i.e., the Corrective Revolution], we are continuing the building of the State of Institutions to replace the State of Personalities, and we are striving to afford the Executive and Legislative Authorities the opportunities to play their roles in full, and to define the functions vis-à-vis each other."[44] Sadat was not only calling for balance between Egypt's executive and legislative branches, his reference to the "state of personalities" indicated that, at least rhetorically, he also supported the establishment of the "rule of law." Importantly, a society in which no one was above the law would necessarily preclude the emergence of "power centers" that the new president claimed was distorting Egypt's proper political and economic trajectory. Even though Sadat had been a loyal servant and spokesman for the regime, his posture as a reformer and a liberal was politically useful—if not entirely believable.

THE (LONG) ROAD TO WAR

By early 1972, Sadat had greatly strengthened his position by outmaneuvering his opponents and courting new allies. Yet the president's political fortunes were hardly secure. Even before the mandated end of the July 1970 cease-fire, there was pressure building for Egypt to alter the status quo in the Sinai through the force of arms. As noted earlier, opposition to Sadat within the ASU Supreme Executive Committee was based, in large part, on the perception that he was unnecessarily delaying a confrontation with the Israelis. There was good reason for this delay, though. Memoirs of senior commanders at the time, including Mohammed Abdel Ghani el Gamasy and Saad el Shazly, indicate that whatever political pressure was emanating from the ASU or the Egyptian people, the military professionals harbored serious reservations about Egypt's readiness for a new round of warfare with Israel in late 1970 or 1971. Still, Sadat was in the unenviable position of being judged almost solely on how he handled the collective national affront that Israel's occupation of Egyptian land represented.

To a large extent, Sadat was a victim of his own political need to sound tough on the Israelis. The American-sponsored "cease-fire standstill" agreement was not popular in Egypt, and Nasser acceded to it only because he was out of options without an agreement from the Soviets to deepen their commitment to Egypt's defense. Although Nasser's mystique had suffered after the June War, his position within the ASU was unassailable. In contrast, when Sadat became president, he had no such political advantages. Thus, while recognizing that the realities of the military situation did not favor Egypt, the new president not only kept up a drumbeat of rhetoric about the perfidy of Israel and its designs on Arab territory, but he also made it clear that Egypt was preparing for a showdown with the Israelis. In a June speech at the Naval Academy in Alexandria, Sadat declared to the gathered officers, "I tell you and our people very sincerely and clearly that 1971 is a decisive year. We cannot wait forever, but we always have to be ready."[45] Yet Sadat had been preoccupied with consolidating his power through the first six months of the year, and war did not come in the last half of 1971. In January 1972, Sadat appeared on television and radio to explain why 1971 had come and gone and yet the Sinai remained in Israelis hands. The president reassured his audience that Egypt had been on the path of confrontation:

> I said before that 1971 was the year of decision. As I said in the beginning of my talk I actually had taken the decision in the presence of all the members of the Supreme Council of the Armed Forces. My instructions to [Minister of War] General Sadiq were prepared and put into force until they were stopped at the last stage.

Yet, mitigating circumstances—specifically the Indo-Pakistani War—undermined Cairo's planning:

> [I]t was the fogged conditions. The conditions which appeared on Sunday, July 9, 1967 were the same which appeared to me—but in South Asia—and my friend, the Soviet Union, which stands on my side, was in the battle.[46]

Here Sadat was making an odd linkage between the uncertainties surrounding clashes along the Suez Canal after the cease-fire in 1967 and the outbreak of war between India and Pakistan on December 3, 1971. The Egyptian leader claimed that by dint of Moscow's Treaty of Friendship and Cooperation with New Delhi, the Soviet Union was a direct party to the conflict, and Egypt could not go to war while its patron was otherwise occupied.

After invoking the destabilized environment in South Asia as a cause for inaction, Sadat then tacked in a different direction to justify why there had been no Egyptian offensive in 1971. He claimed the Egyptian home front was not ready. In order to galvanize and prepare the population for the trials of war when it did happen, Sadat channeled the late American President John F. Kennedy:

> In this coming stage, I request every citizen . . . every parent, every son, every brother, every sister, and every man living on our land. I request everybody not to ask: What can Egypt offer to him? . . . Every one of us should rather ask himself, in the coming stage: What can he offer Egypt?[47]

Neither of Sadat's justifications for inaction was convincing. Technically, the Soviet Union might have been engaged in the Indo-Pakistan conflict given its existing treaty obligations with India, but Moscow's involvement in the war was limited to a naval operation shadowing the American aircraft carrier USS *Enterprise* in the Bay of Bengal that only began after the brief conflict's conclusion. In addition, it was unclear what Sadat meant by "preparing the home front." In his speech to naval officers six months earlier, President Sadat pronounced "the home front is solid."[48] Egyptians had been on somewhat of a war footing since the June 1967 conflict broke out, and the country was under a state of emergency, which placed it under military rule. To be sure, in the days after what became known as the "fogged conditions" speech, the government announced austerity measures and the military indicated that it was open to student recruits, all in preparation for the battle. Against the background of the expectations that "the decisive year" created, these measures were weak. Sadat was in a difficult position, as he had to say something even though Egypt was unprepared to execute a major offensive against the Israelis. Indeed, Sadat confronted the venerable politician's dilemma of rising expectations versus what could realistically be delivered. This problem was of his own making, but given the political realities he confronted, largely inescapable.

The result was an outpouring of frustration with Sadat's apparent stalling. Once again, university students played a central role. Demonstrations against government policy began at Cairo Polytechnic University and soon spread to Cairo, Ain Shams, Alexandria, and Asyut universities as well as a satellite campus of Cairo University in the Nile Delta town of Mansura. Student sit-ins across the capital city led to the formation of the Higher National Committee of University Students to better coordinate the activities of different groups clustered around separate faculties at various institutions. The students' demands revolved around the stalemated situation between Egypt and Israel, but in important ways the conflict served as the backdrop for continued critiques of the regime and its perceived shortcomings. In a proclamation that the students delivered to Sadat at his home on January 22, the Higher National Committee relayed the consensus among student activists that efforts to implement Resolution 242 were a waste given Israel's intransigence, but the students also called for democracy and demanded that Egyptians sacrifice equally in the confrontation with the enemy.[49] This would not be the first time that opposition activists linked the nature of Egypt's political order with its inability to achieve certain foreign policy outcomes. A little more than thirty years later, the echoes of the student movement would be heard in the thundering demonstrations against the U.S. invasion of Iraq in March 2003.

Sadat refused to meet with the student representatives, but they were granted a meeting at the People's Assembly. By the time the meeting in parliament ended, the leaders of the National Committee believed they had a deal on the table to issue their demands publicly. The government reneged and the Interior Ministry's paramilitary troops, the Central Security Forces (CSF), stormed the campuses on January 24. The following day, tens of thousands of students staged a massive demonstration in Cairo's Liberation Square. They remained there through the afternoon of January 26, when the police and CSF were able to restore order to the streets. Overnight, it had become clear that the opposition was far broader than Sadat and his advisors were willing to admit. The regime's spokesmen and state press accused both Marxists and rightist reactionaries of hijacking the campuses, but only those predisposed to support the president accepted this claim. The sit-in downtown demonstrated that the students' complaints were broadly shared among ordinary citizens and the elite alike. In the months following the demonstrations, professional syndicates, including those of teachers, lawyers, journalists, and engineers, expressed solidarity with the students.[50]

Sadat had significant trouble gaining control of the situation, lurching from one explanation for the delay in fighting Israel to another, dismissing the students' complaints, and reneging on earlier promises to lift the security apparatus that enveloped Egypt's campuses. That is where things stood at the beginning of the 1972–73 academic year. The students and the government remained stalemated, but during the academic year, the complexion of student activism changed markedly. Although the Left had taken the lead role in the demonstrations (as it had done in 1968), there was no discernible ideological cast to the protests. The students responded to Sadat's apparent prevarications out of their deeply held nationalism and a desire for a more open and equitable political order. These were themes that held weight across the ideological spectrum. Yet when students returned to classes in the fall of 1972, the suspended state of the confrontation with Sadat split student activists as they vied for leadership of the entire movement. As a result, ideological differences became more pronounced among the different factions of leftists, Nasserists, Islamists, and rightists.[51] Whether Sadat was aware that the student unity was faltering is unclear, but the president took no chances, arresting student leaders from across the spectrum despite having courted leftists, Islamists, and rightists in the drive to consolidate his power. Still, the fissures demonstrated that the ideological differences of the early 1950s had not been erased, even among a generation that had come of age after the Free Officers' coup.

Egypt's universities simmered throughout the academic year and into the next until October 6, 1973, when Sadat, unable to drag the United States and Israel into any meaningful effort to resolve Israel's occupation of Arab lands, sent his armies into battle.[52] The actual planning for the war began in earnest in 1971 while the Egyptians were negotiating a new shipment of weapons from the Soviet Union. Although Soviet weaponry, technical assistance, and active participation in the defense of Egypt helped make it possible for the Egyptians to take on the Israelis during the War of Attrition, the relationship between Cairo and Moscow was hardly smooth. The Egyptians chafed under Moscow's ability to determine which weapons were delivered and how fast. As a result, a small group of Egyptian military commanders actually developed two distinct plans for the crossing. The first, called Operation 41, planned for Egyptian units to storm the Bar Lev line and drive all the way to the Sinai passes—Giddi and Mitla—between twenty and thirty miles east of the Canal. The operation was developed for the benefit of the Soviets and ultimately Egypt's partner in battle, Syria. The Egyptians wanted to present Moscow with a more ambitious war plan in hopes of securing additional weapons systems that until that time had not been forthcoming. For their part, the Syrians had made it clear that they would not fight if the Egyptians harbored only limited goals. For all intents and purposes, Operation 41 was a ruse that Egypt's senior commanders had no intention of executing. The second plan was called High Minarets, which involved a crossing of the Canal and the development of bridgeheads six to eight miles east of the Canal, well within the umbrella of Egypt's surface-to-air missile (SAM) batteries. The latter plan was far more realistic than the first given what Egyptian commanders believed was possible against the formidable IDF, especially the Israeli air force. High Minarets also conformed to the goals that President Sadat outlined in a meeting with senior commanders on June 3, 1971, when he told them that all he needed was a foothold in the Sinai to alter the political and strategic realities of the conflict.[53]

After training, refining the battle plan, and absorbing the new military equipment the Soviets were willing to provide, by the summer of 1973 the Egyptian command deemed the armed forces ready to take on the Israelis. It had been a long way back for Egypt, though there were some significant bumps along the way to the eve of war. The summer and fall of 1972 were particularly tumultuous. In July, President Sadat issued a decree ending the Soviet Union's training and advisory mission in Egypt. Approximately eight thousand advisors, technical experts, and "friendly forces"—Soviet personnel operating both Egyptian and Soviet weapons systems—were to depart Egypt by August 1. Despite suspicions that Sadat was currying favor with Washington, the fallout with Moscow was over the delivery of weapons systems. The Egyptian president was likely signaling to the Soviets that their position in the region was not secure unless more weaponry was forthcoming. The rift was quickly repaired, however, and Soviet weapons and advisors began returning to Egypt in late 1972. In October, Sadat pushed his handpicked war minister, General Mohammed Sadiq, from office over differences in planning for the offensive against Israel, though there were persistent rumors that the anti-Soviet Sadiq was sacrificed for the sake of improved Cairo-Moscow ties. Sadiq and a number of other anti-Soviet officers, in turn, were then implicated in a plot to overthrow Sadat. The group, which called itself "Save Egypt," believed that Moscow was trying to push Cairo into a war for which the Egyptian armed services were manifestly unprepared. The certain defeat would produce political instability, paving the way for a communist take-over of Egypt. The plot was snuffed out with arrests and detentions beginning on November 12.[54] The uncertainty of the fall of 1972 settled down under the new minister of war, General Ahmed Ismail, and preparations for the coming conflict continued for another eleven months.

AL 'UBUR

At 2:00 p.m. on October 6, operation codename "Badr," began when two hundred Egyptian aircraft—commanded from the ground by General Hosni Mubarak—screamed low over the Suez Canal on their way to Israeli airbases and command and control installations in the Sinai. Five minutes later, under cover of artillery fire, groups of combat engineers paddled across the Canal to ensure that Egyptian commandos had successfully sabotaged Israel's last line of defense the night before. The Israelis had built large reservoirs of oil into their network of forts along the Bar Lev line that were, in turn, connected to the bank of the Canal through pipes. Should the Egyptians mount an attack across the Canal and Israel's defenses were in jeopardy of falling, Israeli soldiers were to release the oil into the Canal and ignite it, creating an inferno that was sure to consume the attackers. Confirming that the commandos had been successful, the centerpiece of the operation was set in motion. Within fifteen minutes, 4,000 Egyptian soldiers

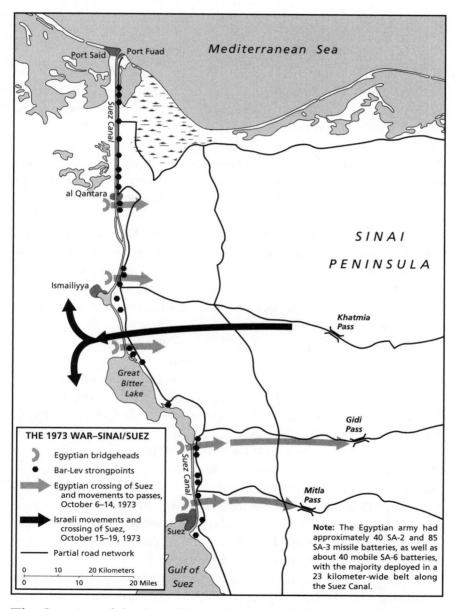

The Crossing of the Suez Canal. Courtesy of Christopher Robinson.

aboard more than 700 rubber dinghies were making their way across the Canal along five fronts to assault the Bar Lev line. The initial battle went better than anyone had expected. By the following morning, the Egyptians had transferred an astonishing 90,000 men, 850 tanks, and 11,000 vehicles into the Sinai and established the planned bridgeheads east of the Canal. In that time, the Egyptians lost only 5 planes, 20 tanks, and an estimated 300 killed in action. The situation for the Israelis was dire. The crossing of the Canal had taken the Israel Defense Forces completely by surprise and inflicted heavy losses on them. (See map in this chapter: The 1973 War—Sinai/Suez.)

The Israelis counterattacked for four straight days, but were largely ineffective until October 11, when they began pushing on Egypt's central bridgehead. The Egyptians made the situation considerably more difficult for themselves through poor command decisions. Someone— whether it was Ismail, Shazly, Sadat himself, or some combination of the three remains subject to debate—determined that Egyptian forces should deviate from the carefully developed battle plan and attempt to take the Sinai passes. This was a dangerous gambit given that the Egyptians would have to move out from under the protection of their SAM batteries. The operation, which began on October 14, proved to be a disaster, as Israel's air force cut the attackers to pieces. Instead of retreating, however, the Egyptians threw caution to the wind and committed their rear reserves to the battle, leaving them dangerously exposed to Israel's determined thrust along Egypt's central battlefront.

The miscalculation left Egypt's forces at the mercy of Israel's Twenty-first and Fourth armored divisions. On the night of the fifteenth, a brigade of Israeli paratroopers under the command of Ariel Sharon broke through the Egyptian lines and crossed the canal. Avraham Adan's force of two tank brigades also made the reverse crossing on the eighteenth. Once ashore, the Israelis began driving north and south in an effort to cut off Egypt's armies in the Sinai. Within ten days it was over. The Egyptians had been brought to their knees after the Israelis encircled Egypt's Third army—about 45,000 men—and refused to allow them to be resupplied. Soviet and American pressure produced a cease-fire that was declared on October 22, but the Israelis ignored it and continued to fight until October 24, when Moscow threatened to intervene to save the Egyptians.

Although the Israelis had hardly been vanquished in the three weeks of fighting, they had clearly been bloodied. The crossing of the Suez Canal was nothing less than an extraordinary feat of courage, tactics, and technical proficiency. Israel's Bar Lev line was a formidable obstacle with its network of forts that rose anywhere from twenty-five to sixty-five feet above the East Bank of the Canal and were equally wide. Few military professionals believed that the line could be breached, no less by the Egyptian armed forces, which the Israelis battered in 1948, 1956, and 1967. Yet had it not been for an American air bridge, which consisted of U.S. air force cargo planes ferrying supplies to the IDF in the Sinai beginning on October 14, the damage would have been greater.[55] When the fighting came to an end, the dire conditions of the Third army overshadowed the fact that Egyptian forces had achieved Sadat's objectives. The war may have been lost once the Egyptians decided to try to drive to the Sinai passes, but as Sadat told the Supreme Council of the Armed Forces in June 1971, even a tenuous hold on the Sinai territory would alter the strategic environment for the Israelis, create enough anxiety about the stability of the Middle East to force Israel from its perceived intransigence, and spur more active American involvement in the region. Although Sadat relied on Soviet goodwill in order to fight the war, he harbored the belief—not articulated until later—that the United States was the critical link to regional peace and prosperity.[56]

"HERO OF THE CROSSING"

Domestically, the Crossing of the Canal had a profound effect on Sadat's political fortunes. He had established full control of the political system with the Corrective Revolution, but his tenure up until October 1973 had been rocky. Sadat remained deeply concerned about potential rivals, economic indicators were mixed with overall economic growth slowing, and he confronted significant frustration and political opposition over his handling of Israel's occupation of the Sinai and other Arab territories. All of this changed suddenly when the collective cries of *Allahu Akbar* (God is Most Great) went up and the assault on the Bar Lev line began. The Crossing and the ability of Egyptian forces to drive the Israelis from the Canal Zone in the opening phase of the war healed the deep nationalist wounds of June 1967 and its humiliating aftermath. Suddenly, Sadat was no longer the prevaricator and second-rate accidental president, but rather *"batal al 'ubur"*—"Hero of the Crossing." The national euphoria invested the Egyptian president with a reservoir of popular support for the first time since he took office. This would prove enormously valuable as

Sadat sought to pursue his agenda unencumbered by regime politics and popular opposition.

Sadat's new status did not mean that he was without antagonists, but the success of the Crossing gave him a significant edge in dealing with any and all potential rivals. Sadat's position was strong enough that in December 1973 he ousted the armed forces chief of staff, General el Shazly, the man who was operationally responsible for planning and executing the Crossing. El Shazly believed that he was made a scapegoat for what he alleges was Sadat's and Ismail's ill-fated plan to take the Sinai passes, but he also let it be known that, after all the Soviet Union had done for Egypt, he opposed Sadat's willingness to give the United States the central role mediating between Egypt and Israel in the aftermath of the war.[57] Mohammed Hassanein Heikal was also relieved of his position as editor of *al Ahram*, for raising similar questions about Sadat's relationship with the United States. To this day, Heikal remains an unceasing opponent of Sadat and his legacy, going so far as to suggest that Sadat poisoned Nasser in order to assume the presidency.[58]

The ouster of Heikal was just the beginning of Sadat's second push (after the Corrective Revolution) to clear away the vestiges of the Nasser era and whatever opposition—real or imagined—to his rule that persisted. In addition to Heikal, other lesser known figures who had served Nasser were turned out of office. Beyond personnel, Sadat began to deepen the policy changes he started in May 1971, moving with greater purpose to make the Egyptian presidency his own. Toward that end, in March 1974, Sadat issued the "October Paper" in which he sought to leverage the "Crossing of the Canal" as a way to chart a new course for Egypt's economic and social development. With the national nightmare of the June 1967 war over and the prestige of the armed forces restored, Egypt was poised to take its next leap forward. Like the modifications to Nasser's rule that he undertook in 1971, Sadat continued to use the July 1952 "revolution" as the basis for his policies and initiatives, but his departure from his predecessor was clearer in the October Paper. For example, Sadat continued to emphasize that he was not abandoning the revolution, but merely fine-tuning it to ensure against future excesses when he declared, "Let me be clear that we are building, not destroying; correcting, not smashing; developing and reinforcing everything that is positive, and liquidating all that is negative."[59] By underscoring that he was placing the revolution back on its proper path, Sadat employed a political tactic that would ultimately make it easier for him to depart from it while continuing to garner political support. Thus, in the October Paper, the president claimed that if not for power centers, political freedom would not have lagged during the first two decades of the revolution. Now that Sadat had disposed of these cliques, it was time to "realize the sovereignty of the law and State of institutions" that were inherent in the Free Officers' original project. Of course, neither Sadat's claims about "political freedom" and the revolution nor his rhetoric about the rule of law was entirely true, but they were politically effective.

The most important innovation of the October Paper was *infitah* (opening). After two decades in which Egypt's leaders expressed their commitment to socialism—though they deviated from statism in practice—Sadat now proposed placing greater emphasis on the private sector and foreign direct investment. Again, Sadat made every effort to demonstrate that his new approach was not new at all. In justifying infitah, Sadat told the People's Assembly:

> The Revolution documents and charters are clear in that they do not provide for total nationalization, nor do they confine activity to the public sector. They adopt the principle of the people's control over the basic means of productions, to ensure that these means are used in the interests of development for the sake of sufficiency and justice.
>
> The private sector has an important role in development, and we should admit that we have not always met its requirements nor created conditions to promote its productive activity.[60]

Sadat was overstating (considerably) what the revolutionary charters and constitutions had to say about Egypt's economic arrangements in order to conceal the true nature of what he was proposing. Infitah would change the way the Egyptians sought to generate economic growth. Although the socialist discourse remained, and the state would continue to be the country's primary economic actor, infitah made it clear that Egypt's future economic development lay with the private sector, foreign investment, and integration of the Egyptian economy with the outside world. There was good economic reason for the shift from Egypt's socialist economy—principally, it was not working. Growth, productivity, and investment were either stagnant or declining by the mid-1970s.[61]

The centerpiece of infitah was Law 43 for Arab and Foreign Investment in Egypt. In order to attract investment, the law allowed for joint projects between state-owned companies and the private sector. This was not much of an innovation, but under Law 43, the entire project would be treated as a private investment even if the state-owned partner firm remained the major shareholder. This had the effect of voiding the range of benefits that workers in strictly state-owned ventures enjoyed. In a reversal of the nationalizations of 1961 and 1964, foreign investors could take controlling positions in state-owned firms. In an additional effort to spur economic growth, the new law provided for the establishment of "free zone" and "in country" projects. Free zones were established in Cairo, Alexandria, and other major cities to stimulate exports. Goods produced in these areas were subject to a 1 percent levy on the total value of the goods moved through the zone, and capital could be repatriated or moved between zones with no restrictions. Products sold into Egypt from the free zone were subject to normal tariffs, however. "In country" projects were given preferential tax treatment for five to eight years and were permitted to import—duty free—the equipment and materials necessary for the enterprise. That said, neither firms in the free zone nor those undertaking in-country projects were permitted to purchase the raw materials for their ventures at highly subsidized prices available to state-owned businesses.[62]

Even with all the important changes, however, Law 43 did not necessarily usher in a period of unfettered capitalism. Local investors doing business in Egyptian pounds continued to confront a range of difficulties in making a profit. They were compelled to offer their workers benefits similar to firms in the public sector and they faced high taxation. Moreover, even under Law 43, the Egyptian state still retained a fair amount of control over economic activity.[63] For example, Law 43 identified investment priorities—exports, technology, and services— and an Investment Authority housed within the Ministry of Economy screened all projects before obtaining approval from other applicable government agencies. Although bureaucratically cumbersome, the process benefited Sadat. Indeed, there was as much a political purpose to infitah as there was an economic rationale. Even as infitah released the power of the private sector, established businessmen—like Osman Ahmed Osman, whose son married one of Sadat's daughters—and a newer wealthy class that emerged were beholden to the government and their contacts within the power structure to make their fortunes. This created a powerful incentive for the business community not only to accommodate Sadat but also to resist any challenges to an emerging status quo in which they benefited above all others. To be sure, there were differences between the regime and business. Osman, for example, was outspoken in his support for privatization, but these dis-agreements could only go so far. The well-being of Osman and his various privately owned consultancies and affiliates were dependent on his ties to the government. If this was the case for someone of tower-ing stature like Osman, it was certainly true for lesser titans of business and industry.

Beyond infitah, Sadat also endeavored to fulfill his commitment to building a state of institutions and political freedom. At the time of the October Paper, he lifted some restrictions on the press, though his boast about ending censorship was, again, not entirely accurate. Certain topics, notably criticizing Sadat, his family, and the armed forces remained decidedly off-limits, as Heikal found out. Sadat's most far-reaching reform was the establishment of *manabir*, or plat-forms, within the Arab Socialist Union in 1976. Notwithstanding the Corrective Revolution, the Crossing, and Sadat's apparent mastery of the political arena by the mid-1970s, the ASU continued to spook him. Although the union and its predecessors were intended to be a way for the state to ensure control over the political arena, the organization was for Sadat decidedly double-edged. It could be both a source of his power and his ultimate undoing if power centers were permitted to develop.

Consequently, Sadat used the power and prestige he garnered from the October War to drive a nail through the Arab Socialist Union bogeyman. In September 1974, Sadat asked a committee of the People's Assembly to study the ASU, its structure, and importantly, what the various constituencies within the ASU wanted. By early 1975, the com-mittee reported back that with the exception of the rightists—who sup-ported privatization, freedom of the press, and multiparty politics—the other constituencies within the union supported the revolution. This must have unnerved Sadat, who had begun moving away from some of the primary aspects of the revolution under the guise of applying its principles more effectively. After about a year of deliberation, Sadat made the decision that would ultimately end the ASU.

From March 1976 on, the union was to feature three formal politi-cal platforms, representing the Left, the Right, and the center. The platform of the Left was called the National Progressive Union Organization (known as Tagammu) under the leadership of Khaled Mohieddin—one of the original Free Officers.[64] The Right was placed under the chairmanship of another Free Officer named Mustafa Kamel Murad and was named the Socialist Liberal Organization, and the center was called the Arab Socialist Organization. In the People's

Assembly elections the following September, the Left won four seats, the Right twelve, the center garnered 280 mandates along with 48 independents. When Sadat opened the People's Assembly a month later, he startled the gathered members and the Egyptian public when he announced that the three platforms within the ASU would heretofore become their own political parties.

Sadat's move was considerably less revolutionary than his supporters suggested at the time or have since. Although it is true that Sadat ushered in an era of multiple parties after more than twenty years of a severely circumscribed political arena, the Egyptian leader had very specific views about the role of political parties. This was linked to Egypt's experiences of the 1940s and early 1950s; indeed, Sadat's statement outlining the creation of the three parties specifically warned of the destructive behavior of the political parties prior to the revolution.[65] In contrast, the president envisioned the Socialist Liberals, Arab Socialists, and National Progressive Union serving as loyal oppositions. But Sadat miscalculated badly. After the first elections in 1976, the parties, though not the Arab Socialists—which would morph into the National Democratic Party in 1978—ended up being more "opposition" than "loyal" and took the government to task on a variety of issues of national import, especially foreign policy. In practice, this did not matter given the Arab Socialists' large majority, but the criticism was embarrassing to Sadat.

Unwilling to crack down on his own creations, the president sought to keep the parties in line through legislation. When the *manabir* were created, they were required to conduct their activities within the parameters of "democratic socialism, social peace, and national unity." In 1977 Sadat forced Law 40, which sought to limit the political arena through the People's Assembly. The law expanded the principles by which parties were to operate to include "the alliance of the working people" and "protecting the basic gains of workers and the *fellahin*" and established the Committee for the Affairs of Political Parties, also known as the Parties' Committee, which the government (and later the ruling party) dominated.[66] The committee was charged with determining whether proposed parties either violated the principles they were expected to uphold or were too similar to existing groups. Either way, Law 40 was a convenient way of keeping undesired factions from the political arena, especially Nasserists and Islamists. Sadat's efforts to circumscribe Egyptian politics were successful over the long run as Law 40 (which was amended in 2005) remained a critical tool of political control until the 2011 uprising that toppled the Egyptian regime.

The passage of the Political Parties Law was an important development, but 1977 was a marker for two other events. The first would shake Sadat, if not the regime, and the second would forever alter the Arab-Israeli conflict and the Middle East. Infitah had proceeded apace, with promising results. Macroeconomic indicators like gross domestic product, balance of payments, and overall domestic production all showed healthy gains between 1974 and 1977.[67] At the same time, the policy coincided with a significant increase in Cairo's trade deficit, which reflected a jump in food imports and an overall wealthier society enjoying the benefits of a new consumer culture. Under normal circumstances, this expansion would have been difficult to finance, but in the mid-1970s, Cairo was enjoying aid from abroad, especially the United States, which, by 1976, was providing Egypt with almost $1 billion in economic support.[68] In addition to the problem of the trade imbalance was Egypt's heavy public indebtedness. This was a function of the Nasser era's unofficial credo, *"me'a b-il me'a farakh b-il-gameah,"* which translates roughly into "a chicken in every pot." This egalitarian ethos was supported with a range of subsidies on basic goods including bread, cooking oil, rice, fuel, sugar, and cigarettes, which put a strain on the budget, especially with a population growing at 2 to 3 percent. In January, at the advice of the International Monetary Fund, Sadat proposed reducing—but not eliminating—these subsidies.

The response from Egyptian society was swift. Across Egypt, the lower-middle and lower classes, and students took to the streets on January 18 to protest policies that would make their lives more difficult. The widely held perception of a society in which the gap between the wealthy—in particular, the nouveau riche—and poor was widening made the response to the proposed subsidy cuts more visceral. Sadat, who was at his rest house in Aswan, was caught off guard by the intensity of the protests, the apparent Nasser nostalgia among many of the demonstrators, and the personal invective directed toward himself and his family. When it became clear that the police were unable to control the cascade of events and restore order, Sadat called on the armed forces. Since returning to the barracks after the 1967 defeat and having restored its prestige with the Crossing in October 1973, the military was reluctant to be responsible for keeping Egypt's streets quiet and was wary of politicians who might be quick to blame commanders if something went wrong. Field Marshal el Gamasy—who had been the director of military operations during the 1973 war and had since risen to become minister of war—demanded that Sadat rescind the proposed subsidy cuts before he put tanks and troops on the streets of Cairo, Alexandria, and other cities. Sadat agreed, and on January 20 the military promptly put down the demonstrations.

The president recovered from what came to be known as the "Bread Riots," but it was clear that the prestige he derived from the October War could not insulate him from the vicissitudes of Egyptian politics and the related challenges of his economic reform program. Clearly, Sadat's efforts to correct the Free Officers' so-called revolution was downright unpopular beyond Egypt's now-thriving traditional and new wealthy classes. It is not hard to see why. Infitah coincided with a warming of Egypt's relations with the United States, the development of a close personal relationship between Sadat and the American Secretary of State, Henry Kissinger, and the noticeable emergence of businesses—bars, clubs, and shops—that catered to Western tastes and mores.[69] These developments raised the old bogeyman of Western penetration, which both Nasserists and Islamists seized on during the riots.

With calm restored to Egyptian cities and towns, Sadat turned his attention back to the conflict with Israel. The better part of the year went by with the new administration of President Jimmy Carter undertaking a policy review and then planning for a peace conference in Geneva. This work continued until November 9, 1977. On that day, Sadat appeared before the People's Assembly and delivered a long speech that addressed issues ranging from democratic developments since the Corrective Revolution, infitah, Sadat's proposed Taxation Law, and terrorism, before turning to the conflict with Israel. Much of what Sadat had to say about Israel was standard boilerplate, but near the end of his address, the president departed from his prepared remarks and declared:

> You must have heard me say that I would go to the end of the world to spare an injury to one of our men, much more the death of one. Israel must be greatly surprised to hear me say that I am even ready to go to the Knesset and discuss with them.[70]

The statement was greeted with a round of applause from the members of the People's Assembly and official guests. One prominent visitor on hand for the speech at the behest of President Sadat—Palestinian Liberation Organization Chairman Yasser Arafat—was outraged, however. As then Foreign Minister Ismail Fahmy explains in his memoirs, the parliament's apparent approval of Sadat's willingness to go to Israel was not to be taken literally. Virtually everyone in the chamber regarded Sadat's statement as "an ends of the earth" rhetorical device intended to demonstrate that Egypt, in contrast to Israel, was serious about peace, but nothing more.[71] The fact that Sadat's declaration came after long passages extolling the value of Arab solidarity and criticizing the Israelis for their perceived intransigence further diminished its apparent importance.

Little did Arafat, or the gathered representatives of the Egyptian people, know that eleven days later, Sadat would deliver another parliamentary speech, but this time it would be before the Israeli Knesset. Sadat's decision to go to Jerusalem was hardly a bolt from the blue. It was the result of a long and circuitous route that began shortly after the cease-fire in October 1973. With the help of Henry Kissinger, the Israelis and Egyptians began negotiations that would result in a disengagement of forces agreement two months later. The war officially came to an end on January 18, 1974, when the Israelis and Egyptians signed an agreement at kilometer 101 of the Cairo-Suez Road—the site of Egyptian-Israeli talks since the cease-fire—that would push the Israel Defense Forces nineteen miles east of the Canal and limit the size and placement of Egyptian forces in the Sinai. A new UN force was deployed to patrol the buffer between the two adversaries.[72] During the negotiations over what became known as Sinai I, the United States and Soviet Union convened a peace conference in Geneva that was intended to be the reference point for future peace negotiations. All the relevant parties except the Syrians and the Palestinian Liberation Organization (which was not invited) attended. Geneva was never intended to be much more than a clever cover for Washington's lead role in negotiating Arab-Israeli peace, providing the fiction of Soviet sponsorship while Kissinger sought to peel the Egyptians away from Moscow.

The initial disengagement agreement was followed nineteen months later by another deal, dubbed Sinai II. Under this plan, the Israelis would withdraw eighteen miles from the positions established with the first disengagement agreement. This would widen the UN buffer zone between the combatants and, importantly for the Egyptians, push the Israelis to the eastern edge of the Sinai passes. The Israel Defense Forces were also required to pullback from the Abu Rudeis and Ras Sudr oil fields. The Israelis and the Egyptians were both granted early warning stations that American civilian personnel would operate. In return for the Israeli redeployments, the Egyptians were only permitted to move their forces—which, like the Israelis, were limited to eight thousand soldiers, seventy-five tanks, and sixty artillery—anywhere from two to four miles further east of their March 1974 positions. The negotiations for the second disengagement had been long and arduous, particularly given Israel's desire for Sadat to make a political gesture such as ending the state of belligerency between the two countries before committing to any additional withdrawal of its forces, especially to the east of the Giddi and Mitla passes, as the Egyptians desired. Sadat balked out of fear that fellow Egyptians and Arabs would conclude that he sought a separate peace.

Kissinger and President Ford were sympathetic to the Egyptian president's position and brought significant pressure to bear on the Israelis—threatening to reassess Washington's entire approach to the Middle East. Ultimately, Washington purchased Israel's agreement through generous commitments of advanced weapons systems; a $2 billion aid package; a promise to ensure Israel's energy supplies; diplomatic commitments that there would be no negotiation with the Palestinian Liberation Organization and no changes to the status quo on the Jordanian front (i.e., Israel's control of the West Bank); and assurances that if there was another disengagement agreement with Syria, only minor changes to Israel's position on the Golan Heights would be required. Israel also received an acknowledgement that there would be no more limited disengagements with Egypt, but rather the next step should be a peace treaty. Finally, Washington assured Jerusalem that in the event of a new threat to Israeli security, the two countries would confer on the best steps to meet the challenge.[73]

On the eve of Sadat's speech expressing his willingness to go to Jerusalem, Egypt and its Arab allies were busily preparing a united Arab front for a second round of talks in Geneva aimed at a comprehensive settlement of the Arab-Israeli conflict. None of the parties had an incentive to continue the limited agreements that Kissinger had spent the better part of the previous three years negotiating. As a result, President Jimmy Carter and his team felt that 1977 was an opportune moment to begin negotiations that would lead to a peace conference in Geneva. The stumbling block was Palestinian representation at the talks—an issue that was a nonstarter for the Israelis. Jerusalem simply would not countenance PLO participation, whereas the Arab countries insisted on the organization's participation as the legitimate representative of the Palestinian people. The Carter administration, stuck between these competing positions, was left to search for a workable compromise along with other pressing issues concerning Soviet participation throughout the fall of 1977.

The Arab states were also hard at work. On November 12, twenty-one of twenty-two Arab foreign ministers met in the Tunisian capital, Tunis, to lay the groundwork for an Arab summit. At the meeting, the Arab world's top diplomats adopted a series of proposals that Egyptian Foreign Minister Fahmy believed would establish greater economic, political, and military coordination among Arab countries. A unified front was central to the Arab strategy for the Geneva conference, which was slated to take place in December.[74] Yet Geneva never took place. Instead, Sadat made good on his word to go to Jerusalem, declaring publicly his intention to the assembled media after a round of talks with his Syrian counterpart on November 16. Few people, including senior Egyptian officials and the Carter administration, knew that Sadat and the Israelis had opened a back channel between Foreign Minister Moshe Dayan and Sadat's trusted aide Hassan Tuhaimi, who had been working on the possibility of a Sadat visit to Israel.

Over the objections of his Arab counterparts, his foreign minister, and his deputy foreign minister (both of whom resigned), Sadat made the 250-mile journey to Israel on the evening of Saturday, November 19. After the presidential plane touched down at Ben Gurion International Airport just outside Tel Aviv, the Egyptian leader made his way to Jerusalem in the company of Israel's president, Ephraim Katsir. Sadat's motorcade traveled along Route 1—the highway that runs southeast from Israel's coastal plain to Jerusalem. The road passes through, or nearby, some of the most important sites in Israel's independence lore such as Latrun, the site of a fierce battle between Israel's Haganah and the Arab Legion; Castel, a strategic hilltop that is a gateway to Jerusalem that Arab forces used to ambush Israeli convoys traveling to the city; and the Burma Road, which runs parallel to Route 1 and was built under cover of darkness so Israeli supply trucks could avoid attacks and relieve besieged West Jerusalem. Security for Sadat's visit was extraordinarily tight, yet thousands of well-wishers still lined the way, hoping to catch a glimpse of the motorcade. That evening the Egyptian leader met with Israeli Prime Minister Menachem Begin before retiring at the King David Hotel across from the Old City of Jerusalem. On the morning of the twentieth, Sadat prayed at al Aqsa mosque, visited the Church of the Holy Sepulcher, and paid his respects to the victims of the Holocaust at the memorial for them, Yad Vashem. The next item on his itinerary was his promised speech at the Knesset.

Located in West Jerusalem's Givat Ram neighborhood, the Knesset, which was completed in 1966, is hardly an inspiring exhibit of modern architecture. In fact, it is downright ugly. For all its visual shortcomings, the symbolism of the building for Israelis and their supporters around the world is probably more important. The Knesset is, after all, the ultimate expression of Jewish sovereignty in the land of Israel. That Anwar Sadat, who had throughout his career engaged in a torrent of anti-Israel propaganda, written in praise of Adolf Hitler, and waged a brutal war against Israel, stood at the rostrum of the Knesset within a few feet of a portrait of Zionism's founding father, Theodore Herzl, was simply extraordinary. Although many remember Sadat's visit to Jerusalem, few recall his speech before the 120 members of the Israeli parliament and the small gaggle of press (of thousands who descended upon Israel) permitted into the Knesset. The Egyptian president engaged in a fair share of religious imagery, quoting from the Quran and the Torah, subtly acknowledged the place in history awaiting him resulting from his visit to Jerusalem, and talked tough to the Israelis. In the most significant passages of his address, Sadat, who spoke in Arabic, declared to his Israeli hosts:

> To tell you the truth, peace cannot be worth its name unless it is based on justice, and not on the occupation of the land of others. It would not be appropriate for you to demand for yourselves what you deny others. With all frankness, and with the spirit that has prompted me to come to you today, I tell you: you have to give up, once and for all, the dreams of conquest, and give up the belief that force is the best method for dealing with the Arabs. You should clearly understand and assimilate the lesson of confrontation between you and us.

> Expansion does not pay. To speak frankly, our land does not yield itself to bargaining. It is not even open to argument. To us, the national soil is equal to the holy valley where God Almighty spoke to Moses—peace be upon him. None of us can, or accept to, cede one inch of it, or accept the principle of debating or bargaining over it . . .

> As for the Palestinian cause, nobody could deny that it is the crux of the entire problem. Nobody in the world could accept, today, slogans propagated here in Israel, ignoring the existence of the Palestinian People, and questioning their whereabouts. The cause of the Palestinian People and their legitimate rights are no longer ignored or denied today by anybody.[75]

Any fair reading of the speech demonstrates clearly that Sadat was asking the Israelis to join him in the implementation of UN Security Council Resolution 242. There were, of course, important differences between the Israeli and Arab parties over the exact interpretation of the resolution, but, before the Knesset, Sadat faithfully articulated the stated position of his government and those of other Arab states. Where he had deviated from the Arab consensus was his visit to Jerusalem. To Sadat's Arab brethren and ultimately many of his own citizens, the Egyptian president had needlessly undermined one of their most potent bargaining chips: recognition of Israel.

Sadat's visit to Jerusalem altered the entire dynamic of Middle Eastern diplomacy. Plans for a Geneva peace conference in December were dropped as the Egyptians and Israelis began bilateral negotiations. At the same time, Sadat's relations with his Arab counterparts deteriorated in the face of withering criticism for the Egyptian president's unilateral step. Sadat would not yield, however. Now that he had made the trip to Israel, he was fully invested in seeing the subsequent process—whatever that was—succeed. Yet for all the importance of Sadat's visit and the Knesset speech as a psychological breakthrough, the ensuing negotiations proved difficult. Not only was there no personal chemistry between the Egyptian president and Israeli Prime Minister Menachem Begin, who was a stern and skillful negotiator, but also the political needs of each leader were diametrically opposed.

Sadat had been clear at the Knesset that his goal was not a separate peace between Egypt and Israel, but rather a comprehensive settlement to the Arab-Israeli conflict. This was presumptuous to say the least, given the broad opposition to Sadat's initiative in the region. Consequently, Sadat needed to demonstrate that he was negotiating with the Israelis both to restore Egyptian sovereignty over the Sinai and, in particular, to realize Palestinian rights. This was a thread that ran through the Knesset speech with Sadat challenging his interlocutors on one of the central myths of Israel's founding:

> I shall not indulge in past events since the Balfour Declaration 60 years ago, for you are well aware of the relevant facts. If you have found the legal and moral justification to set up a national home on a land that did not all belong to you, you should all the more understand the insistence of the Palestinian people to re-establish their State on their land.[76]

Sadat's tough stand was admirable and the politics that drove this position were abundantly clear, but it would ultimately place the Egyptian leader in a bind, giving the Israeli prime minister the upper hand. Indeed, Begin was neither committed to the success of the negotiations in the way that Sadat was nor was he terribly interested in Palestinian rights. Although few realized it at the time, Begin's primary goal was peace with Egypt, but not at the cost of Israeli concessions on the West Bank and Gaza Strip, especially the former.

It was the stalemate in negotiations and the bitter atmosphere surrounding the Sadat-Begin relationship that ultimately led President Jimmy Carter to invite the Egyptians and Israelis to Camp David for twelve days in September 1978. Even at the presidential retreat, hidden away from the press and the grind of politics, Sadat and Begin were unable to get along. President Carter, Secretary of State Cyrus Vance, and National Security Advisor Zbigniew Brzezinski spent their time shuttling between the two leaders and their negotiating teams. On that level, there was a considerable mismatch, however, that placed the Egyptians at a disadvantage. The primary Israeli delegation of Moshe Dayan, Defense Minister Ezer Weizmann, and Aharon Barak was prepared to be considerably more flexible than Begin, whereas Sadat's deputies spent much of their time trying to convince the president to be less flexible lest he agree to a bad deal.[77] In fairness to Sadat, he stuck to the position he laid out before the Knesset, indicating that the Sinai was Egyptian, and, as a result, there was nothing to negotiate. Indeed, Sadat's stance established an important principle—"complete withdrawal"—for subsequent Arab-Israeli negotiations. Still, so long as Begin—whose army still occupied a broad swath of the Sinai—was willing to walk away from negotiations, Sadat was forced to compromise his position on the Palestinians.[78]

During the almost two weeks at Camp David, the final disposition of the West Bank and Gaza Strip and the future of Israeli settlements in these areas were—not surprisingly—sticking points. Although the parties had agreed, in principle, to a five-year transitional period for the territories, the details of what happened after that time were at issue. The Egyptians wanted the transitional period to be used to negotiate a final settlement, but the Israelis were noncommittal. There was also the issue of settlement construction during the mandated five years. In order to cinch the agreement, the United States altered the draft accords to make it more palatable to the Israelis. According to William Quandt, who was present at Camp David as Carter's senior director for Near East Affairs until the last day of the summit, the United States included "language on the applicability of [UN Security Council resolution] 242, including the principle of withdrawal, to the final negotiation of the West Bank and Gaza. And a paragraph calling for a freeze on settlements had always been included."[79]

The importance of Resolution 242 could not be overstated, as it established the core principles of the Arab-Israeli conflict's resolution: Israel's withdrawal "from territories occupied" in the 1967 conflict and the right of all states in the region "to live in peace within secure and recognized boundaries." As important as the resolution was, however, the stipulations of the original American text were scrubbed from the draft. Instead, negotiations would be based on Resolution 242, but not on the outcome of the talks. This was a subtle, but critical shift in semantics, having the effect of releasing the Israelis from any firm commitment to ultimately withdraw from the West Bank and Gaza Strip. Indeed, as Quandt explains, Begin simply did not believe that 242 applied to the Palestinians. Still, the text met the unofficial criteria of being ambiguous enough that both sides could claim victory when Sadat and Begin signed "Framework for Peace in the Middle East Agreed at Camp David" (the official moniker for the Camp David Accords) on September 17, 1978. On the settlement freeze, Carter did ultimately receive a letter from the Israeli prime minister committing Israel to halt construction, but only for three months—the time it was expected to negotiate a final Egypt-Israel peace treaty—and only after the Accords were signed.

PEACE AND ITS AFTERMATH

Although the Camp David Accords envisioned a peace treaty by December 1978, the Israelis and Egyptians missed that goal by a little more than three months. On March 26, 1979, Anwar Sadat and Menachem Begin signed the "Treaty of Peace between the Arab Republic of Egypt and the State of Israel" on the north lawn of the White House. President Jimmy Carter served as the witness. The nine articles of the treaty cover the termination of the state of war between the countries; Israel's withdrawal from the Sinai; the establishment of normal relations; and Israeli navigation and Israel-bound shipping through the Suez Canal, Strait of Tiran, and Gulf of Aqaba. They also dealt with security arrangements in the Sinai, as well as provisions for the settlement of financial claims and a commitment to resolve disputes stemming from the "application or interpretation" of the treaty through negotiations or arbitration. In a letter to President Carter, President Sadat and Prime Minister Begin committed to implementing the provisions of the Camp David Accords relating to the West Bank and Gaza Strip, notably to negotiate the "modalities for establishing a [Palestinian] self-governing authority, define its powers and responsibilities, and other related issues."[80] The letter invited Jordan to participate in the negotiations and noted that the proposed Egyptian and Jordanian delegations "may include Palestinians from the West Bank and Gaza Strip or other Palestinians as mutually agreed."[81] Sadat and Begin also confirmed that the goal of the negotiations was autonomy for the Palestinians of the West Bank and Gaza Strip under an elected Palestinian self-government authority.

The peace treaty was—and remains—a monumental achievement that saved countless lives and gave an opportunity for millions of Egyptians and Israelis to live secure and prosperous lives; yet it produced precisely the results Sadat had so intently hoped to avoid, a separate peace. The Egyptian-Israeli negotiations concerning the occupied territories commenced as promised in Begin and Sadat's joint letter to Carter in late April 1979, but the negotiations went nowhere. The Jordanians and Palestinians refused to participate. In addition, despite Begin's commitments, he was generally unwilling to compromise on the West Bank and the Gaza Strip in a manner that would address Palestinian national aspirations in any substantive way. As a result, there was a certain pointlessness to the whole exercise—though the Carter administration claimed progress on these talks until they were brought to an end by the president's electoral defeat in November 1980.

Sadat had done much to repair the collective nationalist wounds of 1967 by securing the full return of the Sinai through both force of arms and negotiation, but he would pay a steep political price for his accommodation with Israel. Although there was considerable public and elite support for the trip to Jerusalem, by the time the details of the Camp David Accords were revealed, Sadat's dominance of the Egyptian political arena was deteriorating. With the Framework for Peace he had gone well beyond the Egyptian and Arab consensus. Sadat went to Jerusalem to champion the cause of a comprehensive settlement of the Arab-Israeli conflict, but he returned from the mountains of western Maryland with what looked suspiciously like the outline of a separate peace. In response to the framework agreement worked out at Camp David, Foreign Minister Mohammed Ibrahim Kamel resigned; and Sadat's longtime friend, advisor, and father of the president's son-in-law, Sayyid Mar'ei, left his post as speaker of the People's Assembly. Defense Minister Field Marshal Mohammed Abdel Ghani el Gamasy and the armed forces chief of staff, General Mohammed Ali Fahmy, were replaced, though both officers studiously avoided publicly criticizing Sadat.[82]

Despite the rumblings of discontent within the Egyptian executive and the People's Assembly—even before Camp David, the Wafd and the Tagammu parties were openly critical of the peace negotiations—Sadat was able to garner support for the accords by insisting that they were a first step toward comprehensive peace. This position became a significant liability after the actual peace treaty. By coming to terms with Israel without a firm agreement enjoining Begin on Palestinian rights, Sadat gave away Egypt's leverage. With the diplomatic achievement of the treaty in hand, what incentive did Begin have to negotiate in good faith on the Palestinians? After all, this was a step that the Israeli leader was deeply opposed to taking anyway, yet Sadat was willing to settle for little more than a commitment from Jerusalem to negotiate. In all fairness, the Jordanians and Palestinians—with broader Arab support—could have taken advantage of the Egyptian-Israeli offer to negotiate and history might have turned out differently. Still, from the perspective of virtually all factions in Egypt—despite the promised return of the Sinai—Sadat had agreed to a deal that was weighted too heavily in favor of Israel's interests.

Although the sheikh of al Azhar issued a *fatwa* giving the peace treaty religious sanction and Egypt's bourgeoisie and wealthy classes supported the accommodation with Israel, these sentiments were not widely held. Arab governments punished Egypt through economic sanctions: moving the Arab League headquarters to, Tunis; and suspending Cairo's membership in the organization, rendering Egypt a pariah in the Arab world. At home, the People's Assembly, which had already become a hotbed of opposition to Sadat's foreign policy, was in open revolt. The president even had a hard time keeping his own National Democratic Party (which until 1978 was called the Arab Socialist Party of Egypt) in line. As a result, Sadat dismissed the parliament three weeks after the treaty was signed and scheduled new elections for June. Sadat was also harshly critical of the press, deeming the Journalists Syndicate irresponsible. This show of force and threat against the press did not deter his critics, however. Throughout the remainder of 1979 and well into the next year, Sadat confronted an increasingly broad-based and bold opposition. Egyptians looked on as the autonomy talks sputtered without broader Arab participation, while normalization of relations with Israel continued. Israel's first ambassador in Cairo, Eliahu Ben-Elissar, took up residence on February 18, 1980, as Egypt grew increasingly estranged from its Arab brethren. This was an extraordinary shift for a country that was at the forefront of Arab nationalism and sought to lead the region just the decade before. With peace also came the deepening of relations with the United States. Of course, Nasser had done the same thing with the Soviet Union, but the growing ties with Washington were particularly bitter given America's support for Israel. Although it was too early to judge, the general prosperity that Sadat promised would come from peace did not immediately emerge. It seemed that the only groups that stood to benefit from the treaty were the same groups that benefited from infitah—the wealthy classes. By early 1980, a coalition of approximately eighty prominent Egyptians petitioned Sadat to reverse course. Notable signatories included Free Officers such as Abdel Latif al Boghadadi and Kemal al Din Hussein, former Prime Minister Aziz Sidqi, and former Minister of Planning Ismail Sabri Abdallah, who demanded the president freeze relations with Israel, return Egypt to the Arab fold, end the alignment with the United States, and on the domestic front called for independence of the press and the judiciary as part of a broader demand for democracy.[83]

The cordial but wary relationship between the Muslim Brotherhood and regime also came to an end as a result of the treaty with Israel. Although the Brothers were allies of Sadat's de-Nasserization, appreciated his outward religiosity, and supported some aspects of infitah—though certainly not the penetration of Western values and consumer culture that came with it—the trip to Jerusalem, Camp David Accords, and subsequent peace treaty sent the Brothers into open opposition. *Al Da'wa*—the organization's publication, which the regime legalized in 1976—hammered away at Sadat's foreign policy, denouncing both his orientation toward the United States and the agreement with Israel. The Brotherhood regarded both as threats to Egypt's Islamic character and called for an abrogation of the treaty, a return to military options regarding Israel, and nonalignment.[84]

In light of his considerable political challenges, Sadat was briefly conciliatory as he took up the role of prime minister in 1980 in addition to his presidential duties. He admitted that there were shortcomings to infitah, pursued a number of populist economic policies, and lifted the state of emergency that had prevailed since the 1967 war. In an effort to get out ahead of his critics, Sadat engineered five constitutional amendments that the Egyptian people approved in a May referendum. The amended articles of the constitution stressed democracy

The leaders of the Free Officers coup in Cairo, Egypt, on July 31, 1952. From left to right, seated: Lt. Colonel Zakariyya Mohieddin; Squadron Leader Hassan Ibrahim; Lt. Colonel Youssef Saddiq; Lt. Colonel Anwar Sadat; Wing Commander Abdel Latif al Boghdadi; Lt. Colonel Gamal Abdel Nasser; General Mohammed Naguib; and Colonel Ahmed Sawki. From left to right, standing: Major Kamal El Din Hussein and Major Abdel Hakim Amer. Courtesy of the Associated Press.

Gamal Abdel Nasser announces the nationalization of the Suez Canal Company on July 26, 1956, in Alexandria. Courtesy of the Associated Press.

Sayyid Qutb (right) and the president of Colorado State College of Education appeared together in the college's bulletin in 1949 when Qutb was studying in the United States. Courtesy of University of Northern Colorado.

President Anwar Sadat and U.S. Secretary of State Henry Kissinger during a press conference at the Pyramids on February 28, 1974. Courtesy of the Associated Press.

A member of the pro-reform Wafd chants slogans at the party's headquarters, with a picture of the party's founder, Saad Zaghlul in the background. Courtesy of the Associated Press.

A poster supporting Omar Suleiman, Egypt's intelligence chief, for president. The poster reads, "The real alternative, Omar Suleiman for President of the Republic." Courtesy of the Associated Press.

Gamal Mubarak, the president's son and most talked-of heir to the presidency, visits the tomb of former President Anwar Sadat during a ceremony commemorating the twenty-ninth anniversary of his death. Courtesy of Reuters/Amr Dalsh.

Egypt's President Hosni Mubarak addresses the nation in this still-image taken from video February 10, 2011. Courtesy of Reuters/ Reuters TV.

Anti-government protesters celebrate inside Tahrir Square in Cairo after the announcement of Egyptian President Hosni Mubarak's resignation, February 11, 2011. Courtesy of Reuters/Amr Dalsh.

Egyptians cast their votes during a national referendum at a polling station in Cairo, March 19, 2011. Courtesy of Reuters/Amr Dalsh.

and social justice. In addition, the constitution gave official sanction to the multiparty system that Sadat inaugurated in 1976. The changes also included the creation of the Maglis al Shura, or Consultative Council, an upper chamber of parliament with 264 members that was intended "to protect the alliance of the working forces . . . public rights, liberties, and duties, and to entrench the democratic socialist system and widen its fields."[85] The most important change was perhaps amended Article 2, which addressed the issue of religion, specifically the relationship of shari'a to Egypt's legislation. Whereas the previous constitution had, at Sadat's behest, identified shari'a as a basis of Egyptian law, the new text read, "Islam is the religion of the state and Arabic its official language. Principles of Islamic law (shari'a) are *the* principal source of legislation." The change to Article 2 was particularly important given the standard it set. This provided opportunity for Islamist groups, particularly the Muslim Brotherhood, to critique the regime for not upholding the constitution. In addition to the constitutional changes, Sadat introduced the Law for the Protection of the Internal Front and Social Peace, which became known as the "Law of Shame." Among a range of new restrictions, the law essentially criminalized opposition to the government, which, according to the statute, could be interpreted as just about anything and outlawed violation of public, religious, and national morals.[86]

All of these changes were clearly intended to deflect the growing chorus of criticism of the regime. But it was too late. Sadat had come to power promising prosperity and democracy, all the while stressing the importance of Islamic values and his fidelity to the Arab cause. The economic opening, establishment of multiple political parties, and alteration of the constitution—in particular the additional emphasis on shari'a—could not insulate the regime from its critics. After all, only pockets of Egyptian society were prosperous, and neither Sadat nor the government he represented was either credibly democratic or Islamic. Peace with Israel had become a betrayal. To stem the tide of opposition, Sadat diverted further from his rhetorical goal of establishing a state of institutions and, like his predecessor and successor, suppressed his numerous political foes. On September 2, 1981, the regime undertook a massive crackdown. More than 1,500 people across the spectrum of the opposition from political parties such as the Tagammu, Socialist Labor Party, and the already disbanded Wafd to the tolerated Muslim Brotherhood and extremist groups, were arrested. All opposition publications were banned and mosques were placed under the direct supervision of the government. Private mosques under the control of

Islamist groups were shut down. Clearly, Sadat, like Nasser before him, was unable to instill in the public consciousness a set of ideas about the legitimacy and authority of the state that was beyond dispute. At the end of Sadat's rein, the fundamental nature of the political order was more contested than ever.

A Tale of Two Egypts

I N A CITY of innumerable interests, oddities, and contradictions, the viewing platform and stands along Al Nasr Road are among the strangest. White with black trim and a large black marble panel in the center featuring the golden Eagle of Saladin, the stands have sat empty, ghostlike, since October 1981. Traffic speeds by as if nothing out of the ordinary happened in this place. To the uninitiated, the blocks-long platform is oddly out of place, standing vigil over nothing in particular—just another abandoned structure in Cairo that the authorities have neglected to tear down. Look long and hard, though, and a grainy video some three decades old comes to life.

The military parade on October 6, 1981, commemorating the Crossing of the Suez Canal was a spectacle. President Anwar Sadat along with the senior military command and a long list of Egyptian, as well as foreign, dignitaries were on hand to pay tribute to Egypt's greatest military achievement. Vice President Mohammed Hosni Mubarak—known more commonly by his middle name—and Minister of Defense Field Marshal Abdel Halim Abu Ghazala flanked Sadat in the front row as they observed the display of Egypt's firepower. As French-made Mirage fighter jets streaked low across the sky, a flat-bed military vehicle towing an artillery piece stopped in front of the grandstand. Eyewitnesses assumed that the vehicle had broken down, but suddenly two soldiers riding in the back of the truck tossed stun grenades and opened fire in the direction of Sadat and the dignitaries. At the same time, a third soldier leapt from the passenger side of the vehicle and ran toward the viewing stand raking it with AK-47 fire.

The shooting came to halt in about thirty seconds as both Lieutenant Khaled Islambouli and Reserve Officer Engineer Atta Hamida Rahim were subdued when security guards wounded them with return fire. Sergeant Hussein Abbas Mohammed tried (successfully for a short time) to make a getaway. The stands were engulfed in chaos and blood. Within moments, a black Mercedes raced from the scene, driving through the still-parading soldiers as the pilots conducting the air show above, unaware of what had taken place, continued their maneuvers.

In all, nine people were killed and thirty-eight wounded that day, including three U.S. military officers on temporary duty in Egypt. Among those who died were Bishop Samweel, leader of the Coptic Church; President Anwar Sadat's aide-de-camp, General Hassan Allam; Sadat's private secretary, Fawzi Abdel Hafiz; and the president. Sadat was pronounced dead of wounds to his neck, chest, and lower torso at a military hospital in Ma'adi two hours after the attack. It is widely accepted that Lieutenant Islambouli, the soldier who disembarked from the truck first, was Sadat's intended assassin. He certainly planned to be. Islambouli devised the plan, recruited accomplices, and ensured that he had a religious justification for killing the president. Yet although Islambouli was responsible for shooting Sadat at close range, Sergeant Hussein Abbas Mohammed probably fired the fatal shot to Sadat's neck from atop the flatbed.

Despite the confusion in the immediate aftermath of the attack, Sadat's assassination did not throw the country into chaos or produce prolonged instability. The military and internal security forces quickly and quietly assumed control of Egypt's streets as the presidential succession was prepared. In keeping with the procedures laid out in the Egyptian constitution, the president of the People's Assembly, Sufi Abu Taleb, was named acting head of state within hours of Sadat's assassination.[1] Unlike the United States, the Egyptian vice president is not in the direct line of succession. Instead, in the event that the office of the president becomes vacant, a successor needs to be selected within sixty days after the vacancy. Still, there was never any doubt that Vice President Mubarak would follow Sadat.

Mubarak, a bomber pilot by training, had an impressive rise in Free Officers' Egypt. He was born to a middle-class family in 1928 in a village in Menoufiya Province, located in the Nile Delta. Mubarak's father—a petty bureaucrat in the Justice Ministry—wanted his son to attend the Higher Teachers College, but young Hosni opted for a military career. He graduated from the military academy in 1948 and two years later successfully completed pilot training, after which he became an instructor at the Air Force Academy. Mubarak's time at the academy, both as a student and instructor, was critical to his subsequent rise through the ranks, as he built up a reservoir of goodwill among subordinates and superiors alike. In 1959, Mubarak assumed control of Egypt's bomber fleet, and three years later he found himself commanding Egyptian squadrons taking part in Yemen's civil war on behalf of Abdallah al Sallal's republican regime. In the mid-1960s, he was detailed to the Frunze Military Academy in Moscow for additional training on Soviet aircraft that were the core of Egypt's air force. Although he perfected his Russian, the two years in the Soviet Union were not happy ones for Mubarak, who disliked his Russian instructors and colleagues, derided Soviet-built military equipment, and openly criticized communism.

After virtually all of Egypt's air force was destroyed on the ground in the opening hours of the June 1967 war, President Nasser tapped Mubarak to replace Air Marshal Gamal Afifi, the disgraced air force chief of staff. In 1972, Sadat made the forty-four-year-old Mubarak commander of the air force. A year and a half after his promotion, Mubarak's service played an important role in the opening phase of the October 1973 war. He was rewarded for his efforts during the Crossing when Sadat presented him with Egypt's three highest military honors and subsequently promoted Mubarak to air marshal. A year later, in 1975, Mubarak replaced Hussein Shaf'ei as Egypt's vice president.

Mubarak, who was seated next to Sadat during the parade commemorating the Crossing, was slightly wounded in the attack. Bodyguards shoved the vice president under overturned chairs to protect him from the incoming fire. The footage of the aftermath shows a clearly shaken Mubarak emerging from the protective cocoon and being hustled off the grandstand while others lay mortally wounded.

At the same time that Sufi Abu Taleb assumed presidential duties, the ruling National Democratic Party (NDP) nominated Mubarak—who was also secretary general of the party—to replace Sadat. A week after Sadat's death, 98.4 percent of the Egyptians who went to the polls in a referendum voted "yes" to Mubarak's nomination to the presidency. On October 14, 1981, Mubarak appeared before the People's Assembly and in accordance with Article 79 of Egypt's constitution recited the oath of office: "I swear by Almighty God to uphold the Republican system with loyalty, to respect the Constitution and the law, to look after the interests of the people fully, and to safeguard the independence and territorial integrity of the motherland." In his first speech to parliament as president, Mubarak struck a modest tone, reaching out to the opposition and promising to use the Emergency Law, which had been reinstated after Sadat's assassination, in a limited way.

Unlike Sadat's elevation to the presidency, Mubarak's transition from vice president to president was not contested. The goodwill Mubarak had built up during his years of service in the air force was a benefit, as was the absence of powerful groups like the Sabri-Guma-Sharaf triumvirate who controlled the Arab Socialist Union when Sadat came to power. Also, the shock of Sadat's assassination seemed to give Egyptians pause, as if the entire society was intent on pulling back from the brink, lowering the rhetoric, and giving the new leader an opportunity to heal the country's wounds. Indeed, Mubarak released the political figures and activists who Sadat had imprisoned during the last months of his life and committed himself to both political and economic reforms. It was a promising start.

Still, Mubarak confronted a number of challenges as the trauma of Sadat's murder faded and Mubarak's honeymoon ended. The first challenge was Mubarak himself. Although he rose through the ranks of the military quickly and was ultimately tapped to become vice president, Mubarak seemed hardly skilled at politics. During the early years of his presidency, Mubarak's reputation as a politician ranged from awkward at best to outright dimwitted at worst. Ultimately, he proved to be neither of these things, but in the early 1980s there was a sense that Mubarak was weak. This concern brought into sharp relief a second challenge facing Mubarak, which came in the form of his minister of defense, Field Marshal Abdel Halim Abu Ghazala, who was an implicit and indirect challenger to the president.

Charismatic, extremely good to his men (Abu Ghazala was the moving force behind the military's foray into a wide array of businesses from which many officers benefited), and on excellent terms with the United States, the field marshal was a natural contender for the top job.[2] Abu Ghazala never actually made a play for the presidency, though rumor had it that he saw himself as presidential material. Even so, the loyalty toward him among Egypt's officer corps, particularly the ground forces, was enough to make Mubarak wary of Abu Ghazala, and Mubarak was forced to look over his shoulder for seven long years. (During which, in the autumn of 1986, he was obliged to call on Abu Ghazala to put tanks and troops in the streets of Cairo and Alexandria to quell rioting troops from the Interior Ministry's Central Security Forces.)

Ultimately, the president was able to dispose of the field marshal in 1988 after Abu Ghazala was caught transferring U.S. military technology to Saddam Hussein's Iraq, which was engaged in an almost decade-long conflict with neighboring Iran. With Washington's blessing, Abu Ghazala had been the primary conduit of weaponry to the Iraqis. Yet after Abu Ghazala attempted the transfer of 430 pounds of carbon-carbon—used to enhance the accuracy of missiles—without U.S. approval, the field marshal fell out of favor in Washington, enabling Mubarak to dispose of him.

Beyond the apparent rivalry with Abu Ghazala, the primary problems that Mubarak confronted in the 1980s and early 1990s were economic. According to the World Bank, at the time of Sadat's assassination and Mubarak's assumption of presidential duties, the Egyptian population was 45.5 million and the country boasted a rather modest gross domestic product of approximately $40 billion, meaning that per capita annual income was slightly less than $900.[3] Egypt's external debt was $22 billion when Mubarak took office, peaking in 1988 at $46 billion before leveling off around $30 billion for most of the 1990s. Egypt's population was rapidly growing, but the economy did not have the capacity to accommodate the hundreds of thousands of people who annually entered the work force. Throughout the first decade of Mubarak's rule, official unemployment ranged from 5 to 7 percent before rising steadily in the first half of the 1990s, peaking in 1995 at 11 percent. Without significant change, Egypt's economic trajectory was troublesome. Massive debt, significant unemployment, a growing population, and an economy that did not produce much of anything—other than cotton products—did not instill confidence in investors or international financial institutions. To be sure, Sadat's "economic opening" of 1974 opened the way for greater private commercial activity, enriched relatively few, and gave the impression that Egypt had embarked on a transition to a capitalist system. Yet infitah did little to establish the rules, regulations, and laws that are critical to successful modern economies. In order for Egypt to arrest the further deterioration of its economy, a consensus of international financial bureaucrats, U.S. officials, and a somewhat reluctant Egyptian government determined that the country needed a reform program that would bring public debt under control, privatize the state-owned sector, and, overall, make the country attractive to the kind of investment that would produce significant job growth.

In 1987, Egypt and the International Monetary Fund (IMF) struck an agreement in which Egypt would be permitted to reschedule its debt in exchange for a series of reforms that included modification of price controls, an increase in the interest rate, a loosening of import restrictions, and steps toward unifying the exchange rate—Egypt had maintained multiple exchange rates for different segments of the markets, providing more favorable rates for importers of certain goods.[4] In only six months, however, the fund terminated the deal because of Cairo's foot dragging. This was to be a pattern throughout the ensuing decade. The IMF would agree to provide loans in return for Egypt's agreement to undertake wide-ranging structural economic reform, but the Egyptians would either drag out the process or fail to comply. In 1994, after initial discussions on what the IMF calls an "Enhanced Structural Adjustment Facility Trust"—a loan specifically for low-income countries—of $100 million, fund officials walked away from the talks because Cairo had failed to realize reforms it had promised to undertake as a conditions of a previous agreement.[5]

Despite the clear and compelling need for economic change, Mubarak was—for the better part of the 1980s and well into the 1990s—largely resistant to anything but piecemeal reform. From the perspective of IMF economists, U.S. officials, and other observers, Mubarak's reluctance to take on reform may have been politically penny wise, but it was economically pound foolish. Egypt's economic future lay in a sustained and serious effort of reform along the lines the IMF recommended. Yet for Mubarak, the potential political consequences of rapid economic change were of great concern. The president needed to look no further than the 1977 "Bread Riots" to understand that while prosperity may be the long-term outcome of economic reform, instability was an immediate possibility. In the same vein, broad-sweeping privatization and devaluation of the pound were bound to evoke popular ire, especially in the labor sector. For Mubarak, the imperative of maintaining order far outweighed whatever economic progress the IMF and by extension the United States—which had significant influence within both the World Bank and the fund—promised. This may have been shortsighted, but it worked politically. To be fair, over the course of the 1990s, Mubarak introduced a value-added sales tax, reduced subsidies for energy, decreased the number of goods banned for export, depreciated the pound, and agreed to sell off a little more than three hundred state-owned companies. These were important changes, but they were episodic and only happened almost always after a bruising battle between Egyptian, American, and fund officials.[6]

Mubarak seemed to understand better than anyone else that there was a geopolitical dimension to the politics of Egyptian economic change that was, despite the tension with the IMF and U.S. officials, decidedly in Egypt's favor. Sadat had turned Egypt into a strategic partner of the United States. With the Iran-Iraq War in full swing, the Cold War heating up, and the ongoing challenge of confronting regional radicals and rejectionists, Egypt was more important to the United States than ever. Indeed, Cairo played an important role in checking Iran's influence, containing Soviet penetration of the Middle East, and leading the camp of Arab moderates, which included Saudi Arabia, Jordan, Morocco, and the small Gulf states. As a result, Mubarak calculated that Washington was not going to let an asset like Egypt sink under the weight of its own economic contradictions. It was not quite so easy for the Egyptians given Washington's emphasis on economic reform, but Mubarak was ultimately proved correct with a little help from his fellow Arab leader, Saddam Hussein.

When the Iraqi army rolled into Kuwait on August 2, 1990, it proved to be an enormous economic windfall for Egypt. The thirty-two country coalition that President George H.W. Bush put together to confront Saddam Hussein ultimately forced his army back across the Iraqi-Kuwaiti frontier; the coalition included Kuwait, Saudi Arabia, Qatar, the United Arab Emirates, Oman, Bahrain, Morocco, Syria, and Egypt. The Egyptian forces totaled 35,000 soldiers and officers, the fourth-largest contingent to participate in Operation Desert Shield and Desert Storm. When the fighting got underway in March 1991, the Egyptians did not perform very well, advancing extremely slowly and cautiously, but Washington was less interested in military efficiency than the optics of Egyptian participation. Even after its long period of estrangement from the Arab world—a situation Mubarak was able to rectify through persistent diplomacy and support for Iraq during its war with Iran that by 1989 brought Cairo back into the fold—Egypt was regarded as the region's most influential state. Agreement from Hosni Mubarak to deploy forces to the Saudi desert provided the United States political cover to force Iraq from Kuwait in what ended up being a forty-two-day war that pummeled the Iraqi army and did considerable damage to the country.

Egypt was justly rewarded for its participation in the Gulf War. In the aftermath of the conflict, the United States and Arab creditors wrote off or cancelled $20 billion of Egyptian debt, and Washington convinced the Paris Club—an informal group of creditor countries—to forgive $10 billion, or half, of what Cairo owed to a group of European countries, the United States, Canada, and Japan. The benefits of debt relief were immediate. Cairo was able to borrow more money on international markets, but because its external debt had been slashed by as much 50 percent, it could do so at a lower interest rate. The combination of much needed additional cash at more favorable repayment terms eased the pressure on the Egyptian budget and helped pave the way for future economic growth.

The Gulf War represented the highpoint in the U.S.-Egyptian strategic relationship that Mubarak nurtured throughout the 1980s. Although prominent voices, especially the Muslim Brotherhood, questioned Egyptian participation in the conflict to reverse Iraq's invasion of Kuwait, Mubarak gave little ground on Cairo's ties to Washington.[7] Like Sadat before him, Mubarak determined that only the United States had the resources to assist Egypt's development. Also, Egyptian officials, starting with Mubarak on down, believed that a strategic partnership with the Americans—especially after 1991 and the fall of the Soviet Union—conferred a certain special status on Cairo as the undisputed regional power. Never mind that Saudi Arabia was also a pillar of Washington's Middle East policy and that the Egyptian opposition was decidedly opposed to the arrangement.

The clear discomfort the strategic relationship caused in some quarters of Egyptian politics—notably the Muslim Brotherhood, the Left, and Nasserist holdovers—revolved around questions concerning national sovereignty, pride, and, importantly, Washington's special relationship with Israel. When, in the aftermath of the Gulf War, the United States (and the Soviet Union) convened the Madrid peace conference, the Muslim Brotherhood's Supreme Guide Mohammed Hamid Abu al Nasr warned that the forum was a "sell out."[8] Indeed, the regime's opponents often asked a version of the following question: If the United States is Israel's patron, and Israel (peace treaty aside) is a threat to Egypt, is not the United States also a threat to Egypt? The internal logic of the question was hard to dispute, but the answer was decidedly no. Throughout the 1980s and 1990s, Washington poured resources into Egyptian social and economic development and worked hard to institutionalize the Egypt-Israel peace treaty. Mubarak—who triumphantly raised the Egyptian flag over Sinai after Israel's final withdrawal from Egyptian territory—always upheld Cairo's commitment to peace, but in the early years of his presidency, in particular, he managed to maintain a certain distance from the Israelis without raising the ire of Washington.

In June 1982, for example, Mubarak resisted calls to abrogate the treaty after Israel's invasion of Lebanon, but he did recall the Egyptian ambassador from Tel Aviv. Beginning with Israeli Prime Minister Shimon Peres' visit to Alexandria on September 11, 1986, Mubarak met a steady stream of Israeli officials in Cairo and Sharm al Shaykh, yet he rebuffed their invitations to Israel. In Mubarak's almost three-decade rule, he visited Israel once in November 1995 on the occasion of Yitzhak Rabin's funeral. The president's unwillingness to make the one-hour flight to Tel Aviv was a result of the regime's suspicion of Israel, which was cultivated during much of Mubarak's tenure.

This was to be sure a function of domestic politics given the profound unpopularity of the peace treaty (discussed in detail in chapter 6) so during the better part of his first two decades of rule, the Egyptian president never went beyond what Egypt was minimally required to do regarding the Israelis.

Even as the Egyptians held Israel at a distance throughout the 1980s, Cairo positioned itself as a broker of peace between Israel and the Arabs, especially between the Palestinians and Israelis. After the September 1993 Oslo Accords, in which Israel and the Palestinian Liberation Organization recognized each other and, through what was called a "Declaration of Principles," committed to negotiating an end to the conflict between Israelis and Palestinians, Cairo played a supporting role by encouraging and cajoling both parties to uphold their commitments. By most measures, the Egyptians took this role seriously, but ultimately they, along with other would-be brokers of peace, especially the United States, gained little traction. After all, Mubarak and his foreign minister at the time, Amr Moussa, were dealing primarily with Palestinian leader Yasser Arafat, whom observers invariably described as everything from shrewd and wily to downright crazy. At times he was all of these things, while passionately defending the rights of the Palestinian people, which, in Arafat's calculation, could never be satisfied by any of Israel's offers. As for the Israelis, Mubarak clearly concluded (quite correctly) that after Rabin's assassination, Israeli leaders— whether it was Shimon Peres, Benjamin Netanyahu, or Ehud Barak—were incapable politically or unwilling to make a deal with the Palestinians. Consequently, the Egyptians lost interest, and by the late 1990s the Americans no longer saw Cairo as a partner in the peace process. To be sure, the Egyptians often hosted summits and lesser meetings at Sharm al Shaykh, but they were responsible for little beyond the catering. When it came to negotiating the January 1997 Hebron Accord, for example, Clinton administration officials sought specifically to work around the Egyptians, favoring instead the good offices of Jordan's King Hussein.

Around the same time as that agreement, the Egyptians began whipping up concern about Israel's potential to dominate the region economically. This was not a theoretical or conspiracy-based concern.

As a result, it was ripe for political exploitation in a country whose vocal opposition was growing increasingly uneasy with the prospect of Israel's integration in the region. Israel boasted the second-largest economy in the Middle East after Saudi Arabia. In the early 1990s, Israeli Foreign Minister Shimon Peres—who would become prime minister for a short period in late 1995 and the first half of 1996—was fond of talking about the "New Middle East" in which Israel would play a central role in the region's economy. This vision seemed plausible as Arab countries dropped their secondary and tertiary boycott of Israel in the wake of the Oslo breakthrough and Israel's 1994 peace treaty with Jordan, and in 1996 Israel established commercial offices in Qatar and Oman to go along with its previously established economic links with Jordan and Egypt.[9] These positive developments coincided with major setbacks on the Israel-Palestinian front including a wave of suicide bombings in Tel Aviv and Jerusalem, as well as the continued expansion of Israeli settlements in the West Bank and Gaza Strip.

Thus, by 1996, the Egyptians began to express unease with the apparent pace of Israel's growing economic ties with the region. At the time, President Mubarak suggested that the third Middle East North Africa Economic Summit (MENA)—an annual meeting that began in 1994, which included Israelis—be changed to a "conference." From a protocol perspective, this meant that participation would be downgraded from the leadership to the ministerial level. In parallel, the Egyptians argued that Israel's business community should be kept at bay until after a final resolution to the Palestinian conflict, lest the Israelis benefit from expanded economic relations with the Arab world without coming to terms with the Palestinians. In 1997, reflecting the deterioration of Israeli-Palestinian ties, most Arab countries boycotted the MENA Conference in Qatar while the Israelis only sent a small low-level delegation. In 1998, the conference was cancelled outright due to lack of progress between Israelis and Palestinians; the Arab side blamed the government of Israeli Prime Minister Benjamin Netanyahu. In the run-up to the 1999 MENA Conference, Egypt's foreign minister, Amr Moussa, again conditioned Israel's participation in the meeting on "substantive progress in the peace process" and, for good measure, he added that there must be "balanced security for all countries in the region based on international standards of disarmament," which was code for Egypt's long-standing demand that the Israelis give up their nuclear weapons.[10] These conditions effectively scuttled the meeting for the second year in a row. As a consolation, a "Middle East North

Africa Business Initiative" that did not include government officials was convened at the annual World Economic Forum in Davos.

The Palestinian issue and relations with Israel were, however, side-shows to the most significant challenge to Egypt's stability during Mubarak's first two decades in power. Indeed, the five years between 1992 and 1997 were particularly bloody in Egypt. Although Khalid Islambouli and his accomplices assassinated Anwar Sadat in the name of a terrorist organization called al Jihad, it was the extremists of al Gama'a al Islamiyya who were primarily responsible for a wave of violence against Egyptian officials, writers, and foreign tourists. The group, under the leadership of Sheikh Omar Abdel Rahman who was known to Americans for his role in the 1993 bombing of the World Trade Center, was actually closely associated with al Jihad through overlapping leadership and a common worldview.[11] Among the approximately 1,300 killed during al Gama'a al Islamiyya's campaign were the writer Farag Foda—a fierce critic of Islamic fundamentalism—and foreign tourists. The group was also responsible for the 1995 attempt on the lives of (the late) Naguib Mahfouz, Egypt's Nobel laureate in literature, and President Hosni Mubarak.

The government responded in three related ways. First, it embarked on an information campaign to delegitimize extremism and violence. Both the grand sheikh of al Azhar and the grand mufti—the highest Islamic legal authority in the country—issued religious legal rulings condemning the violence of al Gama'a. The state-run media was also relentless in its efforts to demonstrate that the extremist worldview was a deviation from Islam and that violence against innocent civilians was forbidden. Second, the government cracked down on the Muslim Brotherhood even though the organization had not engaged in violence in decades. Nevertheless, Mubarak and the people around him strained to make the case that the Brotherhood was the intellectual fount of the violence the country was now confronting. This was a purposeful misrepresentation that provided the government a justification—albeit a flimsy one—to go after the Brotherhood, which had begun to pose its own nonviolent challenge to the authority of the Egyptian state. Indeed, in October 1992, at about the same time that al Gama'a al Islamiyya began intensifying its violence, the Heliopolis earthquake demonstrated the stark differences between the capabilities of the Egyptian state and the Muslim Brotherhood. Whereas the government earthquake-relief efforts were slow and shoddy, the Brothers were quick and efficient. Within hours Brotherhood-affiliated doctors, pharmacists, and engineers began providing relief to thousands in need.

The Brotherhood had long become adept at using their social services to build and nurture a mass movement; a practice that officials generally overlooked because it relieved the government of having to attend to the needs of many of its citizens. Yet the contrasting responses to the quake proved too much for the defenders of the regime, who believed that the Brothers' relief efforts were a direct challenge to the authority of the state. Mubarak's pressure on the Brotherhood may have contributed to the radicalization of the political environment, providing—in what became a self-fulfilling prophecy that benefited the government—further justification for the crackdown.

Finally, Mubarak declared war on the extremists and their supporters. The Interior Ministry rounded up the leaders of al Gama'a al Islamiyya and al Jihad. They were, in turn, tried before military judges who invariably found them guilty and sentenced them to long prison terms, during which they were subjected to harsh conditions and a campaign to persuade them to recant violence, which some of them did beginning in March 2002.[12] The government's paramilitary forces also attacked areas of Cairo that were believed to be hotbeds of extremist sympathizers. These areas were cordoned off as police and interior ministry forces searched them block by block looking for wanted men and weapons. Despite the constant pressure from the security forces, the extremists continued the fighting with random attacks, often occurring between long periods of time. The violence reached a crescendo, however, on November 17, 1997.

Set in a narrow, beautiful valley seventeen miles from the city of Luxor is the Temple of Hatshepsut—the mortuary complex of ancient Egypt's second female king. The temple built in her honor consists of three colonnaded terraces that visitors access via a long ramp. Within each terrace are scenes depicting the important events of Hatshepsut's reign. Along with the Pyramids of Giza, the Step Pyramid of Saqqara, the Egyptian museum, Karnak, the Valley of the Kings, Dandera, Edfu, and Abu Simbal, the Temple of Hatshepsut is on any tourist's "must see" list. On that Monday morning, six members of al Gama'a al Islamiyya disguised as policemen opened fire on the complex, trapping mostly Swiss and Japanese sightseers along the three terraces. After forty-five minutes, the firing ended and the attackers fled into the desert, leaving fifty-eight tourists—including a five-year-old British boy—and ten Egyptians dead.

The massacre stemmed from a struggle among different factions of the extremist network over a proposed cease-fire between the government and al Gama'a. Ayman Zawahiri, now leader of al Qa'ida, and Rifa'i Ahmad Taha, al Gama'a's military chief, were opposed to any accommodation with the regime and drafted al Gama'a extremists to undertake what came to be known as the "Luxor massacre." They achieved their goals. Units of the Egyptian military under the command of General Sami Enan—who Mubarak later tapped to become chief of staff—took over Upper Egypt and hunted down the terrorists. At the same time, the government reversed its offer of compromise and stepped up arrests of suspected militants. Yet Zawahiri, Ahmad Taha, and Egyptian jihadists in places like Afghanistan and East Africa remained beyond the reach of Egypt's security services, free to plan the 1998 bombings of U.S. embassies in Kenya and Tanzania, the assault on the USS *Cole* in 2000, and ultimately the 9/11 attacks.[13] Still, after the Luxor massacre, extremist violence in Egypt abated. Under constant pressure from the combined firepower of the police and the armed forces and little societal support—especially after what happened at the Temple of Hatshepsut—for their methods, al Gama'a al Islamiyya never again posed a challenge to Egypt and President Mubarak.

By the turn of the century, Mubarak had taken the presidential oath four times and was in every way the master of the Egyptian political universe. The self-effacing vice president and air force officer had been transformed over the previous twenty years into a pharaoh. This transformation was reflected in the last decade of Mubarak's reign, during which economic reform became crony capitalism, political change was fortifying the authoritarian system under the guise of reform, and presidential succession that meant a potential inheritance of power. It was an era of official arrogance and popular anger; it seemed that the fabric of Egyptian society was becoming irrevocably frayed.

FROM OMAR EFFENDI TO CITY STARS

As with almost everything in Egypt, a number of parallel narratives have emerged over the 2000s attempting to make sense of the preceding years. In one, Hosni Mubarak was a "transitional figure," though quite obviously not in a temporal sense given his long tenure in office. Rather, when those supporters (rationalizers, even) of the regime spoke of President Mubarak as being transitional, they were referring to politics. True, they argued, almost thirty years was a long tenure, but Mubarak would serve as the bridge from the authoritarianism of the Nasser and Sadat eras to a more democratic and liberal future. This theme became prominent in the president's own speeches and statements. In his 2010 May Day address (which was actually given on May 6) Mubarak reviewed Egypt's economic progress and future plans and then declared: "Egypt is presently witnessing unprecedented social movement, resulting in the enlightened constitutional amendments of 2005 and 2007. We affirm anew our devotion to completing the promised political reform to firmly establish complete democracy, to support the role of the parliament and the parties, strengthen the independence of the judiciary, and to keep religion from politics."[14] The regime's supporters readily acknowledged that problems existed, but they argued that Egypt could not go from a nondemocratic political system to a democracy overnight. The philosophical groundwork and political infrastructure must be laid carefully so as not to undermine social cohesion and thus threaten the very goals of political change and economic development toward which the Egyptian leader had been working all these years. Egyptians have no experience with democracy and thus must be prepared for it. Even so, under President Mubarak, the transition to a democratic future was well under way. The country boasted twenty-four legal political parties; freedom of expression, including criticism of the president and the first family; five hundred "independent" publications; regularly scheduled elections; and a multiparty presidential election.[15] There were three female ministers (out of thirty-two), and eighty-five women sat in the People's Assembly. According to this narrative, Egypt was clearly an "emerging democracy."

Partisans of the regime cited the previous two presidential elections as proof that, short-comings aside, Egypt was moving in the "right" direction. In the late summer and early fall of 1999, Cairo was in full campaign mode. Huge banners hung across Tahrir Square called on Egyptians to vote for President Mubarak "for the sake of stability and development." Government buildings were literally draped in Mubarak campaign propaganda. In one massive poster that was tacked on the Ministry of Social Solidarity and remained there for the next decade, the stout Mubarak appeared five-stories high, shades on, looking off into the future, with a simple message: *Yes, President Mubarak.* Throughout the election season, government workers, students, laborers, and other ordinary Egyptians poured into the streets throughout the country to express their support for Mubarak in his bid for another six-year term. Small posters inserted in magazines, newspapers, and tacked on walls, doors, and metro stations around the Egyptian capital declared:

The President, the Leader, Mohammed Hosni Mubarak
For you and with you always . . . Loyal, Esteemed, Beneficent
Yes, Mubarak
To the Leader who is devoted to his country, his people, and his nation

Egyptian officials reported that on the appointed day of the referendum, September 26, 1999, almost nineteen million Egyptians cast their votes, the vast majority of whom indicated "Yes," confirming the parliament's election of Mubarak. Once he took the oath of office, the president resumed his efforts to forge a more modern and democratic Egypt. A major cabinet reshuffle signaled an emphasis—as promised—on economic development.

Yet, regime loyalists argued that it was the next election season that demonstrated the most dramatic progress toward democratic change. In the early 2000s, the ruling National Democratic Party launched a major initiative under the banner "New Thinking and Priorities" that would lay the groundwork for Egypt's transition to democracy. The vanguard of the party's new agenda was the emerging "Young Turks" of Egyptian politics and finance. The central figure in this group was the president's son, Gamal. Widely believed to be a contender for his father's office, Gamal became something of a cause célèbre in Egypt beginning in the late 1990s. He is the second son of Hosni and his wife Suzanne, who is part Welsh. Their first son, Ala'a, was a businessman who was widely assumed to be corrupt. Gamal had a reputation for being serious, hardworking, and always in control of his environment. He was educated at St. George's College—the oldest private English-language school in Egypt—and the American University in Cairo, where he earned both bachelor's and master's degrees in business administration. After a short stint with the Bank of America (BofA) in Cairo, Gamal was transferred to the bank's London operation, where he was made a junior investment banker.

Despite his buttoned-down persona, there were always persistent rumors that Gamal was involved in questionable practices while he was at Bank of America.[16] In the 1980s and early 1990s, the Egyptian government was confronting an economy-crushing $50 billion in external debt with virtually no means to repay it because Egypt's coffers of foreign reserves were a measly billion dollars. This debt-to-reserves ratio was making it extraordinarily difficult for the Egyptians to issue new debt and raise much needed cash. Indeed, the two biggest foreign players in Egypt's banking sector—Citibank and Bank of America—were lending dollars to the government in limited amounts and only under a strict set of conditions. In an effort to reduce its debt obligations and thus reduce the risk for banks and other entities to lend ever more money to the government, Cairo undertook a debt-buyback program.

According to a Western banker based in Cairo at the time, in order to minimize the government's outlays, the program began with an unofficial, yet officially sanctioned, whispering campaign urging holders of Egyptian debt to accept pennies on the dollar or risk never being repaid. At the same time, the government established a committee consisting of Egypt's three largest state-owned banks—National Bank of Egypt, Banque du Caire, and Banque Misr—as well as BofA and Citibank to oversee the buyback program. Gamal Mubarak was, at the time, in the employ of Bank of America's Cairo operations, the primary identifier of Egyptian debt. This meant that the bank's representatives would fan out across the globe to secure agreement from Egypt's creditors to sell the debt to Bank of America at a greatly discounted rate. BofA would then sell the debt to Egypt's public-sector banks at a hefty profit that was guaranteed by the fact that Gamal Mubarak, the president's son, was an employee of BofA. It would have been inopportune for the representatives of the national banks on the debt-buyback committee to demand a better price from BofA, out of fear that exercising such fiduciary responsibility would have resulted in some form of retaliation from their political masters. After all, as is standard practice in the investment banking industry, Gamal's bonus was based on the profits he generated for BofA.

When Egypt's opposition press got wind of the conflict of interest associated with Gamal's position, he was quickly transferred to Bank of America's European headquarters in London. Although his official title in London had nothing to do with Egypt, Gamal served the same function in London as he did in Cairo. Fear of crossing Egypt's first family ensured that Bank of America could set the price of the Egyptian debt it was selling back to the government at will, thereby ensuring more and more profits. Yet Gamal and a number of colleagues were not completely satisfied with this arrangement. Allegedly, along with Tarek al Amer, another Cairo-based BofA employee who subsequently became chairman of the National Bank of Egypt, and a few others, Gamal set up a company based in the Bahamas that he and his colleagues used to leverage even more personal wealth from Egypt's considerable debt.

Like Bank of America, the Bahamian company would identify Egyptian debt and purchase the obligations at a significant discount. In a twist, the Gamal-controlled entity would then sell the debt to Bank of America—which was wholly unaware of Gamal's conflict of interest—and then BofA would sell it to the government at a profit. In this way, Gamal was benefiting both from the sale of the debt to his own employer *and* from BofA's profit derived from Egypt's debt-buyback program.

As Gamal's business exploits surfaced in the opposition press once again, Bank of America executives began to fear the legal ramifications of its association with the young Mubarak. If BofA's practices were fully exposed, or an unfriendly regime came to power, the Egyptians, by dint of the agreement that the Bank of America was compelled to sign in order to do business in Egypt, could conceivably make claims on BofA's global assets. As a result, by the mid-1990s, Bank of America wound down all of its operations in Cairo and left the country.

At around the same time, Gamal left London and returned to Egypt and set up MedInvest Associates, a private equity firm. Yet business was losing its allure for the younger Mubarak, and he began to devote his energy to public policy. He set up a nongovernmental organization called the Future Generation Foundation, which was dedicated to promoting Egyptian youth in public policy and business. After toying with the idea of setting up his own political party, Gamal became a member of the ruling National Democratic Party. In 2002, the party set up a Policies Secretariat, which would become the vehicle for Gamal's influence and ambition. The secretariat, of which the president's son was the chair, was the place from which the NDP launched its alleged program of economic and political reform.

Gamal's increasing public profile also shed a spotlight on the group of advisors around him who would play central roles advancing the ruling party's agenda throughout the 2000s. Although they had clearly worked hard to ingratiate themselves with the younger Mubarak's inner circle, to Gamal's credit, he did not necessarily surround himself with "yes men" and hangers-on. His associates were accomplished in their own right well before Gamal expressed interest in them and their expertise. The most prominent among Gamal's coterie was Mahmoud Mohieddin, who would become Egypt's minister of investment and subsequently a managing director of the World Bank. Prior to his appointment as minister, Mohieddin served as a senior advisor to the same ministry and was a professor of financial trade at Cairo University. Mohammed Rashid, the former head of Unilever's Middle

East operations, became the minister of industry and trade. There was also the minister of finance, Yousef Boutros Ghali (or YBG, as he became known both affectionately and derisively), an MIT-trained economist (and nephew of former UN Secretary-General Boutros Boutros-Ghali), who has been in government in one form or another since the late 1980s but was nevertheless part of Gamal's circle of advisors.

In addition to the ministers, two political entrepreneurs who had been drawn into Gamal Mubarak's orbit were instrumental in the NDP's ostensible push on political reform. Hossam Badrawi is a physician by training and was a member of the People's Assembly from the Qasr al Aini district of Cairo until he was defeated in the 2005 parliamentary elections. Educated in both Egypt and the United States, Badrawi entered politics in 2000, as an ostensible liberal reformer. Badrawi's star seemed to be on the rise in large part because he was associated with Gamal Mubarak, but his defeat in the People's Assembly election to an NDP old-guard candidate and his reported differences with colleagues inside Gamal's circle of advisors seemed to have left Badrawi somewhat on the outs. Still, he retained a seat in Egypt's upper house of parliament, the Shura Council. After the Egyptian uprising began in early 2011, Badrawi actually became the secretary general of the NDP when the entire executive board, including Gamal Mubarak, of the party was dismissed. Badrawi was supposed to give the party a reformist cast that would help it weather the storm of Egypt's popular uprising, but it was too late. Badrawi ultimately resigned from that post after only six days when it became clear that neither the party nor Mubarak's rule could be salvaged.

The other member of Gamal's coterie of advisors was Mohammed Kamal, a mild-mannered Johns Hopkins trained professor from a modest family in Port Said on the Mediterranean coast. Kamal burst onto the Egyptian political scene unexpectedly at the 2004 NDP national convention as a confidant of Gamal. At that event, the younger Mubarak made broad statements about the party's intentions to undertake reforms in a variety of areas and called upon "Dr. Mohammed" to tell the gathered faithful exactly how it would be done. Kamal's approach was fairly straightforward: Study the institutions of the state in various European countries—Switzerland, France, Sweden, and the Netherlands—and graft them as best as possible onto the Egyptian political system. The strategy provided a measure of defense against those critics both within and outside Egypt who contended that the reforms were not enough or that the measures the NDP was taking did little more than aggrandize the power of the party under the guise of political change. Kamal always responded that his reforms were based on the practices of advanced European democracies—a point often made in NDP literature—with an Egyptian twist.

In early 2005, the president sought to make good on the ruling party's commitment to reform. In a hometown speech at Menoufiyah University, Mubarak directed the NDP's lawmakers to amend Article 76 of the constitution in a way that would allow for multiparty presidential elections. This was unprecedented in Egyptian history. No Egyptian leader dating back to the Pharaoh Menes—who ruled around 2900 BC—had ever permitted a challenge to his rule. After the amendment passed with 83 percent of the vote the following May, President Mubarak embarked on his first competitive presidential campaign. His platform promised, among a host of initiatives in the economic and social spheres, further constitutional amendments to enhance personal and political freedoms, establish checks and balances between the branches of government, and ensure the independence of the judiciary.

In addition, President Mubarak went out on the hustings, taking his case for another term directly to the Egyptian people. If "stability for the sake of development" was the mantra of his 1999 bid for a fourth term in office, Mubarak and his advisors positioned the then seventy-eight-year-old president as the man who could propel Egypt's "crossing into the future." The irony of this was lost on no one other than perhaps the architects of the president's campaign. The use of "crossing" was obviously meant to evoke Egypt's greatest modern military triumph and connect Mubarak ever more closely to that event. Since at least the late 1990s, the presidency's public relations operation sought to associate Mubarak singularly with that military achievement. The roles of President Sadat, General Saad el Shazly, Major General Abdel Ghani el Gamasy, and General Ahmad Ismail Ali were downplayed. It is unclear how exactly the mythology of Mubarak has influenced Egyptians, but on September 9, 2005, the president was returned to office with 88.6 percent of the vote.

On the economic front, the changes that took place during the Mubarak years were, according to the government, impressive. The private sector, which in the late Mubarak period accounted for more than 70 percent of all economic activity, was flourishing. Most of Egypt's macroeconomic indicators were pointing in the right direction, though the massive problems of under- and unemployment and public debt remained. Egypt became an international destination, with its treasures from Egypt's Pharaonic past and world-class diving and five-star hotels in Sharm al Shaykh at the southern tip of the Sinai Peninsula. One television commercial on CNN's international affiliate refers to southern Sinai as the "Red Sea Riviera." In 2008, 12.8 million tourists visited Egypt—the country's best year ever. Egypt, according to some, had the largest concentration of Mercedes Benz automobiles in the world outside of Germany. The story is certainly apocryphal, but it spoke to the widely held notion in a variety of international financial circles that Egypt, after years of economic underperformance, had finally taken the steps to establish a market economy with the capability to generate growth year on year. In 2006, Yousef Boutros Ghali declared that the Egyptian economy was at the "take-off stage."[17] Never mind that this turn of phrase was outdated in the field of development economics, having been popularized in the 1960s and 1970s, but others seemed to agree. The same year, *BusinessWeek* magazine identified Egypt as one of the top emerging markets in the world, and two years later "Egypt Day" at the New York Stock Exchange was, according to investors who attended, a big hit.[18] In 2007, Egypt attracted a record $11 billion of foreign direct investment, more than half of which came from the Houston-based energy company Apache.[19] This progress was reflected in the overall value of Egypt's stock market (the Bourse) which increased almost fourteen-fold between 2002 and 2010.[20]

The contrast between the country Mubarak inherited in 1981 and contemporary Egypt is no more apparent than in the hulking, dusty brown building just off Liberation Square in downtown Cairo that houses the Omar Effendi department store. In its original incarnation, Omar Effendi was actually named Orosdi-Bak, after its founders— Adolf Orosdi, a Hungarian businessman, and his partners, the Bak family. In 1920, six decades after the first Orosdi-Bak opened in Cairo, the company was sold to investors who immediately rechristened the stores "Omar Effendi." In 1957, the store was nationalized.

Like the defunct Abraham & Strauss, Gimbels, Woodward and Lothrop, and other American department stores of years gone by, there is a wistful nostalgia among many Egyptians for Omar Effendi—or more precisely for what the stores once were: the destination of choice for Egyptians in search of everything from sleepwear to kitchen goods. Now the Liberation Square branch on Talaat Harb Street is a few sparse floors featuring very little anyone would possibly want—bad clothing, cheap (both in price and quality) housewares, poorly made furniture, and substandard appliances and electronics. It is not quite the disaster that was GUM—the state-run department store of the late-Soviet period adjacent to Moscow's Red Square—but Omar Effendi is clearly gasping for life. The ample, but generally indifferent, staff far outnumbers the rare shopper who can wander the store virtually alone. Notwithstanding its 2007 privatization, Omar Effendi is on a long, slow slide into oblivion.

Just a few miles away from Omar Effendi lies the stunning contrast to the Egypt that Hosni Mubarak inherited in October 1981: City Stars, Egypt's answer to early twenty-first-century upscale mall Americana. The complex is like northern Virginia's Tysons II or Philadelphia's King of Prussia Mall, only on steroids. Costing $800 million to develop, City Stars features eight million square feet of commercial, entertainment, and hospitality space including three hotels—the Intercontinental, Staybridge Suites, and Holiday Inn. The press guide informs that City Stars' indoor amusement park is the largest in Egypt, which is technically true if only because there are no other indoor amusement parks in the country. In addition, there is a sixteen-screen movie complex, offering first- and business-class service. When it comes to the actual shopping, there is little to the American consumer that would seem out of place with the exception of the chatter of Egyptian Arabic as background noise. Indeed, among the 640 stores that anchor the mall are American standbys like Nine West, Aldo Shoes, the Body Shop, Timberland, Guess, Tommy Hilfiger, and more upscale offerings such as Hugo Boss. The dining options range from McDonald's, Burger King, Subway, Cinnabon, Carvel, and Baskin-Robbins to some of the standard-bearers of the American casual-dining sector—Fuddruckers, Ruby Tuesdays, Chili's, and Macaroni Grill. For Egypt's upper classes and nouveau riche, City Stars is a proud marker indicating that Egyptians can "hang" with the ostentatious wealth of their Persian Gulf cousins. More important, however, the mall represented the endless possibilities of Hosni and Gamal Mubarak's "new Egypt."

Yet the Egypt of high-end shopping centers, gated communities, private jets, and alleged progressive political change was a reality that only a privileged few actually enjoyed. To the vast majority, the plenty available at a place like City Stars is unattainable on wages that average a mere $2,000 a year, not to mention those sixteen million Egyptians who live on about $2 a day. Indeed, for most Egyptians, the economic dream team of 2004 made up of Mahmoud Mohieddin, Rashid Mohammed Rashid, Yousef Boutros Ghali, and Prime Minister Ahmed Nazif, who were brought in to catalyze economic reform, had done much for Egypt's investors, but little else. This was because in order for

Egypt to make the economic strides it made and attract unprecedented foreign investment, its leaders implemented the neoliberal economic programs that were so in vogue during the 1990s, central components of which were accelerated privatization and a free-floating currency.

Privatization had long been a dilemma for Egypt and a primary reason why Cairo's efforts to sell off state assets were episodic—at least until 2004. Indeed, there are a host of social benefits that the state-owned enterprises provide that are critical to their workers and managers, creating vested interests in these firms. This should not be terribly surprising because state-owned firms are not established as purely profit-making entities, but by their very nature have social and political purposes.[21] Regardless of the benefits they provided, however, the state sector did not attract investment and represented a significant drain on state coffers. As a result, after taking up their positions in 2004, the dream team prevailed on President Mubarak to permit privatization in earnest. Between that year and 2009, the Egyptians privatized 191 companies, netting the government 39.4 billion pounds (about $7 billion). This was a significant increase over the rather tepid efforts of 1991 to 2003, when 210 companies were sold off, generating $3.1 billion for state coffers.[22]

There is no reliable data on how privatization specifically affected Egypt's unemployment rate. To be sure, the number of Egyptians that the state-owned sector employed decreased from one million to fewer than six hundred thousand. Still, it is unclear how many of those four hundred thousand-plus workers remained with their newly privatized firms.[23] According to the World Bank, the rate of unemployment decreased about 2 percentage points between 2004 and 2008, but it was not apparent how much of this new employment was directly attributable to privatization or the benefits of the generalized global economic expansion during that time.[24] Regardless of how much the privatization program actually affected employment, the workers' perception was that they were paying a heavy price in the process. They argued that although privatization had been a boon to the Egyptian business class, the sell-off in the state-owned sector had—contrary to the available statistics—contributed not only to unemployment, but also to an ever-increasing income gap in Egyptian society.

Along with privatization, floating the Egyptian pound was the other visible component of Egypt's economic liberalization program. After unifying the exchange rate in the late 1980s, the Egyptian government had valued the pound by what economists call a "managed peg system," which fixed the exchange rate against the U.S. dollar and artificially inflated the value of the Egyptian currency.[25] Over time, the economic costs of this policy became generally unsustainable, as Egyptian exports were relatively more expensive to the rest of the world and the overall weakness of the economy required the Central Bank of Egypt to intervene regularly and spend valuable dollars to shore up the Egyptian currency.

In late 2003, Egypt's then economic decision makers—Prime Minister Atef Obeid, Central Bank Governor Mahmoud Abu Al Oyoun, the head of the Bank of Alexandria, Mahmoud Abdel Latif, Finance Minister Medhat Hassanein, and Minister of Foreign Trade Yousef Boutros Ghali—sought President Mubarak's consent to scrap the managed peg in favor of a free-floating exchange-rate system. The request was controversial and President Mubarak needed to be convinced of its wisdom. Floating the pound, the policy's proponents—among them Gamal Mubarak—argued, would make the Egyptian economy more competitive and, as a result, more attractive to foreign investors, who were critical to resolving what for decades had been the single greatest problem plaguing Egyptian economic planners and officials: high unemployment and massive underemployment.[26] With approximately five hundred thousand people entering the labor market every year, the Egyptian economy did not grow fast enough to absorb these job seekers in addition to the long-term unemployed and underemployed.[27] According to the government, Egypt's unemployment hovered around 10 percent, but the reality was believed to be as much as double that figure.[28] For their part, some members of the old-guard leadership of the National Democratic Party worried about the social impact of releasing the pound from its managed peg. As troublesome as it was from an economic perspective to maintain the policy, there were social benefits to an overvalued currency. An expensive pound gave Egyptians purchasing power that they would not otherwise enjoy. Proponents of the float were aware of the pitfalls of the policy, but they believed (and hoped) that the benefits of Egypt's new competitiveness would outweigh the costs of their policy.[29]

In the end, both camps were correct. Egypt enjoyed a period of unprecedented economic growth in the second half of the 2000s, but Egyptians grappled with a spike in prices as the pound, now subject to global market forces, was worth far less. The impact on the working and lower classes was almost immediate and entirely negative, as food and consumer products became more expensive almost overnight. These problems came to a head in May 2008, when Egyptians encountered a bread shortage. The problem was not actually the lack of bread, but the distorting effect of swings in the pound exchange rate—which made the wheat imports more expensive—combined with the subsidies meant to keep the price of flour artificially low for publicly owned bakeries. Distributors, and even managers of state bakeries, took advantage of this situation and sold their flour to privately held bakeries, where subsequent bread prices were well beyond what many Egyptians could afford. The result was predictable: Enough bread, but in the wrong places at the wrong prices, producing long lines at state-owned bakeries, which, without ample flour, were unable to meet demand, pushing prices even higher at nongovernment bakeries.

The ensuing tide of anger directed at public officials was resonant of the "Bread Riots" of 1977. Although the unrest of three decades prior required the military's intervention to reimpose order, Mubarak—whose prime directive had always been maintaining Egyptian stability—defused the crisis in considerably less dramatic fashion. The president issued a decree banning flour arbitrage and ordered the military and Ministry of Interior bakeries to ramp up production to exorcise the ghosts of 1977. Putting aside why Egypt's military and internal security services controlled bakeries in the first place, the strategy worked and, within a few weeks, bread was once again readily available at state-owned bakeries. Yet the episode revealed the profound unpopularity of the economic reform program and its architects. This posed a perplexing problem for Mubarak. He was the catalyst for Egypt's "crossing to the future" and the dream team—of which Gamal Mubarak was the leading patron—represented that future. Mini-crises like the bread shortage weakened the government's case that economic reform provided society-wide benefits and further reinforced the opposition's counter-narrative that Cairo's pursuit of liberal reforms hatched in Washington, DC, was bringing Egyptian society to its knees.

Egypt's brush with social unrest over the supply of bread did not occur in a vacuum. It came on the heels of almost a decade of worker activism. From 1998 through 2004, Egyptian workers staged one thousand protests. In 2004—the year the new economic team came to office—the number and frequency of these demonstrations picked up considerably. That year alone accounted for a little more than one-quarter of all the protests staged in the preceding six years. Still, 2004 does not compare to 2006, when the protests gathered steam again, with employees in the state-owned sector staging 222 strikes and demonstrations.[30] The center of gravity for worker activism between 2006 and 2008 was Mahalla al Kubra, a city ninety kilometers north of Cairo that is home to Egypt's textile industry. By far the biggest job action occurred at the Mahalla Spinning and Weaving Company on December 7, 2006, when twenty-seven thousand workers went on strike, demanding higher wages and their past bonuses. The dispute over wages was the central factor driving the workers, but the strike was also related to broader concerns about the possibility of privatization. In addition, the walkout came on the heels of elections to the General Federation of Egyptian Trade Unions (GFETU), which were rigged in favor of government candidates. The GFETU is a union in name only. Rather than representing the workers and their interests, the organization actually represents the interests of the state through the General Federation's board.

The dispute between the government and labor was ultimately settled through negotiations, which fell short of everything the workers wanted, but a forty-five-day bonus (instead of the two months they were seeking) and profit sharing in the company should it make more than sixty million Egyptian pounds (about $10 million) was enough for workers to return to the factory.[31] The Mubarak regime's relative flexibility dealing with the Mahalla protests spoke to the weight the workers had. In this case, the government sought to defuse the situation not through a show of force that always carries the risk of getting out of hand, but by satisfying many of the workers' pocketbook demands. Still, the fear within the councils of the Egyptian government was that a state-owned sector in open revolt would threaten the stability of the regime. The leadership wanted to forestall any notions that the economic conditions of the workers had to do with Egypt's domestic political conditions. Yet the weight of Egypt's workers only went so far. Undaunted by the demonstrations and the worker-based protest organization that emerged from it—the December 7 Movement—just a month later, Minister of Investment Mohieddin announced that one hundred state-owned firms would be sold off, sparking two months of demonstrations in Cairo and throughout the Nile Delta that involved 150,000 workers.[32] And, in another flare-up in Mahalla on April 6, 2008—a date that would prove to be important in the Egyptian uprising almost three years later—three protestors were killed in clashes with security forces.

Far from the troubles of Mahalla al Kubra, Egypt's super wealthy and nouveau riche of Mubarak's Egypt came together with the poor in odd places, where irony seems completely lost. The Four Seasons Nile Plaza could be anywhere—New York, Toronto, Kuala Lumpur, Istanbul, Beijing. With slight variations to accommodate local custom and cuisine, for example, the hotel's guests will enjoy virtually the same comforts and level of service no matter where they are in the world. Other than the newspapers and books available in the hotel shop or the large pot of *fuul*—mashed fava beans and olive oil—at the breakfast buffet, there is actually very little about the Four Seasons that is Egyptian or evocative of Egypt. That's likely fine with many of the hotel's Egyptian clientele because the Four Seasons, like them, is in Egypt, but not of Egypt.

This "in, but not of" disconnect was brought into sharp relief at the wedding rehearsal of Amr Badr and his lovely fiancée, Taiba, held on the pool level of the Four Seasons in the early winter of 2006. Amr is a well-known personality in Cairo, being the head of the British travel firm Abercrombie and Kent's Egypt operation. He is the consummate networker, who managed the Mubarak family's travel and served as the discreet fixer who could arrange meetings with ministers and titans of business. It was not unusual for Amr's friends to receive a late-afternoon phone call from him with an invitation to join him by the pool with officials and celebrities alike. At one such gathering, Dr. Zahi Hawass—who under Mubarak served as secretary general of the Supreme Council of Antiquities, vice minister of culture, and a grandmaster of self-promotion—was regaling the table with his exploits on a recent trip to Arizona. In addition to telling stories about being recognized in America's airports, Hawass jovially recalled a brief meeting with John McCain during which he told the senator—a strong supporter of American democracy promotion in the Middle East—that the Egyptian dissident, Saad Eddin Ibrahim, was "an asshole."

Amr's business, his connections, and the universal sentiment that he is a genuinely nice person set up his wedding to be somewhat of an event. Indeed, even the rehearsal dinner was something to behold, even if not entirely the way Amr and his beaming bride-to-be intended. There, young waiters served quiche, canapés, and patés to the extremely well-heeled as the alcohol flowed. A band at one end of the pool played cheesy American lounge classics while toasts went up to the happy couple. In attendance were colleagues from Abercrombie's London headquarters, a few American diplomats, a smattering of Europeans, a couple of Western academics, and a cross-cut of Egypt's political, social, and economic elite. It was a happy occasion. By all measures, the guests were thrilled for Amr and Taiba. Still, one could not help but notice as one of Amr's guests caustically put it the whole event had a "Czarist Russia on the eve of the October 1917 Bolshevik revolution" feel to it—this was a particularly perceptive quip even though it was made not on the "eve" of the Egyptian revolution, but almost five years to the day before the 2011 uprising. The waiters who mingled among the crowd were likely used to such extravagances given their employ at the Four Seasons: but they were, no doubt, from rather modest backgrounds. This was not the Egypt they lived in. Once their shifts were over and they departed the marble palace along the Nile, the wait staff made their way back to places like Shubra, Sayyida Zeinab, and other neighborhoods far from the wealthy enclaves in and around greater Cairo. In another era, Shubra, for example, was an area of tree-lined streets and stately villas of the upper class, but it long ago gave way to Cairo's stresses and strains. Now its defining features are concrete blocks of midsize apartment buildings, overcrowded streets, and a gritty, somewhat rough vibe.

The deterioration of Shubra reflected a more general socioeconomic decay that was manifest in crumbling infrastructure, substandard healthcare, and an inadequate educational system. Egypt's improved macroeconomic and social indicators throughout the 2000s masked the fact that, for the vast majority of Egyptians, the social contract that promised security, a job, health, and an education had not just failed miserably, but was torn asunder. This is why residents of the Sinai—a few of whom spoke wistfully of the Israeli occupation of the area between 1967 and 1982—had been in open revolt for the better part of the past decade. Official indifference only compounded the increasing societal tension over Egypt's broken social contract. Nowhere was this more evident than in the extraordinary string of preventable disasters that befell ordinary Egyptians between late 2002 and mid-2008, killing almost two thousand people. Among these train crashes, fires, building collapses, and other calamities, the sinking of the *al Salam Boccacio 98* and the rockslide that killed more than one hundred in the "unofficial" Cairo neighborhood of Duweiqa stood out as the exemplars of the elite's corruption, predatory policies, and willful disregard of average Egyptians.

Shubra may have been a slum, but it was hardly in the same category as a place like Duweiqa. The shantytown's residents are among the poorest in greater Cairo. Housing is rudimentary (at best) and overcrowded. Founded in the 1960s, Duweiqa was built haphazardly—even by Egypt's almost nonexistent zoning standards—at the foot of the rocky slopes of the Muqattam Hills. Officially, the residents of Duweiqa were (and are) squatting on state-owned land, and as a result, the government does not recognize the settlement. Duweiqa is hardly unique, however. There are 156 unofficial or informal neighborhoods with a population of some six million in greater Cairo.[33]

So long as these areas are deemed unofficial, the government need not expend resources to extend services—notably water, electricity, paved roads—to them.

This is not to suggest that these people are helpless. Indeed, they have developed an enormous capacity to cope in the most adverse of circumstances.[34] But the events of the morning of September 6, 2008, went beyond Duweiqans' well-developed ability to navigate daily life. On that morning, the hills under which many of them lived, crumbled. Dozens of homes were destroyed in the rockslide, and more than one hundred people were killed. No one came to help. Hours went by before the police arrived, and when they did, the officers informed residents they were there to ensure security, not to conduct search and rescue. Eventually, the fire department arrived, but they did not have the heavy equipment or skills necessary to adequately look for potential survivors. In the aftermath, the Cairo governorate bulldozed the area most affected by the rockslides and advised those residents whose houses remained intact to move into the streets for safety. Some survivors were relocated to abandoned buildings nearby, where multiple families were packed into small rooms. After a public outcry and unfavorable media coverage, governorate officials and the People's Assembly promised to relocate the victims to proper housing. Despite this commitment, two years after the rockslide, many victims remained in limbo. The officials responsible for the program insisted that while residents would get new homes, many of those who petitioned for housing were scammers who moved to Duweiqa only after the rockslides in order to get a free home.[35] With their houses demolished along with everything inside, there was no way for many of the people caught in this predicament to prove their prior residency; these Duweiqans have been left with what little they have to fend for themselves. In the end, Cairo's deputy governor and a number of other officials were given suspended sentences and forced to pay modest fines for the response to the rockslides.

The fate of these officials was an all-too-common occurrence for Egyptian officialdom and the well-connected, as the story of the *al Salam Boccacio 98* indicates. The ferry departed the Saudi Arabian port of Duba on February 3, 2006, for an overnight journey to Safaga on Egypt's Red Sea coast, carrying 1,400 passengers and crew. Some seven hours into the journey a fire broke out on board, and after unsuccessful attempts to extinguish the blaze, the ship capsized. Only 376 people survived. In the days and weeks that followed the tragedy, accusations came to light that the fire was only a contributing cause to the sinking.

Shortly after the Egyptian firm al Salam Maritime purchased the vessel from an Italian company, decks were added to accommodate more passengers. Despite protestations on the part of the company and its owner Mamdouh Ismail that the ferry met all international safety standards, those additional decks made the *al Salam Boccacio 98* dangerously unstable. The high winds along the ferry's route that evening, combined with the large amounts of water taken on in the process of fighting the fire, only heightened the boat's instability, and when the vehicle-deck flooded, it pushed the already-listing *al Salam Boccacio 98* over onto its starboard side.

The tragedy was compounded when desperate relatives of the missing passengers descended on the port in Safaga, and were met with only confusion, rumors, and official silence. When protests broke out, the authorities from the Red Sea governorate deployed riot police to the port. The Egyptian police's typically heavy-handed manner of crowd control only further heightened tensions and transformed the catastrophe into a full-blown confrontation between bereaved families and the Egyptian state. This was not all, however. In the immediate aftermath of the *al Salam Boccacio 98*'s sinking, Mamdouh Ismail appeared on Egyptian television and pledged 126,000 Egyptian pounds ($22,000) to the families of each victim, but within two months of the disaster, he disappeared. It was widely believed that Ismail used his connections as a titan of the Egyptian transport industry and a member of Egypt's Consultative Council to slip out of the country to Great Britain, though Egyptian officials denied having a hand in his departure or knowing Ismail's whereabouts and even froze his assets. Yet, in June 2006, the authorities announced that in return for increasing compensation to $50,000 per family, the freeze on Ismail's personal assets would be lifted and his family would be permitted to travel without restriction. Only after considerable public outrage and a fair amount of legal wrangling that lasted the better part of three years, the Safaga Appeals Court sentenced Ismail to seven years in prison for manslaughter and negligence, though Ismail, who never returned to Egypt, did not serve any time.[36]

The differences between the Egypt of City Stars and the Egypt of Duweiqa, as well as the preferential legal treatment for government officials and the well-connected, produced a hotly contested political debate. The standard-bearers for the narrative that depicted Egypt as an emerging market and democracy were the individuals and groups that made up the constituency for autocracy—big business, regime-affiliated intellectuals, the armed forces, the internal security services, and the bureaucracy. The National Democratic Party and the world-view it espoused represented this constituency, and Gamal Mubarak was the prophet of this new Egypt.[37] Broadly speaking, there was a grain of truth in what the younger Mubarak promoted: Egypt's Red Sea coast is beautiful and, indeed, deserving of the appellation "Red Sea Riviera"; the economic reforms pursued since 2004 were generating positive macroeconomic results; and the often lively debate about the future of the country was proof that politics in Egypt was changing. Yet, while this may have been enough for the regime's primary constituents, it clearly did not wash for many of the great reservoir of Egyptians who have suffered at the official indifference to their increasingly grim circumstances.

THE PROBLEM OF THE FINE PRINT

The difficult economic conditions that millions of Egyptians confronted also ran parallel to a political narrative that was strikingly different from the one the regime and its supporters tirelessly advanced. That Egypt boasted two houses of parliament and held regularly scheduled elections did not diminish the fact that Egypt was a police state in which "rule by law" rather than "rule of law" prevailed. The practical effects of the two different prepositions were enormous. The regulations, decrees, rules, and laws of the state provided neither a level legal playing ground for all citizens nor the means to redress their grievances through a neutral legal system, nor, importantly, a mechanism to change their leaders. This may seem odd given that Egypt's constitution set forth a political system resembling a liberal polity. Indeed, many of the important individual and political rights that Americans hold dear were fully elaborated in Egypt's constitution. Yet, protestations of Egypt's elites to the contrary, Egypt was far from a democracy and hardly democratizing.

Since 2003, under both domestic and foreign (primarily American) pressure, the Mubarak regime undertook a series of political reforms. At first blush these changes seemed impressive and reinforced the notion that Egypt was moving toward more democratic politics. In 2005, the lower house of the Egyptian parliament, the People's Assembly, passed two ostensible landmark reforms to the political system. At the direction of President Mubarak, lawmakers established provisions for multicandidate presidential elections and altered the law governing the establishment of political parties. The first of these two changes was potentially momentous, but the amendment turned out to be considerably less than the ruling party, President Mubarak, spokesmen, and a variety of hacks and hangers-on initially claimed. Indeed, the obstacles to challenging the incumbent were formidable. Independent candidates were required to gather support from 250 elected politicians from the People's Assembly; the Shura, or Consultative Council; and provincial councils, all of which the ruling National Democratic Party controlled. There was more, however. Within the requirement was an additional measure laying out the ratio of support from these bodies and the geographic distribution needed in order to qualify. Thus, an independent candidate needed sixty-five signatures of support from the People's Assembly, twenty-five from the Consultative Council, and ten members of municipal councils in at least fourteen of Egypt's twenty-seven governorates.[38]

This would be a tough road for an independent in a political arena rigged in favor of the NDP and where resources for those not affiliated with that party were scarce. Candidates from legal parties confronted a different set of constraints. During the first multicandidate election, which was slated for the fall of 2005, parties were obliged to nominate only individuals who served in party leadership positions. That requirement would be dropped for subsequent presidential elections, but it was replaced with the stipulations that parties could nominate presidential candidates only if the organization had been licensed for the previous five years and held 5 percent of the seats in *both* houses of parliament. There were no parties—other than the ruling National Democratic Party—that met this threshold.

As it turned out, in the 2005 presidential elections President Mubarak faced nine challengers, none of whom were independents. Other than Ayman Nour, the forty-something founder of the al Ghad Party who had run afoul of the Interior Ministry some months before, and Noman Gomaa, the leader of the Wafd Party, the field was virtually unknown even to close observers of Egypt's political scene. The results reflected the asymmetry of power between the National Democratic Party and the opposition. Of the alleged approximately seven million votes cast, President Mubarak's closest competitor, Nour, tallied 7.5 percent and the next runner-up, Gomaa, earned almost 3 percent.[39] None of the remaining candidates registered even 1 percent of the vote.

The leftist Tagammu Party and the Nasserists boycotted the elections over the amendments to Article 76 that made it difficult for the opposition to field presidential candidates, the lack of full judicial supervision of the elections, and the continuing state of emergency in the country. Yet while the boycott was clearly intended to send the message that the presidential election was illegitimate, it made very little difference in the outcome. Neither Tagammu nor the Nasserists had the kind of following to materially alter any election. Even if they did, Egypt's Interior Ministry agents were well-versed in the dark arts of vote rigging, ensuring a Mubarak victory.

The changes to Egypt's Political Parties Law were less newsworthy, but no less controversial. Like the constitutional amendment governing presidential elections, the National Democratic Party and the government-friendly press trumpeted the change as proof positive of President Mubarak's intention to gradually transform Egypt's political system. There was no real reason for the triumphant headlines, though. Close examination of the revised law revealed that it was as restrictive as the one it replaced. While removing stipulations that Egyptian political parties adhere to principles of national unity and Islamic law, as well as uphold the gains of the 1952 revolution, new restrictions were placed on groups seeking to become political parties. Whereas an earlier version of the law required that potential parties be distinct from existing parties, the amended version required that they represent a "new addition" to the political arena. This was a subtle yet important shift that further restricted Egyptian politics. For example, previously there was the possibility of having two parties on the Left, but the changes to the law precluded that chance. Further, would-be parties were required to obtain one thousand signatures of Egyptian citizens from ten governorates. Previously, only fifty signatures were required from anywhere in the country. The amended law also required parties seeking approval to detail their sources of funding, which could not come from foreign sources.[40]

The People's Assembly also made a number of changes to the awkwardly titled Committee for the Affairs of Political Parties. The committee was expanded to nine (from seven) members to accommodate new seats for the ministers of interior and People's Assembly affairs, both of whom were leading members of the NDP. The chairmanship of the committee also remained in the hands of the secretary general of the ruling party.[41] The other members included three retired judges and three independent political figures. Although the Egyptian judiciary has a reputation for guarding its independence, since the Nasser period Egyptian judges had been under assault. The regime used various methods, including judicial appointment and compensation—both of which were under the auspices of the Ministry of Justice—to develop a cadre of judges all too willing to do the regime's bidding.[42] With a leadership that left very little to chance, the three retired justices selected to serve on the committee were expected to serve the regime. But the amendments did not just change the composition of the committee, they also provided it with new powers. For example, if the Political Parties Committee determined that a political party, or one of its leading members, deviated from the party's platform, the party could be shut down. Party activities would also be suspended if the committee believed that it was in the national interest. Moreover, if a party was found to be violating the national interest, the committee had the power to refer the matter to the state prosecutor .

Egyptian lawmakers and the government also often wrote laws or amendments to existing laws in a way that granted citizens certain rights and freedoms and simultaneously restricted them. This was not an accident. Rather, the intrinsic contradictions within many Egyptian laws were intentional, part of a broad effort on the part of those who benefited from the status quo to ensure its longevity. Perhaps the best example of this came from the thirty-four constitutional amendments the People's Assembly passed on March 19, 2007, and set for a public referendum a week later. At the time of the amendments, the government argued that, collectively, these changes constituted a major step toward "rebalancing" the powers of the three branches of government, which had previously favored the executive. As a result, amendments to the constitution required that the government present its budget to parliament at least three months before the end of the fiscal year, and legislators were given the responsibility to approve the budget line by line. Another amendment permitted the People's Assembly to withdraw its confidence in a prime minister without having to submit the decision to the public for a vote. Both of these changes were laudable in terms of strengthening the hand of the People's Assembly and providing a check on executive power.

At the same time, however, another constitutional amendment allowed the president to dissolve parliament at any time without having to answer to the public through a referendum. This constituted a significant addition to the Egyptian executive's already impressive array of powers. This was a power that President Mubarak seemed to relish. On the eve of a visit to Washington in August 2009—his first in five years—Mubarak appeared on the public affairs show *Charlie Rose*. In response to a question about dissolving the People's Assembly, the president responded coyly, "I can't say that I will not dissolve the parliament. There might be some circumstances. I don't have any at the moment, but there might be some circumstances that call for the dissolution of the parliament, but at the moment, there is no single point that merits the dissolution of the parliament. The dissolution of the parliament becomes imperative only when there is a pressing demand."[43] Given that the Egyptian government had long employed broad definitions of everything from national security to political reform, the "pressing demand" that Mubarak invoked could have been literally any issue.

Like the 2005 revisions to the Political Parties Law, the 2007 constitutional amendments further restricted the rights of citizens to organize parties. Amended Article 5 affirmed the right of Egyptians to form political parties, but also proscribed political activity and parties based on religion.[44] The exact wording of the text was subject to different translations and understandings, but at the end of the day, the effect was the same: The Muslim Brotherhood would be banned from all political activity, thereby forestalling, once and for all, the accumulation of Islamist political power.[45] Despite periodic accommodations with the Brotherhood, the regime was intent on keeping the organization outside the legal, but highly circumscribed political arena. Official and unofficial spokesmen for the government argued that the group's ultimate aim was the establishment of a theocratic state, while others—mostly Egyptian and Western academics—argued that the Brotherhood had evolved and could be a force for progressive modernization.[46] As for the Brothers themselves, they have been decidedly cagey on this issue, often using the language of reform, but also leaving much open to interpretation.

The organization's draft party platform of 2007 was intended to demonstrate that the movement was a progressive force for change, but it raised as many questions as it answered. For example, in one part of the document the Brothers staked out a generally moderate position, which recognized the legitimacy of existing government bodies—specifically the Supreme Constitutional Court and the People's Assembly—to harmonize Egyptian law with shari'a.[47] At the same time, the Brothers called for the establishment of a council of religious scholars that the drafters of the platform claimed was merely advisory. Yet the ambiguity of the text raised suspicions that it was intended to be much more than that—an analogue of Iran's Guidance Council that has the authority to strike down legislation for being un-Islamic or outside the norms of the Islamic Republic.[48] The drafting committee also included a provision stating that only Muslims and males could become president or prime minister, which compromised the

Brotherhood's efforts to appear more inclusive.[49] Although there was no consensus within the organization on the document, to many—even committed reformers who had previously been willing to give the Brotherhood the benefit of the doubt—the platform revealed that the Brothers were attempting to leverage the discourse of political change for inherently anti-democratic ends.

In addition to their claims that the Brotherhood sought the establishment of an Islamic state, Egyptian officialdom argued that the proscription on religious parties was connected to their grave concern about what these kinds of parties would do to social cohesion.[50] If the Muslim Brotherhood were permitted to establish a party, they argued, then Egypt's Coptic Christians would likely want to do the same.[51] Indeed, the first decade of the twenty-first century was book-ended with sectarian violence. In early January 2000, a dispute between a Christian shop owner and a Muslim customer left twenty-one Copts dead in the town of al Kosheh—a small town in Upper Egypt. Almost ten years later to the day, in the village of Nag Hammadi, three men with automatic rifles raked parishioners as they were leaving midnight mass on Coptic Christmas, killing seven people. And on New Year's day 2011, a suicide bomber killed twenty-one and wounded ninety-seven at the al Qiddisin Church in Alexandria. In between these events there were countless confrontations between Christian and Muslim Egyptians.

The government's concern about religious parties stoking sectarian differences was legitimate, but there was no getting around the fact that the constitutional amendments were designed to prevent the Islamists from formalizing the political gains they made in the 2005 parliamentary elections when Brotherhood independents secured eighty-eight seats—about 19 percent of the total number of seats in the assembly.[52] This was hardly enough for the Brotherhood to alter whatever the government wanted the NDP-dominated parliament to do, but the result was both unprecedented and demonstrated the movement's potential electoral power. After all, the Brothers won every seat they contested. They did not bother with the other 364 mandates that were open.[53] The results clearly worried the government. Within eight weeks of the polling it announced that local elections scheduled for April 2006 would be postponed for two years.[54]

The context of the Brotherhood's electoral gains was also important. They took place amid both the NDP's much hyped emphasis on "New Thinking and Priorities," which was associated with Gamal Mubarak and his advisors, and the George W. Bush administration's own push for democracy in the Middle East, but especially Egypt. In both Cairo and Washington there was some talk before the polling that the Interior Ministry would make sure the Brotherhood won somewhere around forty seats in an effort to discredit both the younger Mubarak's ostensible reform program and the Bush administration's democracy agenda. When the Brotherhood doubled that target, it certainly put the NDP's young guard on the defensive. For its part, the Bush administration decried violence that had marred the last of three rounds of voting, but the Brotherhood's gains did not convince Washington to back off the Egyptians. That would come a little more than a month later, when the Islamist movement Hamas swept the Palestinian Legislative Council elections, which brought the "Freedom Agenda" to an effective, if not rhetorical, end around the region.

The Egyptian authorities also amended Article 88 of the constitution, which affirmed the importance of election monitoring in order to prevent electoral irregularities and outright fraud—a perennial problem in Egypt. This was a step the opposition should have applauded, but with this reform came other restrictions that simultaneously weakened the prospects of impartial electoral supervision.[55] Previously, Egypt's nine thousand judges oversaw elections at twenty-seven thousand polling sites over a three-week electoral period. No longer. Elections would be held on a single day and monitoring would fall to the Higher Election Commission that would assign a committee to supervise voting and tabulate the results. According to the amendment, "members of judicial bodies" would make up the committee. This stipulation raised a number of red flags for the Egyptian opposition. The amendment made no provision for how the committees would be selected, fueling suspicion that the government sought to staff them with NDP and government-friendly personnel. The phrase "members of judicial bodies" also gave the government a significant amount of leeway in constructing the electoral observation committees. The purposefully vague phrase opened these committees to judges as well as state prosecutors who, unlike idealized notions of U.S. attorneys in the American justice system, were far from politically independent.

The other major area where the 2007 constitutional amendments both giveth and taketh away was in the critical area of due process. Egypt has been under a state of emergency continually since October 1981, when President Anwar Sadat was assassinated.[56] By 2005, there was considerable international (i.e., American) and domestic political pressure to lift the state of emergency and the laws that go with it— a commitment Mubarak made in his run for a fifth term. Yet Mubarak subsequently argued that since Egypt continued to confront the related threats of terrorism and extremism, in order for him to keep his campaign promise, the constitution would need to be amended before he would rescind the Emergency Law. The ensuing constitutional amendments provided a basis for the repeal of the state of emergency and its concomitant laws only because critical components of these regulations were now to be written into the constitution. For example, whereas the Emergency Law once gave the president the power to refer civilians to military tribunals, that prerogative would now be enshrined in Article 179 of the constitution. The same article also allowed Egyptian authorities to ignore protections against arbitrary arrest, warrantless searches, and violations of privacy when prosecuting terrorism cases.[57] Over the years, the Egyptian government used an expansive definition of the term "terrorism" that allowed them to refer not only extremists to military tribunals, but also members of the Brotherhood—which had not been involved in violence since the 1940s—and other opposition activists. The changes to Article 179 did nothing to change this and actually enabled the government's overly broad classification of terrorism and terrorists.

Egyptian leaders and spokespeople claimed that, contrary to the objections of opposition groups, the purpose of the amendments was to strengthen the hand of the legislature against an all-powerful executive, protect the country from terrorism, and provide a more transparent electoral process. The critics, they argued, should not expect quick and dramatic change. Rather, the individuals and groups crying foul over the amendments should take the long view. If given time to "mature," the amendments will pave the way for fairer politics. Yet the bigger picture suggested something else entirely.[58] The government spin aside, the amendments did nothing more than further reinforce the power of the executive and, by extension, the ruling NDP. All the talk of robust checks and balances could not hide the fact that Egypt's political system was rigged in favor of a core constituency. Instead of changing that fact of Egyptian political life, the amendments sought to ensure the nondemocratic status quo under the guise of reform.[59]

Even though few Egyptians or outsiders were willing to accept the government's claims about reform at face value, from the perspective of Egyptian officials there was an intrinsic value to the debate over the 2007 constitutional amendments that was seemingly lost on observers. Regardless of how the opposition greeted the amendments, no matter how repressive the security forces were on the day of the referendum on the amendments, and no matter how tough a stand the *Washington Post* and *Wall Street Journal* took on the Egyptians and their apparent unwillingness to pursue fundamental political reform, Cairo argued that the whole episode proved that progressive politics was, indeed, underway. The government maintained, however incredulously, that the fact that there was a debate at all in Egypt over the constitutional changes was proof positive of how far the government was willing to go to foster a more open political system. This was a valuable talking point, as was the often invoked contention that the changes to Article 179 were similar to provisions contained in the U.S. Patriot Act that passed in both houses of Congress in October 2001 by wide margins.[60] These arguments were superficial, but nevertheless deflected, if not silenced, criticism of the regime in Washington and elsewhere. The disingenuousness of the Mubarak era was reinforced when, despite the amendments to Article 179 that were ostensibly necessary to cancel the state of emergency, the National Democratic Party–controlled parliament renewed the Emergency Law in 2008 and again in 2010. It was no coincidence that after the January 25, 2011, uprising that ousted Mubarak, Egyptians voted to amend Article 88, giving judges the responsibility for all aspects of elections and referenda. In the same vote, Article 179 was deleted from the constitution altogether.

CROSSING THE STREET IN CAIRO

The formal political institutions of the Egyptian state are restrictive, but there is another equally powerful framework that shapes behavior and expectations about politics in Egyptian society: informal institutions. These are the unwritten rules and uncodified norms that, along with formal institutions—constitutions, laws, decrees, and regulations—provide incentives and disincentives for people as they navigate their daily lives. These informal institutions are not unique to Egypt; they exist everywhere. In order to understand how politics and society work, a grasp of both formal and informal institutions is critical. Perhaps the best way to think about informal institutions is to consider Cairo traffic. In 2003, the Cairo governorate commissioned a Japanese engineering firm to study traffic in a city renowned not just for its rich history and culture, but also for its ferocious jam of cars, trucks, buses, and random donkey carts. After months of study, the engineers reported back to Cairo's authorities that they should do nothing because traffic in the city defied explanation. As a result, they made no recommendations to the Cairo authorities, fearing that these suggestions might actually make things worse.

The Japanese engineers remained clueless because, not surprisingly, they only sought to track traffic patterns measuring speed, distances, peak traffic hours, and other data. They are traffic engineers, after all. As important as these factors may be, they are not critical to explaining why traffic in Cairo is the way it is. To the engineers crunching numbers, Cairo's *zahma* is chaotic and hard to explain; but it is not. If it were, Cairenes would not walk in the streets, dart across four lanes of traffic, and think nothing of wading into masses of oncoming cars, buses, and trucks. To be sure, Egypt has its share of traffic deaths— about six thousand per year—but Egyptians do not die in any greater number in traffic accidents than elsewhere. Turkey, a country with a slightly smaller population than Egypt, experiences 4,500 road deaths annually. The data simply does not fit the notion that Cairo traffic is singularly dangerous and chaotic. Observers are clearly missing the informal rules and norms that guide the vast majority of Egyptian drivers and pedestrians to their destinations safely. Somewhere in the Ministry of Transport there must be a compendium of Egyptian traffic laws, but they do not matter as much as the informal rules of the road to which Egyptians have become habituated. That is why when Egyptians step off the curb into traffic, they are not taking as much of a risk as the uninitiated might expect. They have a good sense of when it is a good time to step off the curb and when they should stay put, when a car will swerve and when it will not. Miscalculations, of course, do occur, resulting in injuries and, as noted, deaths.

Yet informal institutions do not just offer insights about the workings of Cairo traffic; they can also tell observers much about the way politics in Egypt work. The past practices and uncodified norms that developed since the Free Officers' coup in 1952 serve as powerful incentives either to conform or remain politically demobilized. This seems strange. After all, despite the authoritarian political order that Mubarak oversaw, Egyptians carried out a lively debate—in which many different political factions participated—about their country's future. Yet notwithstanding the presence of liberal, Islamist, leftist, Nasserist, and a variety of strains in between, for those who defied these incentives there was a price to be paid.

The Muslim Brotherhood consistently ran afoul of the informal (and formal) institutions of the state proscribing questions about the sources of power, legitimacy, and authenticity in Egyptian politics.[61] Liberal voices, like the Egyptian-American sociologist Saad Eddin

Ibrahim and Ayman Nour were imprisoned for violating the same unwritten rules as the Brothers. Ibrahim, who once served as an advisor to President Mubarak and who taught both Gamal and the Egyptian first lady, had the temerity to question whether it was appropriate for the younger Mubarak to be groomed for the presidency in a republic that was, if the regime's rhetoric was to be believed, making the transition from authoritarianism to democracy. Dr. Saad was arrested late at night on the weekend of June 30, 2000, on charges of receiving unauthorized funds from abroad and smearing Egypt's name. After serving fourteen months of a seven-year prison term, he was released, but fearing another arrest, trial, and debilitating stay in prison, Dr. Saad left Egypt. He shuttled among the United States, Qatar, and Turkey between 2007 and mid-2010 before finally returning to Cairo.

For his part, Nour directly challenged Mubarak's claims about reform and positioned himself and his party as authentic challengers to Mubarak (both Hosni and Gamal) and the ruling National Democratic Party's monopoly on power. He was arrested on January 29, 2005, and was accused of forging signatures to meet one of the requirements for legalization of his party. The timing and circumstances of his arrest—on the eve of Iraq's first post-Saddam Hussein elections, embarrassing the Bush administration—helped explain why for a time he became the poster child for American democracy promotion efforts in Egypt. Like Dr. Saad, Nour endured an official smear campaign and a show trial that sent him to prison for four years.

Beyond the Brotherhood, Nour, Dr. Saad and other traditional opponents of the regime, the activists that operated in Egypt's blogosphere during the late Mubarak period also came under increasing state pressure for asking questions about the informal sources of power and legitimacy in Egyptian society.[62] The confrontation began in 2004, when a blogger named Wael Abbas documented police misconduct at a rally protesting Gamal Mubarak's possible succession with pictures and videos that he posted on the Internet. The Egyptian press, which was not permitted to cover anti-regime demonstrations, and international news services began using Abbas's blog as a source for their own reporting on Egypt's emerging political ferment.

Throughout 2005, blogging exploded as a source of both political protest and a way to bear witness to the predatory nature of the Egyptian state. Yet, May 25—the day the Interior Ministry scheduled a public referendum on the 2005 constitutional changes—was a watershed moment. On that day, opposition activists held a peaceful demonstration against the amendments, which they believed were anti-democratic, in Liberation Square and outside the Cairo Press Syndicate. During the protests, riot police and plainclothes thugs set upon the activists and anyone else who happened to be in the area, including journalists. The beatings and even sexual assault of women were, sadly, not out of the ordinary, but unlike after previous episodes, a number of bloggers posted shocking pictures and videos of the events on the Internet. The private Egyptian television channel Dream was first to pick up the disturbing images, which subsequently appeared in the international media.

The bad publicity did not, however, deter the Egyptian leadership. The government dismissed the evidence of official misconduct and turned its attention to gaining the upper hand in the battle with blogger-activists. Determined to no longer be behind the curve when it came to powerful new technologies that lower the obstacles to collective action, the Egyptian government invested heavily in the surveillance of the Internet. The Interior Ministry began systematically targeting bloggers with intimidation, arrest, and in at least one notorious case, rape. Also, the ministries of Foreign Affairs, Defense, and Interior all established units to monitor the Egyptian blogosphere and to follow what was being said about Egypt on foreign-based Internet sites.[63]

The government's stepped-up surveillance of these activists underscored the critical importance of bloggers in the battle over Egypt's competing narratives. Unlike Egypt's emasculated opposition parties, bloggers came to the forefront of exposing the official repression of the Egyptian government, for which some have paid a steep price. For example, Abdel Karim Suleiman, who was first arrested in 2005, was sentenced to four years in prison in 2007 for posting blog entries critical of the Egyptian government and Islam. In May 2006, bloggers Mohammed el Sharkawi and Karim el Shaer, along with *LA Times* stringer and blogger Hossam el Hamalawy, were arrested during a demonstration at the Press Syndicate in Cairo. Given the government's campaign against bloggers, these arrests would not have been all that noteworthy, but for the fact that Egyptian police tortured and raped el Sharkawi in custody. Indeed, 2006 was a very bad year for the Egyptian blogosphere, as over one hundred bloggers and Internet activists, including award-winning blogger Ahmad Said al Islam and the well-known Alaa Abd el Fatah, were arrested. The situation was so bad that year that the Paris-based *Reporters without Borders* added Egypt to its list of "Internet Enemies."[64] Yet the harassment of bloggers continued with arrests of both internationally known and largely anonymous bloggers on an array of charges including Muslim Brotherhood membership, disrupting social harmony, criticizing Islam, spreading false images of Egypt, sending messages about a demonstration, publishing false information about the army, and posting photos of police brutality. Each of these charges was related in some way to breaking informal and unofficial political taboos.

The state repression of new media activists was happening at the same time as a similar campaign against traditional journalists and editors. After years of decline, 2003 and 2004 were a renaissance of sorts for the Egyptian press. Coinciding with both internal and American demands for political change, Egyptian journalists began to ask questions, editorialize, and break stories that were previously off-limits because they touched on the very nature of the Egyptian state and society. Leading the way was *al Masry al Youm* (*The Egyptian Today*), which was founded in 2004 by a human rights activist and media entrepreneur named Hisham Kassem. Ownership of the paper was kept behind a veil and its licensing was a matter of controversy, given Kassem's previous turn as an editor and publisher of the pugnacious, funny, and excellent *Cairo Times*. That weekly was, however, an English-only publication, catering to Cairo's thousands of ex-pat workers, American and British diplomats, and the veritable hordes of foreign graduate students who descended on the city every year to hone their Arabic language skills and undertake dissertation field research. *Al Masry al Youm* was conceived as an Arabic daily with serious journalism and an opposition editorial line. Rumor had it that Egypt's former head of intelligence, Lieutenant General Omar Suleiman, ensured that the paper was licensed. The reasons for this remain murky. Suleiman did not have a reputation for being a progressive on freedom of the press or on pretty much anything. One plausible, but not entirely credible, explanation was that Suleiman nursed presidential ambitions and was thus interested in a publication that would be highly critical of Gamal Mubarak and other members of the political elite. Regardless, if *al Masry al Youm* was intended to be an antidote to the establishment line of *al Ahram*—Egypt's most widely distributed, if not read, newspaper—the jingoism of *al Gumhuriya*, and the yellow journalism of other publications, it was an unmitigated success. Despite having a smaller print run, a function of higher production costs owing to ink and paper subsidies and a cornered market in advertising for the state-affiliated *al Ahram*, *al Masry al Youm* quickly became Egypt's newspaper of record, reporting on official corruption, political malfeasance, and foreign policy in a dispassionate manner combined with investigative journalism and a hard-hitting editorial policy.

Kassem's venture was neither the first opposition newspaper in Egypt nor the most combative, but given that it was founded at a time of political ferment, it quickly developed a mass appeal. The paper was also, of course, not the only reason for what seemed to be a more active media environment. This was more likely the result of a confluence of events including external pressure for reform, growing internal dissent for political change, opposition to a Mubarak dynasty, and economic grievances. Indeed, the moment seemed ripe for *al Masry al Youm* and others to test the boundaries of the regime's tolerance. After all, Egypt's press syndicate had long been on uneasy terms with the government as the Egyptian leadership sought to bring journalists to heel through restrictive laws, regulations, and outright coercion, but it soon became a more open hotbed of anti-regime activity. The group's headquarters in downtown Cairo was the site of a large number of demonstrations beginning in 2005. Reporters were routinely harassed and threatened with prosecution.

The most high-profile case came in March 2008 when a number of opposition dailies reported that President Mubarak had fallen gravely ill. The report turned out to be erroneous, which gave the government an opportunity to exact revenge on the papers and their editors. The following September, the intrepid editor of *al Dustour* (*The Constitution*) Ibrahim Eissa, who had founded the publication almost a decade before *al Masry al Youm* was established; Wael al Abrashy of the weekly *Sawt al Umma* (*Voice of the Nation*); Adel Hammouda of *al Fagr* (*The Dawn*); and Abdel Halim Kandil former editor of *al Karama* (*Dignity*) were convicted of "publishing false information likely to disturb public order."[65] The government argued that the reports caused a precipitous fall in the value of the Egyptian stock market and threatened Egypt's stability. Ultimately, President Mubarak pardoned the editors, though they were forced to pay a fine of 20,000 Egyptian pounds—about $3,500. The editors' transgression was not reporting on the president's well-being per se; rather, by covering his health scare—real or imagined—they too were violating Egypt's informal rules of the political game. It was not so much about succession—this was an issue that had been the subject of near-obsessive discussion for about a decade. More importantly, talk about Mubarak's health and who might come next raised questions about the legitimacy and the power base of the political order.

In October 2010, Eissa became the center of controversy again when new owners of *al Dustour*—one of whom is the leader of the Wafd Party—dismissed him. The trigger was apparently Eissa's intention to print an op-ed on the anniversary of the October 1973 war asking whether, after almost thirty years under President Hosni Mubarak, Egyptian society still had the discipline and sense of self-sacrifice to pull off something like the Crossing of the Suez Canal.[66] That Mohammed ElBaradei, former director general of the International Atomic Energy Agency (IAEA) and opposition figure, asked this obviously rhetorical question compounded the insult to Egypt's leadership. Although the National Democratic Party insinuated that Eissa was fired because of personality differences with the ownership, Eissa was in hot water because he enabled ElBaradei's questions about the legitimacy of the political system after three decades under Mubarak.

The arrests, harassment, and abuse of journalists, bloggers, and editors like Ibrahim Eissa, Saad Eddin Ibrahim, Ayman Nour, and the Muslim Brotherhood were intended to have a chilling effect on the opposition. In this, the regime largely failed. Journalists and activists remained under pressure, but the government was never able to roll back the public debate about reform for which these individuals and groups advocated. Yet even as the Egyptian leadership failed to delegitimize notions of democratic change, it was able to reinforce some of the unwritten codes and norms that contributed to Egypt's authoritarian political order.

These informal institutions, especially the incentives to conform, were powerful. By all measures, the Hazem Salem of 1999 was an activist, dedicated to promoting reform, minority rights, and democratic change as editor of the Ibn Khaldun Center's magazine, *Civil Society*. But Hazem's activism extended only so far. Some years later, he became an Egyptian diplomat, representing the very government that he once agitated against. Hazem is hardly unique, however. Many former students of Dr. Saad and employees of the center have moved on to government positions. Perhaps they changed their minds about the regime and their former activism. Mostly, they protested that they were seeking to change the system from within. This was the argument that Gamal Mubarak's associate, Mohammed Kamal, often made. For anyone who knew Kamal during his time at the Johns Hopkins School of Advanced International Studies, his role as consigliore to Mubarak was a surprise. Rather, his fellow students imagined him as both a serious academic and an activist for political reform and democratic change. Mohammed insisted that he was these things, but one cannot overlook the powerful informal incentives of throwing one's lot in with the regime—in Mohammed's case, the power, prestige, and influence that he would not have otherwise enjoyed if he were just another underpaid professor at Cairo University's Faculty of Economics and Political Science.

Mohammed's experience may have been an extreme case, but the pressures to conform in Mubarak's Egypt were pervasive, if not always effective. Among Egypt's elites, as the end of the Hosni Mubarak era drew closer, there was constant hedging. It was as if thousands of people who operated within the ambit of the regime had their fingers in the air all at once trying to determine the direction of the wind should the president not wake up someday—Egyptians, particularly the elite, never imagined that Mubarak would outlive his own presidency. So privately, people criticized Mubarak, his son, his wife, the regime, the system, but just in case, they remained publicly supportive of the president and all too willing to do the government's bidding. This cognitive dissonance became more acute every autumn when the ruling National Democratic Party convened its annual convention in the cavernous Cairo International Conference Center in Heliopolis—home to the Egyptian armed forces, its officers, and other members of the state elite. There the party faithful gathered for three days of discussion on domestic politics, foreign affairs, and economic policy. Of course, all of it was a stage-managed affair to convey the impression (that no one actually believed) of consultation and democratic practices. Yet there they were—fierce critics of the NDP, the government, and the Mubarak family in private—clapping on cue, their very presence an expression of support for the party, reinforcing the theatrics of the regime, all the while ensuring their careers or access to patronage or both.

Perhaps most telling is Mohammed Nosseir, who was active in the opposition Democratic Front Party. The party was not a force in Egyptian politics with a miniscule following and modest budget. Yet even as the party had virtually no chance of influencing the trajectory of politics under Mubarak, Mohammed nevertheless kept his party affiliation a secret. He feared that his extensive business contacts and broader network of acquaintances would melt away if they learned of his activism within an opposition party, no matter how marginal. So powerful were the disincentives of Egypt's informal institutions that Mohammed freely admitted that while he was committed to a democratic Egypt, he could not risk his livelihood to be open about it until, of course, the 2011 Egyptian uprising when after a week of protests, he joined the demonstrations in Tahrir Square.

Although Mohammed chose—until the last moment—to mask his opposition to Hosni Mubarak's regime, he and his party shared with other activists, parties, and movements a broad narrative of what ailed Egypt. If analysts culled the various positions and statements of the Muslim Brotherhood, some of the legal opposition parties, Ayman Nour, Saad Eddin Ibrahim, human rights organizations, leftists, the centrist Islamist group called the (Center) Party, Nasserists, *Kifaya!*, the April 6 Youth Movement, the Popular Democratic Movement for Change, *Mayehkomsh*, bloggers, journalists, myriad nongovernmental organizations, and a host of lesser known others, their account of Egypt at the end of Mubarak's rule would likely revolve around the following themes:

> Egypt is a proud nation with a long and proud history. It is currently failing. This decline has little to do with its people and everything to do with its government and leadership. Corruption, graft, lack of opportunity, and political repression are hallmarks of the Mubarak regime—a political system that stretches back to the Free Officers' coup of July 1952. As a result, Egypt needs political, economic, and social reform. This will have the combined effects of rooting out corruption, opening up the political arena to voices other than the NDP, and necessarily uplifting the Egyptian people who have been suffering at the hands of an unjust government. An Egypt that is stronger, more equitable, and representative of the people's views will also be equipped to resist the predatory policies of the United States and Israel in the region thereby restoring Egypt's leading role in the Arab world.

To be sure, Egypt's opposition groups vary in emphasis and tone from different factions to individuals, but ultimately each of these groups and activists diagnosed similar pathologies and prescribed comparable policy prescriptions. The opposition's explanation of Egypt's troubles at the end of the Mubarak era and the prescriptions to fix these problems proved to be deeply appealing because it filled the yawning gap between the myths of the "new Egypt" and objective reality. As preceding chapters have made clear, these circumstances were not new. There were moments when the regime and its defenders enjoyed tremendous popular support—after the assassination attempt on Nasser, the nationalization of the Suez Canal, and the Crossing, for example—but their worldview and ideas about how Egypt should be ruled always faced critical challenges. This was the central drama of

Egyptian politics, but until January 25, 2011, the regime always managed to prevail through a combination of bribery and, importantly, coercion. As high as the stakes were over the preceding sixty years, they became even higher over the past decade as Egyptians anticipated a change in leadership.

THE OBSESSION

In the late 1990s, as Mubarak was entering his seventies, Egyptology suddenly changed. It was no longer about Egypt's stunning archaeological treasures of the Valley of the Kings, Karnak, Abu Simbal, the temple of Hatshepsut, the great Pyramids of Giza, and a wealth of other finds. Rather, it became the stuff of policy wonks, big-footed journalists, and intelligence analysts reading Egypt's political tea leaves to divine who would come after Mubarak. Sovietologists used to dissect photos of May Day parades in Moscow's Red Square to gauge who was up and who was down in the Soviet leadership; starting around 1999, observers of Egyptian politics engaged in a similar exercise.

Much of what counted for information about President Mubarak, his fitness, and his state of mind was the stuff of rumor and innuendo. Still, there was no getting around the fact that he was elderly and it was showing. In one of those ham-handed moments when the Egyptian government was seeking to deflect domestic and American pressure to undertake political reform, someone thought it would be a good idea to televise Mubarak as he chaired a meeting on economic reform. This would demonstrate the president's commitment to transparency and change and reinforce the idea that Mubarak himself was a catalyst for Egypt's alleged transformation. It was excruciating to watch. The president sat at the head of the table surrounded by Prime Minister Nazif and the economic dream team along with a few other ministers and advisors. Other than grunting "Uuuh"—agreement—during what seemed like an interminable broadcast, the president appeared to be alternately checked out, flummoxed, and vaguely annoyed. Mostly, he seemed to be having trouble following the conversation. From the vantage point on the other end of the television screen, it did not seem to be just unfamiliarity with the subject matter for a man who came of age as a bomber pilot and became a strongman well versed in the art of power politics. Rather, it was the unmistakable drift of advancing age. Perhaps it was a function of his hearing loss, but Mubarak's body language and facial expressions told it all. He was decidedly less interested in the chatter directed at him than in what seemed to be almost anything else—perhaps tea and a long nap. The overall effect of the broadcast diminished the man who had loomed so large in Egyptian politics for so long.

The issue of who would come next intensified because the president had been resolute about *not* naming a vice president even as he advanced in age. This was in sharp contrast to both Nasser and Sadat, who had eleven and two vice presidents, respectively. In one sense, it remained a mystery why President Mubarak had never named a successor. It seemed reckless for the man at the fulcrum of the state, who had been the target of a number of assassination attempts and who seemed interested solely in maintaining the stability and security of the country, to have studiously avoided this issue throughout his long tenure. Yet Mubarak's unwillingness to identify an heir to the presidency made sense. The unspoken but widely acknowledged rivalry between Mubarak and Abu Ghazala was a searing experience for the president and a primary reason why he resisted appointing a deputy who one day could become a rival for his chair.

Prior to the January 25 revolution, the two most oft-mentioned potential candidates to lead Egypt in the post–Hosni Mubarak era were Gamal Mubarak and Lieutenant General Omar Suleiman, the chief of the General Intelligence Directorate. All of the publicly available evidence suggested that the younger Mubarak had an edge over Suleiman and any other potential contenders. After all, Gamal parachuted into a position of leadership in the National Democratic Party, his profile in the Egyptian media rose dramatically in the late 1990s just as rumors of his possible succession were beginning to make their way around Cairo, and the 2007 changes to Article 76 of the constitution seemed tailor-made to nominate the younger Mubarak president. There were also more subtle signs that Gamal was positioning himself—or as rumor has it, being positioned by his mother—to be president, including his annual performance at the World Economic Forum in Davos and his periodic visits to foreign capitals on what is typically billed as personal business but invariably seemed to include official meetings. For example, he visited Washington twice in 2003, where he met with Vice President Dick Cheney, National Security Advisor Condoleezza Rice, and Pentagon officials. In 2004, the younger Mubarak also accompanied his father to President Bush's ranch in Crawford, Texas. When President Mubarak returned to Washington in 2009 after a five-year absence and again in 2010, Gamal traveled with him, but kept a decidedly low profile.

The April 2004 visit turned out to be disastrous due to a series of Bush administration policy announcements that aligned the United States ever closer with Israel while the Egyptian leader was still in the United States. In the five years between Mubarak visits, Prime Minister Ahmad Nazif and Omar Suleiman—often with Foreign Minister Ahmad Abul Gheit in tow—played the role of interlocutor with Washington. Yet there was one visit in particular that caused a veritable media free-for-all in the Arab press. In May 2006, Wajd Waqfi, an al Jazeera correspondent staking out the White House, noticed Egypt's ambassador, Nabil Fahmy, and a tall man enter the West Wing of the White House. The man with Ambassador Fahmy turned out to be Gamal Mubarak. According to both governments, he was in the United States on a private visit to renew his pilot's license, but he had an audience with the National Security Advisor Stephen Hadley, Vice President Dick Cheney, and Secretary of State Condoleezza Rice. Even President Bush reportedly made himself available for a quick handshake. The innocent explanation suggested that U.S. officials granted a courtesy visit to the son of a long-time ally and friend of the United States.[67] That Gamal was a senior official of Egypt's ruling party made the courtesy call all the more appropriate. For their part, some Egyptians took it as a sign that Washington was signaling its approval of the younger Mubarak's eventual succession to his father's position. This was unlikely, but even to the nonconspiracy-minded, the meeting with Gamal was curious. Although they acknowledged the meeting, neither the Egyptian nor American governments ever explained why Gamal was at the White House that day.

Gamal never publicly stated that he was interested in becoming president of Egypt. At the same time, he never actually denied that he coveted the position. He barnstormed throughout Egypt in what seemed like thinly veiled political campaigns, ostensibly to explain the NDP's reform platform. The unspoken goal of these trips was to develop the image of a man—one who grew up in a palace and consorted with presidents, kings, generals, and foreign ministers most of his life—as authentically Egyptian. It never worked. According to one Egyptian journalist's account, local National Democratic Party officials generally manufactured the crowds that greeted Gamal in Nile Delta villages or faraway towns in Upper Egypt with promises of free *ta'amiyah* (the Egyptian version of falafel) sandwiches.

It was a mistake to assume that all indicators led inevitably to a Gamal presidency. If he were the heir, would it not have made sense to make that clear? This would have reduced significant uncertainty and allowed Egypt's security services to snuff out opposition to a Gamal presidency before he took the presidential oath. The doubts about what became known as the "Gamal succession scenario" fueled hypotheses about an alternative political universe in which Omar Suleiman succeeded President Mubarak. Proponents of this theory were always short on the details of how exactly a Suleiman presidency would come about, other than suggesting that Mubarak would appoint him vice president—a position U.S. officials believe he coveted at one time—but were long on his qualifications.

Suleiman was born to a desperately poor family in Qina, a city of two hundred thousand in Upper Egypt, which is the capital of the Qina governorate. He is a graduate of Egypt's military academy and received advanced training at the Frunze Military Academy in Moscow and the John F. Kennedy Special Warfare School at Fort Bragg, North Carolina. Suleiman is a veteran of both the 1967 and 1973 conflicts with Israel, though the details of his actual service in these wars is unclear. In 1986, he became deputy director of military intelligence, where he first came into contact with President Mubarak. After five years, Suleiman was promoted to director of military intelligence and then appointed head of the General Intelligence Directorate in 1993. He was virtually unknown to most Egyptians until he showed up in Damascus in July 2000 with President Mubarak to attend the funeral of the late Syrian leader Hafez al Assad.

Despite Suleiman's experience in the intelligence world, he tended to be the central figure in most "military succession" scenarios. This was not only a function of the fact that all Egyptian presidents have been military officers and Suleiman was the most visible officer among a senior command that had pursued a low profile since Field Marshal Abu Ghazala was sacked in the late 1980s, but also of the indispensable role Suleiman came to play for President Mubarak. Suleiman's legend actually only began in 1995 when, over the objection of the foreign ministry, he convinced President Mubarak to take his armored limousine to Addis Ababa, the capital of Ethiopia, for a summit of the African Union. Egyptian diplomats were concerned that if Mubarak arrived with an armored car, he would be offending his Ethiopian hosts. Mubarak's decision to heed Suleiman's advice saved both of their lives, as terrorists from the Egyptian extremist group al Gama'a al Islamiyya ambushed Mubarak's convoy as it made its way from the airport to the site of the summit.

After that time, Mubarak came to rely on Suleiman more and more regarding Egypt's most pressing foreign policy issues. The general intelligence director became Egypt's primary interlocutor with the Israelis; played a central role in arranging periodic cease-fires between Israel and Hamas; took the lead seeking the release of an Israeli soldier, Gilad Shalit, who was taken captive in Gaza in 2006; and was the point person in the attempt to reconcile Hamas and Fatah, which controls the Palestinian Authority that is based in the West Bank. Suleiman also controlled the Sudan file, Egypt's most important foreign policy issue given the centrality of the Nile to the survival of the country. His influence in such prominent issues was not surprising given the stakes involved, but it prompted one former Egyptian official to ask sarcastically why Egypt needed a foreign ministry.[68]

There were hints that Suleiman did not see his role as solely confined to geopolitics but domestic concerns as well. This is primarily a matter of where the lieutenant general sat, as the General Intelligence Service is a hybrid organization that is both a foreign espionage and domestic intelligence agency.[69] As a result, Suleiman was among those responsible for Egypt's internal security and stability. To partisans of an Omar Suleiman presidency, his responsibilities in these critical areas, his stature as a military officer, and his apparent gravitas, especially in comparison to the relatively young and inexperienced Gamal Mubarak, made Suleiman an obvious choice.

But there were a number of problems with an Omar Suleiman scenario. On the institutional level, unless there was a turnaround and President Mubarak formalized Suleiman's role as vice president, Suleiman did not meet the criteria for those seeking office other than as an independent candidate. It was not likely that Egypt's head of General Intelligence would go through the humiliating process the National Democratic Party had engineered for independents to qualify for a presidential run. There was, of course, always the possibility that a putsch or a coup d'état would place Suleiman in the top job, but there was no evidence that he had the broad support or network within the officer corps to lead such an effort. While he retained his military rank, he had been out of uniform for more than two decades.

The Suleiman versus Gamal frame, which Western analysts owed largely to a 2003 article in the *Atlantic* magazine by veteran journalist Mary Anne Weaver called "Pharaohs-in-Waiting," ultimately obscured more than it revealed.[70] Weaver's article was published just as Western observers and officials were waking up to Cairo's own emergent succession chatter. The article was eloquent and persuasive, but it had the unintended consequence of locking observers into a particular narrative. Suleiman or Gamal became an *idée fixe*, which naturally hampered the ability of analysts to consider potential alternatives and encouraged them to give less weight to contradictory evidence. These problems were brought into sharp relief when a bespectacled lawyer named Mohammed ElBaradei returned to Egypt after a long absence.

ElBaradei, the secretary general of the International Atomic Energy Agency from 1997 to 2009, was a technocrat whose ties to his native country seemed purposely tenuous, to allow him to more freely contribute to improving global governance. Yet, he caused a political sensation when his plane touched down at Cairo International Airport on February 19, 2010, and—according to international news outlets— as many as one thousand people turned out not just to welcome ElBaradei home but also to implore him to run for president in the 2011 elections. ElBaradei did not douse his supporters' hopes. He coyly told the Egyptian and foreign press that he would consider running if the Egyptian government enacted electoral and party reforms to ensure truly free and fair elections. At the same time, he formed a new political organization called the National Association for Change (NAC), which encompassed a broad swath of Egypt's fractious opposition movement.[71] For its part, even the Muslim Brotherhood, which throughout 2009 and 2010 was under significant state pressure, signaled its support for the NAC and ElBaradei.

As Saad Eddin Ibrahim, Ayman Nour, and countless others discovered, aspiring reformers challenged the legitimacy of the state at their own peril. ElBaradei seemed to understand this fact of Egyptian political life, which is why he refused to commit to a presidential run, opting instead to lay out conditions for his candidacy to which the defenders of the regime were unlikely to accede. This only helped ElBaradei's overall political agenda. In the months after his return to Egypt, he appeared to be the sort of political entrepreneur who could exploit the gap between regime rhetoric—about economic growth, political reform, and social progress—and empirical reality, which was dominated by political repression, poverty, substandard schools, and crumbling national infrastructure.

Once more, ElBaradei did not face the same vulnerabilities as Nour or Dr. Saad, who were easily neutralized with false allegations and farcical court dramas that many members of the Egyptian elite were willing to believe, either out of self-preservation or personal animus toward the defendants. What would seem to have been his biggest weakness—his long absence from Egypt while heading the IAEA— may actually have been his greatest asset. ElBaradei's long tenure in Vienna meant that the regime had nothing on him. It could not taint him with charges of corruption, electoral malfeasance, financial chicanery, Islamist agitation, or of being a stooge of the United States. In fact, ElBaradei clashed repeatedly with Washington while at the IAEA. Still, the Egyptian government did seek to discredit him. President Mubarak kicked off the effort when, referring to ElBaradei, he told a German reporter that Egypt "does not need a national hero." This was a rather odd statement given that the president was the descendant of the Free Officers, whose alleged heroism was critical to Egypt's nationalist pantheon and, more importantly, the connection Mubarak cultivated between himself and the Crossing of the Suez Canal in October 1973.

Following Mubarak's lead, the state-controlled press suggested that ElBaradei provided the legal pretext for the U.S. invasion of Iraq and that he was sowing ethnic and sectarian tensions within Egypt. Neither of these allegations was true, but the government's response to ElBaradei clearly indicated that officials were concerned how he or any other potentially popular figure could complicate Egypt's leadership succession. The early hopes for ElBaradei subsequently dimmed as he darted back and forth between Cairo and Vienna, where he was working on his memoirs, but his declarations about free and fair elections and the need for sweeping institutional reforms were a direct if subtle attack on Gamal Mubarak, who had positioned himself as the avatar of Egyptian political change.

Yet ElBaradei was not the only possible challenger to Gamal or Omar Suleiman for Egypt's top job—he was just the most obvious. There were additional scenarios, which few considered because they did not seem plausible, in which the military might be forced to step in to restore social order. Certainly no one predicted the January 25 uprising—though reports were that the U.S. National Intelligence Council was, indeed, concerned about Egyptian stability—and the ouster of Mubarak that left the country in the hands of the Supreme Council of the Armed Forces, ending the presidential aspirations of both Gamal and Suleiman.

Toward the end of the Mubarak era, the defenders of the regime seemed all too aware of the risks associated with the looming presidential succession and took steps they believed would preclude any "alternative scenarios." State security intensified its effort to break the Muslim Brotherhood as a potential political force through waves of arrests that some believed left more members of that organization in prison that at any time during the Nasser era. Potential opponents like Ayman Nour remained subject to official smear campaigns and legal action. Even though President Mubarak and his allies took a somewhat less confrontational approach to Mohammed ElBaradei given his international standing, Egypt's state-affiliated media continued to try to undermine his domestic prestige. At the same time, a more subtle campaign on the part of regime intellectuals began. They questioned ElBaradei's actual plans, disparaged the people who were affiliated with the National Association for Change, wondered aloud why the former IAEA secretary general kept returning to Vienna, and inquired whether he was willing "to pay the price"—without spelling out what that actually was—necessary to be a national political leader.

The regime-friendly intellectuals who went after ElBaradei also received some help from within Egypt's notoriously fractious opposition. This was not all that surprising, given the long and storied history of Egyptian opposition groups getting bogged down in petty politics that for a long time made it practically impossible for them to mount a coherent and broad-based opposition to the regime.[72] The classic example of this was Makram Ebeid's "Black Book," which chronicled the corruption and graft at the highest levels of the Wafd in the 1930s and 1940s.[73] More recently, Saad Eddin Ibrahim—who supported ElBaradei—published an essay in the May 2, 2010, edition of *al Masry al Youm* in which he demanded to know whether, after his triumphant return to Cairo in February and the creation of the National Association for Change, ElBaradei had a "Plan B." This was, of course, a fair question. At the time, ElBaradei seemed less interested in putting together a coherent strategy for change than in embarrassing the regime and playing coy with the press about his actual intentions. Still, Dr. Saad's piece smacked of no small amount of envy. This was entirely understandable. He had sacrificed much over the preceding decade including his home, family, and life's work to advance the cause of political change, yet he never achieved the kind of traction that ElBaradei had in such a short time. Indeed, though Dr. Saad had a following in Egypt, he seemed far more popular on the shores of the Potomac than on those of the Nile.

What seemed so tragic about the splits and fissures among the disparate opposition was the very fact that Egypt was approaching a moment—presidential succession—when, if they could get their collective acts together, the opposition could have an opportunity to shape the trajectory of Egyptian politics. This was a function of the fact that, despite an ideological spectrum that swept from liberal to Nasserist to leftist to Islamist, the Egyptian opposition shared a similar narrative about the Mubarak years and, in the abstract, some basic notions about Egypt's future as well—free and fair elections, a meaningful parliament, a vibrant press, an independent judiciary, and checks and balances between the different branches of government.

Still, this vision of a more progressive Egypt would, it was almost universally believed, have to wait until after Mubarak died and perhaps then some, especially if, as expected, some regime figure would succeed him. This was not only the gloomy conclusion of Egypt's opposition, but also Mubarak's greatest patron, the United States. Although there had been considerable unease in Washington over Egypt's trajectory during the 2000s, Mubarak remained an ally and as such, a pillar of the American approach to the Middle East.

Radar Contact Lost

A T 1:20 A.M. on October 31, 1999, Captain Ahmad el Habashy, the command pilot of EgyptAir flight 990, eased his Boeing 767 off departure runway 22R at New York's John F. Kennedy International Airport.[1] The big jet roared west at 180 knots over Jamaica Bay momentarily before Captain el Habashy gently rolled the airplane to the left, clearing Long Island's southern beaches, and then out over the open ocean. Six minutes after lifting off, New York Terminal Approach Control, which handles departures and arrivals into the metropolitan area's major airports, instructed el Habashy to climb to "flight level 230" (meaning 23,000 feet) and contact New York's Air Route Traffic Control Center (ARTCC), also known in shorthand as "New York Center." Nine minutes later, an air traffic controller located at ARTCC's nondescript facility in Islip, Long Island, called on el Habashy and directed him to climb to flight level 330 and maintain Mach .80—609 miles per hour—for the long ocean crossing that was to have taken flight 990 almost 5,900 miles and about ten hours to its final destination at Cairo International Airport.

Within a few minutes of reaching cruising altitude, the relief first officer, Captain Gamil el Batouty, entered the flight deck and informed the command first officer, Adel Anwar, that he was being relieved. This was unusual. In keeping with standard EgyptAir and international procedures, flights of 990's duration carry two crews—a command crew consisting of a lead pilot and first officer and a relief crew with the same complement. The lead pilot and first officer are responsible for departure and arrival as well as the first third and last third of the flight.

El Batouty, whose training records revealed a pilot who struggled to achieve proficiency on the 767, was three hours early for his turn in the first officer's right seat.

Fourteen minutes after el Batouty took up his position on the flight deck, Ann Brennan, the New York Center controller, called on flight 990 as it departed the Atlantic sector:

> "EgyptAir 990 radar contact lost recycle transponder squawk one-seven-one-two."
> No answer.
> "EgyptAir 990 New York Center."
> Silence.

Brennan was concerned. Not only had she lost flight 990's transponder but also the primary radar targets on the aircraft. She immediately informed her supervisor that "something was wrong." The two veteran air traffic controllers then called on ARINC—a nonprofit corporation that airlines use to communicate with their aircraft in flight—for assistance: "Mike Sierra Romeo [MSR—EgyptAir's International Civil Aviation Organization airline designator] nine nine zero," called the ARINC operator, but neither el Habashy nor el Batouty replied.

Brennan and her colleague enlisted the help of their counterparts at Boston Center and the pilots of a Lufthansa 747 en route from Mexico City to Frankfurt. After calling EgyptAir 990, the Lufthansa pilot reported back to the New York Controller, "I am sorry there is no reply New York and on one-twenty-one-five we hear no emergency locator transmitter." Next, Brennan hailed "Huntress," the code word for Northeast Air Defense of the North American Aerospace Defense Command (NORAD). Made famous in movies like the 1983 teen drama *War Games*, starring Mathew Broderick and Ally Sheedy, NORAD is responsible for tracking everything that comes into or out of the airspace of the United States, Canada, and Mexico.

> "[Frequency] One-seven-one-two over Dovey [the "intersection" where aircraft begin transoceanic flight] should be maybe a little east of Dovey by now," Brennan informed the airman on duty at Huntress in Rome, New York.
> "Copy standby."
> [Pause]
> "New York. Huntress. Negative. I can't find him."

Brennan then asked Huntress to contact civil and military controllers in Canada for assistance. Her efforts were in vain.

A full twenty minutes before Brennan even placed her call to Huntress at 2:14 a.m., EgyptAir flight 990 had plunged into the Atlantic Ocean sixty miles southwest of Nantucket Island. All 217 passengers and crew were lost. What followed was for most Americans the standard ritual of airplane accidents: saturated media coverage, memorial services for the dead, and a news conference with a group of no-nonsense types declaring that it was too early to make any "determinations" but vowing to "get to the bottom of this" to ensure the safety of the "flying public." These were the investigators of the National Transportation Safety Board (NTSB), who would unwittingly play a central role in the ensuing drama of what happened to flight 990.

For Egyptians, the crash of flight 990 and the immediate aftermath was a tremendous shock. After all, eighty-nine Egyptian nationals, including thirty-three military officers, most of whom were in the United States on official Ministry of Defense business, perished in the crash. In Cairo, the state-run media, much like U.S. networks, focused on the victims' families, broadcasting loops of distraught husbands, wives, fathers, daughters, aunts, uncles, and children. Interviews with the crews' families figured prominently in the coverage. A kind of pall was cast over normally noisy, hectic, lively Cairo. The entire country mourned. The impossibility of a proper burial injected additional pain into an already unbearable situation.

With one hundred Americans also killed, a sense of shared anguish emerged as Egyptian and U.S. officials participated in a memorial service for the dead in Newport, Rhode Island. Yet the palpable grief of the Egyptians soon morphed into collective anger at the United States, specifically the NTSB and Boeing. After the investigators' initial review of flight 990's cockpit voice recorder, they suspected that Gamil el Batouty's early relief of command co-pilot Adel Anwar was an ominous indication of what happened to flight 990.

On the garbled tape, U.S. government Arabic translators discovered that shortly after Captain el Habashy excused himself from the flight deck to go to the lavatory at 1:42 a.m., el Batouty seemed to declare, "I place my fate in the hands of God"—which, to some, indicates a Muslim preparing himself for imminent death—moments before the 767 began a 40 degree dive (most airline passengers never experience anything more than a 5 degree angle of descent). The tapes also indicated that the first officer repeated the phrase a number of times and shut down the plane's massive engines during critical moments when

Captain el Habashy returned to the cockpit and desperately tried to reverse the jet's fall. An NTSB leak to the American press produced speculation that el Batouty committed suicide, taking 216 souls with him in the process.

The news of the NTSB's theory only two weeks after the tragedy was taken in Egypt as an American assault on Egypt's national pride. The Egyptian press, columnists, pundits, and government officials expressed dismay that the investigators had barely begun their investigation when they seemed to have settled on an explanation without considering alternative theories. They also emphasized that the phrase el Batouty allegedly uttered before the 767 began its precipitous drop, *tawakilt al Allah*, is often used when, for example, Arabs start a car and is meant in a way that God should look after them. As a result, the Egyptians rejected the hasty conclusion that Gamil el Batouty, a former military pilot, flight instructor, and long-serving first officer for Egypt's flag carrier was responsible for the crash. Experts informed viewers of Egyptian television that it was impossible for el Batouty to have taken his own life because he was a good Muslim and suicide is *haram* (forbidden) in Islam.

The fact that TWA flight 880 exploded mysteriously off Long Island on its way to Paris in July 1996—after which the American media falsely speculated that Islamist extremists brought the plane down— and that a Swissair MD-11 had crashed in the Canadian Maritimes after experiencing a fire in the cockpit in August 1998 led Egyptians to alternative theories about what caused EgyptAir 990 to fall from the sky. These conjectures included claims that the U.S. military destroyed the plane with a surface-to-air missile; Jewish groups allegedly controlling New York City conspired to have the plane brought down; and Israel's foreign intelligence service, Mossad, planted a bomb aboard the aircraft. Peace treaty aside, the hostility many Egyptians feel toward Israel, the widely held notion that Israel harbors aggressive intentions toward Egypt, and the fact that military officers were among the victims made an Israeli hit entirely possible for many Egyptians. When some months later an Alaska Airlines flight crashed off the West Coast of the United States and it was disclosed that investigators were focusing in on a malfunction in the plane's rear stabilizers, Egyptian commentators were shocked. They argued that the NTSB's focus on defective equipment in the Alaska Airlines crash but not in the EgyptAir case was proof positive that the U.S. government was engaged in a conspiracy to smear Egypt and the national air carrier. But why?

The answer came from more responsible pundits and Egyptian government officials. They argued that the loss of flight 990 was the result of mechanical failure. They also implied that the el Batouty suicide hypothesis was part of an effort to protect the plane's manufacturer, Boeing, and American insurance companies from the liability claims that were sure to come with the result of an objective crash investigation. From the start, the Egyptian government argued that a fair inquiry would reveal that there was something inherently wrong with the design of the 767 that made the crash of flight 990 possible. The Egyptians went so far as to hire a group of retired NTSB officials and former pilots to press their case. In the end, the NTSB's final report on EgyptAir 990 concluded in eerily anodyne language: "The probable cause of the EgyptAir flight 990 accident is the airplane's departure from normal cruise flight and subsequent impact with the Atlantic Ocean as a result of the relief first officer's flight control inputs. The reason for the relief first officer's actions was not determined." Still, Egyptians firmly believe that a mechanical failure in one of the plane's critical systems was the cause, whereas Americans have long concluded that el Batouty downed the plane intentionally.

On a quiet August afternoon six years later, over tuna sandwiches and Diet Cokes in the cafeteria of Princeton University's famed Woodrow Wilson School of Public and International Affairs, retired U.S. ambassador to Egypt, Daniel Kurtzer, described the aftermath of the EgyptAir crash as the most challenging moment of his three years as ambassador in Cairo. This was telling for a man who took up his post amid a cascade of invective aimed at him by the Egyptian press for his adherence to Orthodox Judaism and coincided with the outbreak of the al-Aqsa intifada, which strained Egypt-Israel relations. Kurtzer's Egyptian counterpart, Nabil Fahmy, also identified the crash of flight 990 as the most difficult episode of his tenure in Washington. Almost eleven years later to the day of the crash, sitting in a comfortable chair in his office, now the dean of the American University in Cairo's School of Global Affairs and Public Policy, Fahmy reflected on the grim aftermath of the disaster. Fahmy, who had arrived in Washington only two weeks before the crash, had not even presented his diplomatic credentials to the Clinton administration when news came of the disaster. He remembered how difficult it was for him because he had no answers for devastated relatives. The ambassador was as helpless as they were to make sense of what happened to flight 990. It did not help that within days of the Newport memorial service, Cairo and Washington began a war of words over EgyptAir 990's fate. Although both Kurtzer and Fahmy were clearly relaying what had been upsetting and difficult personal circumstances, the events surrounding the EgyptAir disaster were a metaphor for U.S.-Egypt relations—not the crash per se, but the aftermath—in which two governments were clearly talking past each other. The situation was only made worse by the fact that, despite three decades of partnership and cooperation, the United States had become, unwittingly, a negative factor in Egypt's domestic political struggles.

When Washington and Cairo established strategic ties after the 1979 Egypt-Israel peace treaty, there was a sense of hope and promise. Through the development of Egypt, the United States would go a long way toward constructing a stable, prosperous, and peaceful region that was unwelcome to communism and the Soviet Union. Peeling off the Egyptians was a palliative for a Washington that had been diminished by the events of the previous decade. It proved in part that, after Watergate, the ignominious withdrawal from Vietnam, the Iranian hostage crisis, and the Soviet invasion of Afghanistan, global power and prestige was not shifting inexorably in favor of Moscow. Moving Egypt into the Western camp was also a boost for the typically (even clichéd) American "can-do" spirit. After all, the relationship may have been based on grand strategic considerations, but helping the Egyptians build a successful society would buttress the geopolitics.

More than twenty-five years after the fact, former Ambassador Nicholas Veliotes is still excited. Now long retired, dressed in a black leather bomber jacket and jeans, at eighty-two he has not lost his step. Veliotes relishes recounting his experiences in Egypt and at the State Department. Ronald Reagan appointed him to represent the United States in Egypt when the American military and economic assistance program to Cairo was ramping up in 1983. One of the first things Veliotes did after arriving in Cairo was ask the Egyptians what they needed. An old State Department hand who had served in several senior positions in Washington, as well as postings in India, Europe, and the Middle East, Veliotes wanted to make good on Washington's commitments. The Egyptians responded with a request that would warm the hearts of the coldest of Cold Warriors: Could the United States replace the Soviet designed and manufactured turbines for the Aswan High Dam? Veliotes happily passed on the request to Washington and, when the Soviet equipment was towed up the Nile on its way to the scrap heap, the symbolism was too much for him to resist.

The ambassador recalls that he brought the embassy staff out to the banks of the river to appreciate the occasion. With a broad smile and deep laugh, Veliotes remembers that his staff cheered wildly as the Soviet turbines floated by.

Swapping out Soviet equipment for American technology was just the beginning, though. Eventually, the U.S. Embassy in Cairo grew to be the largest American diplomatic installation in the world (before the behemoth in post-war Iraq dwarfed it) due to the large Agency for International Development (AID) mission in Egypt. Veliotes recalls that much of the embassy staff was working on AID projects. American largesse contributed much to Egypt's infrastructure, agricultural development, and economic progress, but something was amiss. Perhaps it was American naiveté or a fervent belief in the positive use of American power but, as time went on, Egyptians raised questions about this relationship and what, exactly, it meant.

To be sure, people like Mohammed Hassanein Heikal, Saad el Shazly, and others broke with Anwar Sadat early on over what they perceived as his ill-conceived willingness to throw Egypt's lot in with the Americans when it came to dealing with the Israeli challenge. Yet the concern went deeper than tactical and strategic questions related to the disposition of the Sinai Peninsula. By the late 1980s and early 1990s, the American project in Egypt must have seemed to some Egyptians similar to earlier French and British efforts in Egypt, right down to the AID advisors nestled into various government ministries. The Aswan High Dam turbines, sewage systems, communications networks, rural electrification, and road building to which Washington contributed were of course different from Napoleon's printing press or Cromer's agricultural reforms. Yet, only thirty years after a coup that was organized largely around pent up nationalist demands, another global power was on the shores of Egypt, armed with the awesome technology of the West to unlock Egypt's modernization.

Against the backdrop of the broad sweep of Egypt's experience in the twentieth century, the budding relationship with the United States did not make sense. After all, it cut against the grain of the ideas that had animated Egyptian politics for the better part of the preceding one hundred years, whether it was Islamic reformism, social justice, anti-Zionism, Islamist activism, or Egyptian nationalism, all interrelated in a variety of dynamic ways. As a result, the American effort in Egypt was bound to have an impact on the basic question Egyptians had been asking themselves since well before the July 1952 coup—"Who are we and who do we want to be?"

AIDING EGYPT

For all of its exaltation of the coup, the nationalization of the Suez Canal, the positive neutralism, Arab nationalism, and the Crossing—the mythology of Egyptian nationalism—Cairo has long been dependent on foreign assistance. Within weeks of the Free Officers' takeover, American officials in Cairo identified a range of technical areas in which Washington could provide assistance to Egypt. The new Egyptian government under Prime Minister Ali Mahir responded favorably to the U.S. Embassy's overture. He requested that the United States assist Cairo in developing plans for Egypt's economic development. Washington contracted with the engineering firm, Arthur D. Little, to do the study, recommending that Cairo undertake projects that would increase Egypt's manufacturing base, improve its balance of trade, and contribute to public health.[2]

Although nothing came of Little's industrialization proposals, the United States went ahead with smaller-scale projects like the ill-fated "Poultry Improvement Project," which, through the import of one hundred thousand chicks to Egypt, was intended to increase and improve the quality of Egyptian egg production. After three years, the experiment came to an end when disease devastated the American hens.[3] While the Poultry Improvement Project was in its final throes, U.S. Ambassador James Caffery offered the Free Officers $40 million in aid to be split evenly between economic and military aid. The Egyptians were hoping for as much as $100 million. The $60 million difference between Washington and Cairo disappointed the Egyptians. Furthermore, the conditions on the military assistance angered the Free Officers. The Mutual Security Assistance Act of 1954 required that Cairo agree to use U.S.-made weapons for defensive or internal security purposes only and that an American advisory team supervise the use of the equipment.[4] The Egyptians refused these conditions and ultimately settled for increased economic assistance. Cairo also resented Washington's effort to tie military assistance to a resolution of the conflict with Israel. The difficulty of dealing with Washington and the conditions the Eisenhower administration placed on its military aid contrasted sharply with the Soviets. Once Cairo and Moscow came to an agreement, the Czech arms deal of 1955 proceeded swiftly and without onerous political conditions.[5]

After Egypt accepted military assistance from the Soviet bloc, Washington's aid to Cairo was halved to approximately $33 million. The vast majority of this help came under Public Law 480 (PL 480), or the "Food for Peace" program in which developing countries could purchase surplus American agricultural products in their own currencies.[6] Under the provisions of PL 480 Title I, the Egyptians purchased about $13 million worth of goods in Egyptian pounds. Those funds were then "funneled back to Egypt in the form of long-term development loans at low interest rates."[7] This contrasted with Title II, which directed surplus U.S. agricultural goods to relief agencies. By 1960, the PL 480 program accounted for two-thirds of Egypt's grain imports, and three years later Egypt outstripped all other PL 480 participants, becoming the largest consumer of American food aid on a per capita basis.[8] The increasingly PL 480-based relationship between Washington and Cairo reflected the Kennedy administration's view that (1) working with "neutral" countries was preferable to letting these countries just fall into Moscow's orbit, and (2) the process of negotiating short-term food aid agreements would improve U.S.-Egypt ties and concomitantly keep Cairo out of the Soviet camp. The Egyptians liked the program, but the six-month deals made it difficult for their own economic planning, and in 1962 they convinced Washington to agree to a $432 million food aid program that would cover 1963 through 1965.[9]

The food aid program was not entirely without its problems, however. The combination of Egypt's foray into Yemen in 1962 and its widely suspected military buildup led Israel's supporters in the Congress and the government of Saudi Arabia to question the continuation of assistance to Cairo. In the spring of 1963, a report by the Senate Government Operations Committee recommended that additional food aid to Egypt be made conditional on a settlement in Yemen and a halt to Cairo's military expansion. The following November, Congress passed an amendment to the foreign assistance act—clearly aimed at Egypt—that would deny or cut off food aid to any country that threatened other countries also receiving American assistance.[10] Despite the legislation, the food aid continued to flow to Egypt. At the same time, in order to appease Congressional critics and supporters of Israel, the Kennedy administration committed to delivering HAWK surface-to-air missiles to the Israelis.[11]

President Lyndon Johnson took a considerably tougher line on Egyptian aid than his predecessor. After all, Egypt was regarded as a threat to American allies, was a military client of the Soviet Union, and was pursuing socialist-inspired economic policies, but nevertheless received the vast bulk of its food aid from the United States. Although both the House and Senate sought to punish the Egyptians, the president sought to leverage aid to alter Egyptian behavior. In 1965, Johnson informed the Egyptians that the final disbursement of food aid from the multiyear agreement that the Kennedy administration signed in 1962 would be suspended. This came on the heels of an increase in anti-American rhetoric coming out of Egypt and the torching of the United States Information Service Library in Cairo. Johnson's move elicited a positive response from Nasser, who agreed to pay a portion of the library's reconstruction and resumed negotiations with Riyadh over the Yemen war. In turn, Johnson released the last tranche of food aid. Washington's leverage did not last, however. Although the Egyptians continued to lobby for food aid, by 1967 they determined it was no longer worth the trouble. That year, Egypt received $11.8 million in PL 480 Title II aid and an additional $800,000 for a development-assistance loan. Over the course of the next five years, assistance to Egypt totaled a rather modest $2.3 million, the bulk of which was a development-assistance loan.

Aid to Egypt resumed after the October 1973 war, when Washington and Cairo were looking for ways to improve relations (the Egyptians had broken off relations on June 9, 1967). When Egypt and Israel signed the Sinai I accord in 1974, Washington transferred $85 million for the reconstruction of the Canal Zone, providing a boost to bilateral relations.[12] In early 1974, President Nixon requested and received authorization from Congress for $250 million worth of development projects in Egypt. As a result, the U.S. Agency for International Development began its more than three-decade-long (and counting) effort to promote economic and social development in Egypt.[13] Indeed, beginning in 1974, the United States transferred not only food but also consumer goods, raw materials, development aid for reconstruction projects, and technical assistance to Egypt. By 1976–1977, total U.S. assistance to Egypt was about $1 billion a year. On the eve of the peace treaty with Israel in March 1979, aid to Egypt was greater than that to all of the rest of Africa and Latin America.[14] With the signing of the Camp David Accords and the 1979 peace treaty with Israel, the United States added a military component to the aid relationship. Initially, military assistance was set at $1.5 billion over three years in a mix of loans and grants, but it quickly grew. By 1985, the Reagan administration converted all the military loans to grants that exceeded $1 billion, and within two years, military assistance would settle at the now familiar $1.3 billion annually.

For its part, the AID mission in Egypt was charged with administering economic support fund grants that in the mid-1980s grew almost as large as the military assistance package, topping out at $1.065 billion in 1986. American assistance was divided among infrastructure projects and technical assistance that included agricultural improvements, public health, and social work, as well as a program to help Egypt import commodities that would contribute to the country's development.[15] By 1986, as Egypt continued to experience economic difficulties, the focus of AID's mission changed. Program and project-related assistance was replaced with a broader effort to assist Egypt's transition to a free-market economy. This policy change coincided with the Reagan administration's effort to use the economic support as a lever to encourage Egypt to undertake reforms.[16] President Mubarak resented the fact that aid to Israel was not used in the same manner. Indeed, parity with Israel is an issue that has been an irritant for Egyptian officials since aid to Cairo and Jerusalem were linked after the peace treaty. The Egyptian economic assistance package has always been considerably less than Israel's—with the exception of 1985 and 1986—even though Egypt's per capita GDP is far less than that of Israel. Of more significance, however, is the way the aid to the two countries is disbursed. In Israel's case, aid was distributed quarterly directly from the U.S. Treasury to an account located at the Bank of Israel—the Israeli central bank. Moreover, "there were no stipulations as to how the assistance was to be used."[17] In contrast, Egypt's economic support funds were distributed slowly through AID and based on mutually agreed-upon projects under the supervision of agency personnel.[18] AID's efforts in the 1980s carried over into the following decade with a continued emphasis on agricultural reform, deregulation, and the development of market-economy oriented institutions.

After the terrorist attacks on New York and Washington in September 2001, the focus of AID programs placed more emphasis on democracy and good governance programs. This policy shift coincided with the establishment of the Middle East Partnership Initiative (MEPI, discussed in detail later), which was created to promote democratic change in the Arab world. MEPI's programs, in contrast to those of AID, "are generally shorter-term and more focused on addressing specific challenges that must be overcome in order for AID's longer-term development to succeed."[19] According to the AID's own inspector general, this success has been difficult to achieve. A 2009 audit of the agency's democracy and governance activities in Egypt found that it had achieved only limited success during the prior year. Furthermore, AID's good governance and democracy programs suffered from lack of cooperation and support from the Egyptian government.[20]

President Mubarak's resistance to any meaningful political reform in the 2000s, along with concerns about the security of Egypt's border with Gaza after Israel's withdrawal from that area in 2005, changed the nature of the debate in Washington about aid to Egypt. In the twenty-five years between 1979 and 2004, members of Congress, pro-Israel groups, and, most importantly the Egyptians themselves, regarded Cairo's package of economic and military assistance as sacrosanct, tied as it is to the Egypt-Israel peace treaty. That link, however, is informal, and although widely regarded as the price Washington has paid to ensure Egypt-Israel peace, there is nothing in the Camp David Accords or the actual treaty that stipulates the provision of American assistance to the signatories.[21] Three decades later, aid to Egypt had become the subject of much discussion and criticism. Observers from across the American political spectrum, including prominent members of Congress, columnists, Middle East policy analysts, human rights advocates, and democracy promoters questioned the purpose and efficacy of Egypt's aid package. Some called for cutting the aid altogether as a punitive measure for the authoritarian nature of the Egyptian regime, the anti-Semitism and anti-Zionism of the official press, and a perception of Cairo's hostility to a range of U.S. policies in the Middle East, including Washington's approach to the peace process and the military operations in Iraq and Afghanistan. Others called for a reconfiguration of the aid package to address Egypt's needs more effectively. In 1998, the United States, Egypt, and Israel initialed a deal called the "Glide Path Agreement" that would reduce economic aid over the course of the following decade. The idea grew out of a speech that Israeli Prime Minister Benjamin Netanyahu gave before a joint session of Congress on July 10, 1996. In his remarks, Netanyahu committed his government to "begin the long-term process of gradually reducing the level of . . . economic assistance to Israel."[22] Egypt became a party to the agreement by dint of the informal linkage between the two countries' aid packages. In Israel's case, economic support would be wound down completely, given the country's advanced economy and per capita GDP of approximately $18,000 at the time.[23] Egypt's aid would be tapered down by about 5 percent a year until bottoming out at $400 million.

Less than a decade after the Egyptians, Israelis, and Americans agreed to the slow reduction in economic aid, the late Representative Tom Lantos, a Democrat from the San Francisco Bay area, who for many years was the senior-ranking Democrat on what was then called the House International Relations Committee and was founding chair of the House Caucus on Human Rights, proposed H. AMDT (House

Amendment) 694 of H.R. 4818, the Consolidated Appropriations Act of 2005.[24] The Lantos amendment, as the proposal came to be known, sought to shift $325 million from Egypt's military assistance to the country's economic support funds. Lantos reasoned that Egypt did not face any security threats, and thus the kind of military support that Cairo traditionally received was largely unnecessary. At the same time, Lantos argued that the vast reservoir of Egyptians were poor and would be better served if Washington's largesse was spent on promoting economic development.

The amendment provoked anger in Cairo. Egypt's state-owned press portrayed the proposed shift in aid as an overall cut in American assistance that necessarily put Egypt's security at risk and as the work of the Zionist lobby. The editor in chief of the state-owned daily, *al Akhbar*, excoriated Lantos and his amendment: "There is no doubt that this Zionist fanatic who supports Israeli aggression knows no shame, personified by his anti-Egyptian stand in Congress a few days ago. He demands transforming American military assistance to Egypt—less than half of what Israel receives—into economic aid in order to deprive Egypt of the capabilities of defending itself."[25] Gamal Kamal, the military correspondent for *al Gumhuriya* informed his readers, "During my time listening to a hearing of the committee on foreign operations in the House of Representatives last month concerning bilateral Egypt-U.S. relations it was apparent and clear that Democratic representative Tom Lantos supports the state of Israel's campaign against Egypt."[26] *Al Ahram*'s English-language edition acknowledged that the American Israel Public Affairs Committee did not support Lantos' measure, but nevertheless blamed it on the "extreme pro-Israel lobby."[27] The Nasserist weekly, *al Arabi*, ran an article titled, "The Enemy of Egypt Demands Decreasing the Size and Armament of the Egyptian Military" which identified Congressman Lantos as that enemy.[28] In Washington, an ad hoc coalition of Egyptian diplomats, hired lobbyists, members of Congress, who held President Mubarak and Egypt in high esteem, and the Pentagon went into action against the Lantos amendment. They pursued what one participant in the effort described as "a classic Camp David strategy," arguing that Egypt had taken a courageous stand for peace, was a critical player in Israeli-Palestinian negotiations, and that the country and its armed forces were a force for stability in a turbulent region.

In the end, Cairo's efforts paid off. The Lantos amendment was defeated, but in what should have been a wake-up call to the Egyptians, 131 members voted for it. Moreover, Congressman Lantos's proposal forced Egypt's leadership to confront two competing political interests at home as they worked to rescue the full package of military assistance in Washington. The first issue was the ever-important matter of the military. Since he came to power, President Mubarak had been nothing if not scrupulous about ensuring the armed forces' annual allotment of $1.3 billion. Until 2007, U.S. military aid to Egypt was pegged to Israel's assistance package based on a ratio that would give the Egyptians two-thirds of whatever Israel received.[29] In practice, it is more complicated than that, because both countries routinely augment aid packages with supplemental requests and special arrangements or programs. For example, the Egyptians receive Excess Defense Articles from the Pentagon that can be worth hundreds of millions of dollars. Since 2000, Egypt has been permitted to deposit its military assistance in an account held at the Federal Reserve Bank of New York, where it draws interest.[30] Still, the 2:3 ratio had been the general rule, and, as a result, President Mubarak zealously guarded the military component of Egypt's overall assistance package as a principle of bilateral relations. Had the Lantos amendment passed, it would have put Mubarak in an extremely awkward position with the senior command, which had come to expect American aid as a matter of course. Indeed, the Egyptian officers regard the aid not as American generosity but rather as their money.[31]

Second, the government had to contend with the opposition, which was hostile to the United States and its aid program. The Muslim Brotherhood, Nasserists, leftists, and even liberals disliked the relationship. The first three were opposed to the strategic relationship on the grounds that it compromised Egypt's sovereignty and undermined its power. Liberals opposed the relationship even though they shared many of the beliefs that animate American democracy because they regarded U.S. support as a critical pillar of Egypt's authoritarian political system.

Consequently, the Lantos amendment and the government's efforts to defeat it provided a political opportunity for the opposition to call attention to the contradictions of the bilateral relationship. With no way to reconcile the two positions, the government pursued the Lantos amendment on two parallel tracks. At home, it struck a stridently nationalist tone, and in Washington, it lobbied furiously against the proposal. The fact that Lantos was an ardent supporter of Israel made it easier for Cairo and the state-affiliated press to ramp up the domestic indignation. Although the Egyptians ultimately prevailed, it was hard to ignore the irony of staking out a nationalist position at home while working assiduously five thousand miles away to ensure the continued flow of American largesse.

Although the defeat of H. AMDT 694 meant that Cairo's military assistance remained safe for the moment, it no longer seemed so assured. Since the Lantos amendment was offered, there were additional efforts—some more serious than others—to reduce Egypt's military aid where there had been virtually none in the previous two decades.[32] Two years after Lantos was defeated, a new, serious threat to Egypt's assistance package arose when Representative David Obey (D-WI)—the ranking member of the House Appropriations Committee and long regarded as one of Egypt's most reliable friends on Capitol Hill—sponsored an amendment to H.R. 5522 (Department of State, Foreign Operations, and Related Programs Appropriations Act, 2007) that would reduce Egypt's military assistance package by $200 million. The funds, which were to come out of that part of the assistance package used for the purchase of new equipment, would remain available for Egypt, but not until Congress specifically released them. On offering the amendment, Obey justified his position based on what he described as "backsliding on municipal elections, and extension of emergency laws, repression of judicial freedoms and a crackdown on demonstrations and rallies."[33]

Congressional support for the decrease also represented growing frustration with Cairo's inability or unwillingness to crack down on smuggling across the Egyptian-Gaza frontier. After Israel withdrew its settlements and military personnel from the Gaza Strip in September 2005, after thirty-eight years of occupation, a group of 750 specially trained Egyptian paramilitary police were deployed to provide security along the seven-mile border. Although illicit trade between Gazans and Egyptian residents of Sinai was nothing new, the problem became particularly worrisome after the extremist group Hamas won the Palestinian Legislative Council elections in January 2006. The Israelis and the Bush administration were deeply concerned that continued smuggling across the border would further enable Hamas to wage a violent campaign against Israel, something that had been ongoing in the form of rocket attacks on Israeli towns adjacent to Gaza since January 2001.

The amendment's description of Egypt's deteriorating political environment was entirely accurate, and Congress' concern about Israeli security is well known. At the same time, it was also understood among Capitol Hill watchers that Obey was responding to a particularly difficult meeting with Egypt's foreign minister, Ahmad Aboul Gheit. The Egyptian diplomat had risen through the ranks, serving as Egypt's permanent representative at the United Nations for five years before being tapped for the Foreign Ministry's top job in 2004, beating out his rival, Nabil Fahmy, for the position. Aboul Gheit had a reputation for being a hard worker, often boasting that he was at his desk by 7:00 a.m., well before the more relaxed Cairo officialdom made their way into the office. At the same time, however, the foreign minister had an off-putting demeanor. Eager to establish intellectual bona fides with his interlocutors, he often came across as arrogant, dismissive, and patronizing—an odd combination of qualities for the person charged with leading Egypt's diplomatic efforts. When Obey asked Aboul Gheit about the status of Ayman Nour—whose unhappy circumstances had become an important symbol in the Bush administration's effort to promote political change in Egypt—the foreign minister's less diplomatic qualities surfaced as he proceeded to lecture the congressman about Egyptian sovereignty and law. Obey was reportedly deeply offended, having asked about Nour not so that he could engage in a chorus of indignation over Cairo's handling of the activist, but rather so he could learn how to help quiet that criticism. Like the Lantos amendment before it, Obey's amendment failed by voice vote in the committee with only one of his colleagues, Representative Stenny Hoyer of Maryland, in support.

By the time Congresswoman Nita Lowey of New York introduced the Consolidated Appropriations Act, 2008 (H.R. 2764) in June 2007, the case against the Egyptians was even stronger, as Mubarak and his internal security services had continued to brutalize the regime's opponents throughout the previous year. In January 2006, Captain Islam Nabih and noncommissioned officer Reda Fathi were convicted and sentenced to three years in prison for beating and sodomizing a microbus driver named Imad el Kabir with a broom handle. El Kabir's crime? He was taken into police custody after intervening in an altercation between the police and a family member. If it were not for the sheer arrogance of the officers and YouTube, however, Nabih and Fathi would never have been brought to justice. The officers videotaped their misdeeds and sent it to el Kabir's family, neighbors, and co-workers, in an effort both to humiliate their victim and send a warning about crossing the police. Yet the video ultimately found its way to the blogger and human rights activist, Wael Abbas, who posted it on the Internet in November 2006, where the footage horrified viewers around the world.

The prosecution of the officers in the el Kabir case was nevertheless an exception. In another incident that achieved international notoriety, in May 2006 the Egyptian police raped Mohammed el Sharkawi with a cardboard tube. Unlike the Imad el Kabir situation, there was a political angle to the hubris and cruelty of the police in the Sharkawi case. Sharkawi is a well-known blogger and political activist whose campaign against torture is a central feature of his social action. Although there is video evidence against Sharkawi's tormentors, the Egyptian government never took any action against the policemen involved.

Congress was also responding to the iron-fisted methods the Egyptian state used against judges and their supporters who, throughout the spring of 2006, took to the streets to protest for judicial independence. The catalyst for what would become a dramatic confrontation between members of the judiciary's professional association, the Judges Club, and the Egyptian police was the arrest and indictment of two reformist judges—Hisham al Bastawisy and Mahmoud Mekky—who publicly declared that irregularities and fraud had marred the People's Assembly elections of November-December 2005.

The allegations of justices al Bastawisy and Mekky were a blow to the Egyptians, who had been touting an ambitious political reform program during the previous eighteen months. The People's Assembly elections were to be a showcase of how far and how fast the Egyptians had come toward the goals of what the NDP's supposed reformers had been peddling. Yet, for all their efforts, including a Potemkin-village-like room at party headquarters stuffed with earnest young staffers at computer terminals tracking exit polls, the elections were like most other Egyptian elections—rife with irregularities, violence, and the heavy hand of the security services. At a moment when the United States was paying close attention to Egypt's internal politics, the allegations of official duplicity from two respected jurists were deeply troubling to the Mubarak regime. In response, the judges were promptly arrested. Ultimately, Mekky was acquitted, and al Bastawisy was censured. Government spokesmen and Egyptian diplomats sought to portray the entire episode as an internal struggle within the judiciary, which in one sense it was. Mekky, al Bastawisy, and their allies were essentially calling out their colleagues who were all too willing to do the regime's bidding—counter to the best traditions of the Egyptian judiciary. At the core of the conflict was, however, the open secret of the Egyptian leadership's efforts to politicize Egypt's judges, thereby ensuring control of the judiciary.

Like Congressman Obey's amendment the previous year, H.R. 2764 would withhold $200 million from Egypt's military assistance until the secretary of state could verify that the Egyptians (1) enacted a law that protected the independence of the judiciary, (2) undertook police training to "curb police abuses," and (3) destroyed the smuggling tunnels that led from Egypt to Gaza.[34] In a conference committee charged with reconciling the House and Senate versions of the spending bill, legislators agreed to cut $100 million from Egypt's military assistance. The measure became part of Public Law 110–161, the Consolidated Appropriations Act, FY 2008.[35] Congress' successful effort to dock a portion of Egypt's aid produced yet another uproar in Cairo, but the Bush administration ultimately came to the rescue. Secretary of State Condoleezza Rice used what is called a "national security waiver," citing the adverse effects cuts to Egypt's aid would have on American interests in the Middle East to restore the funds.

Efforts to slash Egypt's assistance package reflected the fact that, as time has gone on, the dominant image of the country in Washington was no longer a triumphant Anwar Sadat grasping the hands of Israeli Prime Minister Menachem Begin and President Jimmy Carter after signing the Egypt-Israel peace treaty, but rather of a sixty-something Saad Eddin Ibrahim in his courtroom cage or the paramilitary Central Security Forces beating demonstrators, or haunting photos of Mohammed Atta, the Egyptian ringleader of the September 2001 attacks on New York and Washington. As a result, the Egyptians had few, if any, champions left in official Washington. Congress no longer saw Mubarak's Egypt as an asset, the State Department and Cairo were at odds over human rights, and while the Pentagon placed great value on the Suez Canal and the logistical support the Egyptians extended to American forces in Iraq and Afghanistan, WikiLeaks documents revealed that it had reservations about the Egyptian military's unwillingness to modernize its doctrine or play a more active role in regional counterterrorism. Reportedly, there had been good cooperation between the American intelligence community and its Egyptian counterparts. Yet this hardly seemed like strong pillars on which to continue the aid relationship, a fact the Egyptians seemed slow to recognize in the last few years before the Mubarak regime's collapse.

In order to avoid future battles over aid, beginning in 2008, Cairo latched onto the idea of creating a jointly funded foundation—the Egyptians preferred calling it an "endowment"—that would take the place of the congressionally appropriated annual economic aid package. There is precedent for the establishment of foundations in countries that no longer have a need for direct bilateral aid. In the 1970s, for example, AID helped set up the Korea Development Institute and the Korean Institute of Science and Technology. Portugal and the United States established a binational organization called the Lusa-American Development Foundation with resources left over from AID's economic aid program in 1985. And in 1996, the Costa Rica-USA Foundation for Mutual Cooperation was established.

The idea for an American-Egyptian foundation arose as the ten-year Glide Path Agreement was coming to an end. According to the American ambassador at the time, Francis J. Ricciardone, the question facing officials in Washington and Cairo was: Now what? There had been no understandings between the two countries about what would happen when the agreement expired. In contrast, the Bush administration signed a Memorandum of Understanding with Israel in 2008 covering increases in military assistance through 2018. According to Ricciardone, the Egyptians initially wanted to seek an increase in economic aid, arguing that inflation had cut deeply into the overall value of the assistance. This was unrealistic to say the least. After congressional efforts to shift or withhold Egypt's military assistance, it should have been abundantly clear to Egyptian officials that Capitol Hill was in no mood to augment aid to Egypt.

Although Egypt was not popular among lawmakers, Ricciardone—along with many others—believed that Cairo remained critical to Washington's entire Middle East strategy. Once more, the debate about its aid package was hurting bilateral ties. A foundation would thus serve two purposes. First, it would eliminate the source of tension that the annual debate over the congressionally appropriated aid package had become. Second, it would phase out the economic support funds and ultimately end AID's mission in Egypt—something the Egyptians seemed to desire. Much to Ricciardone's surprise, the Egyptians initially hated the idea because it would have meant "graduating" from the aid program once and for all. As much as they railed about congressional efforts to build ever more conditionality into the aid package and USAID, the Egyptians were reluctant to go off the dole.

By 2009, the Egyptians eventually came around to the idea of a foundation-endowment, arguing to themselves that with the combination of a growing economy and a diminishing assistance program, which did not even cover the annual interest on Egypt's $4.2 billion debt to the United States, it was time to graduate and focus on trade, not aid.[36] In their about-face on the foundation, the Egyptians obviously saw the benefits of shielding themselves from congressional criticism. They also recognized that the proposal was perhaps the best way to continue collaborative projects on education, scientific research, and industrial research and development.[37] The Egyptians proposed funding the foundation beginning in 2011 with $350 million the bulk of which would come from the U.S. accounts that were already designated for Egypt and "an unspecified financial commitment from the Egyptian government."[38] Once funding was in place, an independent board of prominent Egyptians and Americans would be established to oversee the "Egyptian-American Friendship Foundation" as U.S. economic assistance was gradually phased out over a decade. Members of Congress were not enthusiastic about the idea because it meant appropriating funds while giving up their oversight responsibilities, an important form of leverage over the Egyptians. Still, in the Consolidated Appropriations Act for FY 2010, Congress included up to $50 million for the proposed endowment-foundation.[39]

The Obama administration expressed interest in the foundation-endowment idea, but not solely on Cairo's terms. Outside the endowment, during his first two years in office, President Obama supported the $1.3 billion military assistance package and requested that Congress appropriate $250 million in economic aid. Of that economic assistance, the administration requested $20 million for democracy and governance programs. Yet Congress believed that this amount was too low and in the funding legislation determined that "not less than $25 million shall be made available for democracy, human rights, and governance."[40] Even with Congress' directive, the $25 million that the Obama administration programmed represents less than half the amount the Bush administration spent in fiscal year 2008 on initiatives dedicated to building rule of law, protecting human rights, promoting good governance, encouraging political competition, and supporting civil society.[41] The Obama team justified the cuts on the grounds that Egypt could not absorb the higher levels of funding, though some democracy advocates argued that it reflected the president's general lack of interest in political change in Egypt and the Middle East in general. This was a matter of debate. While overall AID funding for democracy and good governance programs fell, the Obama administration increased funding for political reform initiatives through other State Department offices such as the Middle East Partnership Initiative (MEPI) and the Bureau for Democracy, Rights, and Labor. To outside observers this may have seemed like merely shifting money around, but MEPI could fund NGOs that were *not* registered with the Egyptian government unlike AID, which had to operate within stricter parameters that gave Cairo a say in which organizations the agency could fund. More generally, the administration ramped up its funding of the civil society sector—groups that are autonomous from the state that seek to advance a specific set of interests such as human rights, political freedoms, and religious tolerance, to name just three prominent examples—on the whole increasing funding from $9 million in fiscal year 2009 to $14 million the following year.[42]

During the late Mubarak period, the Egyptians regarded the linkage between its domestic political development and American assistance as a betrayal of the historic commitments made at the time of the Camp David Accords and the Egypt-Israel peace treaty. The January 25 revolution has, in a stunning twist of irony, likely saved and perhaps even enhanced the prospects for Egypt to continue receiving American assistance. Given the central role of the armed forces in rescuing the country from potential chaos during the uprising, it is unlikely that Washington will seek to alter the military component of the aid package. On the economic support side, despite the expressed desire of the Egyptian people to build a new political system on their own, Congress will likely want to support a democratic transition in Egypt through continued assistance to civil society groups devoted to forging a more open and liberal order.

THE TRILATERAL LOGIC OF BILATERAL RELATIONS

American assistance to Egypt, especially after its peace treaty with Israel, was traditionally viewed as an acknowledgement of Cairo's prestige and the special role it was to play in the Middle East. Whereas its power once derived, in part, from its capability to make war on Israel, after the accommodation with Israel, Egypt's influence was to be based on its ability to help expand the regional circle of peace. This was a goal both Egyptians and Americans shared, but there were also profound differences in the way they came to view the peace treaty and its consequences. In the West and the United States specifically, there is a narrative about the peace between Egypt and Israel that is not necessarily shared among Egyptians. To be sure, there are many who recognize the courage and vision required for President Anwar Sadat to go to Jerusalem in November 1977. They also recognize the benefits of peace. Egypt no longer bears the economic, political, and diplomatic burdens of being in a state of war with Israel. The human costs were great as well, as tens of thousands of Egyptians perished in the wars and skirmishes fought between May 14, 1948, and October 24, 1973, when the guns finally fell silent on the Egypt-Israel front.

For all the real benefits of peace, the treaty between Egypt and Israel is, in many ways, "orphaned."[43] It is hard for non-Egyptians, and non-Arabs, to grasp that while Camp David and the subsequent peace agreement are Cairo's greatest diplomatic triumphs, they are simultaneously its greatest shame. Supporters of Israel, successive American administrations, and other observers in the West have long decried the cold nature of relations between Israelis and Egyptians. Indeed, while Cairo and Jerusalem have good security coordination and maintain a $400 million volume of trade, and there are regularly scheduled flights between Cairo and Tel Aviv, relations have hardly developed in the way so many had hoped on March 26, 1979.[44] To be sure, there are a few bright spots, notably the establishment in 2004 of Qualified Industrial Zones (QIZs) in Egypt that provide Egyptian goods with preferential access to the American market so long as these products contain at least 8 percent Israeli content. For example, a button made in Israel sewed onto an Egyptian-manufactured shirt would qualify for export to the United States under the terms of the QIZ agreement. These zones have been a success, generating an estimated $1 billion in revenues for the 717 companies that take part, but the QIZs are an exception to a relationship that is, while peaceful and formally normalized, also mistrustful and unfriendly. Set against a close reading of Egyptian history, however, Egypt's ties with Israel cannot be anything but distant.

For many Egyptians, including intellectuals, government officials, and ordinary people, Zionism was—and remains—widely regarded as a version of Western colonialism and thus a direct threat to Egypt. Nasser articulated this view in his *Philosophy of the Revolution*, which was written after the July 1952 coup, when he wrote: "[W]hen the Palestine crisis began [in 1948], I was utterly convinced that the fighting in Palestine was not taking place on foreign soil, nor was our participation going beyond the requirements of simple friendship. It was a duty made obligatory by the necessity of self-defense."[45] Once more, many Egyptians neither recognize the historic Jewish attachment to Palestine nor Zionism as a legitimate movement of national liberation. In the Egyptian narrative, Britain midwifed, France fostered, and the United States nurtured Israel all in an effort to split the region and dominate its resources. In this way, the Palestinian struggle against Jewish statehood was part and parcel of Egypt's own encounter with European penetration in the late nineteenth and first half of the twentieth centuries. In essence, the Egyptians and Palestinians were battling the same foreign forces intent on dividing and exploiting the Middle East. Although the British and French retreated from the region long ago, Israel remains. From the Egyptian perspective, it is a colonial outpost undeterred in its ambitions, due largely to the patronage of the United States.

Against the backdrop of these views of Zionism and the nature of Israel, Egypt's peace with Israel is hardly heroic or courageous (or any other terms of admiration Western observers have appended to it). Rather, in a bout of recklessness that came to characterize his presidency, Sadat sacrificed the Palestinian cause, Egyptian honor, and Cairo's power for very little. The fanfare of the treaty and the reverence for Sadat cannot hide the fact that for many in Egypt it was little more than an Israeli and American ruse. After all, since the treaty was signed, Israel invaded Lebanon twice (1982 and 2006)—and stayed there for almost two decades in between the two conflicts—in addition to having numerous border skirmishes and limited incursions; attacked Iraq; bombed Syria; extended its laws to the Golan Heights; built 135 settlements in the West Bank and Gaza Strip; declared Jerusalem "complete and united"; and killed or jailed untold numbers of Palestinians, including women and children.[46] All the while, Egypt, the most powerful Arab state, stood on the sidelines. Cairo protested lamely at the United Nations, expressed concern at the State Department, and demarched Israeli diplomats, but was otherwise powerless to confront Israel's predatory policies for one reason and one reason only: to ensure the flow of American aid to Egypt's coffers. To Egyptian observers, while the treaty constrained Cairo and made it impossible for the Arabs to go to war with Israel, it had rather the opposite effect on Israeli behavior. No longer unduly concerned with its southwestern border, Israel was free to pursue its policies with virtual impunity.

It was mid-morning in Cairo and Ismail Sabri Abdallah—first vice president, chair of the Institute of National Planning, and minister of planning under Sadat—sat behind his desk at the offices of the Third World Forum and engaged in a wide-ranging discussion of Egyptian politics. Although clearly getting older (this was some years before his death in 2006), Abdallah was profoundly charismatic and illuminating. When the conversation turned to foreign policy, the matter of Israel inevitably dominated. He saw the Egyptian relationship with the Israelis as a function of American global hegemony. This was hardly surprising. Abdallah was an unreconstructed Marxist seemingly unfazed by the fall of communism in Central and Eastern Europe, as well as the countries that were the Soviet Union. For all his opposition to the United States and Sadat, after breaking from the president in April 1975, Abdallah was entirely matter of fact about the logic behind the famous trip to Jerusalem, Camp David, and the peace treaty: "If we [Egypt] wanted to have a good relationship with the United States, we needed to spend the night in Tel Aviv." This characterization of the Egypt-Israel relationship may seem crude in light of the wistful romance surrounding the Camp David era, but Abdallah was entirely correct.

Before his visit to Jerusalem in November 1977, Sadat believed that Egypt could enjoy relations with the United States commensurate with those between Israel and the United States, but only after the Egyptians came to terms with the Israelis. Indeed, William B. Quandt, President Jimmy Carter's senior director for Near East Affairs at the White House, remembers: "When talking to Sadat about the consequences of peace, Carter at some point said that our relationship with Egypt would then be like our relationship with Israel—nothing more specific, but later taken by the Egyptians as a promise of something like parity."[47] Sadat may have misunderstood Carter, or Sadat may have only heard what he wanted to hear, or the American president may have been purposefully ambiguous as a way of prodding the Egyptians, but whatever the interpretation, Quandt's recollection bears out Ismail Sabri Abdallah's point precisely. There is a trilateral logic to the bilateral relationship between the United States and Egypt.

The centrality of Israel in the U.S.-Egypt relationship set an unintended trap for the Egyptians. There may be a strategic relationship between Egypt and the United States, but the informal requirement— good Egyptian-Israeli relations—built into these ties from the very start meant that Washington would almost always view Cairo through the prism of Israel. To be sure, in recent years, Congress repeatedly expressed concern over Egypt's deteriorating human rights situation, but Israel's interests continued to be a priority. Congressional efforts to cut Egypt's military assistance package abated as Cairo tightened its cordon around Gaza in 2008, and Israeli complaints about Egyptian conduct on the border area subsequently stopped. There were a few exceptions, of course. In January 2009, Congressman Anthony Weiner (D-NY) introduced a resolution in the House Committee on Foreign Affairs "to prohibit United States military assistance for Egypt and to express the sense of the Congress that the amount of military assistance that would have been provided for Egypt for a fiscal year should be provided in the form of economic support fund assistance."[48] Weiner's legislation never made it out of committee, however. During the summer of 2010, Senator Russ Feingold (D-WI), on behalf of both himself and John McCain (R-AZ), introduced S. Res. 586, which called on Egypt to repeal the Emergency Law, conduct free and fair elections, end arbitrary detention, abolish torture, and lift restrictions on freedom of assembly. It also encouraged the Obama administration to make human rights and democratic freedoms part of its dialogue with Egypt, to help ensure the independence of the judiciary, and to direct funds to civil society organizations, regardless of whether they are approved by the Egyptian government or not.[49] The resolution was nonbinding and left in limbo after Senator Feingold's electoral defeat in November 2010.

The Egyptians claimed they would like to get out from under the trilateral logic of their bilateral relationship with the United States, but they offered few, if any, good ideas about how to make this happen. Egyptians preferred to reorient ties around trade and investment, issues which, though important to both Cairo and Washington, hardly constitute the basis for a strategic relationship. Even if Washington and Cairo had negotiated some new type of bilateral agreement or understanding before the uprising of January 2011, Congress would have been less inclined to appropriate aid to Egypt. These circumstances deeply rankled and mystified the Egyptians. Before Mubarak's fall, Egyptian officials and regime-affiliated interlocutors took offense that much of their importance to the United States was a function of Israel, or, more specifically, Egypt's geographic proximity and potential threat to the Israelis. From their perspective, Egypt, the inheritor of a great civilization and the largest and most influential Arab country, deserved a special relationship with the United States in its own right. One former senior American official with years of experience in the Middle East likened the United States-Israel-Egypt dynamic to rival siblings fighting for their mother's attention. The analogy may be over the top, but it accurately reflected the unhappy situation in which Egypt found itself.

For its part, the American side also seemed bereft of any ideas about how to make the U.S.-Egypt relationship a truly bilateral one. Inside the Beltway, conferences, reports, and roundtables including Egyptians and Americans bore little fruit. The problem was, as one Washington Egypt expert and former government official declared, Cairo and Washington no longer shared a "big project." After all, peace with Israel had become institutionalized, the Cold War was over, Egypt's economic performance had improved so much that ending the U.S. economic aid program was within sight, and—as quietly helpful as Cairo had been to the United States in Iraq and Afghanistan—the military relationship with Egypt had become largely of secondary importance to Washington.

Of course, the desire to move away from the U.S.-Egypt-Israel relationship to more productive and specifically bilateral ties was confined to Egyptians with direct ties to the government or otherwise within the ambit of Mubarak's regime. Some of Egypt's liberals, many of whom found American support for the Mubarak regime bewildering, nevertheless believed Washington had a critical role to play in helping forge a more democratic Egypt. Still, other liberals did not, believing that Washington could not play a positive role in the region largely due to its connection to Israel. This position was consistent with most of the rest of the activists, factions, groups, and movements that make up Egypt's opposition. It may be too much to suggest that these groups want to undermine American-Egyptian-Israeli relations, but hostility and mistrust of these ties writ large was both pervasive and deeply rooted in Egyptian political discourse.

It is important to underscore that although by the late 1980s and 1990s the servants of the Egyptian regime were generally supportive of the trilateral relationship—challenges and all—this was not always the case. Initially, prominent members of Egypt's senior command, such as Major General Mohammed Abdel Ghani el Gamasy, were either skeptical of the benefits of the relationship with the United States or, like Lieutenant General Saad el Shazly, downright hostile. The memoirs of both el Shazly and el Gamasy betray a considerable wariness of the United States and its intentions. El Shazly wrote critically of U.S. support for Israel's demands in the period immediately following the October 1973 war, whereas el Gamasy voiced unease with U.S. military transfers to Egypt that began in the late 1970s—particularly in comparison to the U.S.-manufactured weapons in Israel's arsenal.[50] When Sadat made his historic visit to Jerusalem later in the decade, his foreign minister, Ismail Fahmy—the father of Ambassador Nabil Fahmy who as Egypt's representative in Cairo had the unfortunate responsibility of dealing with the EgyptAir 990 disaster—resigned in protest as did the deputy foreign minister, Mohammed Riad, and the Egyptian ambassador to Yugoslavia, Murad Ghales. To be fair, Fahmy's resignation did not necessarily reflect an ideological hostility to Israel. There was clearly a difference between him and Sadat over diplomatic strategy. The foreign minister believed that the president was giving away too much at the front end of what would likely be a long and difficult negotiation with the Israelis. Still, the opposition to Cairo's foreign policy reorientation, even within official circles, paled by comparison to the way Egyptian opposition elites responded.

More than any other group, the Muslim Brotherhood has been at the forefront of the opposition to both Jerusalem and Washington. After all, it was the Brothers who first sought to sound the alarm about the dangers of Zionism in the 1930s. In the 1960s, despite the split with Sayyid Qutb's followers, who regarded the Nasserist regime as their primary threat, then Supreme Guide Hassan al Hudaybi and the Brotherhood mainstream considered Israel a greater threat to Egypt and the Islamic movement. The modus vivendi between the regime and the Brotherhood came to a bitter end after Sadat's journey to Jerusalem. Never mind that Sadat had given the Brothers a second life after the repression of the Nasser years—even if it had been in his political interest—the organization went into open opposition with the regime over the outreach to Israel.

During the first few years of the Mubarak era, the Brothers took a less strident tone on the twin issues of the United States and Israel, but they remained steadfast in their abiding opposition to both. Later in the decade, however, they began to take Egypt's leadership to task for failing to look after Cairo's interests and called for Israel's destruction. In February 1987, for example, the Supreme Guide Mohammed Hamid Abu al Nasr's message was implicit, but unmistakable:

Egypt's security . . . is totally linked to the security of Palestine, as Egypt has often been invaded across its eastern border. It is in the homeland's interest to have a sisterly state that will cooperate with Egypt through thick and thin.[51]

Moreover, the Egyptian leadership's failure to do otherwise, according to Abu al Nasr, betrayed not only Egypt's historic position as the guardian of Arab and Islamic interests, but also its national honor.

As the 1987 parliamentary elections approached, the Brotherhood—which remained illegal—entered an electoral coalition with the Socialist Labor and Liberal parties. The platform, subsequently referred to as the "Islamic Alliance," advocated freezing Egypt's obligations under the peace treaty due to Israel's consistent violation of the agreement. This suggested a measure of pragmatism on the issue among the Brotherhood. After all, it implied the legitimacy of the treaty if only Israel would live up to its obligations. This was a potentially important development, but the platform did not actually indicate much of a change in the Brothers' hostility to Israel and the United States, identifying Zionism as "Egypt's most dangerous enemy" and rejecting strategic ties with Washington.[52]

The Brotherhood emphasized this theme when President George H. W. Bush convened the Madrid peace conference in October 1991. On the eve of the opening plenary, the Brotherhood's leader used the tribune of the Socialist Labor Party, *al Sha'ab*, or the People, as a platform to warn its readers that Egyptian participation at Madrid was no less than a "sell out." To the Brothers, the American endeavor was not geared toward forging peace between the Arab states and Israel, but— echoing Islamic reformers and Arab nationalists of an earlier era—it was an "effort to preempt any attempt for a possible renaissance of the [Islamic/Arab] nation to recover its vitality and unity."[53] More specific to Egypt, the Brothers firmly believed that the strategic relationship between Washington and Cairo did not enhance Egyptian security but, rather, was a threat. The Islamic Alliance's platform was clear on this point:

> The danger of the special relationship with America in light of its strategic agreement with Israel based on obvious bias toward Israel damages our national security and thus is all the more reason to refuse to grant them [the United States] facilities and military bases for its forces or tolerating joint maneuvers on our soil.[54]

In this single passage, the drafters of the coalition's electoral plank captured the central problem of U.S.-Egypt ties beginning in the late 1970s and early 1980s. As long as Washington played the role of Israel's patron, the United States was a threat to Egypt.

As the debate in Egypt began to focus more heavily on the political reform and change throughout the 2000s, the Brotherhood and its critique of the United States-Israel-Egypt relationship followed. The chairman of the Brotherhood's political department and member of its Executive Bureau, Mohammed Morsi, captured this change when he observed that contrary to Washington's rhetoric during the Bush years, the United States had done nothing to promote democracy in Egypt. Israel, too, Morsi continued, had no interest in a democratic Egypt because it "would do more to support the Palestinians."[55] Yet the organization has not completely dropped its traditional account of what ails Egypt and the region more generally. In a 2007 interview with the editors of the Brotherhood-affiliated Web site Ikhwanweb.com, Dr. Mohammed al Sayed Habib, the first deputy chairman of the Muslim Brotherhood, declared, "There is an Israeli-American project that aims to humiliate the nation, weaken its beliefs, cause a moral corruption, attempt to steal and loot its wealth, eradicate its cultural privacy. This project aims to dismember the region and redraw its map."[56]

The Brotherhood's most recent authoritative statement on the trilateral relationship is located in its 2010 electoral program, which was somewhat more subtle and circumspect if no less critical of these ties. In the brief section on national security, the Brothers observed that Egypt's diminished leadership in the region and the Islamic world is linked directly to Cairo's relationship with Washington, making Egypt a "subordinate" or "secondary" power in the Arab and Islamic world. On the Palestinian issue, the Brotherhood "re-affirmed resistance to the illegal occupation of Arab and Islamic lands," offered the organization's "hand of assistance and support to the Palestinian people and to the Palestinian resistance to Zionist usurpation," and called for "total resistance to economic, cultural, political, and security normalization with the Zionist entity and nullification of any agreement that supports [it]." In a direct challenge to the Egyptian government, which along with Israel had created a *cordon sanitaire* around the Gaza Strip, the Brothers demanded the "lifting of the blockade on Gaza and permanently opening the Rafah crossing to the inhabitants of the encircled Strip . . . and the establishment of a free area between the Strip and Egypt, helping to save the needy inhabitants of the blockaded Strip."[57] Through its electoral platform, the Muslim Brotherhood was clearly intent on embarrassing the regime on the most sensitive issues surrounding the Egyptian government's standing relations with Israel and the United States, ranging from the whole notion of normal relations between Cairo and Jerusalem, Egypt's policies toward Gaza, and more broadly how strategic ties with the United States compromised Egyptian power and influence.

The Muslim Brotherhood is not the only group that has been in open revolt against the regime over its policies toward Israel, the Palestinians, and the United States. Across the political spectrum, from the Nasserists to the leftist Tagammu Party and the Wafd, Egypt's political parties oppose normalization of relations with Israel and regard the United States as profoundly biased against the Palestinian and Arab cause.[58] These views were not only reflected in the political parties, which were largely ineffective in Egypt's traditionally circumscribed political environment, but were also given life in the more politically active professional syndicates. To be sure, many of these groups have at one time or another been under the control of the Muslim Brotherhood, especially those representing doctors, pharmacists, engineers, and lawyers.[59] The Union of Egyptian Writers, which was founded at the behest of President Anwar Sadat in 1975, has been an exception of sorts.[60] The board's composition has changed only rarely and it has never been under the control of the Brotherhood, though the union tends to be sensitive regarding topics related to religion and religious themes. For example, the syndicate supported the Ministry of Culture's effort to censor books that are deemed offensive to Islam. Not unlike any of Egypt's other professional associations, the writers' union is steadfastly opposed to the normalization of relations with Israel. The writers argue that although Egypt and Israel enjoy diplomatic relations, they need not be party to an unjust peace. As a result, they are determined to hold the line against contact with Israelis, given the ongoing occupation of Palestine; the construction of settlements on Palestinian lands, including East Jerusalem; and, concomitant with this "colonization," the suppression of Palestinian rights. Egypt's writers adhered to the union's official position, with one notable exception. In April 1994, seven months after the signing of the Oslo Accords, which committed Israel and the Palestinian Liberation Organization to negotiate an end to their conflict, one of Egypt's most famous playwrights, Ali Salem, got into his car and drove to Israel. In his book about the trip, *Rihla ila Isra'il* (*A Journey to Israel*), Salem recalls the cognitive dissonance of his three-week visit.[61] It was not adoration or admiration, Salem responds to his critics, that prompted his visit to Israel, but rather curiosity and a desire to relieve himself of the hatred of decades of war and hostile peace. Salem's visit was hardly the first by an Egyptian, but both his stature and total disregard for his syndicate's blanket boycott of all things Israeli, no less Israel itself, was shocking.

After an estimated sixty thousand copies of *A Journey to Israel* sold in Egypt and another six visits to the Jewish state, the Union of Egyptian Writers stripped Salem of his membership in 2001. Salem sued to reverse the decision and won in 2002, but resigned his membership as soon as he was reinstated. The union meanwhile continued its efforts to discredit Salem. His plays remain written but not produced, his pension is frozen, and he is widely shunned. He is Ali Salem, though, and he continues to write for the Saudi-owned pan-Arab daily, *al Hayat*, and he has derived a certain fame in the West for his willingness to visit Israel, his open support for peace, and his outspoken condemnation of al Qa'ida. Still, it is unlikely that, after the Salem affair, very many other writers would break the taboo of normalization, which was precisely what the syndicate's board members intended.

Salem's story may be the extreme. After all, he got into his car and drove to Israel for three weeks, toured the country, wrote a book about it, and then went back again and again. There are professional hazards for those who do far less than Salem, however. In September 2009, for example, a woman named Hala Mustafa ran into trouble with the Journalists Syndicate. Mustafa is an analyst at the government-affiliated al Ahram Center for Political and Strategic Studies, editor of the journal *Democracy*, and was a member of the National Democratic Party's influential Policies Secretariat. She is well-known among the Middle East studies crowd inside the Beltway, having attended the University of Maryland and spent some time as a visiting fellow at the Washington Institute for Near East Policy. Mustafa crossed the syndicate's code of no contact with Israelis when she met with Shalom Cohen, Israel's ambassador in Cairo, who requested her assistance in setting up a conference that would include Israelis, Egyptians, and Americans to discuss the peace process after President Obama's June 4, 2009, Cairo speech. The meeting between Mustafa and Cohen was not secret—even routine movement of the Israeli ambassador in Cairo requires advance notice and security. Mustafa took the meeting but never agreed to assist Cohen. Nevertheless, the courtesy call with the Israeli official was enough for her to land in hot water. Mustafa's syndicate membership was threatened and she was condemned in the press. In the end, Mustafa received a warning from the journalists.[62]

It is no surprise that Egyptian opposition groups oppose Israel, the United States, and Cairo's relationship with both. Besides making the Egyptians feel weak, they contend that the peace treaty constrains Egypt and distorts its foreign policy. For example, the U.S.-sponsored modernization of Egypt's armed forces has been purposefully slow and has emphasized a defensive military posture. Moreover, Egypt's national interests, at least as former President Hosni Mubarak defined them during his three decades in office, were aligned with Israel and the United States on a variety of core regional issues including the Palestinian-Israeli conflict, transnational jihadism, and Iran. Yet many Egyptians support the Palestinian cause, regard Washington's global war on terror as a war on Islam, and are not unduly concerned about Iran's nuclear program. But as one former senior Bush administration official recalls: "The Egyptians may have disagreed on a variety of issues and they let us know, but they always worked with us. This was especially the case on the [2005] Gaza withdrawal. We were allies."[63]

The risk for the Egyptian regime stemming from its ties with Washington and Jerusalem was the undeniable interconnectedness between these relations and domestic political opposition. Some analysts and observers identify the American invasion of Iraq as a critical moment when politics returned to Egypt. The war was a turning point that led to the emergence of the protest movement Kifaya! and thrust Egyptian opposition activists into the national and international spotlight. Yet, it was the appearance of popular committees in 2000–2001 in support of the second Palestinian intifada that presaged Kifaya! and gave impetus to the development of an unofficial opposition comprised not of politicians, but of political and social activists, more generally. As with the July 1952 coup or the student protests of the late 1960s and early 1970s, the emergence of these popular committees indicated a link between Palestine and moments of great domestic political stress in Egypt.

By the time the United States undertook "Operation Iraqi Freedom," the Egyptian opposition, already angry over the second intifada and Cairo's inability or unwillingness to do much about it, was inflamed. On the first full day of the invasion—March 20—the Interior Ministry authorized an antiwar demonstration in Liberation Square. The goal was to allow Egyptians to "let off steam" by venting their anger at Washington within earshot of the U.S. Embassy. By permitting the demonstration, President Mubarak hoped to position himself and the government comfortably within the flow of Egyptian public opinion. Mubarak calculated poorly, however. The demonstrators predictably assailed the Bush administration on Iraq and blasted the Israelis, but then something even more profound and potentially worrying for Mubarak took place. The withering critique of the United States and Israel spilled over onto Mubarak and his presumptive successor— Gamal Mubarak. Using Washington's predatory policies as their pretext, Egyptians heaped scorn on the Mubarak family, disparaged the notion of "dynastic succession," and declared the regime illegitimate on two critical grounds. First, the protestors drove home the point that Cairo's strategic ties to the United States and Israel ran counter to public opinion. Second, they revealed the regime's vulnerability on the ever important issue of nationalism. After all, was not the regime founded in response to Western penetration of the region? Although Mubarak counseled the Bush administration against war in Iraq, he also helped enable the conflict. In other words, the demonstrators in downtown Cairo were saying: A truly democratic Egypt would resist the United States and Israel.

The link could not have been clearer during two subsequent events that shook the Middle East. Israel invaded Lebanon in June 2006 after a border incident in which the terrorist group, Hizballah, killed three Israeli soldiers. During the operation, the Israel Defense Forces pursued a two-prong strategy intended to inflict maximum damage on Hizballah and to convince the Lebanese people through violence that their support for Hizballah was costly. The Egyptian government (along with its counterparts in Europe, Saudi Arabia, Jordan, the Palestinian areas, and other Arab countries) tacitly supported the Israeli invasion, hoping that by striking a blow against Hizballah, the mighty IDF would also set back the regional ambitions of its primary sponsor, Iran. Yet Israel's tactics and the resulting al Jazeera live video feed produced revulsion and outrage in the Arab world and beyond. Egypt's support for Israel placed Mubarak on the defensive. In Cairo, demonstrations broke out condemning the government's position, clearly indicating that the Egyptian public was considerably less concerned about the alleged Hizballah-Iran threat than about standing up to Israel. The combination of inflamed public opinion and the fact that Israel was not winning the war forced Cairo to back away from its position after a few weeks. Mubarak went so far as to dispatch Gamal and other Egyptian officials to Beirut, during a lull in the fighting, in an expression of solidarity with the Lebanese people. By that time, however, the damage had been done. The younger Mubarak's mission to Lebanon could not hide the fact that the Egyptian government stood with the Israelis in their battle with Hizballah.[64] Posters of Hizballah's leader, Hassan Nasrallah, and the Lebanese flags that dotted the Cairo landscape during and after hostilities demonstrated the popular opposition to the government's position.

Indeed, the optics of this opposition were at times startling. At an al Ghad Party rally one evening in September 2006 in the Bab Sharaya area of downtown, the organizers hoisted a large poster of the party's founder, Ayman Nour, who was languishing in an Egyptian prison, next to an equally large portrait of Nasrallah. Given what had transpired in Lebanon some weeks earlier, for the Egyptians present there was understandably no irony to the scene, but to the outside observer it was almost too much to take. The al Ghad faithful were paying homage both to Nour, whose cause the Bush administration was championing as one of the brave liberal voices to speak out against Mubarak's authoritarianism, and Nasrallah, leader of an organization a senior American official once called the "A-team of terrorism." If this was not enough, the al Ghad supporters complemented the Nour and Nasrallah posters by projecting unflattering photos of President Mubarak and his family on an enormous screen.

The second incident that highlights how Egypt's relations with the United States and Israel were a source of opposition to the Mubarak regime occurred in the early morning hours of Memorial Day 2010 about one hundred miles off the coast of Gaza. At 4:30 a.m. local time, Israeli commandos rappelled from helicopters aboard the 305-foot Turkish ferry *Mavi Marmara* and took over the vessel. In the process of commandeering the ship, the Israelis killed eight Turks and one Turkish-American. The ferry was part of a six-ship flotilla bound for the Gaza Strip that was intending to break Israel's blockade of the area and its 1.5 million residents, which—since June 2007—has been under the control of Hamas. The Israelis boarded the vessel after it refused the navy's orders to divert to the port of Ashdod. The Turkish government called Israel's actions "piracy," recalled its ambassador, and demanded an apology. Turkish Prime Minister Recep Tayyip Erdoğan, already popular in the Arab world for his stand on Israeli policy in Gaza, took Israel to task for the incident aboard the Turkish-flagged vessel and the conditions of the Palestinians in Gaza. Indeed, Erdoğan's strident rhetoric and standing among average Arabs left some Turkish and Arab pundits wondering whether the prime minister was the new Gamal Abdel Nasser.

The Egyptian opposition was dumbfounded and angry. Not only were the non-Arab Turks leading the region against Israeli policies—a position they believed should have been Cairo's proper role—but the Egyptian government had been a willing partner of Israel (with the blessing of the Bush and Obama administrations) in keeping Gaza locked up. Egypt's complicity with Israel on Gaza was actually nothing new. During Israel's "Operation Cast Lead" targeting Hamas in Gaza in late 2008 and early 2009, the Egyptian government remained steadfast in keeping the border closed, lest a flood of Palestinians, including militants, enter Sinai to escape the Israelis. The flotilla incident only served to reinforce the full extent of Cairo's alignment with Jerusalem and Washington, fueling further opposition to Mubarak and his regime.

Like the parties and opposition in the era just before the coup, if Egyptians agreed on anything, it was on nationalist grounds. Strip the Brotherhood, Nasserists, Leftists, Kifaya! and the myriad smaller protest groups that emerged over the 2000s of their ideological differences, and it is clear that they share the same nationalist terrain. For them, Washington's interests in the region are malevolent: to divide the region sufficiently in an effort to make it safe both for the extraction of oil, which perpetuates the political, economic, and military supremacy of the West; and the security of Israel, an anachronistic outpost of Western imperialism that has sought to destroy legitimate Arab and Islamic rights in Palestine. In this, the regimes of both Anwar Sadat and Hosni Mubarak were complicit by dint of their strategic relationship with the United States and Israel. These trilateral ties also compromised Egypt's sovereignty and its natural foreign policy orientation. Indeed, if not for the alignment with Washington and Jerusalem—which was only possible under an authoritarian political order—Cairo might have led the region in opposing U.S. policy in the Middle East rather than facilitating it. These sentiments do not portend well for U.S. relations with post-revolutionary Egypt. Although a breach in relations is remote, it is likely that Cairo will diverge from Washington on important regional issues such as the peace process, Hamas, and the approach to Iran (discussed in detail in chapter 7).

A CRUCIBLE OF TERRORISM

If the aid package and the trilateral logic of U.S.-Egypt relations had long caused tension in the relationship, the freighted issue of terrorism injected a whole new level of friction. Like Americans of a certain age can who recall in detail everything they did on November 22, 1963—the day President John F. Kennedy was assassinated—those, especially New Yorkers and Washingtonians, who experienced the September 11 attacks can tell you everything they did that sunny Tuesday: what they ate for breakfast, what they were wearing, who they saw first after hearing the news, and what they said. The shock and enormity of the death and destruction in lower Manhattan and at the Pentagon altered the way Americans live, travel, and look at the world. Jersey barriers, the Transportation Security Administration, and the USA Patriot Act became everyday features of American life whether people noticed or not. Abroad, particularly in the Middle East, U.S. foreign policy experienced something of a revolution. During the 1990s, Washington stood shoulder to shoulder with Cairo in its fight with al Jihad and al Gama'a al Islamiyya. The realities of ground zero changed American policy, however. In one sense, Mubarak remained very much an ally of the United States, offering the services of his intelligence agencies in interrogating al Qa'ida suspects. At the same time, however, there was a strong belief in Washington that the Egyptian leader presided over a regime that by its very authoritarian nature contributed to the scourge of terrorism that was suddenly threatening the security of the United

States itself. This fact produced a shift in Washington's approach to Egypt and the Middle East more generally. The effect was to place the United States at the center of Egypt's own domestic debates about the country, its political system, and its future.

For obvious reasons, there has been considerable focus on Saudi Arabia since 9/11. Of the nineteen hijackers who flew airplanes into the World Trade Center and the Pentagon, killing 2,980, fifteen were Saudis. Osama bin Laden, al Qa'ida's former leader and at one time the most wanted man in the world, was from the Saudi Red Sea coast city of Jeddah and a scion of one of the most prominent and wealthy families in the kingdom. Given these circumstances, it is no wonder that Saudi Arabia has been the subject of no fewer than 139 books and figured into untold numbers of presidential statements, stump speeches, congressional testimony, journal articles, and opinion pieces since that terrible day.[65]

Lost in all the commentary about Saudi Arabia is the role of Egyptians in transnational terrorism. By many measures, Egypt has been an important partner in the battle against terrorism, but it is also a source of this scourge. It was, after all, Mohammed Atta, a stern-looking Egyptian urban planner from the Giza district of Cairo, who led the four teams that perpetrated the 9/11 attacks. Yet Atta was a mere foot soldier in a broader jihadist movement that is notable for the involvement of Egyptians. Sheikh Omar Abdul Rahman, Mohammed Atef (aka Abu Hafs al Masri), Abu Ubaidah al Banshiri, Abu Ayyub al Masri, Saif al Adl, Sayyid Imam al Sharif, Mohammed Hassan Khalil al Hakim, Ahmed Mohammed Hamed Ali, Abdallah Ahmed Abdallah, Mustafa Abu al Yazid, Ali Mohammed, and Ayman Zawahiri are all Egyptians. This group represents the leadership, pamphleteers, logisticians, and military planners of a broad network of global terrorists and their sympathizers. They are the descendants of the Brotherhood vanguard who embraced Sayyid Qutb's *Milestones Along the Way* in the mid-1960s and are motivated to rid Egypt and other societies of jahaliyya—ignorance—and establish the absolute sovereignty of God.

In the years following the 1979 Soviet invasion of Afghanistan, Osama bin Laden became a disciple of a Palestinian preacher named Abdallah Azzam. Trained at Cairo's al Azhar University, Azzam, whom bin Laden met at King Abdel Aziz University in Jeddah, advocated an uncompromising jihad against the godless communism of the Soviet Union and the moral decadence of the West. Azzam was not the only charismatic Islamist in bin Laden's orbit at the time, however. Ayman Zawahiri, whose audiotapes and videos threatening violence have haunted the American people since September 11, also entered bin Laden's inner circle during the 1980s.

At first blush, Zawahiri is an unlikely mastermind of global jihad. A pediatrician with Coke-bottle glasses, he was raised in the Cairo suburb of Ma'adi, which, during his childhood, much like today, is somewhat of a refuge from the din of Cairo proper. Its tree-lined streets off the main thoroughfares are quieter than downtown, and hedgerows obscure the stately villas of the upper class and comfortable apartment buildings of the upper middle class.[66] Zawahiri became radicalized at fifteen and would eventually lead one of Egypt's most notorious extremist groups, al Jihad, which was responsible for Anwar Sadat's assassination. Those old enough will recall Zawahiri from the news footage of his trial for conspiring to murder Sadat. He stood apart from the fracas of his fellow prisoners in a large courtroom cage while calling to the gathered international press:

> We want to speak to the whole world. Who are we? Why did they bring us here and what do we want to say? We are Muslims. We are Muslims who believe in our religion and hence we tried our best to establish an Islamic state and an Islamic society. We have sacrificed and stand ready for more sacrifice. We are here the real Islamic front and the real Islamic opposition. And now as an answer to the second question, why did they bring us here? They bring us for two reasons. First, they are trying to abort the expanding Islamic movement which threatens the dishonest agents of the regime. And secondly, to complete a conspiracy of evacuating the area in preparation for the Zionist infiltration. Such a conspiracy was declared by the stupid agent Anwar Sadat.[67]

These few lines said literally all there needed to be said about the Egyptian president's murder. Zawahiri's justification conformed precisely to central tenets of Islamic radicalism that Sayyid Qutb delineated in *Milestones Along the Way*.

The man who would become a mainstay at bin Laden's side served three years in an Egyptian prison for his part in the conspiracy to kill President Sadat. By the mid-1980s, al Jihad was a crippled organization with its leadership dead, imprisoned, or scattered. Lacking the personnel and financial resources to wage jihad against the Egyptian regime, Zawahiri's only real option upon his release from prison was to make his way to the central hub of the emerging transnational terrorist movement: Peshawar, Pakistan. There Zawahiri discovered bin Laden.

For Zawahiri, the Saudi was an opportunity. The combination of his vast family fortune, uncompromising radicalism, and quiet charisma could rekindle al Jihad's fortunes.[68] The prevailing view among analysts and observers is that Zawahiri's organization became a wholly owned subsidiary of al Qa'ida when the organizations formally merged in June 2001.[69] In a financial sense, this is true. Bin Laden's deep pockets rescued al Jihad from falling into relative obscurity with little means to engage in holy war. If not for his Saudi patron, Zawahiri would likely have ended up in circumstances similar to those as Ahmad Jibril—the leader of the Popular Front for the Liberation of Palestine-General Command—and the Democratic Front for the Liberation of Palestine's Nayef Hawatmeh. These aging radicals have spent the better part of the past three decades fulminating, agitating, and threatening, but never doing much in the way of taking action.

In an entirely different way, however, it is Zawahiri's al Jihad that appropriated al Qa'ida. As Lawrence Wright demonstrates in his astounding work *The Looming Tower*, bin Laden was in many ways a naïf and subject to manipulation. This almost childlike quality, combined with Zawahiri's skills as a master political infighter, doomed all other competitors for bin Laden's trust and patronage. In time, the Egyptian eliminated not only his competitors of would-be counselors and chief ideologues to bin Laden, but also the second rung of al Qa'ida leadership. Indeed, when bin Laden left Sudan in 1996, his security detail, military planners, and bagmen were all Egyptians originally associated in one way or another with Zawahiri and his al Jihad organization.[70] In this way, al Qa'ida "central"—as opposed to its affiliate in Yemen, al Qa'ida in the Arabian Peninsula, or the group operating in Algeria, al Qa'ida of the Islamic Maghreb—has a distinctly Egyptian profile.

Zawahiri and bin Laden were of upper-middle or upper-class origins. Indeed, the leaders of extremist groups tend to be doctors, engineers, pharmacists, veterinarians, and military officers. Why this is the case is a hotly debated topic. Many scholars and analysts have made this observation, but few, if any, have provided a compelling answer.[71] An equally puzzling phenomenon is the foot soldiers in the transnational jihadist movement. Why do these young men answer the call?[72] It seems for large numbers of them, political alienation, limited economic opportunity, and the availability of extremist ideologies—all of which contemporary Egypt manifests in spades—play a significant contributing role in their taking up arms as a means to redress their political grievances. Despite the reams of scholarly work on what drives militancy among young men, the best account emerges from the Egyptian writer Alaa al Aswany's monumental political and social critique titled *The Yacoubian Building*. In the book, which is in its ninth edition, al Aswany traces the lives of the inhabitants of 34 Talaat Harb Street in downtown Cairo during the first Gulf War. One of them is Taha, the bright and talented son of the Yacoubian building's *bawab* (doorman) who wants to improve his socioeconomic standing so that, among other things, he can afford to marry his sweetheart, Busayna. Taha enjoys none of the informal advantages that are prerequisites for success in contemporary Egypt. He has no *wasta*—connections—and little money. As a result, he turns to one of the proven methods of climbing Egypt's steep socioeconomic ladder: Taha tries to enroll in the police academy, but he is denied entry because his father is a lowly doorman. He, in turn, becomes radicalized and joins al Gama'a al Islamiyya while studying at Cairo University and is subsequently arrested for protesting the U.S.-led Operation Desert Storm. He is beaten and raped during his detention.

The arc of al Aswany's social commentary is familiar to those paying close attention to the changes wrought in Egypt since the Sadat period. Indeed, in the abstract, Taha's predicament is similar to the protagonist in Yusuf al Qa'id's *War in the Land of Egypt*. In that penetrating allegory of the false hopes of Nasserism and the hypocrisy of the early Sadat years, the voiceless Masri (literally "Egyptian") and his family are subject to the corruption and cruelty of the upper classes as well as the soulless bureaucracy of Egypt. Reflecting the different eras in which they wrote, al Qa'id's Masri dies heroically in battle during the October 1973 war, whereas al Aswany's Taha achieves martyrdom in a terrorist operation that kills a senior state security officer.

Al Qa'id is clearly interested in mythologizing the average Egyptian, who, despite the humiliations of life, is both noble and devout in his fealty to Egypt. Al Aswany's message is ultimately quite different and is indicative of the changes that have occurred in Egypt in the time between the two books' publication dates. Faced with dwindling options in a society that pays lip service to ideas like community, justice, and honesty but is, in truth, deeply corrupt and brutal, Taha becomes enamored of extremist ideologies, ultimately turning not just from Busayna and his family, but also from Egyptian society. Taha withdraws to a secret encampment in the desert outside of Cairo in what he imagined to be the ultimate expression of a perfect Islamic society before being sent on his mission. Although writing about two different periods, the dynamic that al Aswany illustrates was actually well under way even before al Qa'id published his book in 1978. In April 1974, for example, a group of militants under the leadership of a Palestinian named Salih Siriyya attempted a takeover of the Military Technical Academy as the first step in a coup that would sweep away the Egyptian regime and usher in an Islamic state. The plot failed and Siriyya was sentenced to death, but the attack was shocking nonetheless. It was brazen, targeted the military, and was the first of its kind for a new breed of extremists.

Since the appearance of *Milestones*, and without the benefit of Qutb's guidance due to his execution in 1966, the Islamists engaged in an intense debate over their ideological godfather's prescription for true believers living in a society that was in a state of ignorance. While there was general agreement with Qutb's prescribed "separation" from the world around them, there was a difference of opinion on the extent of "withdrawal."[73] One faction held that out of self-preservation, it was enough to secretly declare *takfir* (excommunication) on Egyptian society—the concept central to the split with the Brotherhood and Supreme Guide Hassan al Hudaybi in 1965—while Muslim activists accumulated enough power to overthrow the government and remake society along their Islamic ideals.[74] Others openly declared takfir and literally withdrew from society so that it would not be necessary to engage in the sort of dissimulation their colleagues were advocating.

The stakes were high in this debate over the proper theological approach to a society that was regarded within the Islamist milieu as beyond the pale, but the practical outcome was the same no matter how it was settled: Egyptian society was in a state of ignorance in which man's law was superior to God's law and thus ripe for jihad. This was the thinking that produced the Military Technical College attack, Sadat's assassination, and the low-level insurgency that Islamist extremists waged against the Egyptian state in the 1990s; as well as the U.S. Embassy bombings in Nairobi and Dar el Salaam in August 1998, the strike on the USS *Cole*, and ultimately the terrorist assaults on New York and Washington in September 2001. It was this last incident that precipitated Washington's interest in Egypt's domestic political development.

WHITE MAN'S BURDEN?

Since the 1950s, three interests have guided the United States in the Middle East: ensuring the free flow of energy resources from the region, helping to protect the security of the state of Israel, and preventing any power—other than the United States—from dominating the Middle East. There have been variations of these three broad policy objectives in six decades. For example, preventing Moscow's penetration of the region ceased to be a central issue for the United States after the Soviet Union collapsed in December 1991. Observers often also include "countering rogue states" and "combating terrorism" in the constellation of U.S. interests. A case can be made for the latter, especially in light of the "cosmic struggle" that al Qa'ida and its affiliates are waging, but confronting the challenge of terrorism is not specific to the Middle East. To be sure, origins of the conflict are in the Middle East, but the battlefield is truly global. As for the problem of so-called rogue states—countries that threaten the regional rules of the game that the United States and its allies have established—it is merely derivative of Washington's interest in oil, Israel, and its own regional predominance. In order to achieve these goals, Washington long pursued a policy that could best be characterized as "authoritarian stability."

In late 1979, a foreign policy intellectual named Jeane Kirkpatrick, who would go on to serve as Ronald Reagan's ambassador to the United Nations, penned an article in the neoconservative flagship publication *Commentary* called "Dictatorships and Double-Standards."[75] All around Kirkpatrick, there were troubling signs that the global correlation of forces—a Soviet concept encompassing broad measures of a country's relative influence, power, and prestige—was shifting away from the United States. In January 1979, the pro-American Shah of Iran fled his country as a revolution unfolded, making way for the emergence of the Islamic Republic of Iran. In July of the same year, the Washington-friendly dynasty that controlled Nicaragua collapsed. In place of the Somoza family, which had ruled the country as an American client since the 1930s, the Cuba-allied Sandinista National Liberation Front came to power. Soon afterwards, Nicaragua fell into the Soviet orbit. Kirkpatrick's piece was published at the same time the Iranian hostage crisis began. On November 4, revolutionaries stormed the American Embassy in Tehran, taking fifty American diplomats and Marines hostage for what would become 444 days. Simultaneous to the takeover, Iran experienced a wave of anti-American protests, during which hundreds of thousands, perhaps millions, turned out in the country's main cities declaring, *Marg bar Am-ree-ka!* (Death to America!). The month after "Dictatorships and Double Standards" appeared, the Soviets invaded Afghanistan. Moscow's adventure would end in a debacle a decade later, but at the time it was seen as a worrisome indicator that the Soviets—taking advantage of American weakness—were embarking on an effort to alter the geostrategic balance of Southwest Asia permanently.

For Kirkpatrick and others, President Jimmy Carter's emphasis on human rights was to blame for Washington's global predicament. The stakes, according to Kirkpatrick, were too high in the global struggle between the United States and the Soviet Union for American policymakers to care about the character of regimes so long as their leaders were aligned with the United States. In practice, this meant that human rights, political and personal freedoms, rule of law, accountability should be of little or no concern to Washington in the conduct of its relations with American allies. Once more, if those rulers should find themselves under threat from anti-American groups, whether Islamist theocrats or Marxist revolutionaries, then Washington had an obligation to support its nondemocratic allies. Regardless of how brutal and repressive their dictatorships were, Mohammed Reza Pahlavi and Anastasia Somoza were far better than Iran's revolutionary leader, Ayatollah Khomeini, and the Sandinistas' Daniel Ortega.

Perhaps spooked by the events of the late 1970s, successive American administrations seemed to take Kirkpatrick's policy recommendation to heart and, in the Middle East especially, pursued a policy that placed an emphasis on the stability that friendly authoritarians could provide. In one of the most stirring speeches of the late Cold War, President Ronald Reagan stood in the shadow of Berlin's Bradenburg Gate and the wall that divided the city and demanded, "Mr. Gorbachev, tear down this wall!" Reagan was imploring his Soviet counterpart to free not just the people of East Berlin but also of East Germany and, indeed, the entire Eastern Bloc.[76] Yet, on the Middle East's clear democracy and freedom deficits, Reagan, who often referred to the United States as a beacon of liberty throughout the world, was mostly silent throughout his presidency.

Foreign policy realism marked George H. W. Bush's turn in the White House, which was consistent with Kirkpatrick's thinking a decade earlier. Bush ordered five hundred thousand troops to the Persian Gulf and the deserts of Saudi Arabia to face down Saddam Hussein, not because of Iraq's version of totalitarianism, but rather because the Iraqi leader had invaded Kuwait and declared it a province of his own country. Had Washington and the international community acceded to Baghdad's aggression, the invasion would have likely set a precedent that would have complicated the United States' global interests.[77] In justifying the dispatch of American troops to the Persian

Gulf, President Bush declared that one of his administration's objectives was the emergence of a "new world order."[78] Yet Bush was interested more in maintaining a peaceful international order—a lofty goal indeed—than in the nature of the states that encompassed the international community.

Bush's successor, Bill Clinton, indicated early on in his tenure that he wanted to move out of the "authoritarian stability" paradigm in favor of a foreign policy that, among other things, placed an emphasis on the "enlargement of democracy" around the world.[79] Yet, in the Middle East, it was business as usual. Clinton was inaugurated at around the same time al Gama'a al Islamiyya's campaign of terrorism in Egypt was in full swing, and, according to an administration official at the time, "We felt the need to stand shoulder to shoulder with Mubarak against the extremists."[80] The same official also revealed that the administration had a policy of promoting democracy in the Middle East, but it ran through the peace process. Clinton's team reasoned that once there was a comprehensive settlement of the Arab-Israeli conflict, the justification for national security states—foremost Egypt—would evaporate, paving the way for more open and accountable governments.

By any objective measure, the policy of "authoritarian stability" worked for thirty years. The flow of oil from the region was only disrupted once, during the 1973 Saudi-led oil embargo, but this was temporary, lasting only six months, though it did cause considerable economic pain to the United States. Israel has remained secure and, since its peace treaty with Egypt in 1979, has not confronted the prospect of fighting an all-out war with its neighbors. And ever since the mid-1970s, when Henry Kissinger flipped Egypt, Washington has been the region's predominant power. There have been setbacks, of course. Besides the oil embargo, the Iranian Revolution was a blow to the United States. In one fell swoop, Iran went from strategic ally to hostile power, making it relatively more complicated and expensive for Washington to pursue its objectives. Still, with the help of countries like Egypt, the United States has managed to achieve its primary regional interests.

It has become cliché to suggest that "on September 11 everything changed." In hindsight, the phrase seems maudlin, but in many ways it is correct. The happy globalization of the late 1990s gave way to a darker, more forbidding view of the world and the threats it posed to the United States. On July 10, 2001, a former senior counterterrorism official at the State Department, Larry C. Johnson, published an op-ed in the *New York Times* called "The Declining Threat of Terrorism" in which he argued that the danger to Americans from terrorism had receded to such an extent that it was largely negligible. Just two months later, the *Times* ran a slew of editorials and op-eds called "The War Against America; An Unfathomable Attack," "War without Illusions," "How to Protect the Homeland," "The Specter of Biological Terror," and "Safe Borders."[81] The vast difference in worldview between Johnson's piece and the subsequent publications in the newspaper of record in just sixty or so days was profound. More than anything, it reflected a sudden and dramatic shift in the national mood.

In the search for answers about what happened on 9/11, some Americans sought to withdraw from the dangerous world; others regarded the attacks as a call to action to defend America's way of life. Still others took a critical look at U.S. foreign policy, especially in the Middle East and Washington's support for Israel, and concluded that the United States itself was to blame for the tragedy. In those heated days after the attacks, when there was a pervasive fear of another hit at any time and any place, this type of debate was most unwelcome in American political discourse. At the same time, a small group of American officials were reevaluating U.S.-Middle East policy, though they were not questioning ties with Israel. While fires were still burning in lower Manhattan and the Pentagon, officials quietly jettisoned the entire framework of U.S. foreign policy that Jeane Kirkpatrick had so eloquently outlined twenty-two years earlier. Although there was a well-developed bureaucracy dedicated to developing, advancing, and coordinating U.S. efforts to promote human rights and democracy, these matters were of generally little consequence when decisions were made in Washington concerning the Middle East up until September 10, 2001.

A day later, what went on inside Arab countries—the human rights violations, limited economic opportunity, availability of extremists ideologies, and overall predatory nature of Middle Eastern governments— was suddenly supremely important to safeguarding the United States, its interests, and the American people. In order to "drain the swamp" of would-be terrorists, the administration of George W. Bush embarked on an effort to promote democratic change in the Arab world. The architects of the policy theorized that the combination of political alienation, economic dislocation, and availability of extremist ideology in the authoritarian regimes in the Middle East—most notably Egypt, but also Saudi Arabia—were more likely to produce terrorists. If disaffected young men could process their grievances through democratic institutions, fewer would want to bomb American embassies, attack

U.S. warships, and fly civilian airliners into buildings in Manhattan and Washington.

The prescription for America's terrorism problem—promoting democracy—was deeply appealing and achieved a near foreign policy consensus. It is not hard to see why. The policy promised to mitigate, if not entirely resolve, what suddenly seemed to be the singular national security threat to the United States. Once more, it promised a foreign policy consistent with American values. This would do much to alleviate—if not again resolve—the problem of anti-Americanism in the region. Besides Washington's unstinting support for Israel, the perceived gap between the principles, practices, and norms by which Americans like to believe they live at home and the conduct of the United States in the Middle East caused considerable anger among average Egyptians and other Arabs. Egyptians would often ask, "Why has the United States historically supported freedom and democracy in Latin America and Eastern Europe but not the Middle East?" The claim about Latin America is certainly debatable, but the broader issue of Arab perceptions about the United States and its support for nondemocratic leaders in the region was both analytically important and has the virtue of being true.

The hasty enthusiasm with which official—and unofficial—Washington embraced democracy promotion could not make up for some of the policy's significant analytical and practical drawbacks, however. There seemed to be a somewhat sunny emphasis on one potential endpoint of transitions—liberal democracy—at the expense of other potential outcomes including illiberal democracy or a "narrowed dictatorship."[82] Never mind that instability—both internal and external—is often associated with countries undergoing transitions.[83] To be fair, there was a general awareness of this risk, but they were often deemed acceptable given the alternative. The report of the Council on Foreign Relations' Independent Task Force on reform in the Arab world was typical in this regard: "While transitions to democracy can lead to instability in the short term, the Task Force finds that a policy geared toward maintaining the authoritarian status quo poses greater risks to U.S. interests and foreign policy goals."[84]

Overall, despite the consensus within the foreign policy establishment, promoting democratic change did not match the threat for which it was developed. Osama bin Laden and Ayman Zawahiri did not send nineteen (or allegedly twenty) young men to attack the United States because Washington supports nondemocratic regimes in Egypt and Saudi Arabia.[85] Rather, the Twin Towers, Pentagon, and possibly the Capitol were in al Qa'ida's crosshairs because not only were U.S. forces stationed on Saudi territory, but also because the United States is a patron of political systems that places man's law above that of God's and, in the process, contributes to the perpetuation of jahaliyya. It is unclear how a more democratic and open Egypt or Saudi Arabia mitigates the problem of people who believe they are engaged in this type of "cosmic" struggle.[86] For al Qa'ida's theoreticians, democracy has precisely the same problem as an authoritarian one—God's law does not rule.

Policymakers and advocates of democracy promotion may have been correct in their assumption that fewer people would be willing to take up arms against their states—and the United States—in more open, transparent, and accountable political systems.[87] Still, Sayyid Qutb's intellectual framework for transnational jihad was revolutionary and uncompromising, distinguishing only between a very specific conception of Islamic society and the rest. To the extent that there will always be people attracted to this worldview, the United States and its allies will be targets of al Qa'ida, its affiliates, and its imitators. There is no policy prescription for this other than good police work, intelligence gathering, and superior firepower.

The other problem for the United States was the uncharted territory of encouraging political change in friendly Arab countries. The critique among democracy advocates in the Arab world that the United States promoted freedom everywhere but the Middle East was, as noted, powerful and largely correct. Yet the implication of some anti-Arab bias in this perceived anomaly was on one level understandable given long-standing American policy in the Middle East, but it was also wrong. Egypt, Saudi Arabia, Jordan, and Morocco are all Arab countries, but that is not the salient characteristic common to all of them. Rather, they are American allies who happen to be Arab. Over the course of six decades, Washington had no interest in promoting democracy in the Arab world because its policy of relying on friendly authoritarians to achieve its objectives in the Middle East seemed to work quite well. Once the United States finally decided that freedom in the Middle East mattered after the September 11 attacks and the articulation of the "Freedom Agenda," policymakers had very little idea how to advance reform in large part because there was no policy memo, playbook, or inkling how to do this within friendly countries.

The places where Washington was most successful in advancing democracy—Germany and Japan—were defeated in total war and occupied. The countries of Eastern and Central Europe were part of the Warsaw Pact, making it easy for Washington to pound away at them and their Soviet masters about human rights and freedom. There were exceptions to this, of course. The Philippines was an authoritarian ally of the United States that made a successful transition to democracy. This had little to do with U.S. policy, however. Washington only swooped in to support "people power" well after it became clear that the Marcos dictatorship was on the verge of collapse. South Korea is another oft-cited example of an American friend that became democratic, but the extent of Washington's role in the Korean transition—or delayed transition—remains subject to considerable academic debate.[88]

In the Middle East and Egypt, in particular, Washington needed to answer two critical questions about democratic change in the Middle East. First, how does it encourage Arab leaders to undertake reform? Second, how does the United States protect its strategic interests in the short and medium terms when transitions tend to be fraught? Neither the Bush nor the Obama administrations answered either question effectively, though the political upheaval in the Middle East in early 2011 made the first query moot as far as Egypt was concerned. Before the end of President Mubarak's reign, analysts and observers suggested pressuring him to change by leveraging economic and military assistance in a manner that would force the Egyptian leader to undertake meaningful political change in order to secure American largesse.[89] This, they argued, posed relatively little risk to U.S. interests because anything Washington asked of Mubarak was in his interest anyway. Actual policymakers did not seem totally convinced of this argument and when it came to the Egyptian uprising, they seemed hamstrung between the uncertainties of political change and American interests. At least during the early stages of the mass demonstrations against Mubarak, the Obama administration walked a very fine line between a nondemocratic ally who had contributed much to U.S. regional interests and popular demands for a democratic transition. Indeed, Washington seemed to position itself in a way that had the Egyptian president managed to hang on, the damage to U.S.-Egypt relations would not have been as great had the White House totally broken from the dictator.

The most profound shortcoming of democracy promotion policy was, however, resistance from the Arabs themselves. This was to be expected of Egyptian leaders who rejected the American intrusion in Egypt's internal affairs. Egyptian nationalism can often be prickly, but more importantly, Cairo did not believe that it should answer to anyone, even those who were providing it with generous aid. In the 1950s and 1960s, Soviet leader Nikita Khrushchev's entreaties on behalf of Egypt's embattled communists were dismissed as "unacceptable interference in Egypt's domestic affairs."[90] Given that the Egyptian regime was founded in large part on resistance to foreign presence and influence in the country, the emerging "Freedom Agenda" in Washington was bound to be met with President Mubarak's opposition.

Yet this view was not confined to the Egyptian officialdom. Even those intellectuals, activists, and ordinary Egyptians who wanted to live in a democracy were uneasy about the post-9/11 discussion in Washington about democracy in Egypt and the Middle East. Here there were three interrelated concerns: First, just as with the Egyptian leadership, there is a deeply ingrained sense of nationalism that breeds contempt of foreigners bearing advice about the way Egyptians should live. Second, the American policy was widely believed to be an effort to "impose" democracy on Egypt. This became a particularly potent issue after the U.S. invasion of Iraq, which, by default, became an actual exercise in imposing democracy on an Arab country. Finally, as Washington was shifting toward a policy emphasizing democratic change, Egyptian intellectuals, students, and other observers argued that the United States sought democratic change out of its "own interests." This was true. Whereas authoritarian stability had been regarded previously as the best way to secure the free flow of oil and Israel's security and maintain American predominance, Bush administration officials now calculated that in fact democratic states in the Arab world would best help Washington achieve these goals. In 2002, an Egyptian political scientist named Hassan Nafa'a appeared on a panel at the Washington Institute for Near East Policy's annual Soref Symposium. During the event Nafa'a, who would later go on to be one of the spokesmen for Mohammed ElBaradei's reformist National Association for Change, articulated widely held suspicions of American democracy promotion in Egypt:

> Everyone would like to see democratic regimes rule, not only in Arab and Muslim countries, but everywhere. You will nevertheless find a lot of skepticism, because once you have democratic ideals that conflict with other objectives of American foreign policy—such as oil supply or the security of Israel—the United States sacrifices the former, being much more keen to achieve the latter. Is there a commitment to restructure the agenda of U.S. foreign policy objectives? I am not so sure.[91]

Nafa'a is hardly representative of Egypt's broad community of democracy activists, but the sentiments he expressed touch precisely on why the United States was widely regarded to be an illegitimate messenger of change.

Even as the Egyptian government—like many other states in the region—was deflecting Washington's pressure for change, the Bush administration was operationalizing what until December 12, 2002, had been a largely rhetorical exercise. On that day, then Secretary of State Colin Powell announced the establishment of the Middle East Partnership Initiative (MEPI) with an initial funding of $29 million.[92] This new layer of bureaucracy within the Near Eastern Affairs Bureau of the State Department was intended to take the lead in implementing the administration's Freedom Agenda. MEPI would fund programs in four critical areas—called pillars—that were deemed important to building liberal democracies in the Arab world: political reform, economic reform, educational reform, and women's empowerment.[93] In practice, MEPI's writ included encouraging trade, mobilizing foreign direct investment, promoting the rule of law, strengthening civil society, helping improve access to quality education, and addressing specific challenges that women face in the Arab world. Some of this work had begun during the 1990s under the auspices of AID, but the exigencies of U.S. foreign policy post-September 11 gave many of these programs new emphasis. While AID had focused on creating constituencies within Arab governments for change, the rationale for MEPI was to work with independent and indigenous NGOs and civil society groups, as well as governments. As noted, initial funding for MEPI was $29 million. The following year, the Bush administration requested $145 million, but Congress appropriated only $45 million for the effort.

Reformers and government spokesmen in the Middle East greeted the establishment of MEPI with a combination of wariness and derision. The level of funding was wholly inadequate for the task at hand, indicating that Washington remained far from serious when it came to reform. There was also the alleged problem that Washington support for local NGOs would undermine the legitimacy of these groups given Washington's long-term support for Israel and its impending invasion of Iraq. In practice, not a single Egyptian civil society organization ever rejected MEPI assistance, though this was largely a function of the fact that they were a self-selecting group. The real concern, however, was the Egyptian government's response. After all, Saad Eddin Ibrahim was imprisoned in part for receiving a grant from the

European Commission designed to educate Egyptians about proper electoral practices. Among the four charges, the professor had run afoul of Articles 1 and 2 of Military Order No. 4 of 1992, which prohibited Egyptians from receiving money from abroad without prior permission, which originally targeted the Muslim Brotherhood and Islamist extremist groups.

Even before the establishment of MEPI, the People's Assembly passed the Law of Associations (Law 84 of 2002, also known as the NGO Law) that restricted the ability of Egyptian civil society organizations to raise money and made it more difficult for them to operate. Central to the law was a requirement that all NGOs—between 16,000 and 19,000 organizations—register with the Ministry of Social Affairs, which gave the government the opportunity to reject applications from a variety of long-standing groups dedicated to human rights, workers' rights, housing rights, and combating torture. The NGOs were also prohibited from engaging in political activity, though there was immediate concern among civil society organizers that the excessively broad view of "politics" among Egyptian functionaries and ministers would place their organizations in jeopardy. While NGOs were permitted to accept donations, they were prohibited from receiving money from abroad without exception. Also, if the organization received funding of twenty thousand Egyptian pounds or more from a single source, the NGO's board was required to submit the details of the donation and supporting documentation to a registered auditor. Violation of these provisions would result in fines equal to the amount of the gift or jail time.[94]

Congress sought to give Egyptian organizations a way out of these restrictions when, eighteen months later, it included a provision—known as the Brownback amendment (for then-Senator Sam Brownback, a Republican from Kansas)—in Public Law 108–447 that stated, "With respect to the provision of assistance for Egypt for democracy and governance activities, the organizations implementing such assistance and the specific nature of that assistance shall not be subject to the prior approval by the Government of Egypt."[95] Before leaving Cairo to become the assistant secretary of state for Near East Affairs, U.S. Ambassador David Welch, tested the Brownback amendment when he announced at a press conference that the United States was providing $1 million to two NGOs and four advocacy groups registered as companies without the prior approval of the Egyptian government, though Welch made it clear that Cairo had been made aware of the grants.

Welch's announcement produced a fierce reaction from members of the People's Assembly. Almost immediately, Abu El Ezz el Harriri from the Tagammu Party demanded that the prime minister investigate what he termed "a blatant breach of diplomatic norms that could open the door wide for more American meddling in Egyptian affairs."[96] Mohammed Abdel Alim, a Wafdist, assailed the government for permitting the United States to fund Egyptian advocacy organizations. Members of the ruling National Democratic Party, in an effort not to be caught on the wrong side of what was clearly a sensitive issue, sided with the opposition and demanded that the restrictions on foreign funding for NGOs be extended to companies as well. In the end, the Egyptian efforts to undermine the Brownback amendment mattered little, as Washington continued to fund civil society groups who sought U.S. support regardless of Cairo's objections.[97]

Indeed, with the establishment of a bureaucracy dedicated to encouraging democratic change in the Middle East, the Bush administration was signaling that political reform in the Arab world was going to be a lasting feature of American foreign policy. Indeed, the administration hammered away at the themes it discovered after 9/11, linking terrorism to authoritarianism, the inherent instability of nondemocratic rule, and the universal values of freedom and democracy. Almost a year after the establishment of MEPI, President Bush made the short trip across Lafayette Park opposite the White House on Pennsylvania Avenue to the colonnaded headquarters of the U.S. Chamber of Commerce. The reason for his visit was a speech marking the twentieth anniversary of the federally funded National Endowment for Democracy, which is "dedicated to the growth and strengthening of democratic institutions around the world." The president's remarks were notable in one important respect. Besides using the clunky phrase "forward strategy of freedom in the Middle East" for the first time to describe his administration's policy, Bush explained to his audience why a push for democratic change had become a central focus of his approach to the Arab world:

Sixty years of Western nations excusing and accommodating the lack of freedom in the Middle East did nothing to make us safe—because in the long run, stability cannot be purchased at the expense of liberty. As long as the Middle East remains a place where freedom does not flourish, it will remain a place of stagnation, resentment, and violence ready for export. And with the spread of weapons that can bring catastrophic harm to our country and to our friends, it would be reckless to accept the status quo.[98]

The president praised countries like Bahrain, Qatar, and Morocco for rather modest steps toward more open politics, and even lauded Saudi Arabia for its plan to hold its first-ever municipal elections, but there were no such plaudits for Egypt. Bush neither complimented nor criticized the Egyptians. Rather, citing Cairo's leadership in peace, he exhorted Egypt to "show the way toward democracy in the Middle East."

The Egyptian response to President Bush was to reject his reasoning and deflect his challenge. A week after the speech, the editor in chief of the government-affiliated daily *al Ahram*, Ibrahim Nafie, argued that the preconditions for democratic change were "obviated, directly or indirectly, by U.S. policy in the region." Nafie was, of course, referring to Washington's support for Israel and the American invasion of Iraq. Yet Nafie went further, harkening back to the Western penetration of Egypt and the region more generally: "By perpetuating its occupation of Iraq, the Bush administration forces us to conclude that it has launched a colonial project aimed at securing control over this region's vital resources, and that this project is cloaked in the old time garb of 'the white man's burden' to civilize non-white people."[99] Makram Mohammed Ahmad, editor of the state-owned weekly *al Musawwar*, expanded on Nafie's central theme declaring that the United States:

[I]nsists on imposing its own cultural patterns on everybody without understanding the culture of others; interferes in every little detail of internal affairs; ignores the limits of religion and social customs in its definition of family and defense of homosexuals and people who violate the traditions of their society; imposes itself as a partner in religious and educational issues which are considered exclusive to national work; and imagines that what is good for the United States can be good for others.

Ahmad ended his column implying that Washington's credibility problem was related to its "blind bias toward Israel."[100] In *Akhbar al Youm*, columnist Galal Arif summed up the position of the state-owned press in a column a little more than a week after President Bush's speech: "The Arabs know that U.S. policies have for the past 60 years been a real enemy for all their hopes in establishing justice and democracy. But they also know that there is no place for any U.S. talk about democracy while American aircraft are killing Palestinian children."[101] In an additional effort to fend off Washington's pressure, other state-affiliated editors and government officials asserted that the Bush administration's critique was unwarranted as Egypt was already well on its way to a democratic future. Still, the core of Cairo's response to Bush was contained in the arguments that Nafie, Ahmad, and Arif articulated. These arguments represented unofficial talking points that Egyptian leaders, and those within the ambit of the regime, had used since Washington began talking about political change in the Arab world shortly after 9/11.

Egyptian officials also seized on the issue of terrorism—the very reason for the "forward strategy of freedom"—rejecting out of hand Washington's hypothesis that the Arab world's democracy deficit causes terrorism in favor of their own widely held theory.[102] Within weeks of the September 11 attacks, Egyptian officials argued that the dispossession of the Palestinian people, denial of their legitimate national rights, and the ongoing Israeli occupation of Palestinian lands were the crucibles of transnational jihadism. On October 14, 2001, President Mubarak appeared on Israeli television and told the interviewer: "It is you who are responsible for terrorism. You are responsible. The Palestinian question is the cause of terrorism."[103]

After he became foreign minister, Ahmad Aboul Gheit in 2004 often argued that resolving the Palestinian problem would not only mitigate the problem of terrorism but also resolve "more than 50 percent of the problems of the Middle East." Although always articulated implicitly, to much of Egyptian officialdom and the intelligentsia that caters to it, Washington—by dint of its support for Israel—was directly responsible for the attacks of September 11 and the subsequent global war on terrorism. The Egyptians had a point, if only a flimsy one. Israel and America's support for that country figure more prominently in al Qa'ida's grievances than is commonly believed, but the Egyptians were being disingenuous by suggesting that there would be a marked decline in terrorism and other problems of the region if the Israelis and Palestinians ultimately agreed to call off their century-long struggle over historic Palestine.[104] As the Egyptians no doubt knew well from their own experience, peace agreements can trigger violence.

For their part, Egypt's varied opposition groups reacted warily to Bush's November 6 speech and the Freedom Agenda more generally. After all, the United States had never before seemed terribly interested in the authoritarian nature of the Egyptian regime so long as

President Mubarak kept the Suez Canal open, maintained peace with Israel, and fought the Islamists. There was a sense of "Where's the catch?" among the opposition figures not quite willing to believe that the United States had altered its approach to the region. Moreover, on the issue of Israel, some of the opposition and the government seemed to be entirely in sync. Mohammed Faeq, the head of the Arab Organization for Human Rights—an Egyptian organization—told the Agence France Presse (AFP) that "There is a lack of democracy but democracy cannot be imposed from the outside. Especially if it comes from the United States because it lacks credibility due to its support of Israel and the occupation of Iraq."[105] Yet the Egyptian opposition was not uniformly cautious. The Muslim Brotherhood was, if anything, downright hostile to Bush, echoing much of the government's critique. On November 7, the Supreme Guide Maamoun al Hudaybi told AFP, "There is a great deal of truth in the fact that U.S. support to tyrannical regimes is one reason for the hatred expressed toward the United States . . . But the most important reason for the Muslim people's hatred of the United States is its total bias toward the Zionist entity . . . and U.S. aggression in Iraq and Afghanistan. Bush ignored these."[106] Washington clearly had a credibility gap that covered the spectrum of the Egyptian opposition.

The criticism from Cairo did not deter the Bush administration, which was determined to show that Washington was serious about the Freedom Agenda. The central themes of President Bush's NED speech would be repeated over and over again not only by the president, but also the administration's principal policymakers including the vice president, secretary of state, and national security advisor. Two notable examples involved Secretary of State Condoleezza Rice in the first half of 2005. First, in March she gave a wide-ranging interview to the editors of the *Washington Post* during which she asked rhetorically, "Do I think there's a strong certainty that the Middle East was not going to stay stable anyway? Yes. And when you know that the status quo is no longer defensible, then you have to be willing to move in another direction. I also think there's some argument to be made that America's association with the freedom deficit was a problem for the United States in the region."[107] Two months later, the secretary of state traveled to Egypt, where, before an audience at the American University in Cairo, she decried the past policy of supporting "stability at the expense of democracy" and declared, "The day must come when the rule of law replaces emergency decrees and when an independent judiciary replaces arbitrary justice. The Egyptian government must fulfill the promise it has made to its people—and the entire world—by giving its citizens freedom to choose."[108]

The cumulative effect of the establishment of MEPI, the 2004 Group of Eight sponsored *Partnership for Progress for a Common Future with the Region of the Broader Middle East and North Africa*—which was intended to give the Freedom Agenda a multilateral component—and the Bush administration's rhetorical support for political change forced Mubarak to act. He and his advisors had been unable from the outset to disarm the administration by invoking either nationalism or Israel—or after March 2003, Iraq—and the Egyptian president sought to defuse both pressure from Washington and the growing drumbeat for reform from Egyptian society. Under the watchful eyes of a newly attentive White House, the Egyptian leader positioned himself as a reformer. In 2004, the National Democratic Party began emphasizing change, and at the party's annual conference that year, Mubarak himself talked about "strengthening" and "deepening" democracy. At the same time, the Shura Council—Egypt's Upper House of parliament—established a National Council for Human Rights charged with issuing reports on the state of human rights in the country. And, of course, there was the constitutional amendment laying the groundwork for multiparty presidential elections. Visiting Cairo during this time was to experience excruciating cognitive dissonance, given that practically anyone who had ever been a regime spokesman, apologist, or henchman declared that they had been a reformer for the previous twenty-five years and were so thankful that the leadership was finally catching up to their progressive thinking.

None of these ostensible commitments to political change was credible, but they did have a critically important effect on Egyptian politics. With Washington watching and Mubarak posturing as a reformer, activists who had previously worked at the margins, or who had been subject to repression, were relatively freer to pursue their agendas in new and innovative ways. Although wary of the U.S. role, seemingly overnight, political activists were organizing summits and writing reform manifestos, and those with invitations to conferences at glitzy hotels in places like Doha, Abu Dhabi, and Dubai sharply questioned Egyptian government ministers who were on the program. Journalists and columnists, in particular, took the opportunity to unleash a torrent of criticism on Egypt's first family. This is not to say that the United States caused the political ferment that Egypt experienced between roughly early 2003 and late 2005. The war in Iraq, Israeli policies in the occupied Palestinian territories, and growing concern that Gamal Mubarak was being groomed to succeed his father were likely more decisive in driving the political agitation. In addition, Washington's watchful eye did not always serve to protect activists. After all, 2005 and 2006 were bad years for Egypt's political activists with the arrest of Ayman Nour, numerous bloggers, and the intimidation of many others.

Still, there was a sense in Egypt that Washington, which for so long had supported Egyptian authoritarianism with military, diplomatic, and financial support, was playing a critical role by supplying political cover for the opposition. Although some of Cairo's reformers were profoundly opposed to U.S. policy in Iraq and Palestine, they nevertheless supported—some more grudgingly than others—the Bush administration's pressure for political change. Hisham Kassem, chairman of the board of the Egyptian Organization for Human Rights and founding editor of *al Masry al Youm*, argued that U.S. policy was decisive in cracking open the door of Egyptian political reform. While not entirely unexpected of Kassem—a liberal who welcomed American democracy promotion—even Abdel Halim Qandil, at the time a spokesman for Kifaya! and editor of the Nasserist *al Arabi* that was fiercely critical of the United States, acknowledged that Washington's outspoken support for democracy was providing him and his movement a certain amount of protection from the Egyptian state. For its part, the Muslim Brotherhood was generally quiet on these issues, but it was taking advantage of the relatively more liberal political environment to press its agenda.

Bush may have been a reviled figure among many Egyptians, but his administration helped them publicly air questions about the sources of power and legitimacy of the regime. This was an astounding turn of events. Previously Washington had been a critical factor in Egyptian politics as various opposition groups sought to leverage the U.S.-Egypt strategic relationship to highlight the regime's vulnerability on issues like nationalism and sovereignty. Now the United States was a source of vulnerability for the regime in an entirely different way. In Washington's efforts to attack the "root causes" of terrorism, it injected itself directly into Egyptian debates over the long unsettled questions: What is Egypt? How is it organized? What is its political trajectory and what does it stand for?

Within months, however, the United States and the Egyptian government would revert to form. The Egyptian leadership would regain its footing through the help of both the Muslim Brotherhood and the Palestinian group Hamas. The Brotherhood's electoral success in Egypt in November–December 2005 and, in particular, Hamas' outright victory in the Palestinian legislative elections in January 2006 spooked Washington. Absent an answer to the question, "How do you protect U.S. interests in the short and medium term?" the soaring rhetoric about democracy, freedom, and change that had become a hallmark of the administration was greatly scaled back and became largely perfunctory, though the work of MEPI and AID continued. This was also a time when the situation in Iraq was deteriorating, and Iran used the opportunity to flex its muscles there. Under these circumstances, there was a strong pull in Washington for retrenchment and a focus on core American interests. The change in U.S. policy only confirmed what Hassan Nafa'a and others had suspected four years earlier—positive rhetoric aside, ultimately Washington would not alter its long-standing approach to the Middle East. Washington's pull back from the Freedom Agenda only substantiated what the Brotherhood's Supreme Guide Maamoun al Hudaybi warned a little more than a month after President Bush's National Endowment for Democracy speech—that the United States was not to be trusted because "[it] does not seek to realize the interests of the Arab world. Otherwise it would have stopped its support for Israel and withdrawn its armies from Iraq."[109] The fact that Hamas' electoral victory appeared to be the reason for the Bush administration's sudden uncertainty about democracy in the Middle East spoke volumes to Egyptian and Arab commentators and activists. Indeed, after spending the better part of the previous four years emphasizing the need for political change, by early 2006 the United States looked more and more like the peddler of pernicious double standards Egyptian and Arab skeptics had long suspected.

The accusations of hypocrisy were more accurate than many believed at the time. To be sure, there was a noticeable "edge" to the bilateral relationship, as one former senior Bush administration official relayed, over U.S. effort to promote democracy. These ill feelings were reflected in Mubarak's decision not to travel to Washington after 2004—though this may have had more to do with the way the Egyptian president felt personally betrayed by Bush over his handling of the Palestinian-Israeli conflict—and the tone of joint press conferences. In one noteworthy incident, Foreign Minister Aboul Gheit ostentatiously contradicted Secretary Rice when the two were asked if the fate of Ayman Nour came up in their discussions. Rice declared that she had raised Nour "each time that I meet with my Egyptian counterparts." To this the foreign minister responded, "You didn't raise it today," implying that the American secretary of state was a liar before the assembled press.[110] In the end, however, the Freedom Agenda never got in the way of the strategic relationship. According to senior Bush administration officials, Cairo remained responsive—though perhaps not as responsive as Washington preferred—on traditional issues like the Arab-Israeli conflict, access to the Suez Canal, and help for Washington in inter-Arab councils.[111] At the same time, the United States did nothing materially to punish Egypt for its distinct lack of interest in reform. The exception may have been the Ayman Nour case. It was generally believed in the United States and Egypt that the Bush administration decided to terminate plans to negotiate a Free Trade Agreement with Egypt to protest Nour's imprisonment. Yet, according to officials present at the deliberations over the proposed pact, the determination to not move forward was far more complicated than Nour's situation. His arrest was a factor in the administration's decision, but it was not the only one. The Bush team weighed several variables—including the U.S. trade representative's workload; higher priority countries like Korea, Switzerland, and Malaysia; the chances of getting the deal through an Egypt-hostile Congress; and the fact that Cairo was not ready for the negotiations on a technical level—and Washington decided to walk away.[112]

FLAWED ASSUMPTIONS?

The debate over the U.S.-Egypt Free Trade Agreement represented many of the problems, contradictions, and ironies of the bilateral relationship that made Egypt policy so puzzling. The United States walked into a relationship with Egypt for a set of compelling reasons: the global struggle with the Soviet Union, Israeli security, and the free flow of oil from the Middle East. Cairo was not only perfectly positioned (literally) in the region to be a partner for Washington, but it also had a host of other assets that the United States could leverage for its benefit. In what became a mantra of Egypt analysts and American diplomats, Egypt is the most populous Arab country; it has the most powerful army, which forces the Israelis to be concerned with Cairo; it is a regional bellwether; and Egypt allegedly has historical weight. What other country in the Middle East possessed that combination of attributes? Not Saudi Arabia. Not Israel. Morocco? Hardly. Turkey is non-Arab. Iran is both Persian and Shi'a. The rest of the countries in the region are trivial. In the words of one Egyptian interlocutor: "We produce [the population of] one Bahrain every year." In comparison, Egypt is strong. Once more, the strategic relationship with Washington would have the dynamic affect of making both countries stronger. This description of Egypt was on one level entirely accurate and what the leaders of the regime told themselves, their citizens, and visiting congressional delegations. Upon closer scrutiny, however, the image of a powerful and influential Egypt—the basic assumptions that have guided U.S. policy toward Egypt—was off.

An ongoing debate among social scientists is how to measure state strength. Is a state strong or weak? The answer to this question is important for understanding the way other societies work and for policymakers crafting foreign policy. Like much in the social sciences, no one ever agrees on a uniform metric. Does the extent to which a state can monitor the political activities of its citizens and manipulate their behavior indicate its relative strength? Not necessarily. Does the arrangement of economic institutions provide a good measure for a state's power? This is a good question, but it may tell analysts more about economic elites than overall state strength. Can the state mobilize society in support of a cause or a particular project? This may be a good indicator, but it may only shed light on certain moments in time.

One of the better, more nuanced ways to capture a state's relative strength explores how its political leaders elicit the compliance of their citizens.[113] First, there are "normative appeals"—compelling visions of society that have some basis in reality. Not all Americans live the "American dream," for example, but enough have that many believe in its positive myths. As a result, the vast majority of Americans believe that the United States is a great place to live due to the freedom and opportunities they enjoy. Second, loyalty or political control can also be achieved through bribery, often referred to as patronage. Leaders will distribute the resources of the state—i.e., money—in a way that reinforces the support of loyalists and to buy new backers. In the United States, this is hard to see on a national level, but it is abundantly clear on the state and local levels. Big city governments in Chicago, New York, Washington, and Philadelphia, to name just a few examples, have at various times been run as large patronage machines to the benefit of sitting mayors and their political parties.

Finally, governments use coercion, or the threat of coercion, to keep people in line. Again, this is hard to see in the United States because the vast majority of its citizens believe in its inherent virtues and the state has rarely needed to resort to force to ensure the American political system. There were, of course, Japanese internment camps during World War II, but this use of coercion was directed at a specific and small ethnic group. More generally, even though most Americans pay their taxes, which is in and of itself a testament to the importance of the normative appeal of the United States, there are heavy penalties for those who fail to do so, including possible time in prison.

These means of gaining loyalty and ensuring political control are not mutually exclusive, however. Normative appeals, bribery, and coercion are all part of the same strategy; what is important is a state's relative dependence on these factors. In the United States, the animating ideas of society about "liberty and justice for all" are widely held, meaning that American political leaders rely less on patronage and coercion. In that way, the United States' political system is relatively strong because most people buy into the American dream, which ensures the loyalty of most citizens. Egypt over the last sixty years was the mirror image of the United States. Since the 1960s, Egypt's leaders have failed to develop a coherent ideological vision that makes sense to most people. As a result, the Egyptian elite have had to rely on bribery and coercion to ensure social cohesion. Even so, the amount of resources available to Egyptian leaders in contrast to their Saudi counterparts, is limited. As a result, President Mubarak only had enough largesse to buy off that constituency for autocracy—big business, the military, security service, regime intellectuals, and the bureaucracy. The rest of society was controlled almost exclusively through violence or the threat of it. This is expensive and risky, revealing the profound weakness of the Egyptian state.

In the process of threatening or actually using force against their own population, the Egyptian leadership only added to an increasingly angry, polarized, radicalized, and potentially unstable political arena. Yet Washington based its approach to the Middle East in large part on a stable Egypt, despite all of the country's pressing problems. This conclusion was based on two observations. First, the Egyptians demonstrated a capacity to muddle through significant challenges—defeat in war, economic stagnation, assassination, and terrorism—in the past. Second, the regime's primary constituents never withdrew their support from the leadership. Both these observations are true, but they did not provide insight into the prospects for Egypt's future stability.

On the eve of the Egyptian revolution, Washington was stuck, locked into a relationship that had certain strategic purposes in the past, but with a country whose regional influence seemed to be waning and not as stable as widely believed. The policy debate over Egypt took for granted that President Mubarak would die in office and once the old man took his last sail up the Nile another regime figure would take his place. As a result, policymakers and analysts tended to think of Egypt policy in terms of two options: authoritarian stability or democracy promotion.

For some of those who regarded the Bush administration's efforts to foster democratic change a mistake, a renewed commitment to President Mubarak, the regime he led, and ultimately to his successor would fortify the Egyptian leadership and renew its flagging international and regional standing. With enhanced American support, Cairo would enjoy new regional prestige, making Egypt a more effective partner than in the immediate past. There were several problems with this approach, however. First, it did nothing to alter the vision-patronage-coercion balance that was at the heart of Egypt's weakness; in fact, a policy of authoritarian stability would have only endorsed Cairo's reliance on coercion. Second, it did not resolve a central yet unintended problem in the U.S.-Egypt relationship: Washington had become a critical albeit largely negative factor in Egypt's domestic political struggles. The opposition used the strategic ties between the two countries—or what they have long suspected about these relations, much of which the November 2010 WikiLeaks' revelations confirmed—as a political cudgel against President Mubarak and the regime, more generally. The government deflected this criticism by striking its own anti-American posture by using force against its domestic opponents. Finally, the argument posited that it was possible to turn back the clock in both Egypt and the United States. Yet, too much had happened over the course of the 2000s. In Egypt, activists were challenging the authority of the state in new and bolder ways. Political reform had become a critical part of Egypt's national debate. In Washington, although critics charged that Washington had essentially abandoned the push for democracy as of 2006, when the Bush administration toned down its Freedom Agenda rhetoric, the American foreign policy bureaucracy continued to encourage democratic change in the Middle East.

The second option that wonks and officials debated was a full return to the Freedom Agenda. To advocates of this approach, democratic leaders in Egypt would have to rely less on coercion because they would enjoy the consent of the governed. Yet a return to the democracy-focused approach of 2003–2005 presented a range of problems for Washington. As noted in detail earlier, Egypt's leadership was manifestly opposed to an American role in promoting political change.

In the run-up to Egypt's 2010 People's Assembly elections, which the *Economist* magazine described as "garishly fraudulent," an unnamed senior Egyptian government official called American democracy promoters "deluded."[114] Although it turns out that this was a more apt description of Egyptian officialdom on the eve of the January 25 uprising, this surprising undiplomatic remark was accompanied by a slew of commentaries in the state-controlled press hurling invective at the United States for its alleged interference in Egypt's internal affairs. This was a fight that the Egyptians seemed determined to make sure that Washington lost. With the exception of MEPI grantees, it was also not entirely clear how much Egyptians wanted Washington's help in this area given their perception of foreigners on ostensibly civilizing missions. The recent record of U.S.-Middle East policy is thus hardly an asset for selling American goodwill to skeptical Egyptians. Operation Iraqi Freedom, Washington's support for Israel in its struggle with the Palestinians, and the notion that Washington sought to "impose democracy" on Egypt remain visceral topics in many quarters.

At the same time, the Bush administration's approach to Egypt and the Arab world writ large held enormous appeal. The "forward strategy of freedom" seemed like an antidote to a great global threat emerging from the Middle East, and it had the great benefit of being entirely consistent with American values—something often unapologetically missing from the conduct of U.S. foreign policy. Yet, too often observers overlook the fact that political change is not linear and is entirely contingent. What may start out as a seeming transition to democracy could end up as the consolidation of a liberal democracy or an illiberal democracy or a dictatorship. Never mind that states moving from one type of political system tend to be more unstable and warlike than others. The question was whether these potential costs outweighed the perceived benefits of a democracy promotion strategy. Few scholars have addressed these issues in a rigorous way, but in January and February 2011 it became largely moot. Until that time, American officials and other outside observers assumed that democratic change in Egypt was a generational project. During that time, American aid and values could, if employed judiciously, encourage a democratic evolution of Egypt's political system. This would have the twin benefit of ensuring the development of democratic institutions and, importantly, protecting American interests. It turned out, however, that after thirty years under Hosni Mubarak, Egyptians could not wait.

Uprising

WITH SOME NOTABLE exceptions—like the Semiramis Intercontinental and Conrad hotels—Cairo exists in a narrow spectrum of various hues of beige, tan, and brown. This is particularly jarring from the air, and the landing pattern at Cairo International Airport requires a number of long meandering turns over the city. The plane glides over a veritable sea of sand-colored buildings and monuments, punctuated only by the dark ribbon of the Nile. The brownscape is a function of Cairo's notorious dust and the, no-doubt, great expense of painting and repainting that would be required to keep the grime at bay. As a consequence, even wealthy sections of the city have a rundown, haphazard look. The sense of dilapidation only grows more acute from ground level. It is not only the façades of many buildings that seem tattered, but also the public spaces. Zamalek is an upscale part of Cairo—sitting in the middle of the Nile, facing downtown in one direction and the poor neighborhood of Imbaba in the other. It was once home to many grand villas. Some of those houses remain, but for the most part Zamalek is now like many of Cairo's core neighborhoods, featuring street after street of apartment buildings, some more splendid than others.

The apartment building lobbies of Zamalek are a fascination. To varying degrees they are in disarray—worn carpets, old newspapers strewn about, cracked decorative mirrors on the walls, nonworking light bulbs, that Cairo dust, and, in some cases, broken glass. Enter the elevator—the kind one might find in Paris or Istanbul that only safely carries two or three people—which also tends to be a mess, and step off at any floor. The hallways off the elevators are generally in better condition than the lobby, but the payoff is the apartments, which can be stunning. Their size is often comparable to the ample square footage of the well-heeled on Manhattan's Upper East Side. At times, the nouveau arabesque furniture is a bit much, but it is far from de rigueur. The multiple bedrooms, high ceilings, wood floors, and in one case at least, a wall-sized fireplace, can be jaw-dropping. Even in more modest buildings, the difference between private and public space is vast. To be sure, this is hardly a uniquely Egyptian phenomenon. The gleaming, glass-cased office towers that mark the New York City skyline stand in pronounced disparity with the caked-on filth of the subway system. Yet, in Egypt, the contrast is much more striking because it can be so close to home, literally. At first, these circumstances are disconcerting. Why would people—whether well-to-do or poor—put up with this situation? One might think, if the residents paid the doorman more, their public spaces would be better maintained; but, unkempt lobbies are so common that it cannot possibly be solely a question of the bowab's pay.

Upon further consideration, however, the difference between the public and private spaces of Zamalek's apartment buildings makes perfect sense metaphorically. The failure of Nasserism, with its rhetorical emphasis on social justice, income redistribution, free education, and guaranteed employment gave way to something entirely different under Anwar Sadat. By the time of Nasser's death in 1970, his project was, like the lobbies of Zamalek, in tatters. Given the myriad problems the regime confronted at the time, Sadat could hardly consolidate his power on the record of the preceding eighteen years. Instead, he chose to "correct" Egypt's course in midstream, emphasizing the private sector, commercialism, and consumer consumption. Many of the apartments in Zamalek are a testament to the return of a wealthy social class that had been under pressure during the Nasser years and the rise of a nouveau riche that coincided with Sadat's reign. The new president's intention was not necessarily to disavow community, but political considerations drove his choices. The shibboleths of Nasser's 1960s leftward tack and alignment with Moscow were discarded on the ground floor, left to yellow, crack, and gather dust in favor of the apartments above, which would ultimately bear the fruits of the free market and strategic relations with Washington. Yet there was something hollow about Sadat's direction as well. Only a relative few—the connected, the previously wealthy, courtiers, and hangers-on—enjoyed the fruits of infitah while the vast reservoir of Egyptians contended with hardship.

When Hosni Mubarak came to power, he chose a middle way between Nasser's leftward tilt and Sadat's correction. The new president hung onto the economic opening, calculating correctly that big business was a critical constituency; he moved Egypt back toward the Arab mainstream, but did not repudiate Sadat's separate peace with Israel; he cooperated with Washington to secure its largesse; and he repressed the political ambitions of almost all groups while simultaneously promising reform and change. Against this backdrop, stability became the catchword of Mubarak's rule. However, thirty years after Mubarak unexpectedly became president, stability paradoxically produced an environment conducive to instability. In this way, the broken lobbies of Zamalek represent something profound about the state of Egyptian society over the past six decades—the steady loss of community and a social contract that was finally torn asunder during the Mubarak era.

Hatem is big and burly, but has a gentle soul. He is a proud Egyptian. He fled Egypt a number of years ago for Germany with his Austrian-born wife and baby daughter. Hatem had a litany of complaints about Cairo—the traffic, noise, and pollution. The incessant beeping of taxis, trucks, and private cars particularly grated on him. As he cruised Cairo in his late-1960s vintage Volkswagen Beetle, he would throw his hands up and ask "Why?" when another driver honked at him. These are common grievances that run across the political spectrum and up and down the social classes. It was not, however, the less appealing aspects of Cairo life that drove Hatem from home. One evening over dinner at a restaurant along the Nile, Hatem—who is as apolitical as they come—seemed particularly upset. He did not say he was leaving, but it was clear what he was thinking. Hatem's natural gregariousness drained away from him that night in favor of an overwhelming melancholy. He could no longer cope with a society in which he felt there was so much rhetorical emphasis on community, but at the same time everyone seemed to be out for themselves. Because there was no rule of law in Mubarak's Egypt, the well-heeled and well-connected had been able to capitalize on their advantages to amass even greater wealth or avoid accountability for their misdeeds. The fact that Mamdouh Ismail, the owner of the ill-fated *al Salam Boccacio 98*, was able to shield his wealth and pay little personal price for his company's obvious negligence is a prime example of a phenomenon that has trickled down and permeated society. Of course, this is not a uniquely Egyptian problem. The recent history of Wall Street executives showering themselves with enormous bonuses even after taxpayer bailouts is a glaring example of the American version of this dynamic. At least in the United States, however, there is the rule of law and a mechanism for citizens to hold their leaders accountable. This is clearly not the case in Egypt.

Hatem was lucky. He could go to Germany, where no doubt he would face many challenges, but he felt it was worth it, especially after the birth of his daughter. Others in Hatem's position and social class were generally forced to accept their circumstances and stick it out. Still others chose to fight the police state that corrupted Egyptian society. To them, there was a direct connection between the political order and the corrosion of community. Mohammed ElBaradei was making precisely this point when he wrote his now infamous op-ed for *al Dustour* questioning whether it was possible anymore for Egypt to undertake a big project—like the Crossing of the Suez Canal—that required dedication and self-sacrifice. In order to arrest the deterioration of society, rebuild the social contract, and bring prosperity to the country, the spectrum of political opposition had long sought what was, in essence, regime change. Although there had been significant attention and opposition to Gamal Mubarak's possible inheritance of leadership, it was unlikely that the opposition would have been satisfied with another regime-affiliated figure coming to power. To be sure, there was an added element of hostility to the younger Mubarak because a familial dynasty was so odious to many activists, but there was no reason to believe that any of the possible contenders for the presidency—including a military figure—would take steps to undermine a political system of which their constituents were the primary benefactors.

This battle over both the trajectory of Egyptian politics and the country's soul actually predates the extraordinary events of January–February 2011. Indeed, the broad sweep of the preceding chapters demonstrates that Egyptians have been in open revolt against their rulers since Urabi's nationalist uprising in 1882. By 2010, the struggle for Egypt grew more intense. Beginning with the Consultative Council elections in early June of that year and followed in late November with the People's Assembly polls, the intensity of opposition activity reflected the end-of-an-era atmosphere that has pervaded Egypt as President Mubarak grew older. Surgery in Germany in February 2010 to remove the president's gallbladder—though it was widely believed to be a more serious illness—and his two-month convalescence out of Cairo only seemed to fuel the anticipation of Egyptians who sensed they were on the cusp of change. Adding to this phenomenon was the return of ElBaradei with his Nobel Prize, gleaming resumé, thin security file, and Twitter feed criticizing the regime.

Through the late winter, spring, and summer of 2010 leading up to the People's Assembly election, there was a dizzying array of opposition political activities, including the formation of ElBaradei's National Association for Change, declarations in support of free and fair elections, debates over whether to boycott the polls, and appeals to Washington to pressure the government to undertake reform. Posters of Gamal Mubarak, with the red circle and backslash indicating "no," started appearing on Cairo buildings with the phrase "Egypt is too big for you." Then posters supporting intelligence chief Omar Suleiman for president also began to appear, but they just as suddenly vanished. All this activity was met with the inevitable security crackdown. The organization that came under the most pressure was, predictably, the Muslim Brotherhood. In the late spring of 2010 some activists had gone so far as to suggest that there were more Brothers in jail than at any other time since the Nasser period. This was surely a product of the Cairo rumor mill, but it spoke to the intensity with which it seemed virtually everyone in Cairo was looking toward the election. The opposition, in its struggle to redefine Egypt and the regime, and intent on clearing the political field and shaping a parliament in the way it saw fit, seemed to be heading toward some moment of truth.

On the eve of the parliamentary election, that sense of anticipation disappeared. In its place was the opposition's palpable sense of despair and the ruling NDP's hubris. Egyptian activists had been telling themselves all along that the election would change nothing, the voting would be rigged, and the ruling party would retain an overwhelming majority in the People's Assembly. As the election drew near and their expectations began looking more and more like reality, opponents of the regime began looking for a sliver of hope. Over late-night cookies and tea in his medical office, Dr. Abdel Galil Mustafa, the seventy-something spokesman for the Kifaya! movement, explained that boycott was the only route for his group and those that make up the National Association for Change. To do otherwise would legitimate a profoundly illegitimate process. Dr. Abdel Galil's heart was in it, but he admitted the boycott would not matter much. The outcome of the elections was predetermined. Perhaps, he offered lamely, the boycott "will help educate people about the injustice of a regime." As if they were not already aware of their own political predicament. Fellow boycotter Osama Ghazali Harb—leader of the Democratic Front—argued that boycotting was meant to embarrass the regime, undermine its legitimacy, and send a signal objecting to the possible nomination of Gamal Mubarak to be Egypt's next president. For his part, Ayman Nour, who leads a rump faction of his original al Ghad party, which agents of the regime commandeered, refused to take part in the elections and declared that he would ask representatives of the European Union to serve as unofficial election observers.[1]

Other opposition activists such as the April 6 Youth movement, which emerged in the spring of 2008 to support the rights of Egyptian workers, remained defiant, but in what seemed like desperation, descended into fanciful ideas. About a month before the elections, the group proposed holding parallel, independent elections if the regime did not respond to the seven-point plan for reform that Mohammed ElBaradei's National Association for Change had endorsed: ending the state of emergency, ensuring judicial oversight of the election process, authorizing local and international observers, providing equal access to the media for all candidates, giving Egyptians abroad the right to vote, permitting presidential candidates to run for office "without arbitrary restrictions" and limiting the president to two terms, and allowing voting by national identity card. What was fanciful was not so much the idea of holding parallel elections—which was creative— or that the government would respond to the NAC's demands, something President Mubarak had no intention of doing, rather, the call for the opposition to hold its own elections as a way to embarrass the leaders of the regime was the element of the plan that was farfetched. Perhaps it was their youth, but it should have been clear to the activists of April 6 that, given the predatory nature of the regime, Egyptian officials actually had little shame.

Ali Eddin Hilal, in many ways, represented the disdain that Egyptian leaders harbored toward their own people. Some weeks before the elections, the former professor of political science at Cairo University turned ruling-party secretary for media affairs dismissed the groups planning to boycott the elections and with a wave of his hand and with a look of incredulity asked, "Who are they? They represent no one." The fact that the Wafd, the Tagammu, a host of smaller parties, and even the Muslim Brotherhood's "independents" planned to participate with the NDP in the parliamentary elections should have been, according to Dr. Ali Eddin, a clear indication to any objective observer that the process was entirely legitimate. Of course, on the eve of the polls, 250 (of 600 arrested) members of the Brotherhood remained in jail, and the government had disqualified 30 percent of the candidates that the Brothers put forward. Other NDP officials were similarly dismissive of the opposition, its charges that the elections would be rigged, and international requests to send election observers to ensure that the polling was free and fair as the government had promised. International observers were off the table: "A violation of Egypt's sovereignty," declared one senior NDP operative—a position, he offered, that the opposition parties shared. According to the same ruling party official, the March 2007 amendment to Article 88 of the constitution established the High Election Commission to ensure the integrity of the elections because the judiciary became politicized while supervising the 2005 parliamentary polls.[2] In fact, members of the judiciary called out the regime for electoral fraud, prompting the arrest and detention of those judges.

Despite—or perhaps because of—the leadership's arrogance, nothing was left to chance in the run-up to the 2010 parliamentary elections. In October, the National Telecommunications Regulatory Authority (NTRA) canceled the permits of all broadcast companies that provided live television news feeds in Egypt in an obvious effort to control the flow of information from polling places around Egypt. These media outlets were welcome to apply for new licenses, but in the interim would be required to use state-owned facilities to broadcast. At the same time, the NTRA handed down new regulations on mass text messaging. If media outlets wanted to distribute news via SMS text message, they would need a new, separate license for the service. The license required that the companies pay a fee amounting to 3 percent of their SMS revenue to cover the cost of government censors who would monitor the content of the material disseminated to subscribers. Once more, groups that did not have official status—meaning the Muslim Brotherhood, the National Association for Change, the Nasserists, smaller groups like the Wasat party, and a host of protest groups—were barred from availing themselves of mass text-messaging services. The new regulations demonstrated learning on the part of Egypt's internal security service, just not the right kind. In the 2005 parliamentary elections, which were deeply flawed, SMS texts became an important tool for Egyptians to receive information about the conduct of the election while it occurred. The government was not about to let that happen again.

As it turned out, the conduct of the 2010 People's Assembly elections violated every principle that the government and the NDP promised to uphold. Rather than free and fair, violence—eight people died—intimidation, ballot stuffing, and counting irregularities marred the polling and produced a parliament with only eight opposition voices against an overwhelming NDP majority. Run-off elections in 166 districts in early December produced a similar result. Overall, the ruling party gained 420 seats (81 percent of the total) against 14 for the opposition parties and 70 independents. The scale of the regime's electoral malfeasance—the government did not even try to make it look like a legitimate election—produced sporadic protests and intensified calls for change that were met with arrests, the clubs of the Central Security Forces, and deaf ears. After telling reporters that the elections were "fine," President Mubarak opened the new parliament on December 13 and declared business as usual.

Members of the opposition were not intimidated, however. On the day before the People's Assembly was seated, hundreds of protesters staged a demonstration in front of the Supreme Constitutional Court, calling the parliament "illegitimate," proclaiming the body "null," and demanding that the authorities respect an administrative court's ruling that "invalidated the results in 92 constituencies, affecting 184 seats."[3] Virtually the entire spectrum of the Egyptian opposition was present including Kifaya!, the Muslim Brotherhood, the National Association for Change, April 6 Youth movement, Ayman Nour's al Ghad, the Wafd, the Tagammu, Nasserists, and a variety of smaller activist groups. That demonstration and another one in front of the State Council Court a day later were relatively small, but they were important because the protests brought Egypt's fractious opposition together. If these groups could maintain even a semblance of unity—a very big "if" given their history—it held out the prospect of a broader-based and potentially more effective opposition to the regime.

Toward that end, Nasserists, independents, individual Wafdists, and Muslim Brothers announced plans to establish a "shadow parliament." Like the April 6 movement's parallel-election idea, the concept of an alternative parliament was inspired. In light of the manifest illegitimacy of the People's Assembly, its unofficial twin of 120 members would demonstrate how an Egyptian legislature in an open, democratic, and transparent environment would operate. The effort almost foundered immediately after the idea was hatched, because the leadership of the Muslim Brotherhood and the Wafd initially seemed ambivalent about the idea. Yet on December 22, the Wafd's chairman, al Sayed al Badawi, agreed to host the shadow parliament. His colleague, Alaa Abdel Monem, who was a principal proponent of the idea, told the Egyptian press that the parallel legislature would focus its efforts on democratic development, protecting civil rights, and social justice. The opposition seemed to have developed a unity of purpose and its leading figures claimed to be committed to working together to maintain pressure on the regime, but the regime was clearly counting on its opponents to cannibalize themselves. While the People's Assembly speaker, Fathi Sorour, threatened legal action against participants in the shadow parliament, President Mubarak dismissed them in his speech opening the new People's Assembly, declaring "Let them have fun."

Lacking legitimacy, the defenders of the regime no longer actually seemed to care whether they enjoyed widespread public support. Rather, the leadership was solely interested in appealing to the military, security services, regime-affiliated intellectuals, certain members of the press, the bureaucracy, and big business. President Mubarak traditionally elicited the support of these groups through patronage, weapons, contracts, and access—to name just a few ways—but the relationship was more complicated than just delivering goodies. The regime's supporters needed a narrative to help them make sense of their world.

That narrative could not be based on outright lies, however. Instead, Egyptian leaders fed their primary constituents on a steady diet of observations, statements, and platitudes that were true enough: "Egypt is an emerging democracy with twenty-four legal political parties and hundreds of newspapers and magazines. The fact that people are asking questions about presidential succession is indicative of how far the leadership is willing to go to reform Egypt. The development of democracy will take a long time, but Egypt has come a long way in the last ten years. President Hosni Mubarak is a transitional figure." With the exception of the last one, each of these statements contained a grain of truth, though they hardly told the whole story. That seemed to have been enough for the regime's supporters, but the conduct and outcome of the 2010 parliamentary elections marked a change. The gap between the truthy narrative and objective reality was wider than ever, making it more difficult for the government's spokesmen to square the story of Egypt's democratic evolution with the ever-more-predatory nature of the leadership's approach to its own people.

Then again, perhaps the narrative did not matter much at all. Maybe the regime's constituents believed that the government could act with impunity. What did it matter, really, if state security repressed the opposition and the police brutalized and even killed ordinary citizens like Khaled Said and Ahmad Sha'aban—both murdered at the hands of Alexandria policemen in 2010—so long as one's profits are up 30 percent a year, or your ministry's share of the state budget grows bigger, or those shiny new F-16s arrive, or you get to be a media personality? This was precisely the kind of outlook that produced Zamalek's apartment lobbies. Yet the assumption that the Egyptian state under Mubarak was strong and that it could defy the will of its own people was flawed. In one sense, Egypt *seemed* strong. The government paid no price for the conduct of the elections, as domestic protests in the immediate aftermath were easily quelled and the United States declared that it was "dismayed" and "concerned" about the vote but was unwilling to do more.

At the same time, the quality of the elections—the security sweeps and wholesale disqualification of candidates in the weeks before the polls combined with a day of vote rigging, intimidation, and violence— indicated the manifest weakness of the Egyptian state: the inability, dating back to the Nasser period, of the regime to capture the imagination of the average Egyptian over the long term. To embed in Egyptians' minds that the regime could not only deliver, but also that its practices matched its principles. This, in turn, would infuse the political system with legitimacy. Lacking this asset, President Mubarak—like his predecessors—relied on coercion to control the Egyptian population. Yet the showdown between the regime and the opposition over the elections only added to an increasingly angry, polarized, and potentially radicalized political arena. This was precisely the dynamic that characterized the period before President Anwar Sadat's assassination and contributed to the low-level insurgency Egypt confronted in the 1990s. It was entirely plausible that, as the Egyptian leadership continued to brutalize its citizens to ensure the regime's grip on power, the opposite might occur, triggering more resistance.

POLICE DAY

Egypt's national Police Day—a relatively new holiday that coincided with the anniversary of the January 25, 1952 British attack on a police station in Ismailiyya—was intended, in the words of President Mubarak in 2004, to be "a valuable symbol of patriotism and sacrifice," that gave Egyptians an opportunity to express pride in the police.[4] These kinds of banalities were typical and utterly devoid of any credibility. Indeed, in the run-up to the 2011 Police Day celebration, opposition groups planned a protest in front of the Ministry of Interior to express outrage over police brutality and demand that the Emergency Law be lifted. There was nothing novel about either the anger toward the police or the possibility of protests, but the timing of the planned demonstration—coming just eleven days after the ouster of Tunisia's longtime strongman—raised both the level of expectation and tension in Cairo and beyond. For frequent visitors, landing in Egypt in the days before the protests was like arriving in a different country. Instead of the cursory glance and wave through at customs, bags were actually inspected. More unsettling was the sudden unwillingness of friends and colleagues to chat politics within earshot of anyone they did not know well. Egypt was an allegedly efficient police state, and there was always suspicion that drivers, waiters, doormen, janitors and tea boys, for example, were informants for state security, but it was not Syria where official paranoia ran extremely high. Among foreigners in Cairo, there was a lot of discussion in the days leading up to January 25 whether the protests would be "big," as the Facebook count of those who indicated they would participate in the demonstrations steadily climbed.

Egyptians themselves seemed undecided about what would happen. One astute political analyst offered at first that the protests would not be large as some predicted only to reverse herself a few hours later via e-mail indicating that the demonstrations could very well be massive. It was hard to know. There had been huge demonstrations in the past, but others had fizzled with police and security forces far outnumbering protesters. Not surprisingly, those invested in the Mubarak regime predicted, as one member of the Shura Council did on the eve of the uprising that, "not more than fifty people" would show up for the protests. Omar Suleiman, the head of the General Intelligence Directorate, boasted to a group of visiting American VIPs that even if large numbers of Egyptians did come out into the streets, there would be no repeat of Tunisia because, "The police have a strategy and the president is not weak." Yet the way officials dismissed the possibility of large-scale protests, shutting down further discussion, betrayed a sense of concern. Indeed, since Tunisian president Zine Abidine Ben Ali's fall, Egypt's official press overloaded on stories about positive economic developments and all that the government was doing to improve the lots of Egyptians. It was all so contrived, but even the people who planned the demonstrations would later reveal that they had modest expectations in terms of both turnout and political impact.

It seemed, indeed, that the Egyptian security service had a strategy for dealing with practically any contingency. Beginning in the wee hours of the morning, the government began flooding policemen, Central Security Forces (CSF) troops, and plainclothes agents in and around the streets near the Ministry of Interior on Sheikh Rihan Street, which runs along the old American University in Cairo campus adjacent to

Tahrir Square. Anyone who wandered near the area was viewed with suspicion and "encouraged" to move off quickly. After daybreak, the police were deployed in large numbers at strategic points around Cairo: Tahrir Square, Arab League Street—an enormous boulevard that runs through a section of the city called Mohandiseen—at Ramses and Ataba squares, near Cairo University, and other locations. Twitter revealed activists warning each other of areas with large concentrations of forces and directing each other to rallying points. Throughout the morning hours with traffic moving well and police on what looked like every corner, square, and bridge in Cairo, it seemed that Minister of Interior Habib al Adly had perhaps succeeded in intimidating all but a few diehard activists.

Around noon, the dynamics of the day began to shift. Once again, Twitter provided the best window on what was happening throughout the city. Rather than a single mass of people, activists were coming together in smaller groups, protesting, clashing with police, and then dispersing, only to regroup somewhere else. It was protest by flash mob. Each group, however, moved in the direction of Tahrir, where a first group of protesters broke the police cordon around the square early in the afternoon, allowing thousands more to flood in. Feeling a sense of empowerment from their ability to overwhelm the security forces by sheer numbers, protesters began to surge out of Tahrir along Qasr al Aini Street toward the Interior Ministry and the parliament. The police unleashed tear gas on the demonstrators, who fought back with stones and bricks pulled from the streets and sidewalks.

The protesters eventually reached parliament, where they fought a pitched battle with police, but were ultimately thwarted from entering the gates. By 6:30 that evening, the mass of people had been pushed back onto Qasr al Aini Street and with a show of force that included hundreds of soldiers from the Central Security Forces, the demonstrators were pushed the half mile back to the Square. The CSF's methods were frightening. Young troopers—not much older than seventeen or eighteen years old from predominantly rural areas or poor urban neighborhoods—were lined up in rows armed with shields, batons, and metal pipes and were ordered to charge the demonstrators, as the large trucks that transported the soldiers to the scene chased closely behind. Once they had the protesters back in Tahrir Square, the security forces sought to seal it along its four entrances.

The night of January 25 provided bizarre juxtapositions. Tourists strolled along the Nile Corniche as tens of thousands of Egyptians demanded that Hosni Mubarak leave and join the former Tunisian leader—Zine el Abidine Ben Ali—in Jeddah, Saudi Arabia, where he had taken exile. In an odd choice for a picnic, Central Security Forces soldiers rested and shared a meal of *koshari* on a grassy area just inside Tahrir Square yards from where their fellow soldiers were trying to control angry protesters. Average Egyptians—launderers, shopkeepers, and butchers—went about their routine business despite the events going on just a few blocks away. This was likely a function of the fact that over the previous seven years protests had become routine and, like almost everyone else, these people must have thought that, at most, what was going on in Tahrir Square would last through the night and perhaps into the next day, but not beyond. By far the most jarring moment of the evening was provided by the Police Day celebration going on inside the Semiramis Intercontinental Hotel, which overlooks the square: as their colleagues worked to keep the throngs in Tahrir under control—many of whom were there because they despised the police—senior officers in dress uniform enjoyed the culmination of a day of rest in their honor.

At each access point to Tahrir Square—Qasr al Aini, al Tahrir, Talaat Harb, and Umar Makram streets—large numbers of CSF troops and trucks blocked the way. With an estimated 15,000–25,000 people in Tahrir Square, it at first seemed that the strategy was to keep the protesters bottled up until they got tired and lost interest. Yet shortly after midnight, as ambulances moved into position, the police let loose with volley after volley of tear gas and moved into the heart of the square with water cannons. The government clearly wanted to demonstrate the costs of defying the authority of the state, but its actions also reflected concern among decision makers that the longer protesters were in the square, the greater the chance that more people would join them, making the Tunisian outcome a distinct possibility.

Within two days, the tens of thousands of people in Tahrir Square morphed—by some estimates—into a million people demonstrating across seven of Egypt's twenty-nine governorates. The crowd in Tahrir grew tenfold while in Alexandria—Egypt's second-largest city—the Corniche along the Mediterranean was packed with tens of thousands of demonstrators. Meanwhile in Suez, the army was called in to try to pacify a city that some journalists described as a war zone. By Friday the twenty-eighth, dubbed Egypt's "Day of Rage," more and more Egyptians from all walks of life—businessmen, professors, laborers, government workers—joined the protests. Although the demonstrations were confined to seven governorates, the fact that they had widened and deepened was a significant development. After confrontations all day long in and around Tahrir Square, including an effort by the protesters to take the Ministry of Interior, which left at least three dead, and a raging fire at the national headquarters of the ruling National Democratic Party, the police and Central Security Forces gave way to officers and conscript soldiers of the Egyptian armed forces who were deployed in tanks and armored personnel carriers (APCs) in and around downtown Cairo. This was a stunning development. For Hosni Mubarak—the Pharaoh—to move the military into the heart of his capital suggested that he was losing his grip on a country that he had mastered for almost thirty years.

To change the momentum, the president took to the airwaves early Saturday morning in a nationwide address. Until then, the government had used two rhetorical tactics to try to undermine and deflect the protests. The first was to suggest that demonstrations themselves were a manifestation of how free Egypt had become during the Mubarak period. Second, regime spokesmen argued that the Muslim Brotherhood was behind the protests. Neither of these claims had any basis in fact, and no one outside the increasingly embattled halls of official Egypt much believed them. If Egypt was so free, then why were there hundreds of thousands—perhaps millions—turning up in the streets to demand Mubarak's ouster and a subsequent transition to a more open and democratic political order? The internal contradiction of this declaration either never occurred to the people who came up with the argument or it was just something, anything to say in the face of a mounting crisis. As for the Brotherhood, there was no evidence at all that they were behind the uprising. Rather, they were behind the curve, only committing themselves to the protests on Friday the twenty-eighth—three days after the demonstrations began. In his speech, Mubarak hit on Egypt's alleged liberalization, the threat of the Islamists, and more. In an obvious reference to the Brothers—his longtime bogeyman—he evinced concern over "attempts by some sides to take advantage of this wave of protests and exploit their slogans" before emphasizing Egypt's purported democratic practices: "These demonstrations and the protests we saw in recent years would never have taken place except with this extent of freedom of opinion, expression, and the press." Mubarak then turned his attention to economic grievances, claiming that he had reined in the government's economic reformers in order to protect the poor. He also appealed to Egyptians' sense of nationalism, warning of instability and calling upon the people to protect the homeland. Mubarak finished the short speech with a call for national dialogue and a commitment to reform, announcing "new steps confirming our respect of the independence of judiciary and its provisions. New steps towards more democracy and more freedoms to the citizens. New steps to curb unemployment, improve living standards and upgrade services. New steps to support the poor and limited income brackets."[5] Some hours later, Mubarak dissolved Prime Minister Ahmed Nazif's government and tapped Omar Suleiman to be vice president. This was intended to be a signal to the people on the streets that—while they would not have the satisfaction of humiliating Mubarak in the same way their Tunisian cousins had forced their longtime dictator from his country two weeks prior—the succession was underway and, importantly, it did not involve Gamal.

Mubarak's appeal and warning, as well as the sudden elevation of Suleiman, made little difference. Egyptians continued to pour into the streets throughout the weekend demanding Mubarak's ouster. The military's presence was in one sense reassuring. The soldiers would be protection against the brutal and widely vilified police, but there was uncertainty as well. After all, had not the military been a pillar of the political and economic orders against which Egyptians were now rebelling? Had they not benefited from the system that their forefathers, the Free Officers, created in the 1950s? Were not the top brass from the defense minister, Field Marshal Mohammed Hussein Tantawi—who became Egypt's highest-ranking soldier not through military acumen or courage, but through allegiance to Mubarak—and the chief of staff, Lieutenant General Sami Enan, the service chiefs, and the commander of the Republican Guard all Mubarak's people? The answer to these questions was yes, which gave some Egyptians and outside observers pause. There was every reason to believe that the senior command would remain loyal to the president. In the event he became a liability to them and they were forced to push Mubarak aside, the officers would nevertheless seek to maintain the political system that had served them and their interests so well.

The military's strategy, it seemed, was to contain the protests and ultimately reestablish stability without resorting to violence. The commanders counted on the fact that they could achieve their objectives because they were not the police and the military had spent the last four decades in the background. This meant that despite serving as a primary constituent of the regime, the commanders were insulated from the opposition to Mubarak, his son, the National Democratic Party, and the government. The military's approach was shrewd. It placed them in the position to be saviors and it did not risk a split within the ranks. Furthermore, if all worked well, they just might reduce the size of the protests to a manageable level. As expected, the demonstrators in Tahrir embraced the soldiers, but that embrace also worked in the opposite direction and to the advantage of the protesters. The warm greeting that the recruits and their officers received from their fellow Egyptians drove a potential wedge between the men on the front lines and those calling the shots at headquarters. If there ever was—despite assurances from the Ministry of Defense to the contrary—an order to crack down, the mutual admiration and respect between the soldiers and protesters made it unlikely that those manning the tanks and APCs would comply.

Even as the military played to the people, the commanders worked to salvage Mubarak and the political order. Over the first weekend of protests, American-built F-16s flew just above the rooftops of Tahrir Square, buzzing protesters in an apparent effort to intimidate them. The demonstrators remained steadfast, however, demanding Mubarak's departure and a transition to democracy. By Tuesday, February 1, with demonstrations continuing throughout the country, President Mubarak was forced to address the nation once again. Although he stressed similar themes to his statement of three days earlier, this time Mubarak—feeling the pressure from the protests—was more detailed, declaring that while he would serve out his term in office, he would not seek reelection and that parliament would amend Articles 76 and 77 of the constitution "to modify the qualifications for candidacy for the presidency . . . and set a fixed number of terms for the presidency."[6] Mubarak also called upon parliament to respect judicial findings nullifying 184 NDP victories in the fraud-ridden November 2010 elections. Mubarak clearly calculated that if he took account of some demands emerging from Tahrir it would be enough to relieve the political pressure and send large numbers of people home.

The military establishment apparently agreed. In the early morning of February 2, the armed forces issued a brief statement that symbolically tied the military to the protesters, warned of instability, and obliquely encouraged protesters to leave Tahrir Square because their message had been "heard" and their "demands understood."[7] Still, the protesters remained. A few hours later, soldiers in the area stood aside as pro-Mubarak forces—hired thugs, policemen, and some genuine supporters of the president—descended upon Tahrir Square and attacked the demonstrators. The subsequent twenty-four hours were harrowing as violence engulfed central Cairo. For hours, rocks and bricks filled the air as Mubarak's partisans and his opponents engaged in close combat just across the street from the famed Egyptian museum, which had become the military's field command. As night fell, Mubarak's thugs dropped Molotov cocktails from the buildings surrounding Tahrir on anti-government protesters, and gunfire could be heard. Foreign journalists were also targets of the pro-government mob. The live feed from al Jazeera, which in media parlance "covered the story wall-to-wall," was stunning. Egypt, a country that was almost universally regarded as politically stable, seemed to teeter on the brink of chaos. Through it all, however, the soldiers and officers on duty in Tahrir and the surrounding area did little, having received no orders from up the chain of command to intervene. Moreover, outside the glare of Tahrir, military intelligence had been busy. The military's agents detained foreign journalists, arrested opposition activists, and otherwise intimidated those whom they deemed to be suspicious. The government's insinuation that the demonstrations were somehow a foreign plot created an atmosphere of mistrust and suspicion in which military intelligence and their counterparts in state security thrived.

The following day, the confrontations continued, but the military did take action to separate the sides, and they were finally forced—by circumstance and the need to maintain the armed forces' credibility— to provide security in Tahrir, especially after five were killed and about a thousand others were injured the night and day before.[8] Yet, rather than instilling fear, the violence of the pro-Mubarak forces actually galvanized the opposition. The next day—the second Friday of pro-tests—was dubbed the "Day of Departure." With the military now controlling access to Tahrir through checkpoints where identification was closely examined, a more relaxed, celebratory mood descended on the Square in which hundreds of thousands had turned up to demand an end to Hosni Mubarak's almost thirty-year reign and concomitant political change. Even as the demonstrators welcomed the security that the military provided, there was also a sense of unease about the checkpoints, which, over Friday the fourth and Saturday the fifth of February, were used to reduce the number of protesters in Tahrir Square. Was this just the cost of security, or was this a deliberate strategy on the part of the military command? It was not entirely clear, but this development coincided with a sense that the demonstrations were losing momentum.

At the same time, the newly installed vice president, Omar Suleiman, and the new prime minister, Ahmed Shafiq—a former air force commander—sought negotiations with the Muslim Brotherhood and an ad hoc committee of wise men, who emerged as potential interlocutors between the regime and the opposition. The composition of the group was curious. It included opposition figures such as George Ishaq—a member of Mohammed ElBaradei's National Association for Change and a former leader of Kifaya!—Abdel Monem al Fotuh, head of the doctors' syndicate and a member of the Brotherhood, and noted columnist Fahmi Howeidy, who was a fierce critic of the regime. There were also heretofore nonpolitical or apolitical figures like Ahmad Zuweil, Egypt's Nobel laureate in chemistry, and another scientist named Farouk el Baz, who in the late 1970s was a science advisor to President Sadat, but who had spent the bulk of his career in the United States. Yet the group also contained establishment types like Amr Moussa, Mubarak's former foreign minister and secretary general of the Arab League, who had distanced himself from Mubarak over the previous decade, but was nevertheless a longtime servant of the regime. Kamal Abu Magd also appeared on the list. Magd had been head of the Arab Socialist Union's Youth Bureau after Sadat's "Corrective Revolution" in 1971 and had most recently led the National Council of Human Rights—a creature of the NDP-dominated upper house of parliament, the Shura Council. Nabil Fahmy—former Egyptian ambassador to the United States and dean of American University's school of international affairs—was also a designated wise man.

Noticeably absent was Mohammed ElBaradei, who sought to be the conscience of the growing revolution, though his National Association for Change was represented. It was unclear what to make of ElBaradei and his posture throughout the uprising. He had rushed back to Cairo from Vienna on the third evening of protests and made an appearance among the demonstrators on Friday. By any number of accounts, he failed—if it was ever his goal—to become the focal point of the uprising. The youth groups that spurred the protests and those he addressed at the Istiqamma Mosque were unimpressed with his performance. After returning to his home near the Pyramids on the outskirts of Cairo, ElBaradei was placed under house arrest, but he nevertheless retained access to the foreign press. In interview after interview, he said all the right things about a peaceful transition to democracy, soothed general concerns about future relations between Cairo and Washington, assured viewers that there would be no breach of the Egypt-Israel peace agreement, and declared that while the Muslim Brotherhood would be a feature of the Egyptian political arena, it would not dominate the politics in a new Egypt.

On the surface, Omar Suleiman and Prime Minister Shafiq's outreach seemed like a positive development. They were apparently making good on Mubarak's commitment to a national dialogue. Yet for many Egyptians and longtime Egypt watchers, this was an ominous development. Suleiman in particular—Mubarak's right-hand man of the previous fifteen years—was the last person to negotiate in good faith. In his role as head of Egypt's intelligence service, Suleiman was responsible, in part, for preventing the Brotherhood and any other opposition group from accumulating political power. This was accomplished through both force and manipulation to ensure that dissenting groups remained divided and weak. The vice president's sudden interest in negotiations, especially with the Brotherhood, which was not above striking a deal with the government if only to save itself, was widely suspected of being more of the same.

By Monday, the opposition seemed exhausted and outflanked. Cairo was getting back to normal, except for Tahrir Square and the immediate vicinity. With Vice President Suleiman seemingly in firm control of the crisis and armed with a strategy to divide and wait out the protesters, there was a sense that the change the hundreds of thousands—at times perhaps millions—of demonstrators demanded would ultimately be thwarted. Then, at that moment when the opposition seemed to be weakening and Mubarak was on the verge of regaining the upper hand, two extraordinary events happened. First, the faculty and dean of Cairo University's school of law issued a statement supporting the demonstrators and all of their demands. The attorneys called for "freedom, democracy, sovereignty of law, the realization of social justice, and accountability for those who are corrupt."[9] To the uninitiated this did not seem like a dramatic development, and in the grand scheme of the fast-moving, complex set of events enveloping Egypt it was certainly not the most high profile, but it was, by February 7, the clearest indication that the end of Hosni Mubarak's reign might actually be approaching. State security had long penetrated the law school—indeed all of Cairo University—and the dean, Dr. Ahmed Awed Belal, was a handpicked government functionary who served as a member of the High Elections Committee that had supervised the fraudulent Shura Council elections the previous June and presided over the stolen People's Assembly elections a few months later. For Belal and his professors to issue their statement indicated that the last remaining pillars of the regime's support were beginning to crumble.

Second, and more spectacularly, a thirty-year-old named Wael Ghonim was released from detention. Ghonim, an Egyptian who ran Google's regional marketing operation from Dubai, was involved in instigating the January 25 Police Day demonstrations that kicked off Egypt's uprising. Ghonim tricked his supervisors into letting him travel to Cairo on business (although he made the trip so he could take part in the campaign against Mubarak). After Tahrir Square had been cleared in the wee hours of the morning of January 26, state security detained Ghonim. From their perspective, Egypt's security services had reason to pick him up. Ghonim was thought to be (and has subsequently confirmed) the anonymous impresario behind the Facebook page "We are all Khaled Said"—the young man beaten to death at the hands of Alexandria policemen on June 6, 2010—which served as a testament to the brutality and hubris of Mubarak's Egypt. On the eve of the protests, 70,000 people had indicated on Ghonim's site that they would take part in the January 25 demonstrations and hundreds of thousands of others had visited the page. This made Ghonim the leader of the largest opposition group in Egypt and to the authorities, a provocateur.

It remains a mystery why Ghonim was released on February 7. It certainly was not the government's sudden appreciation for the principle of due process. Someone in an important decision-making position likely calculated that releasing Ghonim would relieve political pressure on the government, divide the opposition, and take the wind out of the demonstrators' sails. If the police and intelligence services were paying attention to Twitter—and there is no doubt they were—they would have observed many references to Ghonim's fate and declarations that activists would not rest until he was released. At the same time, some sort of struggle occurring in the ranks of what was left of Mubarak's power structure may also have been the reason behind Ghonim's freedom. In the days following the ugly attacks on demonstrators at the hands of pro-Mubarak thugs, there was some evidence of score-settling going on among NDP heavyweights. Mostafa el Fiqi— a stalwart member of the ruling party, a leader of the Shura Council, former diplomat, and at one-time private secretary to President Mubarak—reportedly blamed the violent mob on "businessmen." This cast suspicion on Ahmed Ezz—an ally of Gamal Mubarak, the secretary general for organizational affairs of the NDP, and the proprietor of the Ezz Group, a holding company, whose subsidiaries produce steel, porcelain, and other ceramics. Habib al Adly, the publicly reviled minister of interior, was also dumped on once his tactics became a liability for the people who benefited most from his iron fist.

Whatever the explanation for Ghonim's freedom, his release was ultimately not as important as what happened next. On the evening he was let go, Ghonim appeared on the privately-owned television channel *Dream* and gave a moving interview. He wept when he learned that demonstrators had died, but perhaps the most stirring moment was when Ghonim declared, "My wife is an American. I can apply for U.S. citizenship but I didn't, not even the lottery. Many people want to leave, though. We have to restore dignity to all Egyptians. We have to end corruption. No more theft. Egyptians are good people. We are a beautiful people. Please everybody, this is not a time to settle scores, this is a time to build our country." Ghonim struck a chord. In those few short sentences he captured everything that had plagued Egypt over at least the previous decade, but most of all he underlined how the uprising-revolution was about dignity. It was, if anything, a powerful and poignant riposte to President Mubarak's haughty quip: "Let them have fun." It also stood in stark contrast to Gamal Mubarak. To be sure, as a Google executive who resided in that plastic city-state Dubai, Ghonim was not your average Egyptian, but he came across as authentic and humble next to Gamal's sense of entitlement and arrogance. Whether accurate or not, Ghonim represented a return to what Egyptians knew and loved about their own country—a sense of community, loyalty, and sacrifice, as well as a good joke and the belly laughs that always follow—rather than the Egypt, Mubarak's Egypt, that ultimately forced Hatem to part with his beloved VW Beetle and from his homeland.

Not only did Ghonim provide much needed energy for the thousands of diehards in Tahrir, but he also seemingly galvanized even larger segments of the Egyptian population. The day after his interview, the demonstrations in central Cairo and other cities grew. Lawyers in black robes descended on Tahrir. People who had sat on the sidelines for the thirteen previous days turned out into the streets demanding change. Suddenly, Cairo's transport workers declared a strike, as did their counterparts in the Suez Canal Zone. In the industrial city of Mahalla al Kubra, workers in the state-owned sector went on strike as well. This was a significant turn of events. The uprising achieved what some of its own planners—specifically, the April 6 Youth movement—had failed to realize on previous occasions: workers were now connecting their economic grievances with the rigged political order. This was a development that Mubarak had spent years trying to avoid by offering various pocketbook concessions to labor, which it seemed in this case were not going to work. Doctors marched down Qasr al Aini Street from the hospital of the same name to Tahrir, expressing their solidarity with the demands of the demonstrators. It was not just the symbolically or politically potent sectors of society that were pouring into the streets: average Egyptians turned up in Tahrir Square with their children, grandchildren, nieces, nephews, parents, sisters, and brothers to demand Wael Ghonim's Egypt.

By Thursday, February 10, the expectation that the government may yet regain control had largely dissipated and the mood in Tahrir was festive. By midafternoon Cairo time, there were reports that President Mubarak would be stepping down that evening, though there was much confusion surrounding this news. Dr. Hossam Badrawi—one of Gamal's associates—who had become head of the NDP, told the British Broadcasting Company that he expected the president to "make a move" and "transmit his authorities as president to his vice president."[10] When queried whether Mubarak planned to resign, Prime Minister Shafiq was noncommittal, offering only that President Mubarak would do what was best for the country. Subsequently, when the director of the U.S. Central Intelligence Agency, Leon Panetta, reportedly told the House Permanent Select Committee on Intelligence that "there is a strong likelihood that Mubarak may step down this evening," it seemed inevitable that Mubarak would resign when he appeared on state television at 10:30 p.m. local time.[11] Yet within the first three sentences of the president's statement, which was directed first and foremost to the "youth of Egypt in Tahrir Square," it was clear that Mubarak was not exactly resigning. After invoking himself as their father, he declared:

> Before all else, I say to you that the blood of your martyrs and your wounded will not go unaccounted for, and I assure you that I will not be lax with those who are responsible, and with all firmness and determination, I will impose the maximum punishments of the law against those who have committed crimes against our youth.[12]

In the end, Mubarak only "delegated" presidential authority to the vice president. The mood in Tahrir turned immediately from raucous joy to rage. The president's refusal to heed the will of an ever-increasing number of Egyptians belied his declaration that "this moment is not about me personally, it is not about Hosni Mubarak, it is about Egypt and the present and future of its people." To add insult to injury, the transfer of power to Vice President Suleiman was, technically speaking, temporary. According to Article 82 of the constitution, the vice president can only assume presidential authority under certain conditions and on a provisional basis. This was clearly why Mubarak spoke in a manner that made it clear *he* would ultimately hold those responsible for violence accountable and *he* would oversee the constitutional reform. Despite the best efforts of Egyptian diplomats around the world to convince their interlocutors that Mubarak had, indeed, stepped down, it was abundantly obvious that he had no intention of permanently vacating the office he had held for the prior three decades. His appointment of Suleiman was the biggest indicator of this because, if the president *does* actually relinquish authority, Article 84 of the constitution directs not the vice president but the speaker of the People's Assembly (or, if he is unavailable, then the president of the Supreme Constitutional Court) to assume presidential duties until elections can be organized.[13]

Egyptians were stunned. What more did they need to do to convince Mubarak and the people around him that he was the problem, that they had no trust in him, and that he symbolized all that was wrong with their beloved country? The Twitter feed from Egypt revealed anger, shock, and a determination to bring the Mubarak era to an end once and for all as activists began organizing a march to the presidential residence in Heliopolis. This was a potentially dangerous turn of events because the military was sure to have blocked the route from downtown to Mubarak's palace, and beyond the regular army checkpoints there were likely to be contingents of the Haras Gumhuri—Republican Guard—which were dedicated to protecting the president and the regime. For the first time since the pro-Mubarak thugs had attacked protesters in Tahrir Square on February 2, Mubarak was putting Egypt in jeopardy of sliding into violence and chaos.

It was not to be, however. On the morning of Friday, February 11, millions of Egyptians poured into the streets all over the country to demand Mubarak's ouster. The uprising had now gone nationwide, with protesters challenging the authority of the government in places that had been quiet, like the vice president's hometown of Qina and other towns and small cities of Upper Egypt. Meanwhile, in Cairo a mass of humanity streamed along Salah Salim Street heading northeast from downtown toward Mubarak's compound, with others surrounding the state broadcasting building, which was under the watch of regular army soldiers and Republican Guard personnel, while hundreds of thousands of others kept up their protest in Tahrir. By 6:00 p.m. (Cairo time), Vice President Suleiman appeared on state television and announced:

> Citizens, in these difficult circumstances the country is going through,
> the President Mohamed Hosni Mubarak has decided to leave his

position as the president of the Republic, and has entrusted the Supreme Council of the Armed Forces to administer the nation's affairs.[14]

With those 41 words, Hosni Mubarak's reign of 29 years, 3 months, 28 days, and 6 hours ended. He boarded a flight to Sharm el Shaykh, where he, his family, and his courtiers disappeared under heavy security into the presidential rest house. On February 11, 2011, Egyptians accomplished what only three weeks earlier had seemed practically impossible—they dislodged the Pharaoh. It seemed everything that everyone—Egyptians and foreign observers—had long believed about Egypt's political stability and the durability of Mubarak's rule was turned upside down in just eighteen days.

How did this happen? The seemingly insurmountable barriers to collective action—a divided opposition, efficient internal security services, a cohesive constituency for autocracy—that social scientists claimed would prevent mass uprising were instead easily overcome. To be sure, there was pent-up anger in Egypt leading to the events of early 2011. Different sectors of Egyptian society had been in open revolt against the regime at different times going back to at least 2003, when the large Tahrir Square protests against the U.S. invasion of Iraq became a forum to denounce the regime en masse. Yet those demonstrations, along with protests against the constitutional amendments in 2005 and 2007, the wildcat strikes and worker protests in state-owned enterprises, and various smaller anti-government rallies among petty bureaucrats and villagers, never became a revolution. The defenders of the regime were always able to contain the demonstrations, and they worked hard to ensure that the protesters could not threaten the political system.

There is no way of knowing exactly why the January 25 demonstrations were different from so many that came before them. Wael Ghonim admitted in his television interview that he "wasn't optimistic on the twenty-fifth but now I can't believe it." Dissidents in the old East bloc expressed the same surprise during the wildfire-like revolutions of late 1989 that toppled the once thought to be sturdy communist regimes there. Like those revolutions twenty-two years prior, the timing of Hosni Mubarak's collapse was totally unpredictable. Almost immediately, observers began exploring what conditions existed in Egypt that made it ripe for explosion. Analysts focused on the six months or so before the uprising: the murders of Khaled Said and Ahmad Sha'aban, the continuing rise in food prices, revelations of rapacious thievery on the part of business figures connected to the

NDP, and the terrible Shura and People's Assembly elections. Yet these may or may not have contributed to the uprising. After all, police brutality, corruption, economic grievances, and electoral irregularities had for some time been a permanent feature of Mubarak's Egypt.

Paradoxically, it was the very nature of the way the defenders of the regime maintained political control—fear—that ultimately made Egypt's revolution inevitable. The longer the protesters in Tahrir refused to be intimidated no matter what the defenders of the regime threw at them, the greater the chances that what scholars call a "revolutionary bandwagon" would develop.[15] Suddenly, the young father of a two-year-old daughter who had a good job with a multinational firm, the IT consultant, entrepreneur, housewife, doorman, and laborer all of whom previously believed there was great risk in joining the demonstrations determined that the costs of going to Tahrir Square to demand change were not so high after all. The regime tried to reverse this process with the introduction of hired thugs on February 2 and 3. Once that gambit failed, only a military crackdown—which the senior command had ruled out—had the potential to force Egyptians to rethink their growing support for the demonstrations. Indeed, the pendulum had swung so far in the other direction that by the last days of the uprising, the costs of *not* turning out in the streets were far greater than participating in the demonstrations, fearing that they would be identified as supporters of the old regime—even if they really were—after the revolutionary dust settled. This may be a reason why the dean of Cairo University's law faculty was willing to sign a statement of support for the demonstrations and why regime stalwarts resigned from the National Democratic Party once it became clear that all had been lost. Was this a transparent attempt to "get on the right side of history" no matter how late in the game? Of course it was. Yet this phenomenon was part of an overall dynamic in which Egyptians suddenly changed the way they viewed the world, making it entirely possible for Police Day demonstrations to become a revolution that toppled the mightiest of Middle Eastern dictators.

GHOSTS OF THE 1950S

With the military in control of the country, there was a strange back-to-the-future sense of things. The historical analogies between February 2011 and the summer of 1952 were not entirely correct—Field

Marshal Hussein Tantawi and the Supreme Council of the Armed Forces represented the senior military establishment, not upstart midlevel Free Officers—but in other ways it seemed that the ghosts of the early 1950s had returned to haunt the political arena. The immediate euphoria surrounding the military takeover and the expectations (really, hopes) that the Officers would return a clean parliamentary system to civilian leaders was stunningly familiar. The unrest in the labor sector that broke out on February 14 fleetingly reminded observers of the August 1952 unrest in Kafr el Dawwar. Instead of using force like their Free Officer predecessors, however, the Supreme Council issued a military communiqué—its sixth—that warned of the negative consequences of continuing these demonstrations and called upon labor and professional unions to "fulfill their respective duties" in order to avoid further instability. The uniform desire for Tantawi and the Supreme Council to lift the state of emergency quickly was also reminiscent of the post-1952 political environment in which the parties anxiously lobbied the Officers to hand power over to civilians.

By far the most striking—though far from perfect—analogy and the biggest challenge for Tantawi and his officers was that, like the Free Officers in 1952, the Supreme Council had no plan other than a vague notion about turning the country over to civilian rule as soon as conditions warranted. Of course, Tantawi and his team were thrust into the position by circumstance rather than in a bid for power, so they could be excused for not being entirely prepared. Moreover, the high command unexpectedly found itself in an awkward position. Since the dark days following the shattering June 1967 defeat in the war with Israel, they had remained in the barracks. Suddenly, the generals were forced to contend with the unfamiliar and difficult world of Egyptian politics. Each successive military statement suggested that the Ministry of Defense was putting little strategic thought into its plans; it seemed like they were making it up as they went along.

For example, the Supreme Council's announced timeline for civilian control smacked of ad hoc-ery and sowed no small amount of suspicion about the military's intentions. With regard to the former, the officers announced that an eight-member constitutional committee would rewrite five critical articles of the constitution and delete another over ten days, a referendum would be held within two months, and elections would be carried out in six months.[16] The opposition had long been focused on the judiciary playing a larger role in the conduct of elections—which had been the work of the Ministry of Interior with the help of the National Democratic Party—but it was entirely unclear whether the judges would have the capacity to organize these polls in such a short time. Few lamented the collapse of the previously dominant party or the apparent demise of the power of Interior Minister Habib al Adly's empire, but in the aftermath of Mubarak's downfall, picking up the slack was going to be a challenge. Egypt's relatively robust civil society sector stepped into the breach and immediately began working hard to ensure that both the interim authorities and Egyptians were prepared for the task at hand.

Once more, without a clear roadmap for how to proceed, the military seemed to be groping for some group, any group, with whom it could negotiate. On several levels, this was a dangerous place for the military and its civilian interlocutors to be. The officers' discomfort with being thrust into the day-to-day politics of the country, which was reflected in the short timeline for a transition to civilian rule, fueled suspicions that the Supreme Council was ready to cut a deal with just about anybody. The presence of Sobhi Saleh from the Muslim Brotherhood on the Constitutional Committee led some in Cairo to suspect that the soldiers would, if there were no other options, come to a modus vivendi with the Islamists. These fears were most likely the result of the collective revolutionary hangover that Egyptians felt after a wild, countrywide thirty-six-hour celebration in the wake of Mubarak's departure, but they spoke to the "Now what?" atmosphere of the political arena. Uncertainty was the word of the day.

The other potential trap, which was actually more reminiscent of Egyptian politics of the 1930s and 1940s than the period after the Free Officers' coup, was the deep divisions among the opposition. The activists, established opposition parties, the Muslim Brotherhood, and myriad civil society groups had demonstrated enormous staying power and unity of purpose during the heady days in Tahrir Square; but once Mubarak departed, the ideological and personal differences among the leaders of these groups were likely to return. The Western media and its pundits were fond of suggesting that the uprising was "leaderless." In fact, the Egyptian revolution had many leaders and they liked it that way, at least while they were in Tahrir. When it got down to negotiating a new political order, however, the dizzying array of groups and individuals with equities in building the new Egypt made it hard to imagine the orderly transition that the military sought. Did the Coalition of the Youth of the Revolution—which was itself an umbrella group for the Muslim Brotherhood Youth, Justice and Freedom, National Association for Change Youth, Democratic Front

Youth, and the April 6 Youth movement—independent trade unions, independent Islamists, radical left, the March 9 Professors movement, various human rights groups, the seven parties or groups that made up Mohammed ElBaradei's National Association for Change, the established opposition parties (some of which overlapped with ElBaradei's organization), the Constitutional Committee, and the Muslim and Christian religious establishment, all want the same thing? Yes and no. Certainly, in the abstract, most wanted regime change (the Grand Sheikh of al Azhar an important exception), but with post-Mubarak politics in full swing there were different tolerances for compromise and accommodation. Moreover, the youth groups had a revolutionary street credibility and zeal that politicians like Mohammed ElBaradei or Amr Moussa, who both subsequently declared their intention to run for president, as well as the political parties could not possibly muster. Still, the establishment types were not going to abdicate a prominent role for themselves in the new Egypt to the thirty-somethings who sparked a revolution despite their expectations.

Despite, or perhaps because of, the dynamic politics of Egypt's opposition, the Supreme Council of the Armed Forces remained steadfast in its desire for limited constitutional amendments—an approach that did not track far from President Mubarak's position laid out in his three statements to the nation—that could be accomplished relatively quickly. This was a prudent position for the officers to take. First, the constitutional changes did not represent regime change, something that would have permanently altered the military's influential position in the political system and likely affected its vast economic interests. The Constitutional Committee ultimately recommended the amendment of eight articles, one of which contained a commitment to begin writing a new constitution within six months of the parliamentary elections. Other provisions included limiting presidents to two terms in office lasting four years each; leveling the playing field for those who wanted to run for president; strengthening the independence of the judiciary; giving parliament control over the Emergency Law; and abolishing important aspects of that law, which had been incorporated into the constitution in 2007. In a huge turnout—by the paltry standards of past elections and referenda—Egyptians overwhelmingly (77 percent) voted in favor of the amendments.

Second, limited constitutional change promised to get the officers out of politics. Clearly, they understood that the longer they were in charge of the country, the greater the danger to the military as an organization from governing and the vicissitudes of politics. At the same time, however, the officers desired order. The military's sixth communiqué had already made it clear that Tantawi and his colleagues had little patience for continued demonstrations. Confronted with a fraught political environment, a vested interest in the regime over which Hosni Mubarak presided, and the desire to get out of politics, the officers seemed willing to hand the country over to any individual or group that could guarantee stability and the military's privileges. In the early going after Mubarak's fall, activists suspected that the Ministry of Defense favored an Amr Moussa presidency. The former foreign minister and secretary general of the Arab League had fallen out with Mubarak in the early 2000s, primarily because Moussa had become quite popular because of his tough public stance on Israel and the United States. In 2001 the pop song, "I Hate Israel and I Love Amr Moussa" by the Egyptian singer Shaaban Abdel Rahim was a huge hit. Moussa had studiously distanced himself enough from Mubarak over the ensuing decade that he remained quite popular, but he was still part of the establishment. A Moussa presidency might help the Supreme Council of the Armed Forces salvage what they could— especially their own autonomy—from the old political order.

Of course, in the post-revolutionary glow, no one could quite imagine that such a scenario would unfold. After all, had not the senior commanders just witnessed an outpouring of people power? Yes, but they may have also calculated that what they were offering was quite enough for the vast majority of Egyptians, especially those who jumped on the bandwagon late. The opposition understood this possibility and was deeply distrustful of the officers, claiming that they would return to the streets if the military sought to preserve the old regime under new leadership. The military's intentions were so much of a concern that, less than a week after Mubarak relinquished power, ElBaradei called for civilian oversight of Egypt's transition. Although ElBaradei's plan never got traction, the revolutionary groups demonstrated that they had the capacity to intimidate the armed forces through credible threats of a return to Tahrir Square. This was the way they pressured the Supreme Council to dump Prime Minister Ahmed Shafiq and his cabinet, forced additional constitutional amendments, and hastened the dismissal of senior state-television employees. In order to get their point across, the revolutionary groups designated April 1 as "Save the Revolution Day" and brought twenty thousand people back to Tahrir. The demonstration was in response to the military's apparent unwillingness to—among a range of demands—put

Mubarak and other old regime figures on trial, dissolve the National Democratic Party, lift the Emergency Law, and end military trials for civilians.

The threats, political maneuvers, and countermoves between the revolutionary groups and the Supreme Council were no less than a battle between competing legitimacies. Whereas the officers clearly believed that the armed forces remained the repository for the legitimacy of the Egyptian state, the groups that led the uprising in Tahrir believed that legitimacy rested with them. After all, the military represented a discredited regime whose leader had just been toppled in a popular revolution. As a result, the officers should heed the desires of the Egyptian people as expressed through the revolutionaries. This contest was not likely to be settled soon. Although the leaders of Tahrir had significant moral authority, they could not speak credibly for the Egyptian people. As one activist blogger who goes by the name "Sandmonkey" pointed out, the revolutionaries needed to turn their attention to the hard work of political organizing.[17] Sandmonkey was responding to the fact that the opposition activists had actually urged Egyptians to vote "no" in the March 19 referendum, but only 23 percent of voters heeded its call. It was not so much what the proposed amendments to the constitution said, but rather the short-fuse political process that a "yes" would set in motion. The opposition feared that parliamentary elections in six months and presidential polls within a few months after that would give the advantage to nondemocratic groups, especially remnants of the NDP. There was also considerable fear among liberals and what remained of the establishment that the Muslim Brotherhood, which announced its intention to form the "Freedom and Justice Party" and contest anywhere from 30 to 50 percent of the new parliament's seats and salafi groups would score significant electoral victories. The perceived salafist threat represented the manipulations of the late Mubarak years coming back to haunt post-uprising Egypt. The salafis were not a new feature of Egyptian society, but they had become more visible over the last three or four years of Mubarak's rule. Egyptians and outside observers suspected that the government had a hand in this phenomenon as a way of draining support away from the Brotherhood, believing that the salafists would adhere to their quietist tradition. Yet, the assumptions of the past did not hold up against the reality of the "new Egypt"; this would likely be the case as well when it came to Cairo's relationship with Washington.

THE U.S.-EGYPT BREAKUP?

In the immediate aftermath of the collapse of Hosni Mubarak's rule, a game particular to Washington, DC broke out. It began with, "How did the Obama administration do?" and would end with "Can the Bush administration take any credit for the democratic wave sweeping the Middle East?" The honest answers to these questions are "It does not matter," and "Unlikely." To be sure, the Obama team was somewhat slow to recognize what exactly was happening in Egypt. The political dynamics on the ground were way beyond the administration's declarations on January 25 that it was time for reform. Yet American foreign policy officials can be forgiven for the State Department's tin-eared declarations about Egyptian stability. Senior U.S. officials and their staff lived in the same world where academics and policy analysts alike regarded Egypt's political system as among the most stable in the Arab world. In retrospect, President Obama could have staked out any position, and events in Egypt were likely to unfold as they did no matter what he said once the revolutionary bandwagon took off. For their part, members of the Bush administration freely admit that they failed to impress upon Hosni Mubarak the importance of reform. He was resistant at every turn, claiming that he knew Egypt and how to rule it better than they. Also, the extraordinary events of January–February 2011 had nothing whatsoever to do with the U.S. invasion of Iraq almost eight years earlier. Iraq was regarded as the quintessential example of American hubris and few, if any, Egyptians saw it as an example for their country. Rather, it was the Tunisians taking matters into their own hands and toppling their dictator that provided inspiration for Egyptians.

This all suggests that Washington has far less ability to shape events in Egypt than commonly believed. That may have been a drawback for policymakers in the mid-2000s who were trying to pressure Mubarak to embark upon reform, but it is actually a good thing in post-revolutionary Egypt. Within hours of Mubarak's departure for Sharm el Shaykh, Washington was abuzz with a renewed interest in democracy promotion. Now, according to some, was the time to pour more resources into this area. This policy prescription betrayed not only a fundamental misunderstanding of what had transpired in the previous two weeks, but also a blatant disregard for almost a century and a half of Egyptian history. The last thing that Egyptians—who had entirely on their own dislodged their dictator, renewing a sense of national pride and spirit—wanted was a foreign power offering expertise and advice about how to manage their transition.

Moreover, although the United States was not responsible for the inequity of Mubarak's rule, it did enable it and benefit from it. Mubarak was Washington's man in Cairo: he kept the Suez Canal open, repressed the Islamists, and maintained peace with Israel. In return, the United States provided much for Egypt, contributing billions in economic assistance over the years to build up the country's infrastructure, agricultural technology, and public health programs. Yet U.S. assistance, while certainly contributing to Egypt's development also served to undermine the nationalist legitimacy of the regime. After all, how could Mubarak boast of Egyptian pride and ability when USAID employees and contractors were nestled in many government ministries?

At the same time, Egyptians came to see that their country's foreign policy was being warped for the sake of U.S. largesse. The original sin was Sadat's separate peace with Israel, which Mubarak inherited and scrupulously upheld. From the perspective of many Egyptians, this arrangement hopelessly constrained Cairo's power while it freed Israel and the United States to pursue their regional interests unencumbered. For the United States, Mubarak was pivotal in creating a regional order that made it easier and less expensive for Washington to pursue its interests, from the free flow of oil to the protection of Israel and the prevention of any one country in the region from becoming too dominant. The benefits to Mubarak were clear: approximately $70 billion in economic and military aid over thirty years and the ostensible prestige of being a partner of the world's superpower.

For Egypt, the particular policy ramifications of this deal have been plentiful, including Egypt's deployment of thirty-five thousand troops to Saudi Arabia in the Gulf War of 1991, its quiet support for the 2003 invasion of Iraq, its implicit alliance with Israel during the war in Lebanon in 2006, and its complicity with Israel in the blockade of Gaza. Mubarak believed that these policies served Egypt's interests—at least how he defined them—but they ran directly against the grain of Egyptian public opinion. Mubarak thus faced two irreconcilable positions: he could either be Washington's man or a man of the people—but not both. He chose the former and filled in the resulting legitimacy gap with manipulation and force.

It is no surprise, then, that the relationship between Egypt and the United States ran like a live wire through the popular opposition to Mubarak's rule. Protesters in Cairo declared in March 2003, just as U.S. forces were pouring into Iraq, that only a democratic Egypt would be able to resist Israeli and U.S. policies in the Middle East.

More recently, opponents of Mubarak expressed a similar sentiment, calling Mubarak's presidency the "Camp David regime."

No Egyptian leader will make Mubarak's mistake again, which does not portend well for Washington's position in the Middle East. The United States should greatly lower its expectations of what is possible in the post-Mubarak era and come to terms with the end of the strategic relationship. Where, then, does this leave Washington? The best the United States can do to salvage its position in Egypt is for the Obama administration to emphasize democracy, tolerance, pluralism, accountability, and nonviolence—and then take a hands-off approach as Egyptians build a new political system on their own terms. Washington has become such a negative factor in Egyptian politics that it risks doing more harm than good if U.S. officials give in to the temptation to do much more than emphasize "first principles" on a peaceful, orderly, and transparent political change. Implicit demands that call into question the continuation of the U.S. assistance package or even suggestions on how Egyptians should proceed after the Mubarak era will be met with tremendous resistance from those seeking to lead, if only because Egypt's politicians will need to demonstrate their nationalist credibility.

What sort of political future will emerge in Egypt is hard to predict. At the very least, however, Egypt does have a parliamentary history. The country's 1923 constitution established a parliament that functioned on and off to varying degrees until the Free Officers' revolution in 1952. That era was destabilized by the British presence in Egypt, which ultimately ushered in Nasser and his comrades, who constructed the regime against which Egyptians ultimately rebelled. Washington does not occupy Egypt, but it risks playing a malevolent role in the transition if it tries to interfere. This is not only because of the mistrust many Egyptians have for the United States, but also because the trajectory of Egyptian politics is unknowable and is likely to stay that way for some time. Revolutions rarely end the way their protagonists and participants desire when they are on the barricades.

HOAX?

Hassan was giddy, a word not often used to describe him. Not only was he relieved that Egypt's long nightmare had finally come to an end and the prospects of freedom were seemingly better than at any moment in the previous six decades, but Hassan must also have felt vindicated (though he is too polite to boast about it). He was not among the organizers of the protests and his activism had not been as high profile as many others, but Hassan had worked tirelessly to raise awareness among his network of Egyptian and foreign contacts of the perfidy of the Mubarak regime. He was also entirely correct on another level, having little patience for the claim that Egypt's political system was stable and thus durable. Hassan argued quite the opposite; that it was a house of cards built only on a foundation of fear, which was meaningless once Egyptians could no longer be intimidated. He could not predict when that would happen, but he believed it was inevitable.

It did not take long, however, for Hassan's great hopes for the future to turn sour. Within thirty-six hours of Mubarak's flight to Sharm el Shaykh and ignominy, Hassan was back at the computer burning up his keyboard. His first dispatch was titled "Hoax" and mixed Hassan's typical bravado with painful and sudden disillusion:

> I believe a big conspiracy is being perpetrated against the people of Egypt.
>
> Following almost three weeks of nationwide protests leading to the apparent downfall of a dictator, jubilation fills the streets of Egypt, in effect drugging the people into believing they have really become free. They are convinced their interim government will really keep its promises and steer them peacefully to the democracy everyone so valiantly fought for . . . Egypt will remain a military dictatorship indefinitely. How I wish I am wrong.

This message was surely a result of that "revolutionary hangover" that observers had expected. After all, uncertainty breeds fear. Yet in the weeks and months after Mubarak's departure, Hassan remained deeply concerned over the ebb and flow of events. Most of all, he was suspicious of the senior military commanders, whom he quite correctly tied directly to Mubarak. They were, indeed, his officers and while they ultimately pushed the president from office, they were loyal to him to a fault. Mubarak had threatened their cherished order nine days before his departure when he released thugs on Tahrir Square, yet the military stood aside during the chaos and stuck with their dictator.

To be sure, there were bright moments for Hassan. For example, when the revolutionary groups forced the resignation of Mubarak's last prime minister and loyal servant, Ahmed Shafiq, on March 3, Hassan's outlook improved considerably. He was under no illusions, however;

he never believed that Egypt's transition would be easy, but he was also well aware that remnants of the National Democratic Party, elements of the police, state security agents—even after the State Security Investigations was abolished on March 15—business interests, and the military would do whatever they could to salvage the old regime. That is why he voted "no" in the March 19 referendum. Hassan, like the many others who rejected the amendments, feared that previously well-organized and well-funded groups would be in a better position to contest parliamentary elections in six months time than groups confronted with the job of transforming themselves from protest movements into political parties—no easy task. Indeed, there was nothing about the post-Mubarak order that would be easy, but many Egyptians firmly believed that whatever the outcome of their revolution it had to be better than the Mubarak era.

There is a tendency to believe that Egyptians rebelled against Hosni Mubarak in early 2011. That is true, but it is not entirely accurate. They revolted against a regime—a political order—that he led, but that Mubarak inherited from Sadat who had inherited it from Nasser. It was a system that was founded in the ideological and power politics of the early 1950s, when the Free Officers discovered they could dispose of their opponents through nondemocratic laws, rules, regulations, and decrees. Egyptians unexpectedly cracked open that regime and dislodged its caretaker—Mubarak—and for the first time in sixty years have an opportunity to define Egypt as they desire rather than as a line of now discredited military officers have defined it. All the questions that Egyptians have been asking themselves: What is Egypt? What principles and values should guide Egypt at home and abroad? What is the role of religion and nationalism in the life of the country? What kind of foreign policy should Egypt pursue? Can Egypt be a regional leader again? Suddenly Egyptians—through their own bravery and dignity—gave themselves an opportunity to provide their own answers to these questions. Without a compelling and coherent account of Egyptian society and politics in response, their extraordinary efforts could be for naught. Indeed, it is entirely possible that Egypt's elections, the seating of a new parliament, or the inauguration of an elected president may ultimately not matter much. Although among the vast majority, there is great hope that Egyptians can construct a new political system and rebuild their society peacefully, that is unlikely as long as the underlying and antecedent debates about Egypt and what it stands for remain unresolved. There is no way of knowing how this process will unfold or how long it will take. In the immediate post-revolutionary period it is clear that the contest over legitimacies is the first step in what will likely be a bruising battle to define Egypt. Consequently, it is extraordinarily difficult to determine how the country will end up. There are only hints, albeit mixed ones— positive developments about democratic change coinciding with ominous signs of authoritarianism. For now, one thing is clear: the struggle for Egypt continues.

Notes

Introduction

1. Hassan el Sawaf, "Is a Fourth Term Right?" *Civil Society* 8, no. 93 (September 1999): 30–31.

One

1. Howard M. Sachar, *A History of Israel: From the Rise of Zionism to Our Time* (New York: Alfred A. Knopf, 1993), 341.
2. Gamal Abdel Nasser, *The Philosophy of the Revolution* (Cairo: Dar al-Maaref, 1954), 12.
3. The Shura Council, the Upper House of Egypt's parliament, has compiled important documents and declarations dating back to the monarchy. The compilation can be found at: http://www.shoura.gov.eg/const_pdf/const6.pdf. The Free Officers' announcement of their coup can be found on page 284.
4. In August, the British dispatched a contingent of twenty thousand troops to the Suez Canal Zone.
5. John Marlowe, *A History of Modern Egypt and Anglo-Egyptian Relations: 1800–1956*, 2nd ed. (Hamden, CT: Archon Books, 1965), 43, 365.
6. James Gelvin, *The Modern Middle East: A History* (New York: Oxford University Press, 2005), 93. With the purchase of Ismail interests in the Canal, the British assumed control of 40 percent of the Suez Canal Company's outstanding ordinary stock, making London the largest shareholder in the company. Yet, Disraeli was unable to exercise the control that he sought. The bylaws of the firm prevented any one shareholder from having more than ten votes (out of twenty-four) on the Board of Directors and Ismail had given up the voting

rights related to his share until 1894 anyway. See Marlowe, *A History of Modern Egypt and Anglo-Egyptian Relations: 1800–1956*, 61–84.

7. Prior to 1867, Egypt's rulers were calls "pashas," but Ismail convinced the Ottoman to change his title to Khedive, which is a Persian word that means viceroy. See Eugene Rogan, *The Arabs: A History* (New York: Basic Books, 2009), 100.

8. The Turkish Postal Service Law of March 1930 officially renamed the city Istanbul in 1930, though the name had been used unofficially since the fifteenth century. See Richard Robinson, *The First Turkish Republic: A Case Study in National Development* (Cambridge, MA: Harvard University Press, 1963), 298.

9. William L. Cleveland, *A History of the Modern Middle East*, 3rd ed. (Boulder, CO: Westview Press, 2004), 71.

10. See William B. Hesseltine and Hazel C. Wolf, *The Blue and Gray on the Nile: With American Soldiers in the Arab World . . . in 1870* (St. Petersburg, FL: Hailer Publishing, 2006).

11. P.J. Vatikiotis, *The History of Modern Egypt: From Muhammad Ali to Mubarak*, 4th ed. (Baltimore: Johns Hopkins University Press, 1991), 165–66.

12. Marlowe, *A History of Modern Egypt and Anglo-Egyptian Relations: 1800–1956*, 93.

13. For a full discussion of the origins of the Egyptian press and its nationalist influences see Vatikiotis, *The History of Modern Egypt*, ch. 9.

14. The Egyptian nationalist Mustafa Kamil originated the phrase "Egypt for the Egyptians." Kamil was the founder of the National Party and editor of the party's daily newspaper, *al Liwa* (*The Standard*).

15. Albert Hourani, *Arabic Thought in the Liberal Age, 1798–1939* (Cambridge: Cambridge University Press, 1991), 114–115.

16. Ibid., 139.

17. Charles D. Smith, "The 'Crisis of Orientation': The Shift of Egyptian Intellectuals to Islamic Subjects in the 1930s," *International Journal of Middle East Studies* 4, no. 4 (October 1973): 390.

18. Hourani, *Arabic Thought in the Liberal Age, 1798–1939*, 161.

19. Ibid., 172.

20. Emad Eldin Shahin, "Muhammad Rashid Rida's Perspectives on the West as Reflected in al Manar," *The Muslim World* 72, no.2 (April 1989): 113–132.

21. Quintan Wiktorowicz, "Anatomy of the Salafi Movement," *Studies in Conflict and Terrorism* 29, no. 3 (April/May 2006): 207–239.

22. Omayma Abdel-Latif, "Trends in Salafism," in *Islamic Radicalization: The Challenge for Euro-Mediterranean Relations*, eds. Michael Emerson, Kristina Kausch, and Richard Youngs (Brussels: Centre for European Policy Studies, 2009), 69.

23. Hourani, *Arabic Thought in the Liberal Age, 1798–1939*, 230.

24. The Legislative Assembly was the short-lived successor to a Consultative Council and General Assembly that existed between 1882 and 1913. The

Consultative Council consisted of thirty members of whom sixteen were elected. The General Assembly was the lower of house and boasted eighty-four mandates. Of those forty-six were elected and the remaining were appointed by the government.

25. Tom Little, *Egypt* (New York: Frederick A. Praeger, 1958), 100. For more on the concepts of mobilization and assimilation, see Ernst B. Haas, *Nationalism, Liberalism, and Progress: The Rise and Decline of Nationalism* (Ithaca, NY: Cornell University Press, 1997).

26. Eugene Rogan, *The Arabs: A History* (New York: Basic Books, 2009), 164–165.

27. With the establishment of the protectorate, the title consul general became high commissioner.

28. Vatikiotis, *The History of Modern Egypt*, 268.

29. David Fromkin, *A Peace to End All Peace: The Fall of the Ottoman Empire and the Creation of the Modern Middle East* (New York: Henry Holt, 1989), 397.

30. Vatikiotis, *The History of Modern Egypt*, 281.

31. Afaf Lutfi al-Sayyid Marsot, *Egypt's Liberal Experiment: 1922–1936* (Berkeley: University of California Press, 1977), 87.

32. Vatikiotis, *The History of Modern Egypt*, 294.

33. John Sabini, *Islam: A Primer*, rev. ed. (Washington, DC: Middle East Editorial Associates, 1990), 48–49. Also see Carl W. Ernst, *The Shambhala Guide to Sufism* (Boston: Shambhala, 1997) and Julian Baldick, *Mystical Islam: An Introduction to Sufism* (New York: New York University Press, 1989).

34. *Dar al Ulum* increasingly took on a conservative religious cast in response to the secular orientation of Egyptian University (later King Fuad I University and later Cairo University), which was founded in 1908.

35. Richard P. Mitchell, *The Society of the Muslim Brothers* (New York: Oxford University Press, 1993), 4. The attacks on religion that al Banna perceived were in part the result of the disestablishment of Islam that Turkish nationalists undertook after the defeat of the Central Powers in World War I and the subsequent collapse of the Ottoman Empire.

36. Mitchell, *The Society of the Muslim Brothers*, 5.

37. Caroline Piquet, "The Suez Company's Concession in Egypt, 1854–1956: Modern Infrastructure and Local Economic Development," *Enterprise & Society* 5, no. 1 (March 2004): 107–127.

38. Max Rodenbeck, *Cairo: The City Victorious* (New York: Vintage Books, 2000), 165–66.

39. Mitchell, *The Society of the Muslim Brothers*, 14.

40. Ibid., 16–17.

41. Charles D. Smith, "4 February 1942: Its Causes and Its Influences on Egyptian Politics and on the Future of Anglo-Egyptian Relations, 1937–1945," *International Journal of Middle East Studies* 10, no. 4 (November 1979): 461–462.

42. Mitchell, *The Society of the Muslim Brothers*, 24.

43. The relationship between the Muslim Brotherhood and nationalist-minded army officers is well known. Gamal Abdel Nasser, Anwar Sadat and virtually the entire first tier of Free Officers were interlocutors of the Islamists. Sadat's memoir, *In Search of Identity*, emphasizes the former president's prominent role in these contacts. Although there is little disagreement about Sadat's religiosity or his contacts with the Brotherhood prior to the July 1952 coup, Sadat's autobiography is widely regarded among both Egyptian and Western scholars to be self-serving in the extreme.

44. Mitchell, *The Society of the Muslim Brothers*, 27, 65.

45. After 1942, the Wafd actually no longer enjoyed the support of a majority of Egyptians.

46. Mitchell, *The Society of the Muslim Brothers*, 41.

47. Ibid., 56.

48. The actual number of Brothers who took part in the fighting in Palestine is not known.

49. Mitchell, *The Society of the Muslim Brothers*, 58.

50. Ibid, 67.

51. Vatikiotis, *The History of Modern Egypt*, 370.

52. Ibid., 372.

53. Ibid., 378.

54. Joel Gordon, *Nasser's Blessed Movement: Egypt's Free Officers and the July Revolution* (Cairo: The American University in Cairo Press, 1996), 36.

Two

1. Raymond William Baker, *Egypt's Uncertain Revolution under Nasser and Sadat* (Cambridge, MA: Harvard University Press, 1978), 13.

2. On the social composition of Egypt's officer corps, see Eliezer Be'eri, *Army Officers in Arab Politics and Society* (New York: Praeger, 1970), 321. See also, Amos Perlmutter, *Egypt: The Praetorian State* (New Brunswick, NJ: Transaction Books, 1974); and Anouar Abdel-Malek, *Egypt: Military Society; The Army Regime, the Left, and Social Change under Nasser* (New York: Vintage Books, 1968).

3. Walid Khalidi, "Nasser's Memoirs of the First Palestine War," *Journal of Palestine Studies* 2, no. 2 (Winter 1973): 3–32; Robert H. Stephens, *Nasser: A Political Biography* (New York: Simon & Schuster, 1971); Anthony Nutting, *Nasser* (New York: E.P. Dutton, 1972); Dan Hofstadter, ed., *Egypt and Nasser*, 3 vols. (New York: Facts on File, 1973).

4. Be'eri, *Army Officers in Arab Politics and Society*, 91.

5. The British maintained a large presence in Bahrain, Qatar, and the seven states that made up the United Arab Emirates until the early 1970s. For a complete discussion of British and Western interests in the Persian Gulf, see Jeffrey R. Macris, *The Politics and Security of the Gulf: Anglo-American Hegemony and the Shaping of a Region* (New York: Routledge, 2010).

6. Abdel-Malek, *Egypt: Military Society*, 97.

7. Ray Takeyh, *The Origins of the Eisenhower Doctrine: The US, Britain, and Nasser's Egypt, 1953–1957* (New York: St. Martin's Press, 2000), 27.

8. P.J. Vatikiotis, *The History of Modern Egypt: From Muhammad Ali to Mubarak*, 4th ed. (Baltimore: Johns Hopkins University Press, 1991), 357.

9. Joel Gordon, *Nasser's Blessed Movement: Egypt's Free Officers and the July Revolution* (Cairo: American University in Cairo Press, 1996), 54, 93.

10. Vatikiotis, *The History of Modern Egypt*, 394–395.

11. Ibid., 395.

12. Saad M. Gadalla, *Land Reform in Relation to Social Development: Egypt* (Columbia: University of Missouri Press, 1962), 13.

13. Vatikiotis, *The History of Modern Egypt*, 399.

14. R. Hrair Dekmejian, *Egypt under Nasir: A Study in Political Dynamics* (Albany: State University of New York Press, 1971), 23–27.

15. Be'eri, *Army Officers in Arab Politics and Society*, 105–106.

16. In 1943, Makram Ubayd—who came to be known as the conscience of the party—publicly disclosed the details of the Wafd's alleged corruption, sullying the party's image as an organization dedicated to uplifting all classes of Egyptians.

17. Donald Malcolm Reid, "Fu'ad Siraj al-Din and the Egyptian Wafd," *Journal of Contemporary History* 15, no. 4 (October 1980): 721–744.

18. Gordon, *Nasser's Blessed Movement*, 72.

19. Kirk J. Beattie, *Egypt during the Nasser Years: Politics, Ideology, and Civil Society* (Boulder, CO: Westview Press, 1994), 81.

20. Vatikiotis, *The History of Modern Egypt*, 381.

21. Gordon, *Nasser's Blessed Movement*, 69.

22. Jean Lacouture and Simonne Lacouture, *Egypt in Transition*, trans. Francis Scarfe (New York: Criterion Books, 1958), 169; Be'eri, *Army Officers in Arab Politics and Society*, 107.

23. Gordon, *Nasser's Blessed Movement*, 74.

24. Ismail Sabri Abdallah quoted in Selma Botman, *The Rise of Egyptian Communism: 1939–1970* (Syracuse, NY: Syracuse University Press, 1988), 123; Joel Beinin and Zachary Lockman, *Workers on the Nile: Nationalism, Communism, Islam, and the Egyptian Working Class, 1882–1954* (Princeton, NJ: Princeton University Press, 1987), 419.

25. Vatikiotis, *The History of Modern Egypt*, 382.

26. Antonio Gramsci, *Selections from the Prison Notebooks*, trans. Quintin Hoare and Geoffrey Nowell Smith (New York: International Publishers, 1971), 161.

27. Gamal Abdel Nasser quoted in Gehad Audah, "The State of Political Control: The Case of Nasser, 1960–1967," *The Arab Journal of the Social Sciences* 2, no. 1 (April 1987): 98.

28. Derek Hopwood, *Egypt: Politics and Society 1945–1984*, 2nd ed. (Boston: Unwin & Hyman, 1985), 87.

29. Beattie, *Egypt during the Nasser Years*, 80.

30. Abdel-Malek, *Egypt: Military Society*, 92–93; P.J. Vatikiotis, *The Egyptian Army in Politics: Pattern for New Nations?* (Bloomington: Indiana University Press, 1961), 82–83; Perlmutter, *Egypt: The Praetorian State*, 51–52.

31. Under the new cabinet, the constitutional project, launched with much fanfare six months earlier, was left to wither. For a full discussion see Salah Eissa, *Constitution in the Garbage Can* [in Arabic] (Cairo: Cairo Center for Human Rights, 2001).

32. Jon B. Alterman, *Egypt and American Foreign Assistance, 1952–1956: Hopes Dashed* (New York: Palgrave Macmillan, 2002), 3.

33. Gordon, *Nasser's Blessed Movement*, 168.

34. Ibid., 167.

35. Beattie, *Egypt under Nasser*, 73.

36. Ibid., 73; Be'eri, *Army Officers in Arab Politics and Society*, 112–113.

37. Vatikiotis, *The History of Modern Egypt*, 383–384.

38. Reid, "Fu'ad Siraj al-Din and the Egyptian Wafd," 739.

39. Gordon, *Nasser's Blessed Movement*, 71; Reid, "Fu'ad Siraj al-Din and the Egyptian Wafd," 738–739.

40. Reid, "Fu'ad Siraj al-Din and the Egyptian Wafd," 739.

41. Ibid., 739–740.

42. Abdel-Malek, *Egypt: Military Society*, 92.

43. Vatikiotis, *The Egyptian Army in Politics*, 94.

44. Gordon, *Nasser's Blessed Movement*, 114.

45. Abdel-Malek, *Egypt: Military Society*, 95.

46. Botman, "Egyptian Communists and the Free Officers: 1950–1954," 363.

47. Richard P. Mitchell, *The Society of Muslim Brothers* (New York: Oxford University Press, 1993), 130–131.

48. As early as 1950–1951, the American embassy was counseling the Egyptians to demonstrate flexibility on the Sudanese questions, arguing that it would make negotiations over Britain's status in Egypt proper easier.

49. James Jankowski, *Nasser's Egypt, Arab Nationalism, and the United Arab Republic* (Boulder: Lynne Rienner, 2002), 43.

50. Abdel-Malek, *Egypt: Military Society*, 98.

51. George Lenczowski, *The Middle East in World Affairs*, 4th ed. (Ithaca, NY: Cornell University Press, 1980), 526–527.

52. Mitchell, *The Society of Muslim Brothers*, 134–135.

53. Abdel-Malek, *Egypt: Military Society*, 94.

54. Mitchell, *The Society of Muslim Brothers*, 139; Gordon, *Nasser's Blessed Movement*, 178.

55. Mitchell, *The Society of Muslim Brothers*, 150.

56. George Tsebelis argues persuasively that institutions result from the conscious choice of individuals who determine that previous institutions did not serve their interests. See George Tsebelis, *Nested Games: Rational Choice in Comparative Politics* (Berkeley: University of California Press, 1990).

57. Kiren Aziz Chaudhry, *The Price of Wealth: Economies and Institutions in the Middle East* (Ithaca, NY: Cornell University Press, 1997), 16.

58. Douglass C. North, *Structure and Change in Economic History* (New York: Norton, 1981); Douglass C. North and Barry R. Weingast, "Constitutions and Commitment: The Evolution of Institutions Governing Public Choice in Seventeenth Century England," *Journal of Economic History* 59, no. 4 (December 1989): 803–832; Margaret Levi, *Of Rule and Revenue* (Berkeley: University of California Press, 1988). Peter A. Hall and Rosemary C. R. Taylor, "Political Science and the Three Institutionalisms," *Political Studies* 44, no. 4 (December 1996): 936–957.

59. David Collier and Ruth Berins Collier, *Shaping the Political Arena* (Princeton, NJ: Princeton University Press, 1991), ch. 1; Paul Pierson, "Increasing Returns, Path Dependence, and the Study of Politics," *American Political Science Review* 94, no. 2 (June 2000): 251–267; Hall and Taylor, "Political Science and the Three Institutionalisms," 941.

Three

1. Howard M. Sachar, *A History of Israel: From the Rise of Zionism to Our Time* (New York: Alfred A. Knopf, 1993), 475, 481.

2. Gamal Abdel Nasser, *Speech Nationalizing the Suez Canal: Public Address of President Gamal Abdel Nasser on the 4th Anniversary of the Revolution from Alexandria,* July 26, 1956, [in Arabic] http://www.nasser.org/Speeches/browser.aspx?SID=495&lang=ar. All translations in this volume are mine unless otherwise noted.

3. Zachary Karabell, *Parting the Desert: The Creation of the Suez Canal* (New York: Vintage Books, 2004).

4. Donald Neff, *Warriors at Suez: Eisenhower Takes America into the Middle East* (New York: Simon & Schuster, 1981), 206.

5. Ibid., 161.

6. See Eitan Barak, "Between Reality and Secrecy: Israel's Freedom of Navigation Through the Straits of Tiran, 1956–1967," *Middle East Journal* 61, no. 4 (Autumn 2007): 657–679.

7. Sachar, *A History of Israel,* 505.

8. Vaughan Lowe et al., eds., *The United Nations Security Council and War: The Evolution of Thought and Practice since 1945* (New York: Oxford University Press, 2008), 293.

9. Maurice Vaïsse, "France and the Suez Crisis," in *Suez 1956: The Crisis and its Consequences,* eds. William Roger Louis and Roger Owen (New York: Oxford University Press, 1991), 141–142.

10. Brazil, Canada, Colombia, Denmark, Finland, India, Indonesia, Norway, Sweden, and Yugoslavia contributed forces to the United Nations Emergency Force. For additional information, see United Nations, "Middle East—UNEF 1: Facts and Figures," http://www.un.org/en/peacekeeping/missions/past/unef1facts.html (accessed January 5, 2011).

11. World Bank, "Data: Egypt, Arab Rep," http://data.worldbank.org/country/ egypt-arab-republic (accessed December 22, 2010).

12. Robert Mabro, *The Egyptian Economy: 1952–1972* (Oxford: Oxford University Press, 1974), 222–223; World Bank, "Data: Egypt, Arab Rep," http://data. worldbank.org/country/egypt-arab-republic.

13. Ahmed Abdalla, *The Student Movement and National Politics in Egypt, 1923–1973* (Cairo: American University in Cairo Press, 2008), 104.

14. Raymond A. Hinnesbusch, *Egyptian Politics under Sadat: The Post-Populist Development of an Authoritarian-Modernizing State* (Boulder, CO: Lynne Rienner, 1988), 27.

15. Patrick Seale, *Asad: The Struggle for the Middle East* (Berkeley: University of California Press, 1988), 54.

16. Ibid.

17. Ibid.

18. James Jankowski, *Nasser's Egypt, Arab Nationalism, and the United Arab Republic* (Boulder, CO: Lynne Rienner, 2002), 118.

19. Derek Hopwood, *Egypt: Politics and Society, 1945–1984*. 2nd ed. (Boston: Unwin Hyman, 1985), 64; Robert Stephens, *Nasser: A Political Biography* (New York: Simon & Schuster, 1971), 399–408.

20. Eric Croddy, *Chemical and Biological Warfare: A Comprehensive Survey for the Concerned Citizen*, with Clarisa Perez-Armendariz and John Hart (New York: Copernicus Books, 2002); Nuclear Threat Initiative, "Egypt Profile: Chemical Overview," October 2009, http://www.nti.org/e_research/profiles/Egypt/ Chemical/index.html. The Egyptians denied using these weapons, though there were enough eyewitness accounts at the time that it is now widely believed to be true. On Egypt's death toll, see Kenneth M. Pollack, *Arab at War: Military Effectiveness, 1948–1991* (Lincoln: University of Nebraska Press, 2002); and David Witty, "A Regular Army in Counterinsurgency Operations: Egypt in North Yemen, 1962–1967," *Journal of Military History* 65, no. 2 (April 2001).

21. Alan Richards and John Waterbury, *A Political Economy of the Middle East: State, Class, and Economic Development* (Boulder, CO: Westview Press, 1990), 195–196.

22. Kirk J. Beattie, *Egypt during the Nasser Years: Politics, Ideology, and Civil Society* (Boulder, CO: Westview Press, 1994), 175.

23. Julie Taylor, "Prophet Sharing: Strategic Interaction between Muslim Clerics and Middle Eastern Regimes," *Journal of Islamic Law and Culture* 10, no. 1 (April 2008): 50.

24. Donald Reid, *Cairo University and the Making of Modern Egypt* (Cambridge: Cambridge University Press, 1990), 210.

25. Joel Beinin and Zachary Lockman, *Workers on the Nile: Nationalism, Communism, Islam, and the Egyptian Working Class, 1882–1954* (Princeton, NJ: Princeton University Press, 1987), 420.

26. The exceptions were Khaled Muhieddin, Ahmad Fuad, and a prominent Free Officer who was not a member of the RCC named Ahmad Hamrush. All three

were leftists and at one time or another members of the Democratic Front for National Liberation, which was the largest of Egypt's leftist factions.

27. Robert Bianchi, *Unruly Corporatism: Associational Life in Twentieth-Century Egypt* (New York: Oxford University Press, 1989), 125.

28. Beinin and Lockman, *Workers on the Nile*, 432–435; Joel Beinin, "Labor, Capital, and the State in Nasserist Egypt, 1952–1961," *International Journal of Middle East Studies* 21, no. 1 (February 1989): 79–90.

29. Beinin and Lockman, *Workers on the Nile*, 432–435.

30. Marsha Pripstein Posusney, *Labor and the State in Egypt: Workers, Unions, and Economic Restructuring* (New York: Columbia University Press, 1997), 47, 70–73.

31. Abdalla, *The Student Movement and National Politics in Egypt, 1923–1973*, 120.

32. Ibid., 122–123; Marilyn Booth, "Exploding into the Seventies: Ahmad Fu'ad Nigm, Sheikh Imam, and the Aesthetics of a New Youth Politics," *Cairo Papers in Social Science* 29, no. 2/3 (Summer/Fall 2006): 28.

33. Abdalla, *The Student Movement and National Politics in Egypt, 1923–1973*, 125–127.

34. Carrie Rosefsky Wickham, *Mobilizing Islam: Religion, Activism, and Political Change in Egypt* (New York: Columbia University Press, 2002), 31.

35. Nathan J. Brown, *The Rule of Law in the Arab World: Courts in Egypt and the Gulf* (New York: Cambridge University Press, 1997), 82–83.

36. For a complete text of the Emergency Law, see Abdul al Moneim Husni, *A Compendium of Egyptian Law and Statutes*, vol. 6 [in Arabic] (Giza: Merkaz Husni l-il-Dirassat al Qaanuniyah, 1987), 292–306.

37. Barbara Zollner, "Prison Talk: The Muslim Brotherhood's Internal Struggle During Gamal Abdel Nasser's Persecution, 1954 to 1971," *International Journal of Middle East Studies* 39, no. 3 (August 2007): 417; See also, Barbara Zollner, *The Muslim Brotherhood: Hassan al-Hudaybi and Ideology* (New York: Routledge, 2009).

38. John Calvert, *Sayyid Qutb and the Origins of Radical Islamism* (New York: Columbia University Press, 2010), 235.

39. Ibid., 95–96.

40. Ana Belén Soage, "Islamism and Modernity: The Political Thought of Sayyid Qutb," *Totalitarian Movements and Political Religions* 10, no. 2 (June 2009): 189–203.

41. Sayyid Qutb, " 'The America I Have Seen': In the Scale of Human Values (1951)," trans. Tarek Masoud and Ammar Fakeeh, in *America in an Arab Mirror: Images of America in Arabic Travel Literature: An Anthology*, ed. Kamal Abdel-Malek (Gordonsville, VA: Palgrave-Macmillan, 2000), 11. Qutb's article was originally serialized in the Egyptian journal *al Risala* in November and December 1951.

42. Sayyid Qutb, " 'The America I Have Seen': In the Scale of Human Values (1951)" in *America in an Arab Mirror*, 12–15.

43. Calvert, *Sayyid Qutb and the Origins of Radical Islamism*, 183.

44. Zollner, "Prison Talk," 417.

45. Sayyid Qutb, *Milestones Along the Way* (Salmiah, Kuwait: International Islamic Federation of Student Organizations, 1978), 55.

46. Ibid., 9.

47. William E. Shepard, "Sayyid Qutb's Doctrine of Jahiliyya," *International Journal of Middle East Studies* 35, no. 4 (November 2003): 527–528.

48. Qutb, *Milestones*, 87.

49. Ibid., 89.

50. Ibid., 18.

51. For a complete discussion, ibid., ch. 7.

52. Ibid., 99.

53. Ibid., 127.

54. Ibid., 100.

55. Ibid., 164.

56. Zollner, *The Muslim Brotherhood*, 40.

57. Gamal Abdel Nasser, *Statement of President Gamal Abdel Nasser to the People and the Nation Announcing his Resignation from the Presidency of the Republic*, June 9, 1967, http://www.nasser.org/Speeches/browser.aspx?SID=1221&lang=ar.

58. Ibid.

59. Mehran Kamrava, *The Modern Middle East: A Political History since the First World War*. (Berkeley: University of California Press, 2005), 120; Hisham Sharabi, "Prelude to War," in *The Arab-Israeli Confrontation of June 1967*, ed. Ibrahim Abu-Lughod (Evanston, IL: Northwestern University Press, 1970), 57.

60. United Nations, "Key Issues in a Permanent Settlement," United Nations Information System on the Question of Palestine, http://unispal.un.org/unispal.nsf/iss.htm?OpenForm (accessed January 6, 2011).

61. Nadav Safran, *Israel: The Embattled Ally* (Cambridge, MA: Belknap Press of Harvard University Press, 1982), 417; for a comprehensive discussion of American policymaking during the 1967 crisis, see William B. Quandt, "Lyndon Johnson and the 1967 War: What Color was the Light?" *Middle East Journal* 46, no. 2 (Spring 1992): 198–228.

62. There are competing theories as to why the Israelis attacked the *Liberty*. Some historians argue that it was just a mistake. The combination of human and technical errors that are part of the perennial "fog of war" conspired in a tragic error for which the Israelis immediately took responsibility. Although on one level this argument is compelling, it stretches credulity to believe that Israeli air crews and sailors could not tell the difference between a late nineteenth-century vintage Egyptian supply vessel and an American spy ship. Other scholars and *Liberty* survivors have long argued that the Israeli pilots and torpedo boats deliberately attacked the lightly armed American ship to blind Washington of Israel's intention to drive to the East Bank of the Suez Canal. These analysts hypothesize that Israeli Prime Minister Levi Eshkol, Defense Minister Moshe Dayan, and Chief of Staff Rabin feared

that if Washington fully understood their intentions, the Johnson administration would pose a ceasefire. Others claim similarly that Israel wanted to
foil Washington's ability to monitor Israeli military communications so the
Johnson administration would not learn of the IDF's intention to take the
Golan Heights in the following days. These related arguments do not stand
up to scrutiny either for several reasons. Johnson gave his word that he would
not impose a ceasefire as Eisenhower had done in 1956; by the time the attack
began at 2:00 p.m., Israeli forces were already within striking distance of the
Canal, and Israel was open about its intentions regarding Syria. Finally, some
Liberty survivors and their supporters argue that Israeli forces attacked the
Liberty to cover up Israel's alleged massacres of Egyptian prisoners of war.
There is, however, no credible evidence that these war crimes ever took place.

63. League of Arab States, "Khartoum Resolution," September 1, 1967, http://
unispal.un.org/UNISPAL.NSF/0/1FF0BF3DDEB703A785257110007719E7.

64. Richard B. Parker, *The Politics of Miscalculation in the Middle East*
(Bloomington: Indiana University Press, 1993), 3.

65. There are a number of hypotheses—some better than others—to explain the
Soviet warning. One suggests that Moscow invented the Israeli troop build-up
in order to improve its position in the Middle East by coaxing Cairo into
supporting its client regime in Damascus and/or forcing Egypt into a deeper
relationship with the Soviet Union. Another variation of the hypothesis is
that Moscow made up the report and that the Soviets wanted to get Egypt out
of Yemen, and if Cairo believed the Israelis were mobilizing, the Egyptian
military would surely withdraw from the Arabian Peninsula. It seems unlikely
that Moscow was involved in such an elaborate hoax given the stakes involved
and the downside potential for the Soviets if hostilities broke out. A second,
more compelling, theory holds that the Soviets believed the reports of Israel's
military build-up, which fit well within their set of beliefs about Israel and the
Middle East conflict at that moment. There are a number of other explanations, including rank Soviet incompetence and conspiracies about Syrian and
Israeli disinformation campaigns, but there is little evidence to support these
claims. See Richard B. Parker, *The Politics of Miscalculation in the Middle East*
(Bloomington: Indiana University Press, 1993).

66. Rabin's threats were controversial among Israel's leaders, but there is no evidence that he openly threatened the Syrians. Upon the mobilization of Israeli
forces, Prime Minister Eshkol warned his chief of staff to refrain from making
threatening public statements. David Ben Gurion, who held no official role,
but who loomed large politically due to his status as Israel's founder and first
prime minister took Rabin to task for his threats against the Syrians. See
Michael Oren, *Six Days of War: June 1967 and the Making of the Modern Middle
East* (New York: Oxford University Press, 2002), 80.

67. Mohammed Fawzi, *The Three Year War, 1967–1970: Memoirs of General Mohamed
Fawzi*, vol. 1 (Cairo: Dar al Mustaqbal al-Arabi, 1984), 117–125 [in Arabic].
U Thant's notes from his May 24, 1967 meeting with the Egyptian foreign

minister indicate that the Egyptian move on UNEF was intended to apply enough pressure on the Israelis in an effort to ward off what the Egyptians believed to be an imminent IDF strike on southern Syria. See The Secretary-General, *Notes from Secretary General's Meetings in Cairo, 24 May 1967 with President Nasser and Foreign Minister Mahmoud Riad, UAR,* Container S-0865–0001: Peacekeeping Operations Files of the Secretary General: U Thant-Middle East (May 24, 1967).

68. Before the outbreak of hostilities, U Thant denied that his "prompt compliance with the [Egyptian] request for withdrawal of the [United Nations Emergency] Force" caused the 1967 crisis. This is certainly true, but the removal of UNEF contributed to an environment that made the conflict possible. The Secretary-General, *Report by the Secretary-General, delivered to the Security Council,* U.N. Doc. S/7906 (May 26, 1967).

69. Safran, *Israel,* 407.

70. Ibid., 395–397.

71. For an exposition of this argument, see Fouad Ajami, *The Arab Predicament: Arab Political Thought and Practice since 1967* (New York: Cambridge University Press, 1992).

72. For a discussion of the Egyptian military's performance during the June War, see Kenneth M. Pollack, *Arabs at War: Military Effectiveness, 1948–1991* (Lincoln: University of Nebraska Press, 2002), 58–88.

73. Raymond A. Hinnesbusch, *Egyptian Politics under Sadat* (Boulder, CO: Lynne Rienner, 1988), 30–31.

74. Beattie, *Egypt during the Nasser Years,* 124–125.

75. Mona El-Nahhas, "By His Own Hand?" *Al-Ahram Weekly On-line,* February 1–7, 2001, http://weekly.ahram.org.eg/2001/519/eg8.htm.

76. Confidential communication with a former student activist, September 4, 2010.

77. Abdalla, *The Student Movement and National Politics in Egypt, 1923–1973,* 152.

78. Ibid., 156.

79. Ibid., 158.

80. See Gamal Abdel Nasser, *Nasser Speaks: Basic Documents,* trans. E.S. Farag (London: Morsett Press, 1972), 155–167 for the complete text of the March 30 Program.

81. Sachar, *A History of Israel,* 691.

82. Abdallah, *The Student Movement and National Politics in Egypt, 1923–1973,* 162.

83. Makram Muhammad Ahmad, "Students of al Mansoura," [in Arabic] *Al-Ahram,* November 26, 1968; Abdalla, *The Student Movement and National Politics in Egypt, 1923–1973,* 161–162.

84. R. Hrair Dekmejian, *Egypt under Nasir: A Study in Political Dynamics* (Albany: State University of New York, 1971), 259–261.

85. See Mark N. Cooper, "The Demilitarization of the Egyptian Cabinet," *International Journal of Middle East Studies* 14, no. 2 (May 1982): 203–225 for a complete discussion of the civilianization of the government. In *Ruling But Not*

Governing: The Military and Political Development in Egypt, Algeria, and Turkey (Baltimore: Johns Hopkins University Press, 2007), Steven A. Cook argues that while the raw numbers of military officers serving in cabinet positions may have declined, demilitarization of the political system was not as thoroughgoing as Cooper implies.

Four

1. Mohamed Abdel Ghani El Gamasy, *The October War: Memoirs of Field Marshal El Gamasy of Egypt* (Cairo: American University in Cairo Press, 1993), 107.

2. For a detailed discussion of the Bar Lev line, see Kenneth M. Pollack, *Arabs at War: Military Effectiveness, 1948–1991* (Lincoln: University of Nebraska Press, 1991); and Nadav Safran, *Israel: The Embattled Ally* (Cambridge, MA: Belknap Press of Harvard University, 1982).

3. The agreement, which went into effect on August 7, 1970 prohibited the parties from establishing new positions or weapons fifty kilometers east or west of the Suez Canal.

4. United Nations Security Council, Resolution 242 of November 22, 1967 (New York, 1967), http://domino.un.org/unispal.NSF/796f8bc05ec4f30885256cef00 73cf3a/7d35e1f729df491c85256ee700686136. The Rogers Initiative should not be confused with the Rogers Plan of December 1969, which was a ten-point plan for resolving the Arab-Israeli conflict. Both Egypt and Israel rejected the proposal. The Israelis were concerned that while the plan—which was the result of negotiations between the United States, Great Britain, France, and the Soviet Union—envisaged negotiations between the parties, it left very little for discussion. For his part, Nasser regarded the proposal biased in favor of the Israelis and declared "the United States is [the] number one enemy of the Arabs." See Howard M. Sachar, *A History of Israel: From the Rise of Zionism to Our Time* (New York: Alfred A. Knopf, 1993), 93–95; and Safran, *Israel: The Embattled Ally*, 434–435.

5. In the UN Secretary General's report on Jarring's efforts during the latter part of 1970, U Thant regretted that "the parties showed continued serious diveregences" and the "conditions for a useful series of meetings" on the implementation of Resolution 242 did not exist.

6. For a detailed discussion of the PLO in Jordan, see Yezid Sayigh, *Armed Struggle and the Search for State: The Palestinian National Movement, 1949– 1993* (Oxford: Oxford University Press, 1999); Philip Robins, *A History of Jordan* (Cambridge: Cambridge University Press, 2004); Avi Shlaim, *Lion of Jordan: The Life of King Hussein in War and Peace* (New York: Vintage Books, 2007).

7. Shlaim, *Lion of Jordan*, 339; Robert H. Stephens, *Nasser: A Political Biography* (New York: Simon & Schuster, 1971), 554–555.

8. Raymond Anderson, "Egyptians in the Street and Chiefs of State Mourn Death of Nasser," *New York Times*, September 30, 1970.

9. The six Principles of the Revolution—the eradication of all aspects of imperialism; the extinction of feudalism; the abolition of monopolies and capitalist control of the system of government; the development of a strong national army; the institutionalization of social justice; and the establishment of a sound democratic society—first appeared in the 1956 constitution and then in the 1962 National Charter.

10. Raymond William Baker, *Sadat and After: Struggles for Egypt's Political Soul* (Cambridge, MA: Harvard University Press, 1990), 18. See also John Waterbury, *The Egypt of Nasser and Sadat: The Political Economy of Two Regimes* (Princeton, NJ: Princeton University Press, 1983); and Alan Richards and John Waterbury, *A Political Economy of the Middle East: State, Class, and Economic Development* (Boulder, CO: Westview Press, 1990).

11. According to Sadat's memoir, *In Search of Identity*, Under Secretary of State Eliot Richardson who led the American delegation to Nasser's funeral, reported that Sadat would "not remain in power for more than four or six weeks." See Anwar el Sadat, *In Search of Identity* (New York: Harper Colophon Books, 1979), 277. Cable from US Interest Section Cairo (Bergus) to Secretary of State, September 28, 1970, GR-State, Political-UAR 1970–1973, Egypt, NARA II, RG 59, Entry 1613, Box 2642, quoted in Kirk J. Beattie, *Egypt during the Sadat Years* (New York: Palgrave, 2000), 289 n. 58.

12. Terence Smith, "U.S. Officials See Period of Instability in Mideast," *New York Times*, September 28, 1970.

13. Beattie, *Egypt during the Sadat Years*, 42–43.

14. After he became president, Sadat established a museum in Marsa Matruh on Egypt's north coast near El Alamein in honor of Rommel who is widely regarded to be one of the most brilliant military strategists of all time. The modest museum recounts the battle of El Alamein and displays some alleged Rommel artifacts.

15. David Hirst and Irene Beeson reproduce the letter in their book *Sadat* (London: Faber & Faber, 1981), 88.

16. Sadat, *In Search of Identity*, 24.

17. Mohamed Hassanein Heikal, *Autumn of Fury: The Assassination of Sadat* (New York: Random House, 1983), 26.

18. Beattie, *Egypt during the Sadat Years*, 27.

19. Heikal, *Autumn of Fury*, 231–241.

20. Anwar el Sadat, *Address by the UAR President Designate, Anwar el Sadat, Before the National Assembly*, October 7, 1970, Anwar Sadat Archives , http://www.sadat.umd.edu/archives/speeches%5CAADV%20Speech%20to%20 NatlAssemb%2010.7.70pdf.pdf.

21. Ibid.

22. Galal Amin, *Egypt's Economic Predicament: A Study of the Interaction of External Pressure, Political Folly, and Social Tension in Egypt, 1960–1990* (New York: E.J. Brill, 1995), 7; World Bank, "Data: Egypt, Arab Rep," http://data.worldbank.org/country/egypt-arab-republic (accessed December 22, 2010); International

Labour Organization, *Labour Statistics Database*, http://laborsta.ilo.org/STP/ guest (accessed December 17, 2010).

23. Nahal is an acronym for *Noar Halutzi Lohem*, meaning "Fighting Pioneer Youth." A primary function of the Nahal brigade is the development of new settlements, in particular kibbutzim and moshavim, and defense of existing ones. Given this mission, it makes perfect sense that Nahal soldiers were among the first to establish settlements in Sinai.

24. Gershom Gorenberg, *The Accidental Empire: Israel and the Birth of Settlements, 1967–1977* (New York: Times Books, 2007), 179–181.

25. Ann Moseley Lesch, "Israeli Settlements in the Occupied Territories, 1967–1977," *Journal of Palestine Studies* 7 no. 1 (Autumn 1977): Appendix 2.

26. In his memoirs, General Mohamed Abdel Ghani El Gamasy reflects that General Fawzi "was a strict disciplinarian to the point of cruelty," though he admits this may have been a positive quality in the post-1967 environment, when military discipline had all but collapsed. See el Gamasy, *The October War*.

27. Beattie, *Egypt during the Sadat Years*, 48.

28. John Waterbury, *The Egypt of Nasser and Sadat*, 168.

29. Ibid., 168.

30. Yahya M. Sadowski, *Political Vegetables? Businessman and Bureaucrat in the Development of Egyptian Agriculture* (Washington, DC: Brookings Institution Press, 1991), 2.

31. Hamid Ansari, *Egypt: The Stalled Society* (Albany: State University of New York Press, 1986), 159; Waterbury, *The Egypt of Nasser and Sadat*, 130.

32. Beattie, *Egypt during the Sadat Years*, 74–75.

33. The following section is based on Kirk J. Beattie's detailed and extraordinary account of Sadat's consolidation of power in *Egypt during the Sadat Years*, especially pages 57–73. See also, Raymond A. Hinnesbuch, *Egyptian Politics under Sadat: The Post-Populist Development of an Authoritarian-Modernizing State* (Boulder, CO: Lynne Rienner Publishers, 1988), 40–43.

34. Anwar el Sadat, *Speech by President Mohamed Anwar Sadat before the National Assembly*, [in Arabic]. February 4, 1971, http://sadat.bibalex.org/sadatdata/ Sadat-Speech-Files/19710204.html. There is some confusion about what Sadat actually said in the speech. For example, Saad el Shazly, the chief of staff of the Egyptian armed forces during the run up and during the October 1973 war indicates that Sadat offered a six-month extension to the cease-fire. Kirk J. Beattie also reports the six-month time frame. Yet, both the original Arabic and various English translations of Sadat's speech clearly indicate that he only offered a thirty-day extension of the cease-fire. For the English versions of the speech, see a compendium of Sadat's speeches at the Anwar Sadat Archives, http://www.sadat.umd.edu/archives/index.htm. Also, for a relevant excerpt see Raphael Israeli, *The Public Diary of President Sadat: Part One, The Road to War, October 1970–October 1973* (Leiden: E.J. Brill, 1978), 30–32.

35. Hirst and Beeson, *Sadat*, 117–118.

36. In 2004, the chairman of Egypt's Shura Council—the upper house of parliament—appointed Kamel Abu al Magd to be deputy chairman of the newly established National Council for Human Rights. Although the council included a number of prominent human rights activists, it could not be taken seriously as a government watchdog. As a creation of the regime, it is more an effort on the part of Egypt's leadership to deflect criticism of Egypt's human right record by allowing government officials to declare without completely stretching credulity that Egypt has a National Council for Human Rights. The group issues reports on human rights violations that the government routinely ignores.

37. "Constitution of the Arab Republic of Egypt 1971, Articles 2 and 71," [in Arabic] in *al–Dasatir al Misiriya, 1805–1971* (Cairo: Al Ahram Foundation, 1977).

38. Beattie, *Egypt during the Sadat Years*, 106.

39. For a full discussion of the Muslim Brotherhood and the professional syndicates, see Carrie Rosefsy Wickham's extraordinary book, *Mobilizing Islam: Religion, Activism, and Political Change in Egypt* (New York: Columbia University Press, 2002).

40. Baker, *Sadat and After*, 261.

41. Beattie, *Egypt during the Sadat Years*, 107.

42. Barbara H.E. Zollner, *The Muslim Brotherhood: Hassan al-Hudaybi and Ideology* (New York: Routledge, 2009), 64–71.

43. Anwar el Sadat, *Statement to the Nation by President Anwar el Sadat*, September 16, 1971, Anwar Sadat Archives http://sadat.bibalex.org/sadatdata/Sadat-Speech-Files/S19.htm.

44. Israeli, *The Public Diary of President Sadat: Part One*, 109.

45. Anwar el Sadat, *Address to the Naval Officers*, June 22, 1971, Anwar Sadat Archives, http://www.sadat.umd.edu/archives/speeches/BACI%20Speech%20to%20Naval%20Officers%206.22.71.PDF.

46. Anwar el Sadat, *Address to the Nation*, January 13, 1972, Anwar Sadat Archives, http://www.sadat.umd.edu/archives/speeches/BACA%20Address%20to%20the%20Nation%201.13.72.PDF.

47. Ibid.

48. Sadat, *Address to Naval Officers*, June 22, 1971.

49. In February 1972, the Middle East Research and Information Project compiled the students' demands based on Western and Arab media sources. See "Egyptian Students Press Demands," *MERIP Reports* 7 (February 1972): 12.

50. Abdalla, *The Student Movement and National Politics in Egypt, 1923–1973*, 186.

51. Haggai Ehrlich, *Students and University in 20th Century Egyptian Politics* (London: Frank Cass, 1989), 211–212.

52. Ibid., 212.

53. Saad el Shazly, *The Crossing of the Suez* (San Francisco: American Mideast Research, 1980), 106.

54. Ibid., 190–192.

55. Israel's first request for assistance from the United States actually went out on October 6, but was rejected on the grounds that Washington did not want to antagonize the Arab states or the Soviet Union. The Israelis made a second request on the eighth. Two days later, the United States authorized EL AL cargo planes to carry supplies to Israel from Oceana Naval Air Station in Virginia Beach. It was not until two days later that Israeli Prime Minister Golda Meir made an urgent request for immediate assistance that the Nixon administration began the resupply effort in earnest. What came to be known at Operation Nickel Grass lasted until November 14 and included both air and seaborne resupply. It is important to note that the Soviets supplied the Egyptians with weaponry during the war, but it was nowhere near the American effort to assist the Israelis.

56. Sadat, *Address to Naval Officers*, June 22, 1971.

57. El Shazly, *The Crossing of the Suez*, 285, 287.

58. Sadat's daughter Ruqaya immediately responded to Heikal's claim with a libel suit filed in September 2010. See Jack Shenker, "Sadat's Daughter to Sue over Claims He Poisoned Nasser," *The Guardian*, September 20, 2010.

59. *The October Paper* (Cairo: State Information Service, April 1974), 40.

60. Ibid., 60.

61. For a complete discussion, see Galal A. Amin, *Egypt's Economic Predicament: A Study of the Interaction of External Pressure, Political Folly and Social Tension in Egypt, 1960–1990* (Leiden: E.J. Brill, 1995).

62. "Law No. 43 of 1974," in *A Compendium of Egyptian Law and Statutes*, vol. 5, ed. Abdul al Moneim Husni (Giza: Merkaz Husni l-il-Dirassat al Qaanuniyah, 1987), 229–261; Waterbury, *The Egypt of Nasser and Sadat*, 128–134.

63. Beattie, *Egypt during the Sadat Years*, 141.

64. P.J. Vatikiotis, *The History of Modern Egypt from Muhammad Ali to Mubarak*, 4th ed. (Baltimore: Johns Hopkins University Press, 1991), 384–385.

65. Excerpts of Sadat's speech are reproduced in Raphael Israeli, *The Public Diary of President Sadat, Part Three: The Road of Pragmatism, June 1975–October 1976* (Leiden: E.J. Brill, 1979), 1377–1381.

66. Maye Kassem, *Egyptian Politics: The Dynamics of Authoritarian Rule* (Boulder, CO: Lynne Rienner, 2004), 54.

67. Egyptian Ministry of Economic Development, "Major Economic Indicators 1967–1980."

68. Hinnesbusch, *Egyptian Politics under Sadat*, 70.

69. Diplomatic relations between Cairo and Washington were officially reinstated in February 1975.

70. Anwar el Sadat, "Speech by President Anwar el Sadat at the Inaugural Session of the People's Assembly, November 9, 1977," in *Speeches and Interviews by President Mohamed Anwar El Sadat on the Occasion of his Visit to Jerusalem* (Cairo: State Information Service, 1978), 5–54.

71. Ismail Fahmy, *Negotiating for Peace in the Middle East* (Baltimore: Johns Hopkins University Press, 1983), 266.

72. For a detailed discussion of the disengagement agreement, see Henry Kissinger, *Years of Upheaval* (Boston: Little, Brown, 1982), 799–853, 1250–51; Also William B. Quandt, *Peace Process: American Diplomacy and the Arab-Israeli Conflict since 1967* (Washington: Brookings Institution Press, 1993), 183–220.

73. Sachar, *A History of Israel*, 818–825; Quandt, *Peace Process*, 240, 259, 265.

74. Fahmy, *Negotiating for Peace in the Middle East*, 267–273.

75. Anwar el Sadat, "The Speech of President Anwar Sadat to the Knesset," November 20, 1977, in *Speeches and Interviews by President Mohamed Anwar el Sadat*, 145–171.

76. Ibid., 164–165.

77. Quandt, *Peace Process*, 280.

78. Ibid; William B. Quandt, *Camp David: Peacemaking and Politics* (Washington, DC: Brookings Institution Press, 1986): 219.

79. Ibid., 281.

80. "Letter from Israeli Prime Minister Menachem Begin and Egyptian President Anwar el-Sadat to President Jimmy Carter, March 26, 1979," reprinted in Quandt, *Peace Process*, 472–473.

81. Ibid.

82. Hinnesbusch, *Egyptian Politics under Sadat*, 74.

83. Beattie, *Egypt during the Sadat Years*, 260.

84. Baker, *Sadat and After*, 254–256.

85. Arab Republic of Egypt, "Constitution of the Arab Republic of Egypt (amended 1980), Article 194," (Cairo: State Information Service, 1980).

86. Beattie, *Egypt during the Sadat Years*, 263; Eberhard Kienle, *A Grand Delusion: Democracy and Economic Reform in Egypt* (London: I.B. Taurus, 2001), 20.

Five

1. Paragraph 1 of Article 84 states, "In case of the vacancy of the presidential office or the permanent disability of the President of the Republic, the President of the People's Assembly shall temporarily assume the Presidency and, if at that time, the People's Assembly is dissolved, the President of the Supreme Constitutional Court shall take over the Presidency, however, on condition that neither one shall nominate himself for the Presidency." Paragraph 2 outlines how long the office of the president may remain vacant: the People's Assembly shall then proclaim the vacancy of the office of the President. The President of the Republic shall be chosen within a maximum period of 60 days from the date of the vacancy of the presidential office.

2. Robert Springborg, "The President and the Field Marshal: Civil-Military Relations in Egypt Today," *Middle East Report* (July–August 1987): 5–16.

3. Despite the apparent progress in critical socioeconomic areas over the course of the Mubarak years, the World Bank's data should be handled with care if only because it has been derived from official Egyptian sources. Still, the improvement of a variety of critical economic and social indicators is not

only important to the drama being played out in Egypt not only over how Egyptians should interpret Hosni Mubarak's legacy, but also the way forward.

4. Eberhad Keinle, *A Grand Delusion: Democracy and Economic Reform in Egypt* (London: I.B. Tauris, 2001), 146; Bassem Kamar and Damyana Bakardzhieva, "Economic Trilemma and Exchange Rate Management in Egypt," (presented at the 10th Annual Conference of the Economic Research Forum of the Arab Countries, Iran, and Turkey; Marrakesh, Morocco, December 16–18, 2003).

5. Alison Elizabeth Chase, "The Politics of Lending and Reform: The International Monetary Fund and the Nation of Egypt," *Stanford Journal of International Law* 93 (2006): 221.

6. Chase, "The Politics of Lending and Reform," 213; and Kienle, *A Grand Delusion*, 148. An eligible country could borrow up to a maximum of 140 percent of its IMF quota under a three-year arrangement, although this limit could be increased under exceptional circumstances to a maximum of 185 percent of quota. Loans under the ESAF carried an annual interest rate of 0.5 percent, with repayments made semiannually, beginning five and half years and ending ten years after the disbursement.

7. According to Brotherhood spokesman Maamoun Hudaybi, Saddam "has become a symbol of resistance for having resisted a formidable coalition" and in doing so "has the people and their conscience." Yves Heller and Alexander Buccianti, "International Repercussions: The Impotence of Opposition in Egypt," [in French] *Le Monde*, February 19, 1991. The Muslim Brotherhood also expressed its opposition to Egypt's participation in the Gulf War through the newspaper *al-Sha'ab*, the organ of the Socialist Labor Party that the Brothers had for all intents and purposes taken over. See Abdel Hayy Mohamed, "Faculty and Student Unions, the Professional Associations Reject the Military Alliance," [in Arabic] *al- Sha'ab*, September 18, 1990; Magdi Ahmad Husayn, "We Reject an American Framework Giving it a Blank Check for [the United States] to Control Policy, Oil, and Security in the Gulf," [in Arabic] *al-Sha'ab*, September 18, 1990; Adbel Hayy Mohamed, "All Political Parties and Forces Express their Support for the Iraqi People," [in Arabic] *al-Sha'ab*, January 29, 1991.

8. "Muslim Brotherhood Rejects 'Sell Out' Talks," Foreign Broadcast Information Service Report FBIS-NES-91-209, October 29, 1991.

9. The opening of Israel's trade office in Qatar and Oman complemented the low-level diplomatic relations it established with Morocco, Tunisia, and Mauritania in the mid-1990s.

10. "MENA Terms," *al Ahram Weekly*, September 16–22, 1999.

11. See Montasser al-Zayyat, *The Road to Al-Qaeda: The Story of Bin Laden's Right-Hand Man*, ed. Sara Nimis, trans. Ahmed Fekry (Sterling, VA: Pluto Press, 2002).

12. It is important to note that the al Gama'a al Islamiyya renounced violence in 2002, admitting the error of their violent ways in favor of a qualified jihad in

which costs and benefits must be carefully considered and harming civilians is not permitted. Al Gama'a's leaders also contended that jihad cannot be an end in and of itself. They also emphasize a milder version of the concept of *hisba*, which relates to eliminating "deviant practices from Muslim societies," and *da'wa*, or proselytizing. Al Gama'a's recantation of violence indicates the tantalizing possibility of the eventual demise of al Qa'ida, but the external leadership at the time under Mohamed Hassan Khalil al Hakim, also known as Abu Jihad al Masri, rejected the cease-fire.

13. In 2006, Ayman Zawahiri announced the merger of al Gama'a and al Qa'ida—a move that the leadership of al Gama'a in Egypt rejected. When Sayyid Imam al Sharif (aka Dr. Fadl) a founder and leading al Gama'a theoretician sided with the internal leadership in the spring of 2007, Zawahiri issued a videotape the following July severely criticizing both Fadl and al Gama'a leadership in Egypt. See Ewan Stein, "What Does the Gama'a Islamiya Want Now?" *Middle Eat Report* 254 (Spring 2010): 41–42; Amr Hamzawy and Sarah Grebowski, "From Violence to Moderation: Al-Jama'a al-Islamiya and al-Jihad," *Carnegie Papers: Middle East Series* 20 (April 2010), http://www.carnegieendowment.org/files/Hamzawy-Grebowski-EN.pdf.

14. Hosni Mubarak, *Speech of President Mohamed Hosni Mubarak on the Occasion Celebrating the Workers Holiday* [in Arabic] State Information Service, May 6, 2010, http://www.sis.gov.eg/Ar/Story.aspx?sid=35152.

15. Egyptian Press and Information Office, e-mail message to the author, May 11, 2010; State Information Service, "Political Parties," http://www.sis.gov.eg/en/LastPage.aspx?Category_ID=259 (accessed May 11, 2010).

16. The following discussion is based on the firsthand account of a Western banker based in Egypt during the 1990s.

17. Remarks of Yousef Boutros Ghali, National Democratic Party Conference, September 20, 2006.

18. *BusinessWeek*, "Angling to Be the Next Bangalore," January 30, 2006. http://www.businessweek.com/magazine/content/06_05/b3969409.htm.

19. Ministry of Investment–Egypt, "Foreign Direct Investment," http://www.investment.gov.eg/en/investment/pages/foreigninvestment.aspx.

20. The Egyptian Exchange, "Historical Statistics," http://egyptse.com/english/marketindicator.aspx (accessed May 20, 2011).

21. John Waterbury, *Exposed to Innumerable Delusions: Public Enterprise and State Power in Egypt, India, Mexico, and Turkey* (New York: Cambridge University Press, 1993).

22. Sherine Bakir, "Public Promise: Uncertainty Surrounds Privatization Scheme," American Chamber of Commerce in Egypt, January 2009, http://www.amcham.org.eg/resources_publications/publications/business_monthly/issue.asp?sec=4&subsec=Uncertainty%20Surrounds%20Privatization%20Scheme%20&im=1&iy=2009.

23. Bruce K. Rutherford, *Egypt after Mubarak: Liberalism, Islam, and Democracy in the Arab World* (Princeton, NJ: Princeton University Press, 2008), 198.

24. World Bank, "Data: Egypt, Arab Rep.; Unemployment in Egypt," http://data. worldbank.org/country/egypt-arab-republic (accessed October 23, 2010).

25. On the black market, the pound was considerably weaker than the official core exchange rate of one dollar to 4.51 pounds. Once the managed peg system was abolished, the pound immediately depreciated some 17 percent, settling on the black market rate of 5.4 pounds to the dollar. Although Egypt's central bankers did initially intervene to ensure that the currency would not depreciate even more, that burden was considerably less than maintaining an overvalued currency. Ayman M. Ebrahim, "The Growth Effects of Financial Liberalisation Programme in Egypt: Developments and Drawbacks," *Scientific Journal of the Faculty of Commerce and Business, Helwan University* 2 (2006), http://faculty.ksu. edu.sa/ahendy/Published%20Papers/Forms/AllItems.aspx; Massoud Derhally, "Floating to Credibility," *Arabian Business.com*, March 6, 2003, http://www. arabianbusiness.com/floating-credibility-206710.html.

26. Interview with an Egyptian government official in Cairo, February, 16, 2006.

27. World Bank, "Data: Egypt, Arab Rep.," http://data.worldbank.org/country/ egypt-arab-republic (accessed December 22, 2010). Underemployment is a particular problem in Egypt where it comes in all of its definitional forms— high-skilled workers stuck in low skill, low wage positions; people can only find part-time work; and there are too many employees and not enough work to go around.

28. After the January–February 2011 uprising, newly installed Minister of Manpower and Immigration placed the unemployment figure at 19 percent, with the number of those under-employed greater still; Jonathan Wright and Edmund Blair, "Egyptians Grapple with Political Overhaul," Reuters, March 30, 2011, http://af.reuters.com/article/egyptNews/idAFLDE72S0TI2011033 0?feedType=RSS&feedName=egyptNews&utm_source=feedburner&utm_ medium=feed&utm_campaign=Feed%3A+reuters%2FAfricaEgyptNews+%28 News+%2F+Africa+%2F+Egypt+News%29&sp=true.

29. Interview with an Egyptian government official in Cairo, February 16, 2006.

30. Joel Beinin and Hossam el-Hamalawy, "Strikes in Egypt Spread from Center of Gravity," *Middle East Report Online*, May 9, 2007, http://www.merip.org/ mero/mero050907.html.

31. Joel Beinin and Hossam el-Hamalawy, "Egyptian Textile Workers Confront the New Economic Order," *Middle East Report Online*, March 25, 2007, http:// www.merip.org/mero/mero032507.html; Faiza Rady, "The Struggle is One," *Al-Ahram Weekly On-line*, November 8–14, 2007, http://weekly.ahram.org. eg/2007/870/eg5.htm.

32. Beinin and el-Hamalawy, 'Strikes in Egypt Spread from Center of Gravity," http://www.merip.org/mero/mero050907.html.

33. Amnesty International, *Buried Alive: Trapped by Poverty and Neglect in Cairo's Informal Settlements* (London: Amnesty International, 2009).

34. For a fascinating study of informal networks in poor areas of Cairo, see Diane Singerman, *Avenues of Participation: Family, Politics, and Networks in Urban Quarters of Cairo* (Princeton, NJ: Princeton University Press, 1995).

35. Ian Lee, "Homeless in Duweiqa," *Daily News Egypt* video, posted July 28, 2009, www.youtube.com/watch?v=i3HMumcqWNQ.

36. Brian Whitaker, "Crew Accused over Egypt Ferry Disaster," *Guardian*, February 6, 2006, http://www.guardian.co.uk/world/2006/feb/06/egypt.travelnews1; BBC News, "Payout over Egypt Ferry Disaster," June 7, 2006, http://news.bbc.co.uk/2/hi/middle_east/5054358.stm; Reuters, "Deadly Sinking: Egypt Ferry Owner Sentenced to Seven Years," *Welt Online*, March 11, 2009, http://www.welt.de/english-news/article3358219/Egypt-ferry-owner-sentenced-to-seven-years.html?print=true#reqdrucken.

37. It is important to note that Egyptian military officers are prohibited from having a party affiliation.

38. *Constitution of the Arab Republic of Egypt (as amended March 26, 2007)*, Article 76, State Information Service, http://constitution.sis.gov.eg/en/2.htm.

39. According to the government, only 22.95 percent of eligible voters actually voted.

40. The amendments to the Political Parties Law were contained in Law 177 of 2005; see "Law No. 177/2005: Regulating Political Parties System," State Information Service, July 6, 2005, http://www2.sis.gov.eg/En/Politics/PElection/election/Laws/040202040000000005.htm. The changes were based on the National Democratic Party, "Citizens Rights and Democracy," position paper, September 2004, 16–18. [in Arabic]

41. Gamal Essam El-Din, "A Controversial Law," *Al-Ahram Weekly On-line*, July 7–13, 2005, http://weekly.ahram.org.eg/2005/750/eg2.htm.

42. Tamir Moustafa, *The Struggle for Constitutional Power: Law, Politics, and Economic Development in Egypt* (Cambridge: Cambridge University Press, 2007).

43. Hosni Mubarak, interview by Charlie Rose, *Charlie Rose*, PBS, August 17, 2009.

44. *Constitution of the Arab Republic of Egypt (as amended March 26, 2007)*, Article 5, State Information Service, http://constitution.sis.gov.eg/en/2.htm.

45. In their article "Egypt's Controversial Constitutional Amendments," Carnegie Endowment for International Peace, March 23, 2007, http://www.carnegieendowment.org/files/egypt_constitution_webcommentary01.pdf, Nathan J. Brown, Michele Dunne, and Amr Hamzawy translate the operative phrase of the amendment as "within any religious frame of reference" whereas the official English document that the Egyptian government issued stated that political parties and activity "on the basis of religion" were prohibited.

46. See for example, Carrie Rosefsky Wickham, "The Muslim Brotherhood after Mubarak," *Foreign Affairs*, February 3, 2011; Bruce K. Rutherford, *Egypt After Mubarak: Liberalism, Islam, and Democracy in the Arab World* (Princeton, NJ: Princeton University Press, 2009); Kristen Stilt, "'Islam is the

Solution': Constitutional Visions of the Egyptian Muslim Brotherhood," *Texas International Law Journal* 63 no. 73 (Fall 2010): 74–108; Samer Shehata and Joshua Stacher, "The Brotherhood Goes to Parliament," *Middle East Report* 240 (Fall 2006), http://www.merip.org/mer/mer240/shehata_stacher.html.

47. Nathan J. Brown and Amr Hamzawy, "The Draft Party Platform of the Egyptian Muslim Brotherhood: Foray into Political Integration or Retreat into Old Positions?" *Carnegie Papers: Middle East Series* 89 (January 2008): 3–4, http://carnegieendowment.org/files/cp89_muslim_brothers_final.pdf.

48. Muslim Brotherhood, *Program of the Party of the Muslim Brotherhood—First Draft*, Section I, Chapter 2: "Objectives," [in Arabic] August 25, 2007.

49. Muslim Brotherhood, *Program of the Party of the Muslim Brotherhood—First Draft*, Section II, Chapter 1: "The State," [in Arabic] August 25, 2007.

50. Interview with a National Democratic Party official, October 19, 2010.

51. Ibid.

52. Prior to the 2005 elections, seventeen "Brotherhood independents" sat in the People's Assembly, up considerably from their single-seat victory in 1995. Although the Brotherhood boycotted the 1990 parliamentary elections, they sat in the People's Assembly throughout the 1980s. In the 1984 elections in coalition with the Wafd, the Brothers occupied eight seats and in the 1987 elections, when they participated in an alliance with the Socialist Labor and Liberal parties, the Muslim Brotherhood won thirty-eight seats.

53. There have been 454 seats in the People's Assembly of which 444 are open to election. The remaining ten are filled through presidential appointment. In 2009, the People's Assembly passed a provision adding an additional sixty-four seats to the body reserved exclusively for women. Those seats were contested for the first time in 2010.

54. From the Nasser period until the mid 1990s, local elections had been relatively free, but Law No. 26 of 1994 had transformed local elected officials into government-appointed functionaries. The 2006 elections were set to return the status quo ante in local affairs.

55. *Constitution of the Arab Republic of Egypt (as amended March 26, 2007)*, Article 88, State Information Service, http://constitution.sis.gov.eg/en/2.htm.

56. President Anwar Sadat had actually lifted the state of emergency beginning in 1980, but it was quickly reinstated after his assassination.

57. *Constitution of the Arab Republic of Egypt (as amended March 26, 2007)*, Article 179, State Information Service, http://constitution.sis.gov.eg/en/2.htm; Brown, Dunne and Hamzawy, "Egypt's Controversial Constitutional Amendments," http://www.carnegieendowment.org/files/egypt_constitution_webcommentary01.pdf.

58. Karim Haggag, "Part One: Rebalancing Powers and Rebuilding the Political Center," *Arab Reform Bulletin* 5, no. 3 (April 2007), http://www.carnegieendowment.org/publications/index.cfm?fa=view&id=19113#haggag.

59. Gamal Essam El-Din, "A Controversial Law," http://weekly.ahram.org.eg/2005/750/eg2.htm.

60. In the House of Representatives 357 members voted in favor of the Patriot Act against 66 nays. Of the 99 members of the Senate voting on the legislation, 98 voted for it. House of Representatives, "Final Vote Results for Roll Call 398," October 24, 2001, http://clerk.house.gov/evs/2001/roll398.xml; Senate, "U.S. Senate Roll Call Votes 107th Congress—1st Session," October 25, 2001, http://www.senate.gov/legislative/LIS/roll_call_lists/roll_call_vote_cfm.cfm?congress=107&session=1&vote=00313.

61. See Hassanein Tewfiq Ibrahim and Hadi Rageb Audah, *The Muslim Brotherhood and Politics in Egypt: A Study in the Electoral Alliances and Parliamentary Practices of the Muslim Brotherhood in the Framework of Limited Political Pluralism, 1984–1990* [in Arabic] (Cairo: Mahroussa Books, 1995), 310; *Al Sha'ab*, "Electoral Program of the Labor Party List," [in Arabic] March 17, 1987.

62. According to the Egyptian government, Egypt boasts 162,000 bloggers, about 30 percent of all bloggers in the Arab world. Egyptian Press and Information Office, "100 Facts about Egypt," http://www.modernegypt.info/one-hundred-facts-about-egypt/ (accessed January 7, 2011).

63. Interview with Egyptian government officials in Cairo, September 14, 2006.

64. *Reporters without Borders*, "List of the 13 Internet Enemies," November 7, 2006, http://en.rsf.org/list-of-the-13-internet-enemies-07-11-2006,19603.

65. *Committee to Protect Journalists*, "Four Editors Sentenced to Jail," September 13, 2007, http://cpj.org/2007/09/four-editors-sentenced-to-jail.php.

66. The article was eventually published on *al Dustour's* Web site; see Mohamed ElBaradei, "The Victory Itself Would be Bigger than the October War," [in Arabic] *al Dustour*, October 5, 2010, http://dostor.org/politics/egypt/10/october/5/31194.

67. Interview with a former U.S. government official in Washington, DC, November 22, 2010.

68. Interview with a former Egyptian official in Cairo, May 10, 2010.

69. Denis J. Sullivan and Kimberly Jones, *Global Security Watch: Egypt; A Reference Handbook* (Westport, CT: Praeger Security International, 2008).

70. Mary Anne Weaver, "Pharaohs-in-Waiting," *Atlantic Monthly*, (October 2003).

71. The organization has also been referred to invariably as the "National Coalition for Change" and the "National Front for Change."

72. For a contemporary account of this dynamic, see Shadi Hamid, "Can't We All Just Get Along?" *Foreign Policy*, June 2, 2010, http://www.foreignpolicy.com/articles/2010/06/02/cant_we_all_get_along?page=full.

73. Mohamed Hassanein Heikal, one of Egypt's most famous journalists and confidante of both Nasser and Sadat before he fell out with the latter, reveals that Makram Ebeid's "Black Book" was, in part, the work of a group of army officers called the Iron Guard whose members were angry at the Wafd's capitulation to the British in February 1942 and were intent on upholding the honor of the Egyptian monarchy.

Six

1. The section on EgyptAir 990 is based on transcripts from the NTSB investigation into the crash. See National Transportation Safety Board, *Group Chairman's Factual Report: Air Traffic Control Group, NTSB Identification: DCA00MA006,* January 13, 2000, http://www.ntsb.gov/events/ea990/docket/Ex_3A.pdf; National Transportation Safety Board, *Aircraft Accident Brief: NTSB/AAB-02/01 (PB2002–910401); EgyptAir Flight 990, Boeing 767-336ER, SU-GAP, 60 Miles South of Nantucket, Massachusetts, October 31, 1999,* March 13, 2002, http://www.ntsb.gov/publictn/2002/AAB0201.pdf; National Transportation Safety Board, *EgyptAir Flight 990, October 31, 1999: Reports and Other Investigative Material for the Docket,* March 21, 2002, http://www.ntsb.gov/events/ea990/docket/EAContents.htm. Also see William Langewiesche, "The Crash of EgyptAir 990," *The Atlantic Monthly* 228, no. 4 (November 2001).

2. Robert Vitalis, *When Capitalists Collide: Business Conflict and the End of Empire in Egypt* (Berkeley: University of California Press, 1995), 203; John B. Alterman, *Egypt and American Foreign Assistance, 1952–1956: Hopes Dashed* (New York: Palgrave-Macmillan, 2002), 50.

3. Alterman, *Egypt and American Foreign Assistance,* 54.

4. *Mutual Security Act of 1954,* Pub. L. No. 83-665, 68 *Statutes* 937 (1954). Originated as *Mutual Security Act of 1954,* H.R. 9678, 83rd Cong. (1954); William J. Burns, *Economic Aid and American Policy toward Egypt, 1955–1981* (Albany: State University of New York Press, 1985), 16–17.

5. Robert Stephens, *Nasser: A Political Biography* (New York: Simon & Schuster, 1971), 160–161.

6. Burns, *Economic Aid and American Policy toward Egypt, 1955–1981,* 115.

7. Department of Agriculture, "Public Law 480, Title I," Foreign Agricultural Service, http://www.fas.usda.gov/excredits/foodaid/pl480/pl480.asp (accessed December 27, 2010). Food Aid and Security, "Food for Peace," Food Aid Programs, http://foodaid.org/food-aid-programs/food-for-peace/ (accessed December 27, 2010).

8. Burns, *Economic Aid and American Policy toward Egypt, 1955–1981,* 121.

9. Ray Bush, "Crisis in Egypt: Structural Adjustments, Food Security, and the Politics of USAID," *Capital and Class* 53, no. 18 (Summer 1994): 24.

10. Burns, *Economic Aid and American Policy toward Egypt, 1955–1981,* 144–145.

11. Warren Bass, *Support Any Friend: Kennedy's Middle East and the Making of the U.S.-Israel Alliance* (New York: Oxford University Press, 2003), 146, 148–149, 169.

12. Marvin Weinbaum, "Politics and Development in Foreign Aid: U.S. Economic Assistance to Egypt, 1975–1982," *Middle East Journal* 37, no. 4 (Autumn 1983): 639.

13. Ray Bush, "Crisis in Egypt," 22.

14. Burns, *Economic Aid and American Policy toward Egypt, 1955–1981,* 192.

15. Ibid., 186; Staff of House Committee on Foreign Affairs, 96th Cong., 1979, *Report of a Staff Study Mission to Egypt, Syria, Jordan, the West Bank, and Gaza* Committee Print April 1979.

16. William Habeeb, "U.S.-Egyptian Aid Negotiations in the 1980s and 1990s," in *Power and Negotiation*, eds. I. William Zartman and Jeffrey Z. Rubin (Ann Arbor: University of Michigan Press, 2000), 92–93.

17. Ibid, 95.

18. Ibid.

19. Stephen McInerney, *The Federal Budget Appropriations for Fiscal Year 2011: Democracy, Governance, and Human Rights in the Middle East,* Project on Middle East Democracy, April 2010, http://pomed.org/wordpress/wp-content/uploads/2010/04/fy11-budget-analysis-final.pdf, 11.

20. Jacqueline Bell, *Audit of USAID/Egypt's Democracy and Governance Activities: Audit Report No.6-263-10-001-P* (Cairo: U.S. Agency for International Development, Office of Inspector General, October 27, 2009), http://www.usaid.gov/oig/public/fy10rpts/6-263-10-001-p.pdf.

21. "A Framework for Peace in the Middle East Agreed at Camp David (September 17, 1978)," reprinted in William B. Quandt, *Peace Process: American Diplomacy and the Arab-Israeli Conflict since 1967* (Washington, DC: Brookings Institution Press, 1993), 445–456; "Treaty of Peace Between the Arab Republic of Egypt and the State of Israel (March 26, 1979)," reprinted in Quandt, *Peace Process*, 466–475.

22. Benjamin Netanyahu, *Speech by Prime Minister Benjamin Netanyahu to a Joint Session of the United States Congress,* Israel Ministry of Foreign Affairs, July 10, 1996, http://www.mfa.gov.il/MFA/MFAArchive/1990_1999/1996/7/PM Netanyahu- Speech to US Congress- July 10- 1996.

23. International Monetary Fund, *World Economic Outlook Database,* April 2006, http://www.imf.org/external/pubs/ft/weo/2006/01/data/.

24. *Consolidated Appropriations Act of 2005,* H.R. 4818, 108th Cong., H. Amdt. 694 (2004).

25. Galal Duwaydar, "You are Not Welcome, Mr. Lantos," [in Arabic] *al Akhbar,* August 15, 2004.

26. Gamal Kamal, "The Biggest Issue Concerning a Large Portion of the Aid," [in Arabic] *al Gumhuriya,* July 22, 2004.

27. Khaled Dawoud, "Military Aid Crisis," *Al-Ahram Weekly On-line,* July 22–28, 2004, http://weekly.ahram.org.eg/2004/700/index.htm.

28. Cited in Aziza Sami, "At Every Corner," *Al Ahram Weekly On-line,* August 26–September 1, 2004, http://weekly.ahram.org.eg/2004/705/pr1.htm.

29. The 2:3 ratio was agreed upon by all parties after the Egypt-Israel peace treaty, but the United States made no formal commitment to uphold this formula for as long Washington supplied the assistance package.

30. Jeremy M. Sharp, *Egypt: Background and U.S. Relations,* Congressional Research Service, September 2, 2009, 35–36, http://www.fas.org/sgp/crs/mideast/RL33003.pdf.

31. In any discussion of the aid package with Egyptian military officers, they tend to refer to "our money" when it comes to American assistance.

32. Additional efforts to cut aid to Egypt came in the form of the Pitts amendment, sponsored by Congressman Joseph R. Pitts (R-PA). The legislation sought to strip Egypt of more than half its military assistance and to transfer those resources to the USAID Child Survival and Health Program Fund. Pitts was defeated soundly in June 2005 with 87 members of the House voting for the amendment and 326 opposed. Another illustrative, more serious example came in May 2005, when Representative Chris Smith (R-NJ) introduced H.R. 2601, the "Foreign Relations Authorization Act, Fiscal Years 2006 and 2007." Smith proposed cutting Egypt's military assistance by $40 million per year over 2006–2008 and redirecting those funds to the annual economic assistance package. The intended infusion of $120 million of economic support funds came with strings attached, however. Smith inserted into the legislation six requirements—promoting economic growth, reducing poverty, improving humanitarian conditions for the poor, upgrading the education and health systems, fighting corruption, and "strengthening democratic institutions and individual freedoms"—that Cairo would need to fulfill in order for the funds to be made available to Egypt. The congressman also directed the president to alter the "cash-flow financing" program to reflect the reduction of military assistance that Smith was proposing while making sure that the Egyptians could maintain existing weapons systems. Congress watchers pointed out at the time that this change would have crippled the Egyptian military's ability to purchase new (American-manufactured) equipment. Finally, Smith sought to transfer any interest that the military aid earned from a special account at the New York Federal Reserve Bank to the Middle East Partnership Initiative and designated specifically for democracy promotion programs. Although the House passed H.R. 2601 in July by a vote of 351 to 78, the legislation did not become law.

33. Congressional Record, 109th Congress, Foreign Operations, Export Financing, and Related Programs Appropriations Act, 2007 (House of Representative, June 8, 2006), http://thomas.loc.gov?cgi-bin/query/D?r109:1:./temp/~r1097IEW12:b105275.

34. H.R. 2764, 110th Cong. (as reported by House, June 17, 2007).

35. *Consolidated Appropriations Act of 2008*, Pub. L. No. 110-161, 121 *Statutes* 1839 (2007).

36. Sharp, *Egypt: Background and U.S. Relations*, 34.

37. "The U.S. Economic Assistance Program to Egypt: FY 2011 and Beyond," August 17, 2009, *Foreign Policy*, http://www.foreignpolicy.com/files/fp_uploaded_documents/100512_USEconomicAssistance.pdf.

38. Ibid., 5–6.

39. *Consolidated Appropriations Act of 2010*, Pub. L. No. 111-118, 123 *Statutes* 3409 (2010).

40. Ibid.

41. McInerney, *The Federal Budget Appropriations for Fiscal Year 2010*, 25.

42. Department of State, "Fact Sheet on Civil Society & Democracy Promotion in Egypt," Middle East Partnership Initiative, Fall 2010.

43. Fouad Ajami, *The Dream Palace of the Arabs: A Generation's Odyssey* (New York: Pantheon Books, 1998).

44. Central Bureau of Statistics (Israel), "Imports by Countries of Purchase and Exports by Country of Destination," in *Statistical Abstract of Israel* (Jerusalem: Central Bureau of Statistics, 2010), 698.

45. Gamal Abdel Nasser, *The Philosophy of the Revolution* (Cairo: Dar al Maaref, 1954), 61.

46. B'Tselem, "Land Expropriation and Settlements," http://www.btselem.org/english/settlements/statistics.asp (accessed December 6, 2010). According to B'Tselem there are about one hundred additional nonofficial settlements on the West Bank. In 2005, Israel withdrew from its twenty-one settlements in the Gaza Strip.

47. William B. Quandt, e-mail messages to the author, August 14, 2007 and November 19, 2010.

48. *Egyptian Counterterrorism and Political Reform Act*, H.R. Res 696, 111th Cong. (2009).

49. S. Res. 586, 111th Cong. (2010).

50. Saad el Shazly, *The Crossing of the Suez* (San Francisco: American Mideast Research, 1980); Mohamed Abdel Ghani El Gamasy, *The October War: Memoirs of Field Marshal El Gamasy of Egypt* (Cairo: American University in Cairo Press, 1993).

51. Mohamed Hamid Abu al-Nasr, "Open Letter to President Mubarak," [in Arabic] *al Sha'ab*, February 17, 1987.

52. *Al Sha'ab*, "Electoral Program of the Labor Party List," Section VII: National Security and Foreign Relations [in Arabic] March 17, 1987.

53. Mustafa Mashour, "This Conference . . . Between Whom? With Whom? To Whose Benefit?," [in Arabic] *al Sha'ab*, October 22, 1991.

54. *Al Sha'ab*, "Electoral Program of the Labor Party List," Section VII [in Arabic].

55. "Interview with Chairman of the MB Political Department," by Ikhwanweb, August 8, 2008, http://www.ikhwanweb.com/print.php?id=17489.

56. "Habib on MB Party Program, Dialogue with West: An Interview with Deputy Chairman Mohamed Al Sayed Habib," by Ikhwanweb, November 11, 2007, http://www.ikhwanweb.com/print.php?id=14658.

57. Muslim Brotherhood, "Section 4: Regional Leadership," in *Electoral Program of the Muslim Brotherhood—2010 People's Assembly Elections*, 34–36 [in Arabic].

58. United Nations Development Program, "Arab Political Parties Database: Egypt: The New Wafd Party," Program on Governance in the Arab Region, http://www.arabparliaments.org/countries/bycountry.asp?pid=62&cid=5 (accessed December 6, 2010).

59. For a full discussion of the Brotherhood's relationship to the professional syndicates, see Carrie Rosefsky Wickham, *Mobilizing Islam: Religion,*

Activism, and Political Change in Egypt (New York: Columbia University Press, 2002).

60. "Law No. 65/1975: Regarding the Union of Writers" in *Egypt Encyclopedia of Legislation and Law*, vol. 13, ed. Abdel Monem Hosni, [in Arabic] (Cairo: Hosni Center for Legal Studies, 1988), 466–490.

61. The English title is *A Drive to Israel: An Egyptian Meets his Neighbors*, Dayan Center Paper 128 (Tel Aviv: Tel Aviv University, 1994).

62. Agence France-Presse, "Egypt Editor Challenges Union over Israel 'Warning,'" *Asharq Alawsat*, February 3, 2010, http://www.aawsat.com/english/news.asp?section=5&id=19745.

63. Interview with a former U.S. government official in Washington, DC, November 22, 2010.

64. Ibid.

65. This tally does not include children's or self-published books.

66. In *The Search for Al Qaeda: Its Leadership, Ideology, and Future* (Washington, DC: Brookings Institution Press, 2008), Bruce Reidel identifies Zawahiri's background as "upper middle class." The Zawahiri family was, indeed, prominent. His father was a professor of pharmacology at Ain Shams University and his maternal grandfather had been president of Cairo University, a founder of Kind Sa'ud University in Saudi Arabia, and Egyptian ambassador to Pakistan, Yemen, and Saudi Arabia. As Lawrence Wright reports, however, young Ayman's parents raised him in an environment that was a rung or two below the family's social status.

67. Peter L. Bergen, *The Osama bin Laden I Know: An Oral History of al Qaeda's Leader* (New York: Free Press, 2006), 65.

68. For a full exposition of the initial encounter between Zawahiri and bin Laden see, Lawrence Wright, *The Looming Tower: al Qaeda and the Road to 9/11* (New York: Vintage Books, 2006), especially chapter 6.

69. See Fawaz Gerges, *The Far Enemy: Why Jihad Went Global* (New York: Cambridge University Press, 2009) and Wright, *The Looming Tower*.

70. Ibid., 220.

71. One exception to this dearth of explanation is Diego Gambetta and Steffen Hertog, "Engineers of Jihad," (Sociology Working Papers No. 2007–10, Department of Sociology, University of Oxford, Oxford, UK, 2007), http://www.nuff.ox.ac.uk/users/gambetta/engineers%20of%20jihad.pdf.

72. Bruce Hoffman, *Inside Terrorism*, rev. ed. (New York: Columbia University Press, 2006); Mia Bloom, *Dying to Kill: The Allure of Suicide Terrorism* (New York: Columbia University Press, 2005); Robert A. Pape, *Dying to Win: The Strategic Logic of Suicide Terrorism* (New York: Random House, 2005); Robert A. Pape, "The Strategic Logic of Suicide Terrorism," *American Political Science Review* 97, no. 3 (August 2003): 343–361; Marc Sageman, *Understanding Terror Networks* (Philadelphia: University of Pennsylvania Press, 2004): Alan B. Krueger and Jitka Maleckova, "Education, Poverty, and Terrorism: Is There

a Causal Connection?" *Journal of Economic Perspectives* 17, no. 4 (November 2003): 119–144; Martha Crenshaw, "The Logic of Terrorism: Terrorist Behavior as a Product of Strategic Choice," in *Origins of Terrorism: Psychologies, Ideologies, Theologies, States of Mind*, ed. Walter Reich (Washington, DC: Woodrow Wilson Center Press, 1998), 7–24.

73. Gilles Kepel, *Muslim Extremism in Egypt: The Prophet and the Pharaoh*, trans. Jon Rothschild (Berkeley: University of California Press, 1993), 74–76.

74. Ibid.

75. Jeane J. Kirkpatrick, "Dictatorships and Double Standards," *Commentary* (November 1979): 34–45.

76. Ronald Reagan, *Remarks on East-West Relations at the Brandenburg Gate in West Berlin*, June 12, 1987, http://www.reagan.utexas.edu/archives/speeches/1987/061287d.htm.

77. See Richard N. Haass, *War of Necessity, War of Choice: A Memoir of Two Iraq Wars* (New York: Simon & Schuster, 2009), 132–133.

78. George H. W. Bush, *Address Before a Joint Session of the Congress on the Persian Gulf Crisis and the Federal Budget Deficit*, George Bush Presidential Library and Museum, September 11, 1990, http://bushlibrary.tamu.edu/research/public_papers.php?id=2217&year=1990&month=9; President Bush also used "new world order" in an address to a joint session of Congress on March 6, 1991: George H.W. Bush, *Address Before a Joint Session of the Congress on the Cessation of the Persian Gulf Conflict*, George Bush Presidential Library and Museum, March 6, 1991, http://bushlibrary.tamu.edu/research/public_papers.php?id=2767&year=1991&month=3.

79. Anthony Lake, *Remarks of Anthony Lake: 'From Containment to Enlargement' at Johns Hopkins School of Advanced International Studies, Washington, DC*, September 21, 1993, http://www.mtholyoke.edu/acad/intrel/lakedoc.html.

80. Interview with a former U.S. government official, Washington, DC, September 5, 2007.

81. Larry C. Johnson, "The Declining Terrorist Threat," *New York Times*, July 10, 2001; *New York Times*, "The War against America; An Unfathomable Attack," September 12, 2001; *New York Times*, "War without Illusions," September 15, 2001; Joseph S. Nye, "How to Protect the Homeland," *New York Times*, September 25, 2001; *New York Times*, "The Specter of Biological Terror," September 26, 2001; Stephen E. Flynn, "Safer Borders," *New York Times*, October 1, 2001.

82. See Adam Przeworski, *Democracy and the Market: Political and Economic Reforms in Eastern Europe and Latin America* (New York: Cambridge University Press, 1999).

83. Edward D. Mansfield and Jack Snyder, *Electing to Fight: Why Emerging Democracies Go to War* (Cambridge, MA: MIT Press, 2005).

84. Madeleine K. Albright and Vin Weber, "In Support of Arab Democracy: Why and How," with Steven A. Cook, *Independent Task Force Report* 54 (New York: Council on Foreign Relations, 2005): 13.

85. In May 2006, a federal jury in Alexandria, Virginia convicted Zacarias Moussaoui for being a co-conspirator in the September 11 attacks on New York and Washington. Although he was arrested three weeks before the attacks on an immigration violation, his enrollment in a Minnesota flight school at the time of his arrest suggested to many that he was the twentieth hijacker.

86. Reza Aslan, *How to Win a Cosmic War: God, Globalization, and the End of the War on Terror* (New York: Random House, 2009). It is important to note that as Aslan's title implies, he believes that there is an effective way to fight a "cosmic war."

87. For some preliminary findings, see Dalia Dassa Kaye, et al., *More Freedom, Less Terror?: Liberalization and Political Violence in the Arab World* (Santa Monica, CA: RAND, 2008).

88. James Fowler, "The United States and South Korean Democratization," *Political Science Quarterly* 114, no. 2 (Summer 1999): 265–288; David Ariel Adesnik and Michael McFaul, "Engaging Autocratic Allies to Promote Democracy," *Washington Quarterly* 29, no. 2 (Spring 2006): 7–26; Robert A. Scalapino, "Democratizing Dragons: South Korea and Taiwan," *Journal of Democracy* 4, no. 3 (July 1993): 70–83; James Cotton, "From Authoritarianism to Democracy in South Korea," *Political Studies* 37, no. 2 (June 1989): 244–259.

89. There is an enormous literature on aid conditionality and economic reform. A number of analysts have begun to explore whether conditionality can be used to elicit political change. See Steven A. Cook, "The Right Way to Promote Arab Reform," *Foreign Affairs* 84, no. 2 (March/April 2005): 91–102; Shadi Hamid, "The Cairo Conundrum," *Democracy* 15 (Winter 2010): 34–45.

90. Robert O. Freedman, *Soviet Policy toward the Middle East since 1970*, 3rd ed. (New York: Praeger, 1982), 11.

91. Abdullah Akayleh, et al., "Democracy, Peace, and the War on Terror: U.S.-Arab Relations, Post-September 11" (2002 Soref Symposium, The Washington Institute for Near East Policy, Washington, DC, April 8–9, 2002), http://www.washingtoninstitute.org/templateC07.php?CID=102.

92. Department of State, "Middle East Partnership Initiative: History," Department of State Archive: 2002–2009, http://2002-2009-mepi.state.gov/c10130.htm (accessed December 15, 2010).

93. Tamara Cofman Wittes, *Freedom's Unsteady March: America's Role in Building Arab Democracy* (Washington, DC: Brookings Institution Press, 2008), 89.

94. "Law No. 84/2002," in *Official Gazette* no. 22 [in Arabic] (Cairo: State Information Service, June 5, 2002), especially articles 17, 21, 42, and 76; Law 84 was a descendant of Law 32 of 1964, which gave the Ministry of Social Affairs the power to oversee and regulate the activity of civil society groups. In 1999, the government replaced Law 32 with a new regulation on the activities of the NGO sector, Law 153, which was more restrictive than its predecessor. Under the new law, foreign NGOs were required to register with the Ministry of Social Affairs and the practice of registering some civil society

groups as "civil companies" as a way of getting around the Ministry's restrictions was prohibited.

95. Consolidated Appropriations Act of 2005, Pub.L. No. 108-447, 118 Stat. 2809 (2004).

96. Gamal Essam El-Din, "Opposition Snipes at Government," *Al-Ahram Weekly On-line*, March 31–April 6, 2005, http://weekly.ahram.org.eg/2005/736/eg1.htm.

97. Interview with a U.S. government official in Washington, DC, December 3, 2010.

98. George W. Bush, *Remarks by President George W. Bush at the 20th Anniversary of the National Endowment for Democracy*, November 6, 2003, http://www.ned.org/george-w-bush/remarks-by-president-george-w-bush-at-the-20th-anniversary.

99. Ibrahim Nafie, "Double Trouble," *Al-Ahram Weekly On-line*, November 13–16, 2003, http://weekly.ahram.org.eg/2003/664/op1.htm.

100. Foreign Broadcast Service, "Cairo Editor Reacts to Bush's Speech, Explains Why Muslims Hate US," Foreign Broadcast Information Service Report FBIS-NES-2003-1115, November 14, 2003.

101. *Akhbar al-Youm*, "Egyptian Columnist Comments on 'Admissions' by President Bush, US Ambassador," trans. Foreign Broadcast Information Service, *Akhbar al-Youm*, November 15, 2003.

102. In this, the Egyptians are not alone. See for example F. Gregory Gause, "Can Democracy Stop Terrorism?" *Foreign Affairs* 84, no. 5 (September/October 2005): 62–76; Robert Jervis, "Why the Bush Doctrine Cannot be Sustained," *Political Science Quarterly* 120, no. 3 (2005): 351–377; James A. Piazza, "Do Democracy and Free Markets Protect us From Terrorism?" *International Politics* 45, no. 1 (January 2008): 72–91.

103. Public Broadcasting Service, "Newsmaker: El Sayed; A NewsHour with Jim Lehrer Transcript," November 28, 2001, http://www.pbs.org/newshour/bb/middle_east/july-dec01/al_sayed_11-28.html.

104. For a collection of al Qa'ida statements and messages from Osama bin Laden and Ayman Zawahiri see Raymond Ibrahim, ed. and trans., *The Al Qaeda Reader* (New York: Broadway Books, 2007); Bruce Lawrence, ed., *Messages to the World: The Statements of Osama bin Laden* (London: Verso, 2005).

105. Maher Chmaytelli, "Bush Speech on Democracy Missed the Point: Arab Commentators," Agence France-Presse, November 7, 2003.

106. Ibid.

107. *Washington Post*, "An Interview with Secretary of State Condoleezza Rice," by *Washington Post* editors and reporters, March 25, 2005, http://www.washingtonpost.com/wp-dyn/articles/A2015-2005Mar25.html.

108. Condoleezza Rice, *Remarks at the American University in Cairo*, June 20, 2005, Department of State Archive: 2002–2009, http://2001-2009.state.gov/secretary/rm/2005/48328.htm.

109. BBC News, "Egypt: Muslim Brotherhood Discusses Exclusion from National Dialogue," *BBC Summary of World Broadcasts*, December 19, 2003.

110. Condoleezza Rice and Ahmed Aboul Gheit, *Remarks with Egyptian Foreign Minister Ahmed Aboul Gheit After their Meeting in Cairo*, October 6, 2003, http://web.archive.org/web/20061101021542/http:/www.state.gov/secretary/rm/2006/73525.htm.

111. Interview with a Bush administration official, December 2, 2010.

112. Interview with a Bush administration official, November 22, 2010.

113. Ian S. Lustick, "Hegemony and the Riddle of Nationalism," in *Ethnic Conflict and international Politics in the Middle East* ed. Leonard Binder (Gainesville: University of Florida Press, 1999), 332–359.

114. *Economist*, "Great Sacrifices, Small Rewards: Has America's Obsession with this Region Been Worth It?" December 29, 2010.

Seven

1. "Egypt Daily Update," e-mail from Project on Middle East Democracy, November 9, 2010; Eric Trager, "A Tale of Two Parties," *Foreign Policy*, November 18, 2010, http://www.foreignpolicy.com/articles/2010/11/18/a_tale_of_two_parties.

2. Interview with a National Democratic Party official in Cairo, October 19, 2010.

3. George Sadek, "Egypt: Supreme Administrative Court Rules Parliamentary Elections Void," Library of Congress, December 21, 2010, http://www.loc.gov/lawweb/servlet/lloc_news?disp3_l205402430_text.

4. Nevine Khalil, "Human Rights Message on Police Day," *al Ahram*, January 29–February 4, 2004.

5. *Speech by President Mohammed Hosni Mubarak to the Egyptian People*, January 29, 2011, State Information Service, http://www.sis.gov.eg/En/Story.aspx?sid=53519.

6. Hosni Mubarak, *Statement of the President of the Republic, Mohammed Hosni Mubarak*, February 1, 2011, http://www.sis.gov.eg/EN/Story.aspx?sid=53530.

7. Statement by Military Spokesman Ismail Etman, al Jazeera English News, February 2, 2011, http://english.aljazeera.net/news/middleeast/2011/02/201122105166916914.html.

8. Throughout the seventeen-day uprising 384 people were killed and approximately 6,500 were injured, See *Ahram Online*, "Death Toll from Protests Stands at 384; Egyptian Health Ministry," February 22, 2011, http://english.ahram.org.

9. Dr. Ahmed Awed Belal, "Statement from the Faculty of Law at Cairo University," [in Arabic] February 7, 2011.

10. For video footage of Bradawi's interview with BBC Channel 4, see http://bcove.me/yjgxyw7i.

11. William Branigin and Greg Miler, "CIA Director Cites 'Likelihood' that Mubarak May Step Down," February 10, 2011, http://www.washingtonpost.com/wp-dyn/content/article/2011/02/10/AR2011021003172.html.

12. Hosni Mubarak, *Speech by H.E. President Mohammed Hosni Mubarak*, February 10, 2011, http://www.sis.gov.eg/EN/Story.aspx?sid=53668.

13. "Constitution of the Arab Republic of Egypt (as amended March 26, 2007)," State Information Service, http://constitution.sis.gov.eg/en?2.htm.

14. Omar Suleiman, *Statement of the Vice President of the Republic*, Egypt State Information Service, February 11, 2011, http://www.sis.gov.eg/En/Story.aspx?sid=53676.

15. Timur Kuran, "Now Out of Never: The Element of Surprise in the East European Revolution of 1989," *World Politics* 44, no. 1 (October 1991): 7–48. Also see, Charles Kurzman, *The Unthinkable Revolution in Iran* (Cambridge: Harvard University Press, 2004).

16. The articles of the constitution the military identified for revision were 76, 77, 88, 93, and 189. Article 179 was to be removed altogether.

17. "10 Points," posted March 28, 2011, http://www.sandmonkey.org/2011/03/28/10-points/.

Bibliography

Abbas, Wael. "Help Our Fight for Real Democracy." *Washington Post*. May 27, 2007.

Abdalla, Ahmed. *The Student Movement and National Politics in Egypt, 1923–1973*. Cairo: American University in Cairo Press, 2008.

Abdel-Baky, Mohamed. "Judging Obama." *Al-Ahram Weekly On-line*. February 4–10, 2010. http://weekly.ahram.org.eg/2010/984/sc2.htm.

Abdel-Khalek, Gouda, and Robert Tignor, eds. *The Political Economy of Income Distribution in Egypt*. New York: Holmes & Meir Publishers, 1982.

Abdel-Latif, Omayma. "Trends in Salafism." In *Islamic Radicalization: The Challenge for Euro-Mediterranean Relations*, edited by Michael Emerson, Kristina Kausch, and Richard Youngs, 69–86. Brussels: Centre for European Policy Studies, 2009.

Abdel-Malek, Anouar. *Egypt: Military Society; The Army Regime, the Left, and Social Change under Nasser*. New York: Vintage Books, 1968.

Abdel Salam, Mohamed. "Egypt: Liberal Conference Raises Controversy." *Bikya Masr*. November 3, 2009. http://bikyamasr.com/wordpress/?p=5435.

Abdo, Geneive. *No God But God: Egypt and the Triumph of Islam*. New York: Oxford University Press, 2000.

Abdoun, Safaa. "Lawyers Blame Ferry Verdict on Referral to Misdemeanors Court." *Daily Star Egypt*. August 3, 2008. http://www.dailystaregypt.com/article.aspx?ArticleID=15492.

Adesnik, David Ariel, and Michael McFaul. "Engaging Autocratic Allies to Promote Democracy." *Washington Quarterly* 29, no. 2 (Spring 2006): 7–26.

Abbas, Kelidar. "Shaykh Ali Yusuf: Political Journalist and Islamic Nationalist." PhD diss., University of London, 1967.

Abid, Mounir, Khaled Kamel, and Nadia Shabour. "Security Service 'Urge' MB Parliamentary Candidates to Bow Out." *Al-Masry Al-Youm*. November 10,

2010. http://www.almasryalyoum.com/en/news/security-services-urge-mb-parliamentary-candidates-bow-out-elections.

Abu Almagd, Ahmed Kamal, Said Elwani Alnaggar, Abdelmeneim Saeed Ali, Mohamed Ibrahim Shaker, Munir Fahkri Abdelnour, Ali Mohamed Ali Salem, Mohamed Mahmoud Algohari, Ahmed Mahmoud Abdelhaim, and Hossam Hassan Badrawi. *The Prosecution of Dr. Saad Eddin Ibrahim and His 27 Associates before the Egyptian State Security Court (2000–2003)*. Center for Development Studies, November 2, 2009. http://www.eicds.org/english/publications/reports/Prosecution_and_Trial.pdf. (Accessed December 10, 2010.)

Abu al-Nasr, Mohamed Hamid. "Open Letter to President Mubarak." *al Sha'ab*. February 17, 1987. [In Arabic]

Abu Tomeh, Khaled. "Egypt Editor Slammed for Meeting Israeli Ambassador." *Jerusalem Post*. September 18, 2009. http://www.jpost.com/home/article. aspx?id=155382.

Abu-Zeid, M.A. "Egypt's High Aswan Dam." *International Journal of Water Resources Development* 13, no. 2 (June 1997): 209–217.Agence France-Press. "Al-Qaeda Propaganda Chief Killed in Pakistan Strike: Officials." November 1, 2008. http://afp.google.com/article/ALeqM5hFRjo5wy4-L2HckvAXmlqSQKJ-yQ.

———. "Egypt Editor Challenges Union over Israel 'Warning.'" *Asharq Alawsat*. February 3, 2010. http://www.aawsat.com/english/news. asp?section=5&id=19745.

———. "Egypt Fire Damages Church of 'Jesus Footprint.'" June 17, 2008.

———. "Egypt Islamists Say over 600 Arrested in Election Campaign." November 16,2010. http://www.google.com/hostednews/afp/article/ALeqM5hWT8GsnlIjPMpJBxOJxNM_J7IzPg?docId=CNG. b493bfe628055a8f9dfe53f4004c8ab3.51.

———. Zayan, Jailan. "Egypt Launches Probe into Senate Blaze." August 20, 2008.

———. Aiba, Ines Bel. "Egyptian Villages Fight Water War." August 16, 2007.

———. "Timeline of the July War 2006." *Daily Star Lebanon*. http://www.dailystar. com.lb/July_War06.asp#axzz16horbG50. (Accessed December 1, 2010.)

Ahmad, Makram Muhammad. "Students of al Mansoura." *Al-Ahram*. November 26, 1968. [In Arabic]

Ahmed, Jamal Mohammed. *The Intellectual Origins of Egyptian Nationalism*. London: Oxford University Press, 1960.

Ahram Online. "Death Toll From Protests Stands at 384; Egyptian Health Ministry." February 22, 2011. http://english.ahram.org.

Ajami, Fouad. *The Arab Predicament: Arab Political Thought and Practice since 1967*. New York: Cambridge University Press, 1992.

———. *The Dream Palace of the Arabs: A Generation's Odyssey*. New York: Pantheon Books, 1998.

———. "A Master of the Realm." *U.S. News & World Report*. June 26, 2000.

Akayleh, Abdullah, Shafeeq Ghabra, Lisa Anderson, Amy Hawthorne, Chas W. Freeman, and Hassan Nafaa. "Democracy, Peace, and the War on

Terror: U.S.-Arab Relations, Post-September 11." 2002 Soref Symposium, The Washington Institute for Near East Policy, Washington, DC, April 8–9, 2002. http://www.washingtoninstitute.org/templateC07.php?CID=102.

Akhbar, Youm al. "Egyptian Columnist Comments on 'Admissions' by President Bush, US Ambassador." November 15, 2003. Translated by Foreign Broadcast Information Service.

Al-Ahram Weekly On-line. "All the Revolution's Men." July 18–24, 2002. http://weekly.ahram.org.eg/2002/595/sc7.htm.

———. "Dambuster on the Bar Lev Line." October 9–15, 2008. http://weekly.ahram.org.eg/2008/917/fo6.htm.

———. "Newsreel: Marking 9 March." March 15–21, 2007. http://weekly.ahram.org.eg/2007/836/eg1.htm.

Al Jazeera. "Court Aquits Egyptian Ferry Owner." July 28, 2008. http://english.aljazeera.net/news/middleeast/2008/07/200872794038702694.html.

Al Jazeera Magazine. "Hosni Mubarak." May 24, 2007. http://aljazeera.com/news/articles/40/Hosni-Mubarak.html.

Al-Masry Al-Youm. "Does ElBaradei Have a Plan B?" May 2, 2010. http://www.almasryalyoum.com/en/opinion/does-elbaradei-have-plan-b.

———. "Elections Commission Announces 5720 Parliamentary Candidates." November 8, 2010. http://www.almasryalyoum.com/en/news/electoral-commission-announces-5720-election-candidates.

———. "MB Unveils Electoral Platform under the Banner 'Islam is the Solution.'" November 4, 2010. http://www.almasryalyoum.com/en/news/under-banner-islam-solution-mb-unveils-electoral-program.

———. "NAC 'Weak,' Say Wafd Party Officials." July 8, 2010. http://www.almasryalyoum.com/en/news/nac-weak-say-wafd-party-officials.

———. "Parliament Electoral Campaigning Kicks Off Amid Violence." November 16, 2010. http://www.almasryalyoum.com/en/news/parliamentary-electoral-campaigning-kicks-amid-violence.

———. "Parliamentary Elections Set for November 28." October 20, 2010. http://www.almasryalyoum.com/en/news/opposition-demands-unheeded-elections-set-28-november.

———. "Second Autopsy Ordered for Alexandria Police Victim." June 16, 2010. http://www.almasryalyoum.com/en/news/second-autopsy-ordered-alexandria-police-victim.

Al Sha'ab. "Electoral Program of the Labor Party List." March 17, 1987. [In Arabic]

Albright, Madeline K., and Vin Weber. "In Support of Arab Democracy: Why and How." With Steven A. Cook. *Independent Task Force Report* 54. New York: Council on Foreign Relations, 2005.

Ali, Wael, and Mahmoud Gaweesh. "Mixed Reaction in Egypt to Human Rights Bill in US." *Al-Masry Al-Youm*. July 30, 2010. http://www.almasryalyoum.com/en/news/mixed-reaction-egypt-human-rights-bill-us-senate.

All Headline News. "Normalization with Israel? Not Here." April 1, 2010. http://www.allheadlinenews.com.

Alterman, Jon B. *Egypt and American Foreign Assistance, 1952–1956: Hopes Dashed*. New York: Palgrave Macmillan, 2002.

Amer, Pakinam. "Chronology: Egypt's Sectarian Violence." *Al-Masry Al-Youm*. January 12, 2010. http://www.almasryalyoum.com/en/news/chronology-egypts-sectarian-violence.

———. "Legislative Roundup." September 15, 2004. http://peacenow.org/entries/archive477.

Americans for Peace Now. "Legislative Roundup." June 10, 2005. http://peacenow.org/entries/archive909.

Amin, Galal A. *Egypt's Economic Predicament: A Study in the Interaction of External Pressure, Political Folly and Social Tension in Egypt, 1960–1990*. Leiden: E.J. Brill, 1995.

Amin, Mohammed Nuri al. "The 1924 Sudanese Uprising, and the Impacy of Egypt on the Sudan." *International Journal of African Historical Studies* 19, no. 2 (1986): 235–260.

Amnesty International. *Buried Alive: Trapped by Poverty and Neglect in Cairo's Informal Settlements*. London: Amnesty International, 2009.

Amrani, Issandr el. "Controlled Reform in Egypt: Neither Reformist nor Controlled." *Middle* Aref el, Nevine. "Eyeing the Goal Posts." *Al-Ahram Weekly On-line*. September 3–9, 2009. http://weekly.ahram.org.eg/2009/963/eg4.htm.

Anani, Khalil al. "The Mismanagement of the Bread Crisis." *Daily News Egypt*. March 18, 2008. http://www.dailystaregypt.com/article.aspx?ArticleID=12547.

Anderson, Raymond. "Giant Among Communists Governed Like a Monarch." *New York Times*. May 5, 1980.

———. "Hussein, Arafat, Sign Arab Pact to End Clashes." *New York Times*. September 28, 1970.

Ansari, Hamid. *Egypt: The Stalled Society*. Albany: State University of New York Press, 1986.

Anti-Defamation League. "Ayman al-Zawahiri." http://www.adl.org/NR/exeres/EE96E327-DB3E-4344-92F2-A4BDB495C761,DB7611A2-02CD-43AF-8147-649E26813571,frameless.htm. (Accessed December 7, 2010.)

Aref, Nevine el. "Eyeing the Goal Posts." *Al-Ahram Weekly On-line*. September 3–9, 2009. http://weekly.ahram.org.eg/2009/963/eg4.htm.

A'sar, Marwa al, and Heba Fahmy. "NDP's Decision to Let Its Members Vie for the Same Seats is Sign of Weakness, Say Analyst, Opposition." *Daily News Egypt*. November 8, 2010. http://thedailynewsegypt.com/egypt/ndps-decision-to-let-its-members-vie-for-the-same-seats-is-sign-of-weakness-say-analyst-opposition.html.

Ashour, Sherif, Mohamed Megahed, and Omar el-Hadi. "SMS Messaging Restricted in Bid to Preempt Pre-election Activism." *Al-Masry Al-Youm*. October 11, 2010. http://www.almasryalyoum.com.

Aslan, Reza. *How to Win a Cosmic War: God, Globalization, and the End of the War on Terror*. New York: Random House, 2009.

Associated Press. "Fire Hits Historic Building in Downtown Cairo." March 14, 2009. http://gulfnews.com/news/region/egypt/fire-hits-historic-building-in-downtown-cairo-1.57712.

Attalah, Lina. "6 April Protests Stifled by Police." *Al-Masry Al-Youm.* April 6, 2010. http://www.almasryalyoum.com.

———. "Alexandria Policemen Beat Young Man to Death, Says Rights Group." *Al-Masry Al-Youm.* June 11, 2010. http://www.almasryalyoum.com.

———. "Controversial Funds?" *Cairo Magazine.* March 24, 2005.

Audah, Gehad. "The State of Political Control: The Case of Nasser, 1960–1967." *The Arab Journal of the Social Sciences* 2, no. 1 (April 1987): 95–111.

Awad, Marwa. "Egypt President's Son Wants Justice in Activist Death." Reuters. July 6, 2010.

Ayubi, Nazih N.M. *Bureacracy & Politics in Contemproary Egypt.* London: Ithaca Press, 1980.

Azuri, L. "Rising Tensions between Muslims, Christians in Egypt." *Inquiry & Analysis Report* 646 (November 15, 2010). http://www.memri.org/report/en/0/0/0/0/0/0/4765.htm.

Badry, Yousry el. "Preparation for Voter List Registration Complete." *Al-Masry Al-Youm.* October 22, 2010. http://www.almasryalyoum.com/en/news/preparation-voter-registration-lists-complete-0.

Baker, Raymond William. *Egypt's Uncertain Revolution under Nasser and Sadat.* Cambridge, MA: Harvard University Press, 1978.

———. *Sadat and After: Struggles for Egypt's Political Soul.* Cambridge, MA: Harvard University Press, 1990.

Bakir, Sherine. "Public Promise: Uncertainty Surrounds Privatization Scheme." American Chamber of Commerce in Egypt. January 2009. http://www.amcham.org.eg/resources_publications/publications/business_monthly/issue.asp?sec=4&subsec=Uncertainty%20Surrounds%20Privatization%20Scheme%20&im=1&iy=2009.

Baldick, Julian. *Mystical Islam: An Introduction to Sufism.* New York: New York University Press, 1989.

Banna, Hassan al. *Mudhakkirat al-da'wah wa-al-da'iyah.* Beirut: The Islamic Office, 1979. [In Arabic]

Barak, Eitan. "Between Reality and Secrecy: Israel's Freedom of Navigation Through the Straits of Tiran, 1956–1967." *Middle East Journal* 61, no. 4 (Autumn 2007): 657–679.

Barry, Dan, and Matthew L. Wald. "Storm Complicates Search." *New York Times.* November 3, 1999.

Bass, Warren. *Support Any Friend: Kennedy's Middle East and the Making of the U.S.-Israel Alliance.* New York: Oxford University Press, 2003.

BBC News. "Amnesty Calls for Inquiry into Egypt 'Police Torture.'" November 16, 2010. http://www.bbc.co.uk/news/world-middle-east-11764969.

———. "Egypt: Muslim Brotherhood Discusses Exclusion from National Dialogue." *BBC Summary of World Broadcasts.* December 19, 2003.

———. "Egyptian Theatre Fire Convictions." May 23, 3006. http://news.bbc. co.uk/2/hi/middle_east/5007602.stm.

———. "Hundreds Defy Egypt Protest Ban." March 30, 2005. http://news.bbc. co.uk/2/hi/middle_east/4394915.stm.

———. "Israel Approves Gaza Pullout Plan." June 7, 2004. http://news.bbc.co.uk/2/ hi/middle_east/3780457.stm.

———. "Palestinians Shun Israeli Settlement Restriction Plan." November 25, 2009. http://news.bbc.co.uk/2/hi/8379868.stm.

———. "Payout over Egypt Ferry Disaster." June 7, 2006. http://news.bbc.co.uk/2/ hi/middle_east/5054358.stm.

———. "Possible Causes of Ferry Disaster." February 3, 2006. http://news.bbc. co.uk/2/hi/middle_east/4678352.stm.

———. "Q&A: Gaza Conflict." January 18, 2009. http://news.bbc.co.uk/2/hi/ middle_east/7818022.stm.

———. "Timeline: Lebabnon." November 26, 2010.

BBC Channel 4 News. "Interview with Hossam Badrawi." February 10, 2011. At *New York Times* Web site http://thelede.blogs.nytimes.com/2011/02/10/latest-updates-on-day-17-of-egypt-protests/.

Beattie, Kirk J. *Egypt during the Nasser Years: Ideology, Politics, and Civil Society.* Boulder, CO: Westview Press, 1994.

———. *Egypt during the Sadat Years.* New York: Palgrave, 2000.

Be'eri, Eliezer. *Army Officers in Arab Politics and Society.* New York: Praeger, 1970.

Beinin, Joel. "Egyptian Workers Demand a Living Wage." *Foreign Policy.* May 12, 2010. http://mideast.foreignpolicy.com/posts/2010/05/12/ egyptian_workers_demand_a_living_wage.

———. "Labor, Capital, and the State in Nasserist Egypt, 1952–1961." *International Journal of Middle East Studies* 21, no. 1 (February 1989): 79–90.

———. "Review: Egypt's Transition Under Nasser." *MERIP Reports* 107 (July–August 1982): 23–26, 31.

Beinin, Joel, and Hossam el-Hamalawy. "Strikes in Egypt Spread from Center of Gravity." *Middle East Report Online.* May 9, 2007. http://www.merip.org/mero/mero050907.html.

Beinin, Joel, and Joe Stork, eds. *Political Islam: Essays from "Middle East Report."* Berkeley: University of California, 1997.

Beinin, Joel, and Zachary Lockman. *Workers on the Nile: Nationalism, Communism, Islam, and the Egyptian Working Class, 1882–1954.* Princeton, NJ: Princeton University Press, 1987.

Bell, Jacqueline. *Audit of USAID/Egypt's Democracy and Governance Activities: Audit Report No.6-263-10-001-P.* Cairo: U.S. Agency for International Development, Office of Inspector General, October 27, 2009. http://www.usaid.gov/oig/ public/fy10rpts/6-263-10-001-p.pdf.

Belal, Ahmed Awad. "Statement from the Faculty of Law at Cairo University." February 7, 2011.http://bikyamasr.com/wordpress/?p=26182.

Bellin, Eva. *Stalled Democracy: Capital, Labor, and the Paradox of State-Sponsored Development*. Ithaca, NY: Cornell University Press, 2002.

Bergen, Peter L. *The Osama bin Laden I Know: An Oral History of al Qaeda's Leader*. New York: Free Press, 2006.

Bey, Doaa el. "Fires Too Many." *Al-Ahram Weekly On-line*. March 19–25, 2009. http://weekly.ahram.org.eg/2009/939/pr1.htm.

Bianchi, Robert. *Unruly Corporatism: Associational Life in Twentieth-Century Egypt*. New York: Oxford University Press, 1989.

"Biography of Prof. Hossam Badrawi M.D." http://www.upregypt-nchr.org/files/Dr.Hossam%20Badrawi%20C.V..pdf. National Council for Human Rights. (Accessed January 11, 2011.)

Blair, David. "The Fixer in the Shadows Who May Emerge as Egypt's Leader." *Daily Telegraph*. February 24, 2009.

Bloom, Mia. *Dying to Kill: The Allure of Suicide Terrorism*. New York: Columbia University Press, 2005.

Booth, Marilyn. "Exploding into the Seventies: Ahmad Fu'ad Nigm, Sheikh Imam, and the Aesthetics of a New Youth Politics." *Cairo Papers in Social Science* 29, no. 2/3 (Summer/Fall 2006): 19–44.

Borne, John E. "The USS *Liberty*: Dissenting History vs. Official History." PhD diss., New York University, 1995.

Bossone, Andrew. "Bread Prices Stretch Egyptians—and Their Government." *National Geographic News*. July 16, 2008. http://news.nationalgeographic.com/news/2008/07/080716-egypt-food.html.

Botman, Selma. "Egyptian Communists and the Free Officers: 1950–54." *Middle Eastern Studies* 22, no. 3 (July 1986): 350–366.

———. "The Liberal Age, 1923–1952." In *The Cambridge History of Egypt: Modern Egypt, From 1517 to the End of the Twentieth Century*, vol. 2, edited by M.W. Daly, 180–197. Cambridge: Cambridge University Press, 1998.

———. *The Rise of Egyptian Communism, 1939–1970*. Syracuse, NY: Syracuse University Press, 1988.

Boukhars, Anouar. *Politics in Morocco: Executive Monarchy and Enlightened Auhtoritarianism*. London: Routledge, 2011.

Boutros-Ghali, Boutros. *Egypt's Road to Jerusalem: A Diplomat's Story of the Strrugle for Peace in the Middle East*. New York: Random House, 1997.

Brady, Simon. "Egypt Keeps Going Its Own Way." *Euromoney*. September 2003. http://www.euromoney.com/Article/1002178/BackIssue/50031/Egypt-keepsgoing-itsown-way.html.

Bregman, Ahron. *Israel's Wars: A History since 1947*. 2nd ed. London: Routledge, 2002.

Brendon, Piers. *The Decline and Fall of the British Empire: 1781–1997*. New York: Alfred A. Knopf, 2008.

Briggs, Herber W. "Rebus Sic Stantibus Before the Security Council: The Anglo-Egyptian Question." *The American Journal of International Law* 43, no. 4 (October 1949): 762–769.

Broad, William J. "Mohamed ElBaradei." *New York Times.* September 8, 2010. http://topics.nytimes.com/top/reference/timestopics/people/e/mohamed_elbaradei/index.html.

Brown, Archie. "Reform, Coup, and Collapse: The End of the Soviet State." BBC News. October 15, 2010. http://www.bbc.co.uk/history/worldwars/coldwar/soviet_end_01.shtml.

Brown, Nathan J. *The Rule of Law in the Arab World: Courts in Egypt and the Gulf.* New York: Cambridge University Press, 1997.

Brown, Nathan J., and Amr Hamzawy. "The Draft Party Platform of the Egyptian Muslim Brotherhood: Foray into Political Integration or Retreat into Old Positions?" *Carnegie Papers: Middle East Series* 89 (January 2008). http://carnegieendowment.org/files/cp89_muslim_brothers_final.pdf.

Brown, Nathan J., Michele Dunne, and Amr Hamzawy. "Egypt's Controversial Constitutional Amendments." Carnegie Endowment for International Peace. March 23, 2007. http://www.carnegieendowment.org/files/egypt_constitution_webcommentary01.pdf.

B'Tselem. "Land Expropriation and Settlements." http://www.btselem.org/english/settlements/statistics.asp. (Accessed December 6, 2010.)

Burns, William J. *Economic Aid and American Policy toward Egypt, 1955–1981.* Albany: State University of New York Press, 1985.

Bush, George H.W. *Address Before a Joint Session of the Congress on the Cessation of the Persian Gulf Conflict.* March 6, 1991. At the George Bush Presidential Library and Museum Web site, http://bushlibrary.tamu.edu/research/public_papers.php?id=2767&year=1991&month=3.

———. *Address Before a Joint Session of the Congress on the Persian Gulf Crisis and the Federal Budget Deficit.* September 11, 1990. At the George Bush Presidential Library and Museum Web site, http://bushlibrary.tamu.edu/research/public_papers.php?id=2217&year=1990&month=9.

Bush, George W. *Remarks by President George W. Bush at the 20th Anniversary of the National Endowment for Democracy.* November 6, 2003. National Endowment for Democracy. http://www.ned.org/george-w-bush/remarks-by-president-george-w-bush-at-the-20th-anniversary.

Bush, Ray. "Crisis in Egypt: Structural Adjustments, Food Security, and the Politics of USAID." *Capital and Class* 53, no. 18 (Summer 1994): 15–37.

BusinessWeek. "Angling to Be the Next Bangalore." January 30, 2006. http://www.businessweek.com/magazine/content/06_05/b3969409.htm.

Calvert, John. "The Individual and the Nation: Sayyid Qutb Tifl Min Al-Qarya (Child From the Village)." *Muslim World* 90, no. 1/2 (Spring 2000): 108–132.

———. *Sayyid Qutb and the Origins of Radical Islamism.* New York: Columbia University Press, 2010.

———. "'The World is an Undutiful Boy!': Sayyid Qutb's American Experience." *Islam and Christian-Muslim Relations* 11, no. 1 (March 2000): 87–103.

Carnegie Endowment for International Peace. "The April 6 Youth Movement." http://egyptelections.carnegieendowment.org/2010/09/22/the-april-6-youth-movement. (Accessed December 9, 2010.)

———. "Chemical and Biological Weapons in the Middle East." http://www.carnegieendowment.org/publications/index.cfm?fa=view&id=11745. (Accessed January 11, 2011.)

———. "Egypt's Election Primer." http://egyptelections.carnegieendowment.org/2010/09/10/egypt%E2%80%99s-elections-primer. (Accessed December 9, 2010.)

———. "Egypt's Parliamentary Elections Begin." *Arab Reform Bulletin*. November 20, 2005. http://www.carnegieendowment.org/arb/?fa=show&article=21089.

———. "The Nasserist Party: Party Platform." *Carnegie Guide to Egypt's Elections*. November 22, 2010. http://egyptelections.carnegieendowment.org/2010/09/13/party-platform-5.

———. "National Association for Change." http://egyptelections.carnegieendowment.org/2010/09/22/national-assocation-for-change. (Accessed December 9, 2010.)

———. "National Progressive Unionist (Tagammu') Party: Party Platform." *Carnegie Guide to Egypt's Elections*. November 22, 2010. http://egyptelections.carnegieendowment.org/2010/09/13/party-platform-4.

———. "New Wafd Party: Party Platform." *Carnegie Guide to Egypt's Eelctions*. November 22, 2010. http://egyptelections.carnegieendowment.org/2010/09/10/party-platform-3.

———. "Tomorrow (al-Ghad) Party: Party Background." http://egyptelections.carnegieendowment.org/2010/09/13/background-6. (Accessed December 9, 2010.)

Carter Center. "Saad Eddin Ibrahim (Egypt): Seating an Agenda for Arab Democracy." November 2008. http://www.cartercenter.org/peace/human_rights/defenders/defenders/Egypt_saad_eddin_ibrahim.html.

"Ceasefire Agreement." In *Arab Report and Record*, edited by Peter Kilner. Vol. 15, August 1–15, 1970.

Charbel, Jano. "Critics Say New Text-messaging Rules Target Pre-election Political Opposition." *Al-Masry Al-Youm*. October 14, 2010. http://www.almasryalyoum.com.

Chaudhry, Kiren Aziz. *The Price of Wealth: Economies and Institutions in the Middle East*. Ithaca, NY: Cornell University Press, 1997.

Chmaytelli, Maher. "Bush Speech on Democracy Missed the Point: Arab Commentators." Agence France-Presse. November 7, 2003.

Cleveland, William L. *A History of the Modern Middle East*. 3rd ed. Boulder, CO: Westview Press, 2004.

CNN. "Egyptian Doctor Emerges as Terror Mastermind." http://www.cnn.com/CNN/Programs/people/shows/zawahiri/profile.html. (Accessed December 7, 2010.)

Coll, Steve. *Ghost Wars: The Secret History of the CIA, Afghanistan, and bin Laden, From the Soviet Invasion to September 10, 2001*. New York: Penguin Books, 2004.

Collier, David, and Ruth Berins Collier. *Shaping the Political Arena.* Princeton, NJ: Princeton University Press, 1991.

Commission on Growth and Development. "Mahmoud Mohieldin." May 3, 2008. http://www.growthcommission.org/index.php?option=com_content&task=view &id=41&Itemid=138.

Commission on International Religious Freedom. *Annual Report 2006.* May 1, 2006. http://www.uscirf.gov/images/AR2006/uscirf_2006_annualreport.pdf.

———. *Annual Report 2007.* May 1, 2007. http://www.uscirf.gov/images/AR_2007/ annualreport2007.pdf.

———. *Annual Report 2008.* May 1, 2008. http://www.uscirf.gov/images/annual%20 report%202008-final%20edition.pdf.

———. *Annual Report 2009.* May 1, 2009. http://www.uscirf.gov/images/final%20 ar2009%20with%20cover.pdf.

———. *Annual Report 2010.* May 1, 2010. http://www.uscirf.gov/images/annual%20 report%202010.pdf.

Committee to Protect Journalists. "Four Editors Sentenced to Jail." September 13, 2007. http://cpj.org/2007/09/four-editors-sentenced-to-jail.php.

"Constitution of the Arab Republic of Egypt 1971." In *al-Dasatir al Misiriya, 1805–1971.* Cairo: Al Ahram Foundation, 1977. [In Arabic]

Consolidated Appropriations Act of 2008. Pub. L. No. 110-161, 121 *Statutes* 1839 (2007).

Consolidated Appropriations Act of 2010. Pub. L. No. 111-118, 123 *Statutes* 3409 (2010).

Cook, Steven A. "The Right Way to Promote Arab Reform." *Foreign Affairs* (March/April 2005): 91–102.

———. *Ruling But Not Governing: The Military and Political Development in Egypt, Algeria, and Turkey.* Baltimore: Johns Hopkins University Press, 2007.

Cooper, Mark N. "The Demilitarization of the Egyptian Cabinet." *International Journal of Middle East Studies* 14, no. 2 (May 1982): 203–225.

———. *The Transformation of Egypt.* Baltimore: Johns Hopkins University Press, 1982.

Cooper, William H., and Mark E. Manyin. *The Proposed South Korea-U.S. Free Trade Agreement (KORUSFTA).* Congressional Research Service. May 24, 2006. http://pards.org/crs_country/CRSReportTheProposedSouthKoreaU.S.FreeTra deAgreement%28KORUSFTA%29%28May24,2006%29.pdf.

Cordesman, Anthony H. *Arab-Israeli Military Forces in an Era of Asymmetric Wars.* Westport, CT: Praeger Security International, 2006.

———. *Weapons of Mass Destruction in the Middle East: Regional Trends, National Forces, Warfighting Capabilities, Delivery Options, and Weapons Effects.* Washington, DC: Center for International and Strategic Studies, September 2001. http://www.denvergov.org/Portals/326/documents/WMDMiddleEast.pdf.

Costigliola, Frank. *France and the United States: The Cold Alliance since World War II.* New York: Twayne Publishers, 1992.

Cotton, James. "From Authoritarianism to Democracy in South Korea." *Political Studies* 37, no. 2 (June 1989): 244–259.

Cowell, Alan. "Cairo's Aid Ouster Tied to Effort to Get Missle Parts in U.S."
New York Times. April 18, 1989.

Crenshaw, Martha. "The Logic of Terrorism: Terrorist Behavior as a Product of
Strategic Choice." In *Origins of Terrorism: Psychologies, Ideologies, Theologies, States
of Mind*, edited by Walter Reich. Washington, DC: Woodrow Wilson Center
Press, 1998.

Cristol, A. Jay. *The Liberty Incident: The 1967 Israeli Attack on the U.S. Navy Spy Ship.*
Washington, DC: Brassey's, 2002.

Croddy, Eric. *Chemical and Biological Warfare: A Comprehensive Survey for the
Concerned Citizen.* With Clarisa Perez-Armendariz and John Hart. New York:
Copernicus Books, 2002.

Crowley, Philip J. "Daily Press Briefing." November 15, 2010. U.S. Department of
State. http://www.state.gov/r/pa/prs/dpb/2010/11/150914.htm.

Daily Star Lebanon. "About The Daily Star." http://www.dailystar.com.lb/aboutus.
asp.(Accessed January 5, 2011.)

Daly, M.W. "The British Occupation, 1882–1922." In *The Cambridge History
of Egypt: Modern Egypt, From 1517 to the End of the Twentieth Century*, vol. 2,
edited by M.W. Daly, 239–250. Cambridge: Cambridge University Press,
1998.

Dawoud, Khaled. "Military Aid Crisis." *Al-Ahram Weekly On-line.* July 22–28, 2004.
http://weekly.ahram.org.eg/2004/700/index.htm.

———. "Profile: Egypt's Great Survivor." BBC News. November 24, 2003. http://
news.bbc.co.uk/2/hi/africa/3234012.stm.

Deeb, Marius. *Party Politics in Egypt: the Wafd & its Rivals, 1919–39.* London: Ithaca
Press, 1979.

Dekmejian, R. Hrair. *Egypt under Nasir: A Study in Political Dynamics.* Albany: State
University of New York Press, 1971.

Democracy Now. "Global Condemnation of Israeli Armed Attack on
Gaza-Bound Freedom Flotilla: At Least 10 Dead, Hundreds Remain
in Detention." June 1, 2010. http://www.democracynow.org/2010/6/1/
global_condemnation_of_israeli_armed_attack.

Derhally, Massoud. "Floating to Credibility." Arabian Business.com. March 6,
2003. http://www.arabianbusiness.com/floating-credibility-206710.html.

Devenny, Patrick. "List: The Middle East's Most Powerful Spooks." *Foreign
Policy.* July 20, 2009. http://www.foreignpolicy.com/articles/2009/07/20/
the_list_the_middle_easts_most_powerful_spies.

Din, Gamal Essam el. "The Business of Taking over Politics." *Al-Ahram Weekly
On-line.* November 2–9, 2005. http://weekly.ahram.org.eg/2005/767/eg2.htm.

———. "A Controversial Law." *Al-Ahram Weekly On-line.* July 7–13, 2005. http://
weekly.ahram.org.eg/2005/750/eg2.htm.

———. "Drowning Twice Over." *Al-Ahram Weekly On-line.* July 31–August 6, 2008.
http://weekly.ahram.org.eg/2008/908/fr2.htm.

———. "Get the Most Through the Door." *Al-Ahram Weekly On-line.* November
4–10, 2010. http://weekly.ahram.org.eg/2010/1022/eg7.htm.

———. "New Look Shura." *Al-Ahram Weekly Online*. June 24–30, 2010. http://weekly.ahram.org.eg/2010/1004/eg1.htm.

———. "Opposition Snipes at Government." *Al-Ahram Weekly On-line*. March 31–April 6, 2005. http://weekly.ahram.org.eg/2005/736/eg1.htm.

———. "Scramble for the Shura." *Al-Ahram Weekly Online*. April 29–May 5, 2010. http://weekly.ahram.org.eg/2010/996/eg5.htm.

———. "Shura Election Results Contested." *Al-Ahram Weekly Online*. June 17–23, 2010. http://weekly.ahram.org.eg/2010/1003/eg3.htm.

———. "Sifting Through the Embers." *Al-Ahram Weekly On-line*. August 21–27, 2008. http://weekly.ahram.org.

———. "US Throws $1 Million into the Fray." *Al-Ahram Weekly On-line*. March 10–16, 2005. http://weekly.ahram.org.eg/2005/733/eg2.htm.

———. "Waiting for Action." *Al-Ahram Weekly On-line*. June 11–17, 2009. http://weekly.ahram.org.eg/2009/951/eg4.htm.

Dockrill, Michael L., and J. Douglas Goold. *Peace without Promise: Britain and the Peace Conferences, 1919–1923*. Hamden, CT: Archon Books, 1981.

Dockrill, Michael L., and John Fisher, eds. *The Paris Peace Conference , 1919: Peace Without Victory?* Hampshire, England: Palgrave, 2001.

Drajem, Mark. "U.S. Mulling Free-Trade Deals with Egypt, South Korea, Malaysia." *Bloomberg*. September 8, 2005. http://www.bloomberg.com/apps/news?pid=newsarchive&sid=aFtGZzKnwo3Y&refer=asia.

Dunstan, Simon. *The Yom Kippur War: The Arab-Israeli War of 1973*. Oxford: Osprey, 2007.

Duwaydar, Galal. "You are Not Welcome, Mr. Lantos." *al Akhbar*. August 15, 2004. [In Arabic]

Dykstra, Darrell. "The French Occupation of Egypt, 1798–1801." In *The Cambridge History of Egypt: Modern Egypt, From 1517 to the End of the Twentieth Century*, vol. 2, edited by M.W. Daly, 180–197. Cambridge: Cambridge University Press, 1998.

Ebrahim, Ayman M. "The Growth Effects of Financial Liberalisation Programme in Egypt: Developments and Drawbacks." *Scientific Journal of the Faculty of Commerce and Business, Helwan University* 2 (2006). http://faculty.ksu.edu.sa/ahendy/Published%20Papers/Forms/AllItems.aspx.

Economist. "Great Sacrifices, Small Rewards: Has America's Obsession with this Region Been Worth It?" December 29, 2010.

———. "Those Patient Egyptians Lose Their Patience." January 22, 1977.

Efrat, Elisha. *Geography and Politics in Israel since 1967*. London: Frank Cass, 1988.

"Egypt Assistance: Endowment Counterproposal." In Rogin, Josh, "State Department Considers New Endowment As Egypt Extends Emergency Law," May 12, 2010. http://thecable.foreignpolicy.com/posts/2010/05/12/state_department_considers_4_billion_endowment_as_egypt_extends_emergency_law. (Accessed May 24, 2011)

Egypt, Arab Republic of. "Aswan." State Information Service. http://www.sis.gov.eg/En/Story.aspx?sid=402. (Accessed January 11, 2011.)

————. *Constitution of the Arab Republic of Egypt (amended 1980). Article 79.* State Information Service, 1980.

————. *Constitution of the Arab Republic of Egypt (amended March 26, 2007).* State Information Service. http://constitution.sis.gov.eg/en/2.htm.

————. "Law No. 84/2002." In *Official Gazette* 22. Cairo: State Information Service, June 5, 2002. [In Arabic]

————. "Law No. 177/2005: Regulating Political Parties System." State Information Service. July 6, 2005. http://www2.sis.gov.eg/.

————. *The October Paper.* Cairo: State Information Service, April 1974.

————. "Political Parties." State Information Service. http://www.sis.gov.eg/en/LastPage.aspx?Category_ID=259. (Accessed May 11, 2010.)

————. Ministry of Economic Development. "Major Economic Indicators 1967–1980."

————. Ministry of Foreign Affairs. "H.E. Mr. Ahmed Aboul Gheit—Minister of Foreign Affairs." http://www.mfa.gov.eg/MFA_Portal/en-GB/minister/cv/. (Accessed December 1, 2010.)

————. Press and Information Office. "100 Facts about Egypt." http://www.modernegypt.info/one-hundred-facts-about-egypt/. (Accessed January 7, 2011.)

Egypt News. "Egypt National Theatre Hit by Blaze." September 28, 2008. http://news.egypt.com/en/200809284047/news/-egypt-news/egypt-national-theatre-hit-by-blaze.html.

Eisenhower, Dwight. "U.S. Statement and Note to Bulganin." *New York Times.* November 5, 1956.

Eissa, Salah. *Constitution in the Garbage Can.* Cairo: Cairo Center for Human Rights, 2001. [In Arabic]

ElBaradei, Mohamed. "The Victory Itself Would be Bigger than the October War." *al Dustour.* October 5, 2010. http://dostor.org/politics/egypt/10/october/5/31194. [In Arabic]

Ennes, James M. *Assault on the Liberty: The True Story of the Israeli Attack on an American Intelligence Ship.* New York: Random House, 1979.

Erlich, Haggai. *Students and University in 20th Century Egyptian Politics.* London: Frank Cass, 1989.

Ernst, Carl W. *The Shambhala Guide to Sufism.* Boston: Shambhala, 1997.

Etman, Ismail. "Statement." *Al Jazeera English News,* February 2, 2011. http://english.aljazeera.net/news/middleeast/2011/02/201122105166169I4.html.

Ezzat, Dina. "Summit Stops." *Al-Ahram Weekly Online.* March 24–30, 2005. http://weekly.ahram.org.eg/2005/735/sc1.htm.

Fadiman, James, and Robert Frager, eds. *Essential Sufism.* San Francisco: HarperSanFrancisco, 1997.

Fahmy, Ismail. *Negotiating for Peace in the Middle East.* Baltimore: Johns Hopkins University Press, 1983.

Fawzi, Mohamed. *The Three Year War, 1967–1970: Memoirs of General Mohamed Fawzi.* Vol. 1. Cairo: Dar al Mustaqbal al Arabi, 1984.

Federal Bureau of Investigation. "Most Wanted Terrorists: Abdullah Ahmed Abdullah." http://www.fbi.gov/wanted/wanted_terrorists/abdullah-ahmed-abdullah. (Accessed December 1, 2010.)

———. "Most Wanted Terrorists: Ahmed Mohammed Hamed Ali.". http://www.fbi.gov/wanted/wanted_terrorists/ahmed-mohammed-hamed-ali. (Accessed December 1, 2010.)

Fernea, Elizabeth Warnock, ed. *Women and the Family in the Middle East: New Voices of Change.* Austin: University of Texas Press, 1985.

Feron, James. "Eshkol Indicates Israel Will Stay in Occupied Areas." *New York Times.* October 31, 1967.

Finkleston, Joseph. *Anwar Sadat: Visionary Who Dared.* London: Frank Cass, 1996.

Fisk, Robert. "Egypt is a Nation Caught Between Islam and the West." *Independent.* October 12, 2001. http://www.independent.co.uk/opinion/commentators/fisk/robert-fisk-egypt-is-a-nation-caught-between-islam-and-the-west-631094.html.

Fleishman, Jeffrey. "In Egypt, Artists Pay a Price for Reaching out to Israelis." *Los Angeles Times.* December 25, 2008.

Flynn, Stephen E. "Safer Borders." *New York Times.* October 1, 2001.

Fowler, James. "The United States and South Korean Democratization." *Political Science Quarterly* 114, no. 2 (Summer 1999): 265–288.

Foreign Broadcast Information Service. "Cairo Editor Reacts to Bush's Speech, Explains Why Muslims Hate US." Foreign Broadcast Information Service Report FBIS-NES-2003-1115. November 14, 2003.

———. "Muslim Brotherhood Rejects 'Sell Out' Talks." Foreign Broadcast Information Service Report FBIS-NES-91-209. October 29, 1991.

Freedman, Robert O. *Soviet Policy toward the Middle East since 1970.* 3rd ed. New York: Praeger, 1978.

Freedom House. *Freedom of Association under Threat—Egypt.* November 21, 2008. At the UN Refworld Web site http://www.unhcr.org/refworld/country,,FREEHOU,,EGY,,492a751728,0.html.

———. "UPR Stakeholder Submission—Egypt." February 2010.

Freiberger, Steven Z. *Dawn Over Suez: The Rise of American Power in the Middle East, 1953–1957.* Chicago: Ivan R. Dee, 1992.

Fromkin, David. *A Peace to End All Peace: The Fall of the Ottoman Empire and the Creation of the Modern Middle East.* New York: Henry Holt, 1989.

Gabbat, Adam, and Harriet Sherwood. "Freedom Flotilla Ship MV Rachel Corrie Continues to Head for Gaza." *Guardian.* June 4, 2010. http://www.guardian.co.uk/world/2010/jun/04/gaza-flotilla-mv-rachel-corrie.

Gadalla, Saad M. *Land Reform in Relation to Social Development: Egypt.* Columbia: University of Missouri Press, 1962.

Gamasy el, Mohamed Abdel Ghani. *The October War: Memoirs of Field Marshal El Gamasy of Egypt.* Cairo: American University in Cairo Press, 1993.

Gambetta, Diego, and Steffen Hertog. "Engineers of Jihad." Sociology Working Papers No. 2007-10, Department of Sociology, University of Oxford, Oxford,

UK, 2007. http://www.nuff.ox.ac.uk/users/gambetta/engineers%20of%20jihad. pdf.

Gause, F. Gregory. "Can Democracy Stop Terrorism?" *Foreign Affairs* 84, no. 5 (September/October 2005): 62–76.

Gawrych, George W. *The Albatross of Decisive Victory: War and Policy Between Egypt and Israel in the 1967 and 1973 Arab-Israeli Wars*. Westport, CT: Greenwood Press, 2000.

Gelvin, James. *The Modern Middle East: A History*. New York: Oxford University Press, 2005.

Gerges, Fawaz. *The Far Enemy: Why Jihad Went Global*. Cambridge: Cambridge University Press, 2009.

Gharib, Mohamed. "NDP Candidates Say They Were Pressured to Bow Out for Minister." *Al-Masry Al-Youm*. October 25, 2010. http://www.almasryalyoum.com.

Ghitany el, Magda. "Awaiting the Prosecution." *Al-Ahram Weekly On-line*. February 16–22, 2006. http://weekly.ahram.org.eg/2006/782/eg5.htm.

Ghobasy, Mona el. "The Metamorphosis of the Egyptian Muslim Brothers." *International Journal of Middle East Studies* 37, no. 3 (August 2005): 373–395.

Gin, Ooi Keat, ed. *Southeast Asia: A Historical Encyclopedia, From Angkor Wat to East Timor*. Santa Barbara, CA: ABC-CLIO, 2004.

Glain, Stephen. "Pyramid of Hope." *Newsweek*. June 27, 2005.

GlobalSecurity. "Homeland Security: Mohamed Atta." http://www.globalsecurity. org/security/profiles/mohamed_atta.htm. (Accessed December 7, 2010.)

———. "Military: Ayman al-Zawahiri." http://www.globalsecurity.org/military/ world/para/zawahiri.htm. (Accessed December 7, 2010.)

———. "Operation Nickel Grass [Yom Kippur War]." http://www.globalsecurity. org/military/ops/yom_kippur.htm. (Accessed December 7, 2010.)

Goldschmidt, Arthur. *Biographical Dictionary of Modern Egypt*. Boulder, CO: Lynne Rienner, 2000.

Goldschmidt, Arthur, Amy J. Johnson, and Barak A. Salmoni, eds. *Re-Envisioning Egypt, 1919–1952*. Cairo: American University in Cairo Press, 2005.

Gordon, Joel. *Nasser's Blessed Movement: Egypt's Free Officers and the July Revolution*. Cairo: American University in Cairo Press, 1996.

———. *Nasser: Hero of the Arab Nation*. Makers of the Muslim World. Oxford: Oneworld Publications, 2006.

Gorenberg, Gershom. *The Accidental Empire: Israel and the Birth of Settlements, 1967–1977*. New York: Times Books, 2007.

Gottheil, Richard. "Mohammed 'Abdu, Late Mufti of Egypt." *Journal of the American Oriental Society* 28, no. 1 (1907): 254–270.

Govrin, David. "Hala Mustafa and the Liberal Arab Predicament." *Middle East Quarterly* 18, no. 2 (Spring 2010): 41–52.

GovTrack. "Amendments, H.R. 2764: Consolidated Appropriations Act, 2008." http://www.govtrack.us/congress/bill.xpd?bill=h110-2764&tab=amendments. (Accessed December 3, 2010.)

Gramsci, Antonio. *Selections from the Prison Notebooks*. Translated by Quintin Hoare and Geoffrey Nowell Smith. New York: International Publishers, 1971.

Haass, Richard N. *War of Necessity, War of Choice: A Memoir of Two Iraq Wars*. New York: Simon & Schuster, 2009.

Habeeb, William M. "U.S.-Egyptian Aid Negotiations in the 1980s and 1990s." In *Power and Negotiation*, edited by I. William Zartman and Jeffrey Z. Rubin, 81–106. Ann Arbor: University of Michigan Press, 2000.

Haggag, Karim. "Part One: Rebalancing Powers and Rebuilding the Political Center." *Arab Reform Bulletin* 5, no. 3 (April 2007). http://www. carnegieendowment.org/publications/index.cfm?fa=view&id=19113#haggag.

Hail, J. A. *Britain's Foreign Policy in Egypt and Sudan, 1947–1956*. Berkshire, UK: Ithaca Press, 1996.

Hall, Peter A., and Rosemary C. R. Taylor. "Political Science and the Three Institutionalisms." *Political Studies* 44, no. 4 (December 1996): 936–957.

Hallman, Louise. "Egypt Clamps Down on Media ahead of November Elections." International Press Institute. October 18, 2010. http://www.freemedia.at/ singleview/5197/.

Hamid, Shadi. "Can't We All Just Get Along?" *Foreign Policy*. June 2, 2010. http:// www.foreignpolicy.com/articles/2010/06/02/cant_we_all_get_along?page=full.

———. "The Cairo Conundrum." *Democracy* 15 (Winter 2010): 34–45.

Hamzawy, Amr, and Sarah Grebowski. "From Violence to Moderation: Al-Jama'a al-Islamiya and al-Jihad." *Carnegie Papers: Middle East Series* 20 (April 2010). http://www.carnegieendowment.org/files/Hamzawy-Grebowski-EN.pdf.

Hatina, Meir. *Identity Politics in the Middle East: Liberal Thought and Islamic Challenge in Egypt*. London: Tauris Academic Studies, 2007.

Hawley, Caroline. "Egyptian Muslims Kill at Least 20 Christians." *Independent*. January 4, 2000. http://www.independent.co.uk/news/world/africa/egyptian- muslims-kill-at-least-20-christians-727149.html.

Heikal, Mohamed Hasanayn. *Autumn of Fury: The Assassination of Sadat*. New York: Random House, 1983.

Heller, Yves, and Buccianti, Alexander, "International Repercussions: The Impotence of Opposition in Egypt," *Le Monde*. February 19, 1999. [In French]

Hennawy, Noha el. "Skeptics Question Muslim Brotherhood's Support for ElBaradei." *Al-Masry Al-Youm*. July 14, 2010. http://www.almasryalyoum.com/ en/news/skeptics-question-muslim-brotherhoods-support-elbaradei.

Hess, John. "Egypt Marks Completion of Aswan Dam Project." *New York Times*. July 22, 1970.

Hesseltine, William B., and Hazel C. Wolf. *The Blue and Gray on the Nile: With American Soldiers in the Arab World . . . in 1870*. St. Petersburg, FL: Hailer Publishing, 2006.

Hinnesbusch, Raymond A. "Egypt under Sadat: Elites, Power Strucure, and Political Changes in a Post-Populist State." *Social Problems* 28, no. 4 (April 1981): 442–464.

Hill, Richard. *Egypt in the Sudan, 1820–1881.* New York: Oxford University Press, 1959.

———. *Egyptian Politics under Sadat: The Post-Populist Development of an Authoritarian-Modernizing State.* Boulder, CO: Lynne Rienner, 1988.

Hirst, David, and Irene Beeson. *Sadat.* London: Faber & Faber, 1981.

Hoffman, Bruce. *Inside Terrorism.* Rev. ed. New York: Columbia University Press, 2006.

Hofstadter, Dan, ed. *Egypt and Nasser.* Vol. 1, *1952–1956.* New York: Facts on File, 1973.

Hopwood, Derek. *Egypt: Politics and Society, 1945–1984.* 2nd ed. Boston: Unwin Hyman, 1985.

Hosenball, Mark, and Daniel Klaidman. "'I Put My Trust in God.'" *Newsweek.* November 29, 1999.

Hosni, Abdel Monem, ed. *Egypt Encyclopedia of Legislation and Law.* Vol. 13. Cairo: Hosni Center for Legal Studies, 1988. [In Arabic]

Hourani, Albert. *Arabic Thought in the Liberal Age, 1798–1939.* Cambridge: Cambridge University Press, 1991.

Howeidy, Amira. "A Chronology of Dissent." *Al-Ahram Weekly On-line.* June 23–29, 2005. http://weekly.ahram.org.eg/2005/748/eg10.htm.

Human Rights First. "Prosecution & Trials: Egypt's Best Known Activist on Trial." Ibn Khaldun Center for Development Studies. November 8, 2009. http://www.eicds.org/index.php?view=article&id=79&option= com_content&Itemid=63.

Human Rights Watch. "Gaza: Hamas Report Whitewashes War Crimes." January 28, 2010. http://www.hrw.org/en/news/2010/01/28/gaza-hamas-report-whitewashes-war-crimes.

———. "Investigate Torture, Rape of Activist Blogger." March 18, 2007. http://www.hrw.org/en/news/2007/03/18/egypt-investigate-torture-rape-activist-blogger.

———. "The Situation Since June 2003." *Egypt: Margins of Repression.* July 3, 2005. http://www.hrw.org/en/node/11675/section/7.

Humphreys, R. Stephen. *Between Memory and Desire: The Middle East in a Troubled Age.* 2nd ed. Berkeley: University of California Press, 2005.

Hunter, F. Robert. "Egypt under the Successors of Muhammad Ali." In *The Cambridge History of Egypt: Modern Egypt, From 1517 to the End of the Twentieth Century,* vol. 2, edited by M.W. Daly, 180–197. Cambridge: Cambridge University Press, 1998.

Husayn, Magdi Ahmad. "We Reject an American Framework Giving it a Blank Check for [the United States] to Control Policy, Oil, and Security in the Gulf," *ash-Sha'ab,* September 18, 1990. [In Arabic]

Husni, Abdul al Moneim, ed. *A Compendium of Egyptian Law and Statutes.* Vols. 5/6. Giza: Merkaz Husni l-il-Dirassat al Qaanuniyah, 1987. [In Arabic]

Ibrahim, Hassan Ahmed. "The Egyptian Empire, 1805–1885." In *The Cambridge History of Egypt: Modern Egypt, From 1517 to the End of the Twentieth Century*, vol. 2, edited by M.W. Daly, 198–216. Cambridge: Cambridge University Press, 1998.

Ibrahim, Hassanein Tawfiq, and Hadi Rageb Audah. *The Muslim Brotherhood and Politics in Egypt: A Study in the Electoral Alliances and Parliamentary Practices of the Muslim Brotherhood in the Framework of Limited Political Pluralism, 1984–1990*. Cairo: Mahroussa Books, 1995. [In Arabic]

Ibrahim, Raymond, ed. and trans. *The Al Qaeda Reader*. New York: Broadway Books, 2007.

Ibrahim, Saad Eddin. "Egypt's Unchecked Repression." *Washington Post*. August 21, 2007.

———. "Reform and Frustration in Egypt." *Journal of Democracy* 7, no. 4 (October 1996): 125–135.

Ibrahim, Youssef M. "Egyptian Group Says It Tried to Kill Mubarak." *New York Times*. July 5, 1995.

Ikhwanweb.com. "Habib on MB Party Program, Dialogue with West: An Interview with Deputy Chairman Mohamed Al Sayed Habib." November 11, 2007. http://www.ikhwanweb.com/print.php?id=14658.

———. "Interview with Chairman of the MB Political Department." August 8, 2008. http://www.ikhwanweb.com/print.php?id=17489.

Inbar, Efraim. *Israel's National Security: Issues and Challenges since the Yom Kippur War*. NewYork: Routledge, 2008.

International Center for Not-For-Profit Law. "News & Information: 03-07-2010." April 15, 2010. http://www.icnl.org/knowledge/news/2010/03-07_special.htm.

International Labour Organization. "Labour Statistics Database." http://laborsta.ilo.org/STP/guest. (Accessed December 17, 2010.)

International Monetary Fund. *World Economic Outlook Database*. April 2006. http://www.imf.org/external/pubs/ft/weo/2006/01/data/.

———. *International Financial Statistics, 1990–2009*. http://www.imfstatistics.org/imf/. (Accessed December 1, 2010.)

International Trade Centre. "Conversion Factors." http://www.cottonguide.org/conversion-factors. (Accessed January 3, 2011.)

Inter-Parliamentary Union. "Egypt." PARLINE. http://www.ipu.org/parline-e/reports/arc/EGYPT_1979_E.PDF. (Accessed December 16, 2010.)

IRIN News. "Climate Change Could Threaten Food Security: FAO Report." March 11, 2008. http://www.irinnews.org/Report.aspx?ReportId=77215.

Ismail, Abdel Mawla. "Drinking Water Protests in Egypt and the Role of Civil Society." *E-Joussour*. October 7, 2009.

Israel. Central Bureau of Statistics. "Imports by Countries of Purchase and Exports by Country of Destination." In *Statistical Abstract of Israel*. Jerusalem: Central Bureau of Statistics, 2010.

———. "Table of Population in Each One of the Settlements Since 1967." Quoted in "Settlement List: Table of Population in Each One of the Settlements Since

1967." *Peace Now.* http://www.peacenow.org.il/site/en/peace.asp?pi=57. (Accessed December 1, 2010.)

Israel. Knesset. "A Final Word." The Knesset Building in Giv'at Ram: Planning and Construction. http://www.knesset.gov.il/. (Accessed January 4, 2011.)

———. "The Completion and Its Results, Mid-1956 to Mid-1958." The Knesset Building in Giv'at Ram: Planning and Construction. http://www.knesset.gov.il/. (Accessed January 4, 2011.)

Israel. Ministry of Foreign Affairs. "Golan Heights Law, 14 December 1981." Guide to the Middle East Peace Process. November 21, 2007. http://www.mfa.gov.il/MFA/Peace+Process/Guide+to+the+Peace+Process/Golan+Heights+Law.htm.

Israeli, Raphael. *The Public Diary of President Sadat: Part One, The Road to War, October 1970–October 1973.* Leiden: EJ Brill, 1978.

———. *The Public Diary of President Sadat: Part Three, The Road of Pragmatism, June 1975–October 1976.* Leiden: E.J. Brill, 1979.

Issawi, Ibrahim el. "A Man Apart." *Al-Ahram Weekly On-line.* November 16–22, 2006. http://weekly.ahram.org.eg/2006/820/eg7.htm.

Jacquemond, Richard. *Conscience of the Nation: Writers, State, and Society in Modern Egypt.* Cairo: American University in Cairo Press, 2008.

Jankowski, James. *Nasser's Egypt, Arab Nationalism, and the United Arab Republic.* Boulder, CO: Lynne Rienner, 2002.

Jehl, Douglas. "Dissecting a Man's Life to Understand His Outlook." *New York Times.* November 18, 1999.

Jervis, Robert. "Why the Bush Doctrine Cannot be Sustained." *Political Science Quarterly* 120, no. 3 (2005): 351–377.

Jesri, Manal el. "The Activist." *Egypt Today.* May 2005. http://www.egypttoday.com/article.aspx?ArticleID=5062. (Accessed November 23, 2010.)

Johnson, Larry C. "The Declining Terrorist Threat." *New York Times.* July 10, 2001.

Johnson, Peter. "Egypt under Nasser." *MERIP Reports* 10 (July 1972): 3–14.

Johnston, Cynthia. "In Egypt, Long Queues for Bread That's Almost Free." Reuters. Apr 6, 2008.

Jordan, Michael C. "The 1973 Arab-Israeli War: Arab Policies, Strategies, and Campaign." 1997. http://www.globalsecurity.org/military/library/report/1997/Jordan.htm.

Jorden, William. "Moscow Aroused: Strong Notes Are Sent to Britain, France, Israel on Egypt." *New York Times.* November 6, 1956.

Joscelyn, Thomas. "A Victory for the Muslim Brotherhood: The Obama Administration Allows Tariq Ramadan to Travel to the U.S." *Weekly Standard.* January 20, 2010. https://www.weeklystandard.com/blogs/victory-muslim-brotherhood.

Kamal, Gamal. "The Biggest Issue Concerning a Large Portion of the Aid." *al Gumhuriya.* July 22, 2004. [In Arabic]

Kamar, Bassem, and Damyana Bakardzhieva. "Economic Trilemma and Exchange Rate Management in Egypt," 10th Annual Conference of the Economic Research Forum for the Arab Countries, Marrakesh, Morocco, December 16–18, 2003.

Kamrava, Mehran. *The Modern Middle East: A Political History since the First World War*. Berkeley: University of California Press, 2005.

Karabell, Zachary. *Parting the Desert: The Creation of the Suez Canal*. New York: Vintage Books, 2004.

Kassem, Maye. *Egyptian Politics: The Dynamics of Authoritarian Rule*. Boulder, CO: Lynne Rienner, 2004.

Katatney, Ethar el. "Waiting for 'Aish." *Egypt Today* (May 2008). http://www. egypttoday.com/article.aspx?ArticleID=7989. (Accessed January 12, 2011.)

Kaye, Dalia Dassa, Frederic Wehrey, Audra K. Grant, and Dale Stahl. *More Freedom, Less Terror?: Liberalization and Political Violence in the Arab World*. Santa Monica, CA: RAND, 2008.

Kedourie, Elie. *Afghani and 'Abduh: An Essay on Religious Unbelief and Political Activisim in Modern Islam*. London: Frank Cass, 1966.

Kelsey Museum of Archaeology. "The Building of the First Aswan Dam and the Inundation of Lower Nubia: Images from the Collections of the Kelsey Museum." University of Michigan. http://www.umich.edu/~kelseydb/Exhibits/AncientNubia/PhotoIntro.html. (Accessed January 11, 2011.)

Kenney, Jeffrey. *Muslim Rebels: Kharijites and the Politics of Extremism in Egypt*. New York: Oxford University Press, 2006.

Kepel, Gilles. *Jihad: The Trial of Islam*. London: I.B. Tauris, 2006.

———. *Muslim Extremism in Egypt:The Prophet and Pharoah*. Translated by Jon Rothschild. Berkeley: University of California Press, 1993.

Kerr, Malcolm H. *Islamic Reform: The Political and Legal Theories of Muhammad 'Abduh and Rashid Rida*. Berkeley: University of California Press, 1966.

Khalidi, Walid. "Nasser's Memoirs of the First Palestine War." *Journal of Palestine Studies* 2, no. 2 (Winter 1973): 3–32.

Khalil, Nevine. "Human Rights Message on Police Day." *Al-Ahram Weekly Online*. January 29–February 4. http://weekly.ahram.org.eg/2004/675/eg1.htm

———. "The Forgotten President." *Al-Ahram Weekly Online*. July18–24, 2002. http://weekly.ahram.org.eg/2002/595/sc6.htm

Khallaf, Rania. "A Questionable Reincarnation." *Al-Ahram Weekly On-line*. April 7–13, 2005. http://weekly.ahram.org.eg/2005/737/cu1.htm.

———. "Writers Come Home." *Al-Ahram Weekly On-line*. November 30–December 6, 2006. http://weekly.ahram.org.eg/2006/822/eg4.htm.

Khatab, Sayed. "Arabism and Islamism in Sayyid Qutb's Thought on Nationalism." *Muslim World* 94, no. 2 (April 2004): 217–244.

———. *The Political Thought of Sayyid Qutb: The Theory of Jahiliyya*. Routledge Studies in Political Islam. London: Routledge, 2006.

Khatib, Ahmed el. "Detained Members of Shia Group Released and Deported." *Al-Masry Al-Youm*. November 28, 2010. http://www.almasryalyoum.com/.

Khatib, Ahmed el, Nadia Shabour, and Ahmed Ali. "22 Muslim Brotherhood Candidates Pull out of Parliamentary Race." *Al-Masry Al-Youm*. November 1, 2010. http://www.almasryalyoum.com/.

Kienle, Eberhard. *A Grand Delusion: Democracy and Economic Reform in Egypt*. New York: I.B. Tauris, 2000.

Kimmerling, Brauch. *Zionism and Territory: The Socio-Territorial Dimensions of Zionist Politics*. Berkeley: University of California Press, 1983.

Kirkpatrick, Jeane J. "Dictatorships and Double Standards." *Commentary* (November 1979): 34–45.

Kissinger, Henry. *Years of Upheaval*. Boston: Little, Brown, 1982.

Knickmeyer, Ellen. "In Egypt, Upper Crust Gets the Bread." *Washington Post*. April 5, 2008.

Kober, Avi. *Israel's Wars of Attrition: Attrition Challenges to Democratic States*. London: Routledge, 2009.

Krisinger, Chris J. "Operation Nickel Grass: Airlift in Support of National Policy." *Airpower Journal* 3, no. 1 (Spring 1989). http://www.au.af.mil/au/cadre/aspj/airchronicles/apj/apj89/spr89/krisinger.html

Krueger, Alan B., and Jitka Maleckova. "Education, Poverty, and Terrorism: Is There a Causal Connection?" *Journal of Economic Perspectives* 17, no. 4 (November 2003): 119–144.

Kuisel, Richard F. *Seducing the French: The Dilemma of Americanization*. Berkeley: University of California Press, 1993.

Kuran, Timur. "Now at of Never: The Element of Surprise in the East European Revolution of 1989." World Politics 44, no. 1 (October 1991): 7–48.

Kurzman, Charles. *The Unthinkable in Iran*. Cambridge: Harvard College, 2004.

Lacouture, Jean, and Simonne Lacouture. *Egypt in Transition*. Translated by Francis Scarfe. New York: Criterion Books, 1958.

Lake, Anthony. *Remarks of Anthony Lake: 'From Containment to Enlargement' at Johns Hopkins School of Advanced International Studies, Washington, DC*. September 21, 1993. http://www.mtholyoke.edu/.

Langewiesche, William. "The Crash of EgyptAir 990," *Atlantic Monthly* 228, no. 4 (November 2001).

"Law No. 65/1975: Regarding the Union of Writers" in *Egypt Encyclopedia of Legislation and Law*. Edited by Abdel Monem Hosni. Vol. 13. Cairo: Hosni Center for Legal Studies, 1988. [In Arabic]

Lawrence, James. *Imperial Warrior. The Life and Times of Field Marshal Viscount Allenby, 1861–1936*. London: Weidenfeld & Nicolson, 1993.

League of Arab States. "Khartoum Resolution." September 1, 1967. UNISPAL. http://unispal.un.org/UNISPAL.NSF/0/1FF0BF3DDEB703A785257110007719E7.

Lee, Ian. "Homeless in Duweiqa." *Daily News Egypt*. Posted July 28, 2009. www.youtube.com/watch?v=i3HMumcqWNQ.

Lenczowski, George. *The Middle East in World Affairs*. 4th ed. Ithaca, NY: Cornell University Press, 1980.

Lesch, Ann Moseley. "Israeli Settlements in the Occupied Territories, 1967–1977." *Journal of Palestine Studies* 7, no. 1 (Autumn 1977): 26–47.

Lethen, Jonathan. "My Egyptian Cousin." *London Review of Books*. December 12, 2002.

Levi, Margaret. *Of Rule and Revenue*. Berkeley: University of California Press, 1988.

Little, Tom. *Egypt*. New York: Fredrick A. Praeger, 1958.

Lockman, Zachary, ed. *Workers and Working Classes in the Middle East: Struggles, Histories, Historiographies*. Albany: State University of New York Press, 1994.

Louis, William Roger. *The British Empire in the Middle East, 1945–1951: Arab Nationalism, the United States, and Postwar Imperialism*. New York: Oxford University Press, 1984.

Lowe, Vaughan, Adam Roberts, Jennifer Welsh, and Dominik Zaum, eds. *The United Nations Security Council and War: The Evolution of Thought and Practice since 1945*. New York: Oxford University Press, 2008.

Lustick, Ian S. *For the Land and the Lord: Jewish Fundamentalism in Israel*. New York: Council on Foreign Relations, 1988.

———. "Hegemony and the Riddle of Nationalism." In *Ethnic Conflict and international Politics in the Middle East*, edited by Leonard Binder, 322–359. Gainesville: University of Florida Press, 1999.

Lynch, David J. "Tension in Egypt Shows Potency of Crisis." *USA Today*. April 30, 2008.

Mabro, Robert. *The Egyptian Economy, 1952–1972*. London: Clarendon Press, 1974.

Macmillan, Margaret. *Peacemakers: The Paris Conference of 1919 and Its Attempt to End War*. London: John Murray, 2001.

Macris, Jeffrey R. *The Politics and Security of the Gulf: Anglo-American Hegemony and the Shaping of a Region*. New York: Routledge, 2010.

MacFarquhar, Neil. "Egyptian Reformers Take to Streets to Oppose a 5th Term for Mubarak." *New York Times*. April 28, 2005.

———. "Riot Police Crack Down on Day of Anti-Mubarak Protests Across Egypt." *New York Times*. April 27, 2005.

Mahmood, Saba. *Politics of Piety: The Islamic Revival and the Feminist Subject*. Princeton, NJ: Princeton University Press, 2005.

Mansfield, Edward D., and Jack Snyder. *Electing to Fight: Why Emerging Democracies Go to War*. Cambridge, MA: MIT Press, 2005.

Marlowe, John. *A History of Modern Egypt and Anglo-Egyptian Relations, 1800–1956*. 2nd ed. Hamden, CT: Archon Books, 1965.

Mark, Clyde. "Middle East: U.S. Foreign Assistance, FY2002, FY2003, and Request for FY2004." Congressional Research Service. April 16, 2003. http://www.policyarchive.org/handle/10207/bitstreams/1633.pdf.

Mashour, Mustafa. "This Conference . . . Between Whom? With Whom? To Whose Benefit?" *al Sha'ab*. October 22, 1991. [In Arabic]

Marsot, Afaf Lutfi al-Sayyid. *Egypt's Liberal Experiment: 1922–1936*. Berkeley: University of California Press, 1977.

Marsot, Afaf Lutfi al-Sayyid. *A Short History of Modern Egypt*. 1985. Reprint, Cambridge: Cambridge University Press, 1994.

Mauroni, Al. *Chemical and Biological Warfare: A Reference Handbook*. 2nd ed. Santa Barbara, CA: ABC-CLIO, 2007.

Maxwell, Neville. "Reconsiderations: Jawaharlal Nehru: Of Pride and Principle." *Foreign Affairs* 52, no. 3 (April 1974): 633–643.

Mayton, Joseph. "Egypt Won't Allow Foreign Monitors for Elections." *Bikya Masr*. November 18, 2010. http://bikyamasr.com/wordpress/?p=21018.

McDermott, Anthony. *Egypt: From Nasser to Mubarak; A Flawed Revolution*. London: Croom Helm, 1988.

McDonough, Challiss. "Egyptian Bread Crisis Stirs Anger." *VOA News*. March 24, 2008.

McGreal, Chris. "Egypt: Bread Shortages, Hunger and Unrest." *Guardian*. May 27, 2008. http://www.guardian.co.uk/environment/2008/may/27/food.egypt.

McInerney, Stephen. *The Federal Budget Appropriations for Fiscal Year 2011: Democracy, Governance, and Human Rights in the Middle East*. Project on Middle East Democracy. April 2010. http://pomed.org/wordpress/wp-content/uploads/2010/04/fy11-budget-analysis-final.pdf.

Medzini, Mernon, ed. "Freedom of Navigation: Egyptian Decree Regarding Navigation in the Suez Canal, 6 February 1950." In *Israel's Foreign Relations, Selected Documents*. Vols. 1–2, *1947–1974*. Jerusalem: Ministry of Foreign Affairs, 1976. http://www.mfa.gov.il/MFA/Foreign%20Relations/Israels%20Foreign%20Relations%20since%201947/1947-1974/1%20Egyptian%20Decree%20Regarding%20Navigation%20in%20the%20Suez.

———. "Freedom of Navigation: Introduction." In *Israel's Foreign Relations, Selected Documents*. Vols. 1–2, *1947–1974*. Jerusalem: Ministry of Foreign Affairs, 1976. http://www.mfa.gov.il/MFA/Foreign+Relations/Israels+Foreign+Relations+since+1947/1947-1974/FREEDOM+OF+NAVIGATION-+INTRODUCTION.htm.

———. "The Yom Kippur War and Aftermath: Separation of Forces Agreement, Israel Government Statement, 18 January 1974." In *Israel's Foreign Relations, Selected Documents*. Vols. 1–2: *1947–1974*. Jerusalem: Ministry of Foreign Affairs, 1976. http://www.mfa.gov.il/MFA/Foreign+Relations/Israels+Foreign+Relations+since+1947/1947-1974/23+Separation+of+Forces+Agreement-+Israel+Governme.htm.

Mehrez, Samia. "Take Them Out of the Ball Game: Egypt's Cultural Players in Crisis." *Middle East Report* 219 (Summer 2001). http://www.merip.org/mer/mer219/219_mehrez.html.

Meijer, Roel, ed. *Global Salafism: Islam's New Religious Movement*. New York: Columbia University Press, 2009.

Meital, Yoram. *Egypt's Struggle for Peace: Continuity and Change, 1967–1977*. Gainsville: University Press of Florida, 1997.

Mekay, Emad. "Egypt Press Union to Appeal Egyptian Journalist's Arrest." *New York Sun*. September 30, 2008.

Melman, Yossi. "Israel Pinning Hopes for Hamas Deal in Gaza on Egypt Intel Chief." *Haaretz*. January 20, 2009. http://www.haaretz.com/print-edition/features/israel-pinning-hopes-for-hamas-deal-in-gaza-on-egypt-intel-chief-1.268496.

MERIP Reports. "Egyptian Students Press Demands." *MERIP Reports* 7 (February 1972): 12.

Mesahel, Mohamed Abdel Khaleq. "Press Syndicate Questions Hala Mustapha over Normalization." *Al-Masry Al-Youm*. November 10, 2010. http://www.almasryalyoum.com/en/news/journalists-syndicate-questions-hala-mustapha-over-hosting-israeli-ambassador-0.

Metz, Helen Chapin, ed. *Egypt: A Country Study*. Country Studies/Area Handbook Series. Washington, DC: U.S. Government Priting Office, 1991.

———. *Libya: A Country Study*. Country Studies/Area Handbook Series. Washington, DC: U.S. Government Priting Office, 1988.

Mitchell, B.R. *International Historical Statistics: Africa, Asia & Oceania, 1750–1993*. 3rd ed. London: Macmillan Reference, 1998.

Mitchell, Richard P. *The Society of the Muslim Brothers*. New York: Oxford University Press, 1993.

Mohamed, Abdel Hayy. "All Political Parties and Forces Express their Support for the Iraqi People." *ash-Sha'ab*. January 29, 1991. [In Arabic]

———. "Faculty and Student Unions, the Professional Associations Reject the Military Alliance." *ash-Sha'ab*. September 18, 1990. [In Arabic]

Moore, Clement Henry. *Tunisia Since Independence: The Dynamics of One-Party Government*. Berkeley: University of California Press, 1965.

Morayef, Heba. "Tahrir Sqare Voices Will Never Be Silent," Human Rights Watch. February 11, 2011. http://www.hrw.org/en/news/2011/02/11/tahrir-square-voices-will-never-be-silenced.

Morris, Benny. *The Birth of the Palestinian Refugee Problem, 1947–1949*. Cambridge: Cambridge University Press, 1996.

Morrow, Adam, and Khaled Moussa al-Omrani. "After Summer Shortages, Promise of Water Runs Dry." Inter Press Service. October 11, 2007.

Mostafa, Hadia. "Facing the Consequences." *Business Today Egypt*. July 2010. http://www.businesstodayegypt.com/article.aspx?ArticleID=4066.

Moubayed, Sami M. *Damascus Between Democracy and Dictatorship*. Lanham, MD: University Press of America, 2000.

Moussalli, Ahmad. "Wahhabism, Salafism and Islamism: Who is the Enemy?" A Conflict Forum Monograph. January 2009.

Moustafa, Tamir. *The Struggle for Constitutional Power: Law, Politics, and Economic Development in Egypt*. Cambridge: Cambridge University Press, 2007.

MSNBC. "Who is Ayman al-Zawahri?" March 25, 2004. http://www.msnbc.msn.com/id/4555901/ns/world_news-terrorism/.

Mubarak, Hosni. *Speech of President Mohamed Hosni Mubarak on the Occasion Celebrating the Workers Holiday*. May 6, 2010. State Information Service. http://www.sis.gov.eg/Ar/Story.aspx?sid=35152. [In Arabic]

Mubarak, Hosni. *Speech of President Mohamed Hosni Mubarak to the Egyptian People.* January 29, 2011. State Information Service. http://www.sis.gov.eg/En/Story. aspx?sid=53519.

Murphy, Caryle. *Passion for Islam; Shaping the Modern Middle East: The Egyptian Experience.* New York: Scribner, 2002.

Murphy, Dan. "Egypt's Economic Reform Meets Unprecedented Wave of Labor Resistance." *Christian Science Monitor.* December 7, 2007.

Murtagi, Abdel Muhsin. *General Murtagi Tells the Facts.* Cairo: al Wtan al Harbi, 1976. [In Arabic]

Musallam, Adnan A. *From Secularism to Jihad: Sayyid Qutb and the Foundations of Radical Islam.* Westport, CT: Praeger, 2005.

———. *Sayyid Qutb: The Emergence of the Islamicist, 1939–1950.* Jerusalem: PASSIA, 1990.

Muslim Brotherhood. *Program of the Party of the Muslim Brotherhood—First Draft.* August 25, 2007. [In Arabic]

———. "Section 4: Regional Leadership." In *Electoral Program of the Muslim Brotherhood—2010 People's Assembly Elections.* [In Arabic]

Mutual Security Act of 1954, Pub. L. No. 83-665, 68 *Stat.* 937 (1954).

Nafie, Ibrahim. "Double Trouble." *Al-Ahram Weekly On-line.* November 13–16, 2003. http://weekly.ahram.org.eg/2003/664/op1.htm.

Naggar, Mona el. "ElBaradei Calls for Boycott in Egypt." *New York Times.* September 7, 2010.

Naguib, Mohammed. "A King is Deposed: Six Fateful Hours." *Time.* August 25, 1952.

———. *Egypt's Destiny.* New York: Greenwood Press, 1955.

Nahhas el, Mona. "By His Own Hand?" *Al-Ahram Weekly On-line.* February 1–7, 2001. http://weekly.ahram.org.eg/2001/519/eg8.htm.

———. "'Your Credit is Due to Expire.'" *Al-Ahram Weekly Online.* October 21–27, 2010. http://weekly.ahram.org.eg/2010/1020/eg7.htm.

Nahmias, Roee. "Egypt Deals With Water Uprising." *Ynetnews.* July 29, 2007. http://www.ynetnews.com/articles/0,7340,L-3431255,00.html.

Nakeeb, Anwar M. el. "Egyptian Food Subsidy System: Structure, Performance and Future Perspective." PowerPoint presentation at the World Bank Conference, Singapore, June 2009.

Nasrawi, Salah. "Muslims Torch Christian Homes in Southern Egypt." *Washington Post.* November 16, 2010.

Nasser, Gamal Abdel. "Nasser's Memoirs of the First Palestine War." Translated and Annotated by Walid Khalidi. *Journal of Palestine Studies* 2, no. 2 (Winter 1973).

———. *Nasser Speaks: Basic Documents.* Translated by E.S. Farag. London: Morsett Press, 1972.

———. *The Philosophy of the Revolution.* Cairo: Dar al Maaref, 1954.

———. *Speech Nationalizing the Suez Canal: Public Address of President Gamal Abdel Nasser on the 4th Anniversary of the Revolution from Alexandria.* July 26, 1956. http://www.nasser.org/Speeches/browser.aspx?SID=495&lang=ar. [In Arabic]

————. *Statement of Gamal Abd al-Nasser to the People and the Nation to Declare to Step Down From the Presidency.* http://nasser.bibalex.org/Speeches/browser.aspx?SID=1221. (Accessed November 10, 2010.) [In Arabic]

————. *Statement of President Gamal Abdel Nasser Regarding his Resignation from Government delivered by President of the National Assembly Anwar Sadat.* June 10, 1967. http://www.nasser.org/Speeches/browser.aspx?SID=1222&lang=ar. [In Arabic]

————. *Statement of President Gamal Abdel Nasser to the People and the Nation Announcing his Resignation from the Presidency of the Republic.* June 9, 1967. http://www.nasser.org/Speeches/browser.aspx?SID=1221&lang=ar. [In Arabic]

National Democratic Party. *Citizens Rights and Democracy.* Position paper, September 2004. [In Arabic]

Neff, Donald. *Warriors at Suez: Eisenhower Takes America into the Middle East.* New York: Simon & Schuster, 1981.

Netanyahu, Benjamin. *Speech by Prime Minister Benjamin Netanyahu to a Joint Session of the United States Congress.* Israel Ministry of Foreign Affairs. July 10, 1996. http://www.mfa.gov.il/MFA/MFAArchive/1990_1999/1996/7/PM Netanyahu-Speech to US Congress- July 10- 1996.

New York Stock Exchange Euornext. "NYSE Hosts its First 'Egypt Day' with Egypt's Corporate and Governmental Leaders as well as Leading Middle Eastern Investors." February 4, 2008. http://www.nyse.com/events/1201864190090.html.

New York Times. "Ayman Nour." February 19, 2009.

————. "Basic Facts About the Suez Canal." August 5, 1956.

————. "Egypt Nationalizes Suez Canal Company." July 27, 1956.

————. "Heykal Said to Attribute Ouster to Rift on Nixon." February 11, 1974.

————. "Israelis Confirm Sinai Move." October 30, 1967.

————. "New Plan to Free Egypt." August 23, 1920.

————. "News Summary: International." January 18, 2006.

————. "Sukarno, 69, Dies; Led Indonesians." June 21, 1970.

————. "The Specter of Biological Terror." September 26, 2001.

————. "The War against America; An Unfathomable Attack." September 12, 2001.

————. "Thousands in Egypt Riots Over Price Rise." January 19, 1977.

————. "Thousands of People Protests What They Call Police Torture." June 25, 2010.

————. "Transcript: The Debate." May 3, 2007.

————. "War without Illusions." September 15, 2001.

North, Douglass C. *Structure and Change in Economic History.* New York: Norton, 1981.

North, Douglass C., and Barry R. Weingast. "Constitutions and Commitment: The Evolution of Institutions Governing Public Choice in Seventeenth Century England." *Journal of Economic History* 59, no. 4 (December 1989): 803–832.

Nuclear Threat Initiative. "Egypt Profile: Chemical Overview." October 2009. http://www.nti.org/e_research/profiles/Egypt/Chemical/index.html.

Nutting, Anthony. *Nasser.* New York: E.P. Dutton, 1972.

Nye, Joseph S. "How to Protect the Homeland." *New York Times.* September 25, 2001.

Official Journal of the European Communities. "Sentence Passed on Professor Saad Eddin Ibrahim." June 19, 2001. http://eur-lex.europa.eu/LexUriServ/LexUriServ.do?uri=OJ:C:2002:081E:0058:0059:EN:PDF.

Omar Effendi. "Omar Effendi: A Transformation of Style." http://www.omareffendi.com.eg/myPage.aspx?id=9. (Accessed October 26, 2010.)

Oren, Michael. *Six Days of War: June 1967 and the Making of the Modern Middle East.* New York: Oxford University Press, 2002.

Oteify, Rania. "Coming Up Roses." *Business Today Egypt.* April 1, 2003.

———. "Return of the Bread Lines?" *Business Today Egypt.* October 3, 2003.

Ottaway, David B. "Egyptian Leader Was Key U.S. Ally." *Washington Post.* October 7, 1981.

Owen, Roger. *Lord Cromer: Victorian Imperialist, Edwardian Proconsul.* Oxford: Oxford University Press, 2004.

———. *State, Power and Politics in the Making of the Modern Middle East.* 3rd ed. London: Routledge, 2004.

Pace, Eric. "Egypt Trying 54 Accused of Plot." *New York Times.* January 23, 1968.

———. "Egypt's Ex-Air Chief is Given 15-Year Term for 'Negligence'; 2d Officer is Also Jailed on Charge Resulting From June War with Israel." *New York Times.* February 21, 1968.

Palestine. Central Bureau of Statistics. "Number of Settlements in the West Bank, by Year of Establishment, 1967–2009." In *Israeli Settlements and Land Grab Database* (unpublished data). Ramallah: Palestinian Central Bureau of Statistics, 2009. http://www.pcbs.gov.ps/Portals/_pcbs/Settlements/Table%204.htm. (Accessed December 1, 2010.)

Panama Maritime Authority. *Preliminary Investigation Report on the Sinking of the M/V Al Salam Boccaccio 98.* August 17, 2006. http://www.naviecapitani.it/gallerie%20navi/Ro-Ro%20%20e%20%20Ro-Pax%20%20----%20Ro-Ro%20%20and%20%20Ro-Pax/foto/B/Boccaccio/Relazione%20sul%20naufragio.pdf.

Pape, Robert A. "The Strategic Logic of Suicide Terrorism." *American Political Science Review* 97, no. 3 (August 2003): 343–361.

Parker, Richard B. *The Politics of Miscalculation in the Middle East.* Bloomington: Indiana University Press, 1993.

Perkins, Kenneth J. *A History of Modern Tunisia.* Cambridge: Cambridge University Press, 2004.

Perlmutter, Amos. *Egypt: The Praetorian State.* New Brunswick, NJ: Transaction Books, 1974.

Perry, Glenn E. *The History of Egypt.* The Greenwood Histories of Modern Nations. Westport, CT: Greenwood Press, 2004.

Piazza, James A. "Do Democracy and Free Markets Protect us From Terrorism?" *International Politics* 45, no. 1 (January 2008): 72–91.

Pierson, Paul. "Increasing Returns, Path Dependence, and the Study of Politics." *American Political Science Review* 94, no. 2 (June 2000): 251–267.

Piquet, Caroline. "The Suez Company's Concession in Egypt, 1854–1956: Modern Infrastructure and Local Economic Development." *Enterprise & Society* 5, no. 1 (March 2004): 107–127.

Pollack, Kenneth M. *Arabs at War: Military Effectivens, 1948–1991.* Lincoln: University of Nebraska Press, 2002.

Population Council. *Survey of Young People in Egypt: Preliminary Report.* February 2010. http://www.popcouncil.org/pdfs/2010PGY_SYPEPrelimReport.pdf.

Posusney, Marsha Pripstein. *Labor and the State in Egypt: Workers, Unions, and Economic Restructuring.* New York: Columbia University Press, 1997.

Povoledo, Elizabetta. "Book Fair's Plans to Honor Israel Lead to Protests." *New York Times.* February 9, 2008.

Powell, Eve Troutt. *A Different Shade of Colonialism: Egypt, Great Britain, and the Mastery of the Sudan.* Berkeley: University of California, 2003.

Project on Middle East Democracy. "Egypt: Al-Dostour Editor Ibrahim Eissa Fired." *The POMED Wire Archives.* October 5, 2010. http://pomed.org/blog/2010/10/egypt-al-dostour-editor-ibrahim-eissa-fired.html/.

———. "Egypt: Are International Monitors Only for Failed States?" *The POMED Wire Archive.* October 19, 2010. http://pomed.org/blog/2010/10/egypt-are-international-monitors-only-for-failed-states.html/.

———. ElBaradei Calls for Election Boycott." *The POMED Wire Archives.* September 7, 2010. http://pomed.org/blog/2010/09/egypt-elbaradei-calls-for-election-boycott.html/.

———. ElBaradei Works to Motivate Diaspora." *The POMED Wire Archives.* October 1, 2010. http://pomed.org/blog/2010/10/egypt-elbaradei-works-to-motivate-diaspora.html/.

———. "Egypt: Brotherhood Behind ElBaradei?" *The POMED Wire Archive.* July 14, 2010. http://pomed.org/blog/2010/07/egypt-brotherhood-behind-elbaradei.html/.

———. "Egypt: Brotherhood Will Contest 30% of Parliament." *The POMED Wire Archive.* October 10, 2010. http://pomed.org/blog/2010/10/egypt-brotherhood-will-contest-30-of-parliament.html/.

———."Egypt Daily Update" e-mail messages. October 25, 27–29, 2010, and November 1–16, 2010 .

———. "Egypt: Brutality Charges for Policemen Involved in Khalid Said's Death." *The POMED Wire Archive.* July 1, 2010. http://pomed.org/blog/2010/07/egypt-brutality-charges-for-policemen-involved-in-khalid-saids-death.html/.

———. "Egypt: Gabr Arrives in DC to Fight Resolution." *The POMED Wire Archives.* September 23, 2010. http://pomed.org/blog/2010/09/egypt-gabr-arrives-in-dc-to-fight-resolution.html/.

———. "Egypt: Mubarak More Television Stations Closed, Possible Facebook Ban." *The POMED Wire Archives.* October 21, 2010. http://pomed.org/

blog/2010/10/egypt-more-television-stations-closed-facebook-ban-possible.
html/.

———. "Egypt: Mubarak Will Likely Reject International Monitors Again." *The POMED Wire Archives*. October 4, 2010. http://pomed.org/blog/2010/10/egypt-mubarak-will-likely-reject-international-monitors-again.html/.

———. "Egypt: New Website Seeks to GOTV." *The POMED Wire Archives*. October 7, 2010. http://pomed.org/blog/2010/10/egypt-new-website-seeks-to-gotv.html/.

———. "Egypt: No Free and Fair Oversight of Elections." *The POMED Wire Archives*. September 27, 2010. http://pomed.org/blog/2010/09/egypt-no-free-and-fair-oversight-of-elections.html/.

———. "Egypt: The 'Boycott-Participation' Divide and International Monitors." *The POMED Wire Archives*. October 25, 2010. http://pomed.org/blog/2010/10/egypt-the-boycott-participation-divide-and-international-monitors.html/.

———. "Egypt: TV Broadcasters Targeted as Media Freedom Rollback Continues." *The POMED Wire Archives*. October 14, 2010. http://pomed.org/blog/2010/10/egypt-tv-broadcasters-targeted-as-media-freedom-rollback-continues.html/.

———. "Egypt: Voter Registration Complete. Wafd Announces 176 Candidates." *The POMED Wire Archive*. October 22, 2010. http://pomed.org/blog/2010/10/egypt-voter-registry-complete-wafd-announces-176-candidates.html/.

———. "The Weekly Wire" e-mail message. November 15, 2010.

Przewroski, Adam. *Democracy and the Market: Political and Economic Reforms in Eastern Europe and Latin America*. New York: Cambridge University Press, 1999.

Public Broadcasting Service. "Newsmaker: El Sayed; A NewsHour with Jim Lehrer Transcript." November 28, 2001. http://www.pbs.org/newshour/bb/middle_east/july-dec01/al_sayed_11-28.html.

———. "Push for Democracy: A NewsHour with Jim Lehrer Transcript." July 11, 2005. http://www.pbs.org/newshour/bb/africa/july-dec05/egypt_7-11.html#.

Quandt, William B. *Camp David: Peacemaking and Politics*. Washington, DC: Brookings Institution Press, 1986.

———. *Decade of Decisions: American Policy Toward the Arab-Israeli Conflict, 1967–1976*. Berkeley: University of California Press, 1977.

———. "Lyndon Johnson and the 1967 War: What Color was the Light?" *Middle East Journal* 46, no. 2 (Spring 1992): 198–228.

———. *Peace Process: American Diplomacy and the Arab-Israeli Conflict*. Berkeley: University of California Press, 1993.

———. *The Middle East: Ten Years After Camp David*. Washington, DC: Brookings Institution Press, 1988.

Quigley, John. "The Legal Status of Jerusalem under International Law." In *The Turkish Yearbook of International Relations: 1994*, vol. 24. 11–23. Ankara, University of Ankara, 1997.

Qutb, Sayyid. *Milestones Along the Way.* Salmiah, Kuwait: International Islamic
    Federation of Student Organizations, 1978.
———. "'The America I Have Seen': In the Scale of Human Values (1951)."
    Translated by Tarek Masoud and Ammar Fakeeh. In *America in an Arab Mirror:
    Images of America in Arabic Travel Literature: An Anthology,* edited by Kamal
    Abdel-Malek. Gordonsville, VA: Palgrave MacMillan, 2000.
Rabin, Yitzhak. *The Rabin Memoirs.* Boston: Little, Brown, 1979.
Rady, Faiza. "The Struggle is One," *Al-Ahram Weekly On-line,* November 8–14,
    2007, http://weekly.ahram.org.eg/2007/870/eg5.htm.
Randal, Jonathan. "King Forms New Cabinet; May Fly to Cairo Summit."
    Washington Post. September 27, 1970.
Reagan, Ronald. *Remarks on East-West Relations at the Brandenburg Gate in West
    Berlin.* June 12, 1987. At Ronald Reagan Presidential Library http://www.reagan.
    utexas.edu/.
Reid, Donald Malcolm. *Cairo University and the Making of Modern Egypt.*
    Cambridge: Cambridge University Press, 1990.
———. "Fu'ad Siraj al-Din and the Egyptian Wafd." *Journal of Contemporary
    History* 15, no. 4 (October 1980): 721–744.
Reidel, Bruce. *The Search for Al Qaeda: Its Leadership, Ideology, and Future.*
    Washington, DC: Brookings Institution Press, 2008.
Reitan, Albert G. *Specialists Factual Report of Investigation: DCA00MA006.* National
    Transportation Safety Board. February 10, 2000. http://www.ntsb.gov/events/
    ea990/docket/Ex_12A.pdf.
Reporters without Borders. "List of the 13 Internet Enemies." November 7, 2006.
    http://en.rsf.org/list-of-the-13-internet-enemies-07-11-2006,19603.
Reuters. "Deadly Sinking: Egypt Ferry Owner Sentenced to Seven Years." *Welt
    Online.* March 11, 2009. http://www.welt.de/english-news/article3358219/
    Egypt-ferry-owner-sentenced-to-seven-years.html?print=true#reqdrucken.
———. "Egypt's Bread Lines Turn Deadly Amid Food Crisis." April 6, 2010.
———. "US Defers Decision on Free Trade Talks with Egypt." *Khaleej Times.*
    January 18, 2006. http://www.khaleejtimes.com/DisplayArticle.asp?xfile=data/
    middleeast/2006/January/middleeast_January456.xml&section=middleeast.
Rice, Condoleezza. *Remarks at the American University in Cairo,* June 20, 2005,
    Department of State Archive: 2002-2009. http://2001-2009.state.gov/secretary/
    rm/2005/48328.htm.
Rice, Condoleezza, and Ahmed Aboul Gheit. *Remarks with Egyptian Foreign
    Minister Ahmed Aboul Gheit After their Meeting in Cairo.* October 6, 2003.
    http://web.archive.org/web/20061101021542/http:/www.state.gov/secretary/
    rm/2006/73525.htm.
Richards, Alan, and John Waterbury. *A Political Economy of the Middle East: State,
    Class, and Economic Development.* Boulder, CO: Westview Press, 1990.
Rizk, Yunan Labib. "*Al-Ahram:* A *Diwan* of Contemporary Life (339): Democracy
    is Born." *Al-Ahram Weekly On-line.* May 25–31, 2000. http://weekly.ahram.org.
    eg/2000/483/chrncls.htm.

———. *"Al-Ahram:* A *Diwan* of Contemporary Life (615): The Making of a King." *Al-Ahram Weekly On-line.* September 29–October 5, 2005. http://weekly.ahram. org.eg/2005/762/chrncls.htm.

———. *"Al-Ahram:* A *Diwan* of Contemporary Life (629): Shaky at the Helm." *Al-Ahram Weekly On-line.* February 16–22, 2006. http://weekly.ahram.org. eg/2006/782/chrncls.htm.

Robins, Philip. *A History of Jordan.* Cambridge: Cambridge University Press, 2004.

Robinson, Richard D. *The First Turkish Republic: A Case Study in National Development.* Cambrdige, MA: Harvard University Press, 1963.

Rodenbeck, Max. *Cairo: The City Victorious.* New York: Vintage Books, 2000.

Rogan, Eugene. *The Arabs: A History.* New York: Basic Books, 2009.

Ross, Russell R., and Andrea Matles Savada, eds. *Sri Lanka: A Country Study.* Country Studies/Area Handbook Series. Washington, DC: U.S. Government Priting Office, 1990.

Rubin, Barry. "Muslim Broterhood Declare War on America: Will America Notice?" *The Rubin Report* (blog). October 7, 2010. http://rubinreports.blogspot. com/2010/10/muslim-brotherhood-declares-war-on.html.

Rutherford, Bruce K. *Egypt after Mubarak: Liberalism, Islam, and Democracy in the Arab World.* Princeton, NJ: Princeton University Press, 2008.

Sabini, John. *Islam: A Primer.* Rev. ed. Washington, DC: Middle East Editorial Associates, 1990.

Sachar, Howard M. *Egypt and Israel.* New York: Richard Marek Publishers, 1981.

———. *A History of Israel: From the Rise of Zionism to Our Time.* New York: Alfred A. Knopf, 1993.

Sachs, Susan. "Egypt Clears Rights Activist Whose Jailing Drew World Protest." *New York Times.* March 19, 2003.

Sadat, Anwar el. *Address by the UAR President Designate, Anwar el Sadat, Before the National Assembly.* October 7, 1970. At Anwar Sadat Chair for Peace and Development [ASCPD]. http://www.sadat.umd.edu/archives/ speeches%5CAADV%20Speech%20to%20NatlAssemb%2010.7.70pdf.pdf.

———. *Address to the Nation.* January 13, 1972. At ASCPD. http://www.sadat.umd. edu/archives/speeches/BACA%20Address%20to%20the%20Nation%201.13.72. PDF.

———. *Address to the Naval Officers.* June 22, 1971. At ASCPD. http://www.sadat. umd.edu/archives/speeches/BACI%20Speech%20to%20Naval%20Officers%20 6.22.71.PDF.

———. *In Search of Identity: An Autobiography.* New York: Harper Colophon Books, 1979.

———. *Speech by President Mohamed Anwar Sadat before the National Assembly.* February 4, 1971. http://sadat.bibalex.org/sadatdata/Sadat-Speech- Files/19710204.html. [In Arabic]

———. *Speeches and Interviews by President Mohamed Anwar El Sadat on the Occasion of his Visit to Jerusalem.* Cairo: State Information Service, 1978.

————. *Statement to the Nation by President Anwar el Sadat.* September 16, 1971. http://sadat.bibalex.org/sadatdata/Sadat-Speech-Files/S19.htm.

Sadat, Jehan el. *A Woman of Egypt.* New York: Simon & Schuster, 1987.

Sadek, George, "Egypt: Supreme Administrative Court Rules Parliamentary Elections Void" Library of Congress, December 21, 2010. http://www.loc.gov/lawweb/servlet/lloc_news?disp3_l205402430_text.

Sadowski, Yahya M. *Political Vegetables? Businessman and Bureaucrat in the Development of Egyptian Agriculture.* Washington, DC: Brookings Institution Press, 1991.

Safran, Nadav. *Israel: The Embattled Ally.* Cambridge, MA: Belknap Press of Harvard University Press, 1982.

Sageman, Marc. *Understanding Terror Networks.* Philadelphia: University of Pennsylvania Press, 2004.

Said, Summer. "Unmaking Monopolies." *Business Today Egypt.* October 2004. http://businesstodayegypt.com/article.aspx?ArticleID=2415.

Sakr, Hala. "'It Did Not Fail.'" *Al-Ahram Weekly On-line.* July 18–24, 2002. http://weekly.ahram.org.eg/2002/595/sc13.htm.

Salah, Tarek, and Nesma Abdel Qader. "Brotherhood Begins E-Campaign to Collect NAC Signatures." *Al-Masry Al-Youm.* July 9, 2010. http://www.almasry-alyoum.com/en/news/brotherhood-begins-e-campaign-collect-nac-signatures.

Saleh, Heba. "Egypt Ferry Probe Raps Officials." BBC News. April 19, 2006. http://news.bbc.co.uk/2/hi/middle_east/4924802.stm.

————. "Egypt Weighs Cost of Daily Bread." *Financial Times.* March 8, 2008. http://www.thefinancialexpress-bd.com/more.php?news_id=27734.

————. "Egyptians Hit by Rising Food Prices." BBC News. March 11, 2008. http://news.bbc.co.uk/2/hi/middle_east/7288196.stm.

————. "Storm over Egypt's Israeli Links." *Financial Times.* October 14, 2009. http://www.ft.com/cms/s/0/b4b7d814-b859-11de-8ca9-00144feab49a.html#axzz1B1WkGBi1.

Salem, Ali. *A Drive to Israel: An Egyptian Meets his Neighbors.* Tel Aviv: Tel Aviv University, 1994.

————. "My Drive to Israel." *Middle East Quarterly* 9, no. 1(Winter 2002): 45–52.

Sami, Aziza. "At Every Corner." *Al-Ahram Weekly On-line.* August 26–September 1, 2004. http://weekly.ahram.org.eg/2004/705/pr1.htm.

Sawaf, Hassan el. "Is a Fourth Term Right?" *Civil Society* 8, no. 93 (September 1999): 30–31.

Sayigh, Yezid. *Armed Struggle and the Search for State: The Palestinian National Movement, 1949–1993.* Oxford: Oxford University Press, 1999.

Scalapino, Robert A. "Democratizing Dragons: South Korea and Taiwan." *Journal of Democracy* 4, no. 3 (July 1993): 70–83.

"Scenes for a Sit-in." *Baheyya* (blog). December 6, 2007. http://baheyya.blogspot.com/2007_12_01_archive.html.

Sderot Media Center. "What You Need to Know about Kassams." May 25, 2009. http://sderotmedia.org.il/bin/content.cgi?ID=388&q=6&s=16.

Seale, Patrick. *Asad: The Struggle for the Middle East*. Berkeley: University of California Press, 1988.

———. *The Struggle for Syria: A Study of Post-War Arab Politics, 1945–1958*. London: Oxford University Press, 1965.

Secretary-General, The. *Notes from Secretary General's Meetings in Cairo, 24 May 1967 with President Nasser and Foreign Minister Mahmoud Riad, UAR*. Container S-0865-0001: Peacekeeping Operations Files of the Secretary General: U Thant-Middle East. May 24, 1967.

———. *Report by the Secretary-General, delieverd to the Security Council*. U.N. Doc. S/7906. May 26, 1967.

Semeika, Mohsen, and Mohamed Talaat Dawod. "NDP's Pro-Gamal Mubarak Candidates Banned From Parliamentary Polls." *Al-Masry Al-Youm*. November 8, 2010. http://www.almasryalyoum.com/en/news/ndps-pro-gamal-mubarak-candidates-banned-parliamentary-polls.

Shadid, Anthony. "Apathy Makrs Constitutional Vote in Egypt." *Washington Post*. March 27, 2007.

Shahin, Emad Eldin. "Muhammad Rashid Rida's Perspectives on the West as Reflected in al Manar." *The Muslim World* 72, no.2 (April 1989): 113–132.

Shahine, Gihan. "Labour Market Blues." *Al-Ahram Weekly On-line*. October 23–29, 2003. http://weekly.ahram.org.eg/2003/661/eg7.htm.

Shalakany, Amr. "'I Heard It All Before': Egyptian Tales of Law and Development." *Third World Quarterly* 27, no. 5 (2006): 833–853.

Sharabi, Hisham. "Prelude to War." In *The Arab-Israeli Confrontation of June 1967: An Arab Perspective*, edited by Ibrahim Abu-Lughod. Evanston, IL: Northwestern University Press, 1970.

Sharp, Jeremy M. *Egypt: Background and U.S. Relations*. Congressional Research Service. September 2, 2009. http://www.fas.org/sgp/crs/mideast/RL33003.pdf.

Shazly, Saad el. *The Crossing of the Suez*. San Francisco: American Mideast Research, 1980.

Shehab, Shaden. "The Cabinet's New Look." *Al-Ahram Weekly On-line*. July 15–21, 2004. http://weekly.ahram.org.eg/2004/699/eg1.htm.

Shehata, Samer, and Joshua Stacher. "The Brotherhood Goes to Parliament." *Middle East Report* 240 (Fall 2006). http://www.merip.org/mer/mer240/shehata_stacher.html.

Shenker, Jack. "Sadat's Daughter to Sue over Claims He Poisoned Nasser." *Guardian*. September 20, 2010. http://www.guardian.co.uk/world/2010/sep/20/egypt-president-murder-claim-lawsuit.

Shenon, Philip. "U.S. Accuses 2 Egyptian Colonels in Plot to Smuggle Missile Material." *New York Times*. June 25, 1988.

Shepard, William E. "Sayyid Qutb's Doctrine of Jahiliyya." *International Journal of Middle East Studies* 35, no. 4 (November 2003): 521–545.

Sherbinil, Ramadan al. "Author Sues Israeli Centre for Pirating Book." GulfNews. com. October 31, 2010. http://gulfnews.com/news/region/egypt/author-sues-israeli-centre-for-pirating-book-1.704176.

Shlaim, Avi. *Lion of Jordan: The Life of King Hussein in War and Peace*. New York: Vintage Books, 2007.

Singerman, Diane. *Avenues of Participation: Family, Politics, and Networks in Urban Quarters of Cairo*. Princeton, NJ: Princeton University Press, 1995.

Sivan, Emmanuel. *Radical Islam: Medieval Theology and Modern Politics*. Enlarged ed. New Haven, CT: Yale University Press, 1990.

Six Day War (5–10 June 1967). In *Ground Warfare: An International Encyclopedia*, edited by Stanley Sandler. Vol. 3. Santa Barbara, CA: ABC-CLIO, 2002.

Slackman, Michael. "Assault on Women at Protest Stirs Anger, Not Fear, in Egypt." *New York Times*. June 10, 2005.

Slackman, Michael, and Mona El-Naggar. "Calls in Egypt for ElBaradei to Seek Presidency." *New York Times*. February 19, 2010.

Smith, Charles D. "4 February 1942: Its Causes and Its Influence on Egyptian Politics and on the Future of Anglo-Egyptian Relations, 1937–1945." *International Journal of Middle East Studies* 10, no. 4 (November 1979): 453–479.

———. "The 'Crisis of Orientation': The Shift of Egyptian Intellectuals to Islamic Subjects in the 1930s." *International Journal of Middle East Studies* 4, no. 4 (October 1973): 382–410.

Smith, Henrick. "Anti-Nasser Plot by Military Men Reported Foiled." *New York Times*. August 29, 1967.

———. "U.S. Chides Israelis on Settler Program." *New York Times*. September 27, 1967.

Smith, Lee. "Silencing the Dissent." *Weekly Standard*. September 27, 2009. http://www.weeklystandard.com/Content/Public/Articles/000/000/017/015wxijy.asp.

Smith, Terence. "U.S. Officials See Period of Instability in Mideast." *New York Times*. September 28, 1970.

Smolansky, O.M. "Moscow and the Suez Crisis, 1956: A Reappraisal." *Political Science Quarterly* 80, no. 4 (December 1965): 581–605.

Soage, Ana Belén. "Islamism and Modernity: The Political Thought of Sayyid Qutb." *Totalitarian Movements and Political Religions* 10, no. 2 (June 2009): 189–203.

Sobhi, Samir. "Obituary: Hussein El-Shafei (1918–2005)." *Al-Ahram Weekly On-line*. November 24–30, 2005. http://weekly.ahram.org.eg/2005/770/eg12.htm.

Sorenson, David S. *An Introduction to the Modern Middle East: History, Religion, Political Economy, Politics*. Boulder, CO: Westview Press, 2008.

Sorour, Fathi. "The Newsreel Digest." *Egypt Today*. April 2005. December 10, 2010. http://www.egypttoday.com/article.aspx?ArticleID=4843.

Spencer, Robert. "Muslim Brotherhood Jockeys for Power in Egypt." *Human Events: Jihad Watch* (blog). July 27, 2010. http://www.humanevents.com/article.php?id=38250.

Springborg, Robert. "The President and the Field Marshal: Civil Military Relations in Egypt Today," *Middle East Report* 147 (July–August 1987).

Stacher, Joshua A. "Post-Islamist Rumblings in Egypt: The Emergence of the Wasat Party." *Middle East Journal* 56, no. 3 (Summer 2002): 415–432.

Stack, Liam. "Food Crisis: A Daily Quest for Bread in Cairo." *Christian Science Monitor*. June 6, 2008.

Stayer, Robert W. *Why Did the Soviet Union Collapse?: Understanding Historical Change*. Armonk, NY: M.E. Sharpe, 1998.

Stein, Ewan. "What Does the Gama'a Islamiyya Want Now?" *Middle Eat Report* 254 (Spring 2010): 40–44.

Stephens, Robert H. *Nasser: A Political Biography*. New York: Simon & Schuster, 1971.

Sterling, Brent L. *Do Good Fences Make Good Neighbor?: What History Teaches Us About Strategic Barriers and International Security*. Washington, DC: Georgetown University Press, 2009.

Stilt, Kristen. "'Islam is the Solution': Constitutional Visions of the Egyptian Muslim Brotherhood." *Texas International Law Journal* 63, no. 73 (Fall 2010): 74–108.

Stock, Raymond. "Very, Very Lost in Translation." *Foreign Policy* (September/October 2009).

Sullivan, Denis J., and Kimberly Jones. *Global Security Watch: Egypt; A Reference Handbook*. Westport, CT: Praeger Security International, 2008.

Sullivan, Denis J., and Sana Abed-Kotob. *Islam in Contemporary Egypt: Civil Society vs. the State*. Boulder, CO: Lynne Rienner, 1999.

Symons, M. Travers. *Britain and Egypt: The Rise of Egyptian Nationalism*. Southampton, UK: Camelot Press, 1925.

Takeyh, Ray. *The Origins of the Eisenhower Doctrine: The US, Britain, and Nasser's Egypt, 1953–1957*. New York: St. Martin's Press, 2000.

Tal, David. *War In Palestine, 1948: Strategy and Diplomacy*. New York: Routledge, 2004.

Talhami, Ghada Hashem. *The Mobilization of Muslim Women in Egypt*. Gainesville: University Press of Florida, 1996.

Taylor, Julie. "Prophet Sharing: Strategic Interaction between Muslim Clerics and Middle Eastern Regimes." *Journal of Islamic Law and Culture* 10, no. 1 (April 2008): 41–62.

Terry, Janice J. *The Wafd, 1919–1952: Cornerstone of Egyptian Political Power*. London: Third World Centre, 1982.

Tessler, Mark A. *A History of the Israeli-Palestinian Conflict*. Bloomington: Indiana University Press, 1994.

"The U.S. Economic Assistance Program to Egypt: FY 2011 and Beyond." *Foreign Policy*. August 17, 2009. http://www.foreignpolicy.com/files/fp_uploaded_documents/100512_USEconomicAssistance.pdf.

Time. "Middle East: The Camel Driver." March 29, 1963.

———. "Middle East: Osman the Efficient." July 13, 1970.

———. "Middle East: A Watershed Week for Egypt's Sadat." June 9, 1975.

Trager, Eric. "A Tale of Two Parties." *Foreign Policy*. November 18, 2010. http://www.foreignpolicy.com/articles/2010/11/18/a_tale_of_two_parties.

Tsebelis, George. *Nested Games: Rational Choice in Comparative Politics*. Berkeley: University of California, 1990.

Tucker, Richard P. "Containing Communism by Impounding Rivers: American Strategic Interests and the Global Spread of High Dams in the Early Cold War." In *Environmental Histories of the Cold War*, edited by J.R. McNeill and Corinna R. Unger, 139–166. Cambridge: Cambridge University Press, 2010.

United Nations. "Key Issues in a Permanent Settlement." United Nations Information System on the Question of Palestine [UNISPAL]. http://unispal.un.org/unispal.nsf/iss.htm?OpenForm. (Accessed January 6, 2011.)

———. "Middle East—UNEF 1: Facts and Figures." http://www.un.org/en/peacekeeping/missions/past/unef1facts.html. *(Accessed January 5, 2011.)*

———. "Security Council Resolutions -1981." http://www.un.org/Docs/scres/1981/scres81.htm. (Accessed December 1, 2010.)

———. "Special Sessions." http://www.un.org/en/ga/sessions/special.shtml. (Accessed January 4, 2011.)

———. *Statistical Yearbook* 1953. U.N. Sales No. 1953-XVII-9.

———. *Statistical Yearbook* 1955. U.N. Stat. Y.B., U.N. Sales No. 1957-XVII-10.

———. *Statistical Yearbook* 1957. U.N. Stat. Y.B., U.N. Sales No. 1957-XVII-1.

———. *Statistical Yearbook* 1961. U.N. Stat. Y.B., U.N. Sales No. 62-XVII-1.

———. *Statistical Yearbook* 1963. U.N. Stat. Y.B., U.N. Sales No. 64.XVII.1.

———. *Statistical Yearbook* 1965. U.N. Stat. Y.B., U.N. Sales No. 66.XVII.1.

U.N. Development Program. "Arab Political Parties Database: Egypt: The New Wafd Party." Program on Governance in the Arab Region. http://www.arabparliaments.org/whatwedo/parties.aspx?cid=5&pid=62.

———. "Egypt: Law on Non-Governmental Organizations (2002)." Program on Governance in the Arab Region. http://www.undp-pogar.org/countries/theme.aspx?t=2&cid=5.

———. *Egyptian Counterterrorism and Political Reform Act*. H.R. Res 696. 111th Cong. (2009).

———. *Egyptian Counterterrorism and Political Reform Act*. H.R. 2977, 110th Cong. (2007).

———. *Egyptian Counterterrorism and Political Reform Act*. H.R. 696, 111th Cong. (2009).

———. "Final Vote Results for Roll Call 398." October 24, 2001. At the Office of the Clerk http://clerk.house.gov/.

———. *Foreign Relations Authorization Act, Fiscal Years 2006 and 2007*. H.R. 2601, 109th Cong. § 1021 (2005).

———. Report Together with Minority Views to Accompany H.R. 2764. H. R. Res. No. 110-197 (2007).

———. Report of the Committee on Rules to Accompany H.Res. 878. H. R. Rep. No. 110-497 (2007).Providing for the consideration of the Senate amendment to the bill (H.R. 2764) making appropriations for the Department of State, foreign operations, and related programs for the fiscal year ending September 30, 2008, and for other purposes. H.R. Res. 878. 110th Cong. (2007)U.S. Congress.

House. Committee on Foreign Affairs. *Report of a Staff Study Mission to Egypt, Syria, Jordan, the West Bank, and Gaza.* 96th Cong., 1979, Committee Print.

———. *Results of Referendum on Amending Article 76 of the Constitution—Egypt.* Program on Governance in the Arab Region. May 25, 2005. http://www.pogar. org/publications/elections/results/referenda/egypt-2005-e.pdf.United Nations Security Council. Resolution 242 of November 22, 1967., http://domino.un.org/ unispal.NSF/796f8bc05ec4f30885256cef0073cf3a/7d35e1f729df491c85256ee7006 86136.U.S. Congress. House. *Consolidated Appropriations Act of 2005.* H.R. 4818. 108th Cong. H. Amdt. 694 (2004).

———. *The Department of State, Foreign Operations and Related Programs Appropriations Act, 2008.* H.R. 2764, 110th Cong. (as reported by House, June 17, 2007).

———. *The Department of State, Foreign Operations and Related Programs Appropriations Act, 2008.* H.R. 2764, 110th Cong. (as reported by Senate, July 10, 2007).

U.S. Congress. Senate. S. Res. 586, 111th Cong. (2010).

———. "U.S. Senate Roll Call Votes 107th Congress—1st Session." October 25, 2001. http://www.senate.gov/legislative/LIS/roll_call_lists/roll_call_vote_cfm. cfm?congress=107&session=1&vote=00313.

U.S. Department of Agriculture. "Public Law 480, Title I." Foreign Agricultural Service. http://www.fas.usda.gov/excredits/foodaid/pl480/pl480.asp. (Accessed December 27, 2010.)

U.S. Department of State. *2008 Human Rights Report: Egypt.* February 25, 2009. http://www.state.gov/g/drl/rls/hrrpt/2008/nea/119114.htm.

———. *2009 Human Rights Report: Egypt.* March 11, 2010. http://www.state.gov/g/ drl/rls/hrrpt/2009/nea/136067.htm.

———. "Background Note: Egypt." November 10, 2010. http://www.state.gov/r/pa/ ei/bgn/5309.htm.

———. "Biography: Francis J. Ricciardone, Jr." September 8, 2005. http://web. archive.org/web/20071010070656/http:/www.state.gov/r/pa/ei/biog/52768.htm.

———. "Fact Sheet on Civil Society & Democracy Promotion in Egypt." Middle East Partnership Initiative. Fall 2010.

———. "Middle East Partnership Initiative: History." Department of State Archive: 2002-2009. http://2002-2009-mepi.state.gov/c10130.htm. (Accessed December 15, 2010.)

———. "OPEC Oil Embargo, 1973–1974." *Milestones: 1969–1976.* Office of the Historian. http://history.state.gov/milestones/1969-1976/OPEC.

———. "Settlement Activity in the Israeli Occupied Territories." 1991. Quoted in "Settlement Activity, 1967–1990." Foundation for Middle East Peace. http:// www.fmep.org/settlement_info/settlement-info-and-tables/stats-data/ settlement-activity-1967-1990. (Accessed December 1, 2010.)

U.S. Food Aid and Security. "Food for Peace." Food Aid Programs. http://foodaid. org/food-aid-programs/food-for-peace/. (Accessed December 27, 2010.)

U.S. National Commission on Terrorist Attacks Upon the United States. *The 9/11 Commission Report: Final Report of the National Commission on Terrorist Attacks upon the United States.* Washington, DC: Government Printing Office, 2004. http://www.gpoaccess.gov/911/pdf/fullreport.pdf.

U.S. National Transportation Safety Board. *Aircraft Accident Brief: NTSB/AAB-02/01 (PB2002-910401); EgyptAir Flight 990, Boeing 767-336ER, SU-GAP, 60 Miles South of Nantucket, Massachusetts, October 31, 1999.* Adopted March 13, 2002. http://www.ntsb.gov/publictn/2002/AAB0201.pdf.

———. *EgyptAir Flight 990, October 31, 1999: Reports and Other Investigative Material for the Docket.* March 21, 2002. http://www.ntsb.gov/events/ea990/docket/EAContents.htm.

———. *Group Chairman's Factual Report: Air Traffic Control Group, NTSB Identification: DCA00MA006.* January 13, 2000. http://www.ntsb.gov/events/ea990/docket/Ex_3A.pdf.

U.S. Office of the U.S. Trade Representative. "United States and the Republic of Korea Sign Landmark Free Trade Agreement." June 30, 2007. http://web.archive.org/web/20080527150515/http://www.ustr.gov/Document_Library/Press_Releases/2007/June/United_States_the_Republic_of_Korea_Sign_Lmark_Free_Trade_Agreement.html.

Vaïsse, Maurice. "France and the Suez Crisis." In *Suez 1956: The Crisis and its Consequences,* edited by William Roger Louis and Roger Owen. New York: Oxford University Press, 1991.

Vatikiotis, P.J. *The Egyptian Army in Politics: Pattern for New Nations?* Bloomington: Indiana University Press, 1961.

———. *The History of Modern Egypt: From Muhammad Ali to Mubarak.* 4th ed. Baltimore: The Johns Hopkins University Press, 1991.

Vitalis, Robert. *When Capitalists Collide: Business Conflict and the End of Empire in Egypt.* Berkeley: University of California Press, 1995.

Voll, John O. "Unity of the Nile Valley: Identity and Regional Integration." *Journal of Africa Studies* 3, no. 2 (Summer 1976): 205.

Wahish, Niveen. "Forget Unemployment." *Al-Ahram Weekly On-line.* March 26–April 1, 2009. http://weekly.ahram.org.eg/2005/770/eg12.htm.

———. "Hossam Badrawi: Physician, Parliamentarian, Perfectionist; A Great Many Hats to Wear." *Al-Ahram Weekly On-line.* June 19–25, 2003. http://weekly.ahram.org.eg/2003/643/profile.htm.

Wald, Matthew L. "Many Theories on Final Climb of Doomed Jet." *New York Times.* November 5, 1999.

Wald, Matthew L., and David Johnston. "F.B.I. May Be Asked to Take Over Case of EgyptAir Crash." *New York Times.* November 16, 1999.

Wall, Irwin M. *The United States and the Making of Postwar France, 1945–1954.* Cambridge: Cambridge University Press, 1991.

Walz, Jay. "Nasser Starts Construction of Aswan Dam on the Nile." *New York Times.* January 10, 1960.

Warburg, Gabriel R. *Egypt and the Sudan: Studies in History and Politics.* London: Frank, 1985.

Washington Post. "Clinton's Silence on Egyptian Democracy." November 11, 2010.

———. "Interview with Secretary of State Condoleezza Rice." March 25, 2005. http://www.washingtonpost.com/wp-dyn/articles/A2015-2005Mar25.html.

Waterbury, John. *The Egypt of Nasser and Sadat: The Political Economy of Two Regimes.* Princeton, NJ: Princeton University Press, 1983.

———. *Exposed to Innumerable Delusions: Public Enterprise and State Power in Egypt, India, Mexico, and Turkey.* New York: Cambridge University Press, 1993.

Weaver, Mary Anne. "Pharaohs-in-Waiting." *Atlantic Monthly* (October 2003).

Weinbaum, Marvin. "Politics and Dvelopment in Foreign Aid: U.S. Economic Assistance to Egypt, 1975–1982," *Middle East Journal* 37, no. 4 (Autumn 1983): 636–655.

Whitaker, Brian. "Crew Accused over Egypt Ferry Disaster." *Guardian.* February 6, 2006. http://www.guardian.co.uk/world/2006/feb/06/egypt.travelnews1.

Wickham, Carrie Rosefsky. *Mobilizing Islam: Religion, Activism, and Political Change in Egypt.* New York: Columbia University Press, 2002.

———. "The Muslim Brotherhood After Mubarak." *Foreign Affairs.* February 3, 2011. http://www.foreignaffairs.com/articles/67348/carrie-rosefsky-wickham/the-muslim-brotherhood-after-mubarak.

———. "The Path to Moderation: Strategy and Learning in the Formation of Egypt's Wasat Pary." *Comparative Politics* 36, no. 2 (January 2004): 205–228.

Wiktorowicz, Quintan. "Anatomy of the Salafi Movement." *Studies in Conflict and Terrorism* 29, no. 3 (April/May 2006): 207–239.

———, ed. *Islamic Activism: A Social Movement Theory Approach.* Bloomington: Indiana University Press, 2004.

———. *The Management of Islamic Activism: Salafis, the Muslim Brotherhood, and State Power in Jordan.* Albany: State University of New York Press, 2001.

Wittes, Tamara Cofman. *Freedom's Unsteady March: America's Role in Building Arab Democracy.* Washington, DC: Brookings Institution Press, 2008.

Wittes, Tamara Cofman, and Andrew Masloski. "Democracy Promotion under Obama: Lessons from the Middle East Partnership Initiative." *Middle East Memo* 13 (May 2009). http://www.brookings.edu/~/media/Files/rc/papers/2009/05_democracy_promotion_wittes/05_democracy_promotion_wittes.pdf.

———. "Data: Egypt, Arab Rep." http://data.worldbank.org/country/egypt-arab-republic. (Accessed December 22, 2010.)

———. "Data: Egypt, Arap Rep.; Unemployment in Egypt." http://data.worldbank.org/country/egypt-arab-republic. (Accessed October 23, 2010.)

World Bank. "Egypt: Annual Population Growth, 1977." http://databank.worldbank.org/. (Accessed December 15, 2010.)

———. "World Bank Development Indicators." December 2010. http://data.worldbank.org/data-catalog/world-development-indicators.

Wren, Christopher S. "Arabic Speakers Dispute Inquiry's Interpretation of Pilot's Words." *New York Times.* November 18, 1999.

———. "Ignoring Foes, Cairo Moves ahead on Parley to Prepare Geneva Talks." *New York Times*. December 2, 1977.

———. "Israeli Embassy Opens Quietly in Cairo." *New York Times*. February 19, 1980.

Wright, Lawrence. *The Looming Tower: al Qaeda and the Road to 9/11*. New York: Vintage Books, 2006.

———. "The Man behind Bin Laden," *New Yorker*. September 16, 2002.

Ynetnews. "Report: Settlements Polluting West Bank Streams." June 28, 2009. http://www.ynetnews.com/articles/0,7340,L-3738100,00.html.

"YouTube, Yahoo Censor Human Rights Blogger." *Pajamadeen* (blog). November 30, 2007. http://www.pajamadeen.com/tag/wael-abbas.

Zayyat, Montasser al. *The Road to Al-Qaeda: The Story of Bin Laden's Right-Hand Man*. Edited by Sara Nimis. Translated by Ahmed Fekry. Sterling, VA: Pluto Press, 2002.

Zollner, Barbara H.E. "Prison Talk: The Muslim Brotherhood's Internal Struggle During Gamal Abdel Nasser's Persecution, 1954 to 1971." *International Journal of Middle East Studies* 39, no. 3 (August 2007): 411–433.

———. *The Muslim Brotherhood: Hasan al-Hudaybi and Ideology*. New York: Routledge, 2009.

Index

Amer, Abdel Hakim, 41, 51, 56, 76, 100–101, 104, 111, 116

Amer, Tarek al, 170

American Israel Public Affairs Committee, 222

Anglo-Egyptian Treaty of 1936, 25–26, 30, 36, 41, 58. *See also* British-Egyptian relations

Anwar, Adel, 210

Apache, 174

April 6 Youth Movement, 200, 277, 279, 292, 299

Arab Contractors Company, 112

Arab-Israeli peace negotiations
  bilateral Israeli-Egyptian contacts, 147–49, 150, 151
  Camp David Accords, 148–51
  Carter administration policies, 142, 144–45, 148–49, 150
  Egypt-Israel peace treaty, 149–50, 151, 162, 219, 230–31, 232
  Geneva peace conferences, 143, 144–45
  Hebron accord, 163
  Johnson administration policies, 95
  Jordan-Israel peace treaty, 164
  Madrid conference, 162, 237
  Mubarak and, 162–63
  Muslim Brotherhood views, 236–37
  Nasser and, 109
  normalization of Egyptian-Israeli relations, 151–52
  Oslo Accords, 163, 164, 239
  Rogers Initiative, 109, 127, 320n3
  Rogers Plan, 320n4
  Sadat and, 121–22, 142–43, 144, 145–48, 230, 233
  Security Council Resolution 242, 109, 147, 148–49
  settlement construction issue, 148, 149
  Sinai I agreement (1974), 143–44
  territory gained in Six Day War, 95
  U.S. role, 95, 144–45, 148–51

Arab League, 95, 151

Arab nationalism, 72, 73–74, 98. *See also* pan-Arabism

Arab Organization for Human Rights, 263

Arab Socialist Organization, 139–40

Arab Socialist Union (ASU), 51, 81, 106, 113–14, 121, 122–23, 139–40

Arab summits, 145

Arafat, Yasser, 110, 142, 163

Arif, Galal, 261–62

Assad, Hafez al, 204

Assassinations
  attempts on Mubarak, 165, 204
  attempts on Nahhas, 35, 36, 116
  attempts on Nasser, 60–61, 64, 82, 116–17
  of al Banna, 36
  of Mahir, 32, 35
  of Nuqrashi, 36, 53
  of Sadat, 155–56, 157, 158, 165, 246

ASU. *See* Arab Socialist Union

Aswan High Dam, 66–67, 68, 112, 215–16

Aswany, Alaa al, 248

Atta, Mohammad, 227, 245

Authoritarianism
  stability, 250, 251, 252, 257, 270
  U.S. foreign policy and, 250–52, 255

authoritarianism in Egypt
  in 1930s, 25
  development, 5, 62–63
  institutionalization of regime, 62–63
  under Nasser, 112
  persistence, 106
  U.S. acceptance, 6, 251, 262–63, 269–70

Azhar al, 26, 28, 78, 126, 151, 165, 245

Azzam, Abdallah, 245

Ba'athism, 73, 74, 76–77

Badawi, al, al Sayed, 279

Badr, Amr, 180

ElBaradei, Mohammed
  demonstrations of 2011 and, 289
  editorials, 198, 275
  presidential candidacy, 206–7, 208, 299
  return to Egypt, 206, 275–76
  statements on transition, 300
  See also National Association for
    Change
elections
  constitutional referenda, 299, 301
  Consultative Council, 275, 290
  fraud, 186, 190, 226, 271, 278–79,
    290
  Legislative Assembly, 19
  local, 189, 330n54
  monitoring, 190, 192, 226, 278, 287,
    297–98
elections, People's Assembly
  of 1976, 139–40
  of 1979, 151
  of 1987, 236, 330n52
  of 2005, 189, 190, 278
  of 2006, 226
  of 2010, 271, 276–79, 287
  boycotts, 276–77, 330n52
  parallel, 277
elections, presidential
  candidates in 2011, 299, 300
  multiparty, 168, 173, 184–86, 264
  referenda, 118, 157, 168–69
  requirements for independent
    candidates, 185
elites, 2–4, 179–81, 183–84, 199
Emergency Law, 82, 106, 190–91, 192,
  234, 299
employment policies, 79, 118, 138
  See also labor
Enan, Sami, 167, 286
Erdoğan, Recep Tayyip, 243
Erskine, George, 37
Ethiopia, African Union summit, 204
European Commission, 258–59
exchange rates
  on black market, 328n25

  floating, 177–78, 328n25
  managed peg, 176–77
  overvaluation, 121
  unifying, 160
expatriates, 274–75, 292
Ezz, Ahmed, 291

Facebook, 282, 291
Faeq, Mohammed, 263
Fahmy, Ismail, 142–43, 235
Fahmy, Mohammed Ali, 151
Fahmy, Nabil, 203, 214–15, 225, 289
Faluja, 9–10, 35
Farouk, King
  British and, 30–31, 32–33
  exile, 39, 52
  Free Officers and, 37–38
  Muslim Brotherhood and, 29
  Palestine war (1948), 9
  Sadat and, 116
  son, 55
  Wafd and, 26, 30–31
fascism, 26
Fathi, Reda, 225–26
Fawzi, Mohammed, 97, 113, 114, 119,
  120, 122, 123, 322n26
FCGFETU. *See* Founding Committee
  for a General Federation of Egyptian
  Trade Unions
Feingold, Russ, 234
ferry sinking, 182–83
Fiqi, Mustafa el, 291
Foda, Farag, 165
Food for Peace program, 217–19
food imports, 141, 217–19
Ford, Gerald, 144
foreign direct investment, 137–38, 174,
  177
Foreign Ministry, 225, 235
foreign policy
  Arab rivalries, 75, 96
  estrangement from other Arab states,
    151–52, 161
  in future, 244

renunciation of violence, 326–27n12

terrorist attacks, 165, 166–67, 204, 252

Zawahiri and, 167, 327n13

Gamasy, Mohammed Abdel Ghani el, 119–20, 127, 141–42, 150–51, 235

Gaza Strip

blockade, 233, 238, 243

border with Egypt, 221, 224, 227, 233, 243

Hamas control, 224, 243

Israeli settlements, 148, 164, 335n46

negotiations over, 148, 149, 150

self-government, 150

Shalit capture, 205

United Nations Emergency Force, 97

See also Palestinians

General Federation of Egyptian Trade Unions (GFETU), 179

General Intelligence Service, 204, 205, 282, 290

GFETU. *See* General Federation of Egyptian Trade Unions

Ghad Party, al, 185, 242, 277, 279

Ghales, Murad, 235

Ghonim, Wael, 290–92, 295

Golan Heights, 94, 144, 232

Gomaa, Noman, 185

Google, 290–91, 292

Gorst, Sir Eldon, 19

Green Shirts, 26

Group of Eight, 264

Gulf emirates, 75

Gulf War (1991), 161, 162, 248, 251–52, 303, 326n7

Guma, Sharawi, 113, 114, 119, 120, 122, 123

Habashy, Ahmad el, 210, 212–13

Habib, Mohammed el Sayed, 237–38

Hadi, Ibrahim Abd al, 36, 53, 57

Hamalawy, Hossam el, 195

Hamas, 190, 224, 243, 265–66

Harb, Osama Ghazali, 276–77

Harriri, Abu El Ezz el, 260

Hassanein, Medhat, 177

Hatem, 274–75, 292

Hatshepsut, Temple of, 166–67

Hawass, Zahi, 180

Heikal, Mohammed Hassanein, 116, 117, 136

Heliopolis earthquake, 165–66

High Election Commission, 190, 278, 290

hijackings, 109–10

Hilal, Ali Eddin, 277

Hilali, Nagib al, 37, 38

Hitler, Adolf, 115

Hizballah, 242

hotels, 77–78, 175, 179–80, 284

Hourani, Albert, 18

housing, 181–82, 272–73

Housni, Ahmad, 46

Howeidy, Fahmi, 289

Hudaybi, Hassan al

Free Officers and, 49, 53, 57–58, 60

imprisonments, 57–58, 82, 90

Qutb and, 91, 249

rivals, 46

as supreme guide, 46, 91, 125–26

view of Israel, 236

Hudaybi, Maamoun al, 262, 266

human rights

Carter administration policies, 251

violations, 253, 323n36

human rights organizations, 200, 230, 263, 264, 265

Hungary, 70

Husayn, Taha, 84

Hussein, Kemal al Din, 10, 35, 40, 152

Hussein, King, 94, 98, 110, 163

Hussein, Saddam, 158–59, 161, 251

See also Iraq

Ibn Khaldun Center, 198

Ibrahim, Hassan, 40, 53–54, 116–17

Ibrahim, Saad Eddin, 180, 193–94, 198, 208, 227, 258–59

IBRD. *See* International Bank for
    Reconstruction and Development
IDF. *See* Israel Defense Forces
IMF. *See* International Monetary Fund
income inequality
    decline in, 71–72, 111
    under Mubarak, 175–76, 179, 274
    under Nasser, 104, 111
    under Sadat, 141, 273
    See also elites
independence movement, 20.
    See also nationalism
India
    Non-Aligned Movement and, 74
    war with Pakistan, 128, 129
Indonesia, Non–Aligned Movement and,
    74–75
inequality. *See* elites; income inequality
infitah (opening), 137–38, 141, 142, 159
infrastructure
    problems, 181–82
    U.S. assistance, 220
institutions, 62–63, 192–94, 198–99
intelligence service, 52, 76, 102, 106,
    204, 205, 282
Interior Ministry
    Central Security Forces, 130, 282,
        283, 284
    crackdown on Islamist groups, 166
    Internet monitoring, 195
    Nasser as minister, 51
    party regulations, 47–49
    preparations for demonstrations,
        282–83
    security forces, 80, 123
    vote rigging, 186, 190, 297–98
    See also police
International Bank for Reconstruction
    and Development (IBRD), 67
International Monetary Fund (IMF), 71,
    141, 159–60
international trade, 138, 141, 178, 231
Internet
    bloggers, 194, 195–96, 225, 301

official surveillance, 195
social media, 282, 283, 291
YouTube, 225
Iran
    Baghdad Pact, 66
    coup against Mossadegh, 52
    Guidance Council, 188
    Hizballah and, 242
    Islamic revolution, 4, 250, 251, 252
    U.S. hostage crisis, 250
    war with Iraq, 158–59
Iraq
    Baghdad Pact, 66
    claims to Kuwait, 75
    competition with Egypt, 75
    Gulf War (1991), 161, 162, 248,
        251–52, 303, 326n7
    overthrow of monarchy, 72–73
    proposed union with Syria and
        Egypt, 76–77
    U.S. invasion, 4, 207, 241, 257, 303–4
    war with Iran, 158–59
Iron Guard, 116
Ishaq, George, 289
Islam
    al Azhar, 26, 28, 78, 126, 151, 165,
        245
    intellectuals, 16–18
    jihad, 89, 90, 245, 255, 326–27n12
    nationalism and, 16–18
    Quran, 29
    Qutb on, 85, 86–91
    religious societies, 27
    salafism, 17, 301
    secularism and, 28, 78
    social justice, 85
    as state religion, 153
    Sufism, 27
Islam, Ahmad Said al, 195
Islambouli, Khaled, 155–56, 165
Islamic Alliance, 236–37
Islamic Congress, 117, 124
Islamic law (shari'a), 6, 16, 18, 89–90,
    124, 153, 188

Mubarak regime
    challenges in early years, 158–66
    critics, 2–4, 193–94, 195–96, 199–200
    economic policies, 159–61, 174–76,
        184, 220, 274
    foreign policy, 42, 161, 162–65,
        240–43, 274
    legitimacy, 197–98, 280, 281
    military and, 286–87
    Muslim Brotherhood and, 165, 166,
        188, 189, 193, 207, 236, 279
    opposition, 178, 179, 190, 198,
        207–9, 223, 240–41, 242–44,
        262–63, 270, 275–77, 279–80
    as police state, 184, 225–26, 227, 282
    political reforms, 168, 173, 184–85,
        186–92, 226, 264, 270, 285–86, 287
    relations with United States, 162,
        209, 220–21, 227, 235, 244–45,
        252, 266–67, 302–3 repression,
        195–96, 225–26
    response to 2011 demonstrations,
        285–86, 287, 288–90, 296
    state of emergency, 190–91, 192
    strength, 267–68, 269, 270, 280–81
    Sudan and, 42
    supporters, 280–81, 287–88, 291
    See also National Democratic Party
Murad, Mustafa Kamel, 139
Muslim Brotherhood
    ban, 35–36, 53, 82–83
    in Egyptian military, 54–55
    ElBaradei and, 206
    election of 2010 and, 277, 279
    electoral platforms, 188–89, 236–37, 238
    foreign policy positions, 162, 236–38,
        263
    founding, 27
    Free Officers and, 35, 42
    Free Officers' regime and, 46, 49, 53,
        57–58, 60–61, 86
    growth, 28–29
    Gulf War and, 162, 326n7
    imprisonments, 36, 61, 82–84, 86,

116–17, 276, 277
    leaders, 28–30, 31, 46, 162
    message, 28
    moderation, 126, 188, 265
    monarchy and, 29, 31
    Mubarak regime and, 165, 166, 188,
        189, 193, 207, 236, 279
    Palestine and, 33–34, 35
    People's Assembly members, 189,
        190, 265–66, 330n52
    political activities after revolution
        (2011), 298, 301
    political objectives, 29, 31
    popular appeal, 124
    principles, 29
    professional syndicates and, 238–39
    publications, 31, 33, 125–26, 152
    Qutb's influence, 85–91
    reemergence in late 1950s, 83, 86
    reform rhetoric, 5, 6
    regulations, 188
    on relations with United States, 223
    releases from prison, 125
    repression, 33, 61, 82–83, 90, 91, 165,
        166
    response to 2011 demonstrations,
        285, 288–89
    Sadat and, 11, 31, 115, 117, 124–25,
        152, 236, 311n43
    secret apparatus, 31, 35–36, 61
    Sidqi government and, 33
    social services, 165–66
    split, 90–91
    student cadres, 80
    terrorism links, 165
    use of violence, 30, 31, 35–36
    vanguard, 86–91
    Wafd and, 31–32
    during World War II, 31–32
Muslim Sisterhood, 83–84
Mustafa, Abdel Galil, 276
Mustafa, Hala, 240
Mutual Security Assistance Act of 1954,
    217

Nabih, Islam, 225–26
NAC. *See* National Association for
  Change
Nafa'a, Hassan, 257–58, 266
Nafie, Ibrahim, 261
Naguib, Mohammed
  background, 46
  cabinets, 46, 53
  Free Officers and, 38, 45–46,
    55–56
  house arrest, 61
  as president, 51, 55–56
  as prime minister, 45–47, 49, 55
  relations with United States, 52
Nahhas, Mustafa al
  Anglo-Egyptian Treaty and, 25–26,
    36
  assassination attempts, 35, 36, 116
  British and, 30–31
  corruption charge, 49
  Muslim Brotherhood and, 31
  opposition to Free Officers, 48, 57
  as prime minister, 25–26, 30–31, 36,
    37, 58
Napoleon Bonaparte, 14
Nasrallah, Hassan, 242
Nasser, Gamal Abdel
  accomplishments, 81, 110–11
  attempted assassination of, 60–61, 64,
    82, 116–17
  background, 40–41
  cabinet posts, 51
  death, 110, 136
  foreign policy, 65–66, 67, 72, 96,
    108–10, 112
  leadership of Free Officers, 37–38,
    41–42, 50
  legacy, 110–13
  March 30 Program, 104–5, 106,
    107
  Muslim Brotherhood and, 53, 57–58,
    60–61, 83, 311n43
  Naguib and, 46
  nationalism, 41, 105

opposition, 103–4
political goals, 50
popularity, 64, 81, 83, 92
reforms, 56
regional leadership, 74
relations with United States, 52
resignation, 92
Sadat and, 114, 116
speeches, 67–68, 91–92
succession, 113–14, 117
Suez Canal nationalization, 65,
  67–68
United Arab Republic and, 73–74,
  76–77
war (1967), 91–92, 96–99,
  100
war in Palestine (1948), 10
on Zionism, 231
See also Free Officers Free Officers'
  regime
Nasserism
  decline, 98–99, 103–7
  failure, 105–6, 273
  reform rhetoric, 5, 6, 104–5
  Sadat's policy changes, 123–24,
    126–27, 136–40, 142, 273
Nasserists
  election boycott, 185–86
  foreign policy positions, 238
  under Mubarak, 185
  nationalism, 243
  opposition to Mubarak, 200, 223,
    278, 279
  opposition to Sadat, 130, 140, 142
  on relations with United States, 223,
    238
  students, 130
National Assembly, 103, 114, 117,
  123
National Association for Change (NAC),
  206, 208, 257, 276, 277, 279, 289
National Charter, 78, 321n9
National Council for Human Rights,
  264, 289, 323n36

United States
  Britain and, 65
  Patriot Act, 192
  Public Law 480, 217–19
  Qutb's view of, 85
  retail and restaurant chains, 175
  strength of political system, 268–69
  support of Israeli military in 1973
    war, 135
  visits by Gamal Mubarak, 202–3.
  See also democracy promotion
United States Agency for International
  Development (USAID), 216,
  219–20, 228, 229–30, 258, 266
  See also U.S. aid to Egypt
U.S. aid to Egypt
  after revolution of 2011, 230
  AID projects, 216, 219–20, 228,
    229–30, 266
  amounts, 220, 228, 229
  for Aswan High Dam, 67, 215–16
  conditions, 217, 218–19, 220, 221,
    227, 234, 334n32
  congressional debates, 217–18,
    221–25, 227, 228–29, 233–34,
    334n32
  criticism of, 4, 303
  democracy promotion, 220, 229,
    259–60
  dependence on, 223–24
  economic support, 52, 141, 162, 217,
    220, 229
  food, 217–19
  foundation proposal, 227–29
  Glide Path Agreement, 221, 228
  Lantos Amendment, 221–24
  market reforms and, 220
  MEPI programs, 220, 229–30, 258, 266
  military, 158–59, 217, 219, 222–24,
    227, 228, 229, 230, 240, 334n32
  military training in nineteenth
    century, 13
  peace treaty linkage, 162, 215, 219,
    221, 230

political development linkage, 220,
    229, 230, 234
  public opinion on, 230
  relationship to aid to Israel, 220, 222,
    223, 333n29
  requests, 52, 65
  technical, 215–16, 217, 220
U.S.-Egyptian Free Trade Agreement,
  267
U.S.-Egyptian relations
  after Free Officers' coup, 44, 51–52,
    65
  after Mubarak, 244, 302, 304
  after peace treaty with Israel, 152,
    215, 219, 233
  ambassadors, 52, 203, 214–16, 217,
    228
  authoritarian stability, 6, 262–63,
    269–70
  Britain and, 65
  Cold War considerations, 44, 52, 65,
    70, 218
  debates in Egypt, 216, 223–24, 235,
    240–41, 243–44
  democracy promotion, 256–58,
    259–62, 264–67, 270–71, 302
  EgyptAir crash and investigation,
    210–15
  with Free Officers' regime, 217–19
  free trade agreement proposal, 267
  Gulf War (1991), 161, 162
  Iraq war and, 241
  Israel and, 233, 234–35, 243, 261
  Mubarak and, 162, 209, 220–21, 223,
    227, 235, 244–45, 252, 266–67,
    302–3
  Mubarak's visits, 187–88, 202–3, 266
  Muslim Brotherhood views, 236–38
  nationalism and, 256–58, 302
  as neocolonial, 52, 271, 303
  Nour issue, 194, 225, 242, 266–67
  Obama administration, 229–30,
    234–35, 256, 302, 304
  opposition views, 303–4